Jan/
To Tim
with all good wishes
Malachi J. Horney

THE NARCOTIC OFFICER'S NOTEBOOK

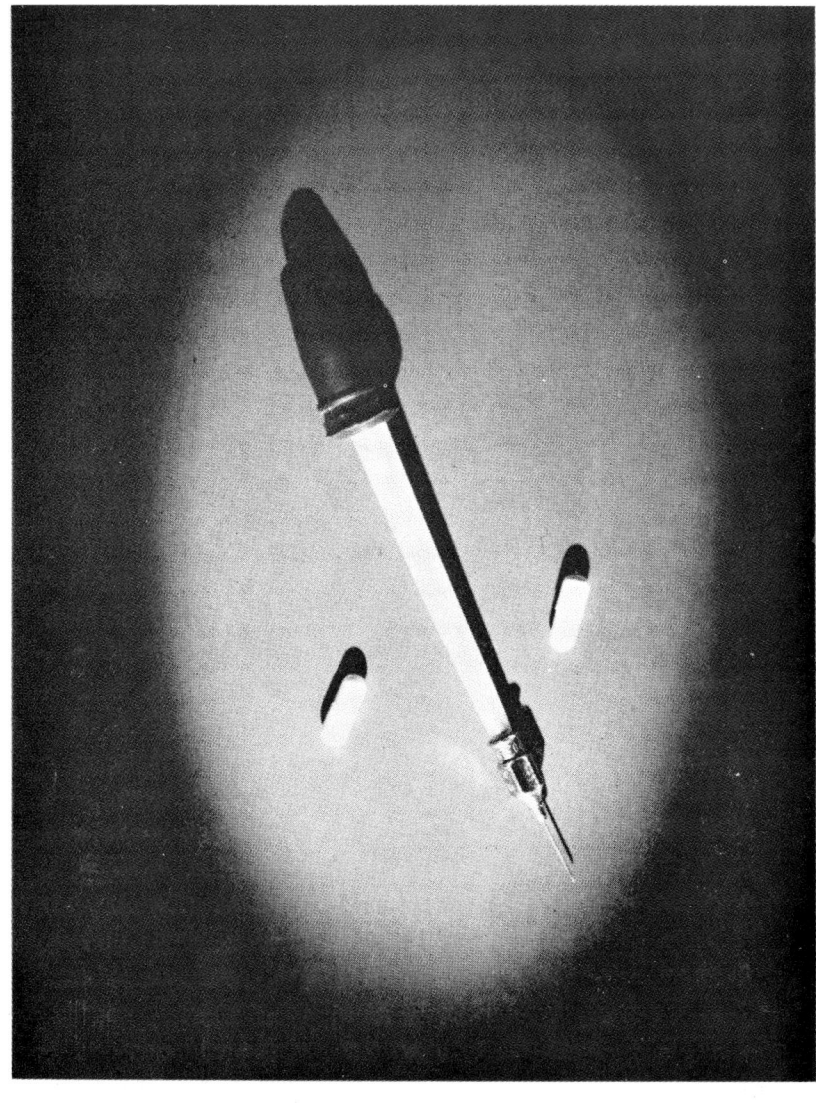

THE NARCOTIC OFFICER'S NOTEBOOK

Second Edition, Second Printing

By

MALACHI L. HARNEY

Formerly, Superintendent, Division of Narcotic Control State of Illinois; Formerly, Assistant to the Secretary for Law Enforcement, United States Treasury Department, Assistant to United States Commissioner of Narcotics, and Treasury Agent

and

JOHN C. CROSS

Formerly, Superintendent, Division of Narcotic Control State of Illinois, Formerly, Treasury Agent United States Bureau of Narcotics

With a Foreword by

H. J. Anslinger

United States Commissioner of Narcotics, Retired United States Representative to the United Nations Commission on Narcotic Drugs, Retired

CHARLES C THOMAS • PUBLISHER
Springfield • Illinois • U.S.A.

Published and Distributed Throughout the World by
CHARLES C THOMAS • PUBLISHER
BANNERSTONE HOUSE
301-327 East Lawrence Avenue, Springfield, Illinois, U.S.A.

This book is protected by copyright. No part of it may be reproduced in any manner without written permission from the publisher.

© *1961 & 1973, by* CHARLES C THOMAS • PUBLISHER
ISBN 0-398-02310-7
Library of Congress Catalog Card Number: 72-180816

With THOMAS BOOKS *careful attention is given to all details of manufacturing and design. It is the Publisher's desire to present books that are satisfactory as to their physical qualities and artistic possibilities and appropriate for their particular use.* THOMAS BOOKS *will be true to those laws of quality that assure a good name and good will.*

First Edition, 1961
Second Edition, 1973
Second Edition, Second Printing, 1975

Printed in the United States of America

To Narcotic Law Enforcement Officers in this country and the world around, a strong fraternity of devoted men whose endeavors to contain the dreadful narcotic evil have borne good fruit and upon whose integrity, strength, intelligence, tireless efforts and ceaseless vigilance our society must greatly depend for protection from an ever present danger, we dedicate this book with admiration and respect.

FOREWORD

THIS BOOK IS A major and much needed contribution to the indoctrination and instruction of police and others engaged in any manner in the enforcement of narcotic control laws and in the handling, cure and rehabilitation of narcotic addicts.

Between them, John C. Cross and Malachi L. Harney have been engaged in law enforcement for more than three quarters of a century. They have personally participated in the prosecution of hundreds of narcotic cases. They have had firsthand acquaintance with hundreds of narcotic traffickers and addicts. They have studied reports on addicts and traffickers by the thousands. They are perceptive observers of the narcotic scene. Few persons indeed could bring to the writing of such a book the long, varied and down-to-earth experiences of the authors with the realities of the narcotic traffic and of narcotic addiction. From that experience they have produced a book which should be must reading for all narcotic officers and for judges, prosecutors, probation and parole officers, social workers and others whose duties bring them in any way into the narcotic field. Also there is much in it of interest for the nonspecialist who seeks a close acquaintance with the problems of narcotic law enforcement and narcotic addiction.

H. J. ANSLINGER

PREFACE

To the authors, this book was a creation of necessity. We are of a generation of law enforcement officers which has seen firsthand much of our national and worldwide effort to curb what was a growing evil of narcotic addiction.

As perhaps no other person, the narcotic law enforcement officer is in a position to come to know the whole picture of narcotic abuse. At first he may visualize the creature only piecemeal as did the several East Indian blind men in the fable, who each found a different conception of the elephant—as a wall, a pillar, a rope, or a spear as one of them grasped a side, a leg, a tail, or a tusk. But with time and experience the narcotic officer has the unique opportunity to comprehend the true form of the whole "elephant."

We said in the preface to our first edition that there was a dearth of good textbook material on narcotic law enforcement. As our small contribution to alleviate this situation we had published *The Informer in Law Enforcement* (Thomas, Springfield, 1968) and the first edition of this volume (1961). With the increasing concern over drug abuse in this country and elsewhere in the last decade, many good books have been published in recent years to augment several fine earlier works which remain outstanding in this field (p. 320). However, there has not been much authoritative writing from the standpoint of the law enforcement officer. Without him, in our opinion, much of the other fine efforts to control drug abuse will be futile or worse.

In this book we emphasized some of the aspects of criminal investigation which are of particular value to the narcotic officer. Often his other detective experience has not made him sufficiently aware of the absolute necessity for expert surveillance, for fine undercover work, and for the skillful employment of informers.

When we published this book in 1961 we did so with the confidence and optimism that came from our intimate knowledge of a long and winning war which the United States and much of the world had waged for some six decades against the narcotic drug traffic as it was then known and described (plate facing p. 9). Some battles had been lost but these had been recouped, and more. Net progress had been good. In less than half a century up to 1960 the number of opiate addicts had been reduced to about one-tenth of the early twentieth century count. Equally as remarkable, because of scarcity, the daily opiate intake per addict, as the authors saw, was reduced by about the same huge proportion.

Unwitting drug abuse by self-medication with the opiates and cocaine had been almost wholly overcome. Positive attitudes and action by the medical profession had practically eliminated the improper prescribing and dispensing of narcotics under the guise of medicine. (see pp. 42-43). Once prevalent, opium smoking had become an historical curiosity. Once common on the streets, morphine was almost unavailable to addicts. Heroin was so reduced in potency (to about 5%) that in this country users had a "needle habit" rather than any rate of dependence which would cause "withdrawal symptoms" if discontinued. Cannabis had never taken on serious importance as a drug of abuse although this relatively new introduction to the American drug scene in the guise of marihuana, and mostly confined to third-rate musicians and their friends, was a matter of some concern because of the proselyting of a younger group of people and the indication that it was expanding a favorable climate for the use of "harder" drugs. The amphetamines and barbiturates were a worrisome problem. There was increasing abuse of these drugs, sometimes hard to distinguish in the very wide legitimate medical application, but abusers then constituted a more mature class of people. Usually introduction to the drug was something other than a hedonistic move toward an exciting, hallucinating, or intoxicating substance.

In the ten years since our first edition of *The Narcotic Officer's Notebook* was published in 1961 there has been a dramatic, an almost incredible deterioration in the drug abuse picture in this country. This had accelerated toward the end of the 1960 decade. An important contribution, but by no means the major factor, was the erosion of the power and effectiveness of the American police, the cumulative effect of slow attrition, the accelerating impact of a long series of Supreme Court decisions. (There are hopeful signs that this now has been well recognized and some remedial steps may be in process.) But the Supreme Court emasculation of police powers with the slowing down of the whole judicial process and the resultant general contempt for law enforcement efforts has made a clandestine traffic more difficult to control. Any road back will be long and slow.

The preponderant factor in the present unhappy development was the sudden change in social climate in this country—and to a greater or lesser degree in some other areas of the world. The change, within a significant minority, makes thinkable that which was formerly unthinkable, makes tolerable or acceptable what formerly was anathema. It elevates a degrading, vicious drug culture to an acceptable mode of life. A full discussion of the reasons and remedy for these suicidal adventures is beyond the purview of this book. But it is necessary to note an obvious social phenomenon and to realize what this may mean in the way of added burdens on law enforcement efforts to check an alarming increase in the abuse of drugs.

The picture as it emerges today is that while the addict does not have regular access to the opiates through medical practice, some of the reported abuses of methadone "cures" may well be leading us in that direction now. Opium is still a rarity in the traffic. Heroin still is relatively scarce and very expensive, but thriving on a generally expanding drug culture it is making inroads. Cocaine, which was an almost unknown rarity for several decades, has become more plentiful to accommodate the insatiable demands of a widening multiple dependence market. The bitter fruit of 24-hour-a-day harping about a "generation gap," round-the-clock musical promotion of drug abuse, and the emergence of pied pipers like Allen Ginsberg and Timothy Leary has made marihuana use a youth protest symbol for many. Much of this may be casual, but there is the inevitable disaster, and grief for their parents and friends, in the harm of marihuana itself and in its more concentrated forms like hashish. Recently importations of this have increased by leaps and bounds. There is the inevitable progress of some marihuana users to harder drugs, inescapable in a society suffering from the cancer of an expanding drug culture. There is a burgeoning abuse of the sedatives like the barbiturates and the tranquilizers, of the stimulants like the amphetamines, and the hallucinogens like LSD (lysergic acid diethylamide) and similar drugs relatively unknown a few years ago and which may be multiplied to a fantastic degree by additional chemical developments.

So the picture is not a pretty one. It is one for alarm, not panic. It calls for all the weight, skill, knowledge, and dedication that law enforcement can muster.

There now exist substantial forces which, perhaps out of ignorance or half-knowledge and in apparent misconception of the very essence of narcotic addiction, have been recommending radical and dangerous departures in drug abuse control programs in this country. As a result, narcotic officers and others directly concerned with narcotic law enforcement and addiction are often called on to comment on these recommendations for change. Consequently in the belief that it was a real necessity in this field we included in the introduction of our first edition a rather extensive discussion of the "British System" myth, in that it was a myth insofar as any conception that the British narcotic law enforcement program was radically different from ours in principle or operation. For its historical value we have retained this comment in the second edition and have added up-to-date developments in the "British System."

We have extended the discussion on cannabis (marihuana, etc.) in view of its increasing importance. We have expanded the discussion of methadone, a synthetic addictive opiate which is now being used in swelling volume as a purported control for heroinism.

In this new edition we hope to preserve for present and future drug abuse control specialists some useful gleanings from an experience which has encompassed much of the history of comprehensive narcotic law enforcement in this country.

MALACHI L. HARNEY
JOHN C. CROSS

ACKNOWLEDGMENTS FOR THE FIRST EDITION

IT IS impossible to make full and adequate acknowledgments of assistance in putting together a document which encompasses experience from the working lifetimes of the authors.

We owe a particular debt of gratitude to the Hon. H. J. Anslinger, United States Commissioner of Narcotics and United States Representative to the United Nations Commission on Narcotic Drugs, under whose direction it was our privilege to work for many years. Mr. Anslinger possesses a more comprehensive knowledge of the illegal narcotic traffic and the world narcotic problem than any man living. His friendly advice was most helpful and his cooperation in making available to us material from some of the unique files of the Federal Bureau of Narcotics was invaluable to our purposes.

Our gratitude likewise goes to Henry L. Giordano, Deputy Commissioner, Wayland L. Speer, Assistant Commissioner, and Charles Siragusa, Assistant Deputy Commissioner, all of the Federal Bureau of Narcotics; to Carl J. DeBaggio, General Counsel and to Samuel H. Breidenbach, Head, Returns Division.

A particular expression of thanks must go to Harry E. Corrick, head of the Statistical and Records Division. Our former longtime co-laborer finds no research project too difficult. A grateful acknowledgment must go to Charles D. Rhodes, statistician, whose handiwork appears in the narcotic history graph which is included as an exhibit in the book.

We are grateful for much help from Marjorie Williamson, Junia E. Shambaugh, and Anne Ostroff of the Commissioner's office.

We are much indebted to Patrick P. O'Carroll, Director of the Treasury's Law Enforcement Officers School and of the FBN Training School, and to his staff. An acknowledgment must go to former directors Harry M. Dengler and Robert L. Bouck. Particular thanks must go to Herman Crookshank, to Joseph Bransky, Irwin I. Greenfeld, and George H. Gaffney of the school lecture staff and to George H. White and Garland Williams.

Our thanks go to Charles C. Fulton, a brilliant chemist in the narcotic field, who graciously permitted us to quote freely from his writings.

We have a special obligation to a fine scientist, Dr. Harris Isbell, Director of the Addiction Research Center of the U.S. Public Health Service Hospital, Lexington, Ky., whose friendly cooperation has been indispensable to us. We make this acknowledgment without any implication that Dr. Isbell agrees with the conclusions and the opinions of the authors. To the many other authors in the U.S. Public Health Service who have given us permission to quote from their writings, we are indeed grateful.

We are indebted to the inspectors of the Division of Narcotic Control, State of Illinois, for some of the incentive to write this book. We owe particular appreciation to Wm. B. (Barney) Myers, Supervising Inspector at Springfield, Illinois, who contributed the section on surveillance photography, the Frontispice and Figures 10, 12, 14, and 20, and who made many helpful suggestions respecting the preparation of this volume.

A particular acknowledgment must go to Dorothy Bundy of the reference section of the Illinois State Library for her patient and productive researching. To Paul Newey, a former chief investigator for the State's Attorney, Cook County, Illinois, and a former U.S. narcotic agent, and to former State's Attorney Benjamin Adamowski of Cook County, Illinois, we are grateful for permission to reproduce photographs in the chapter on the fortified room.

To Dorothea Dorge Kreitner we express our appreciation for her original sketch of the attack on John Brown's fire house fort at Harper's Ferry, as reproduced in our chapter on the fortified room.

For help with the manuscript we owe special thanks to Dorothy Bence and Jean Mann of Springfield, Illinois, and to Florence B. Bridges of Washington, D.C.

Finally we express our very special thanks to Gladys M. Harney who cheerfully carried out the task of typing most of the manuscript and the incidental correspondence.

M.L.H.
J.C.C.

ACKNOWLEDGMENTS FOR THE SECOND EDITION

For our second edition we are again greatly indebted to many of the persons listed in the acknowledgments to the first edition, but we will not repeat these individual acknowledgments here.

In addition, for the new volume we are obligated to many others who helped us in its writing. Here we must emphasize that our recognition of obligation to any or all individuals in no way indicates that these persons may or may not be in accord with the interpretations, conclusions, or opinions expressed in the book. These are specifically and solely those of the authors.

Among the many people who made facilities and information available to use in our research we particularly must thank the following in the Bureau of Narcotics and Dangerous Drugs, U. S. Department of Justice: John E. Ingersoll, Director; John H. Finlator, *Deputy Director; Edward Lewis, M.D.; John T. Maher, Jr.; Paul F. Malherek; William R. Butler; George M. Belk; John R. Enright; Michael G. Picini; Donald E. Miller, Chief Counsel; Gene R. Haislip; Louis F. Bussler; and William M. Lenck. Also we are obligated to Joseph C. Flanders, Marvene R. Sullivan, and Elizabeth J. Nowlan.

In the Laboratory Operations Division we are indebted to John W. Gunn, Donald W. Johnson, William P. Butler, Jack Rosenstein, and Joseph A. Perillo. For excellent and cheerful assistance from the fine library of the BNDD we are particularly indebted to Jane N. Zack and Edith A. Crutchfield.

In the Bureau of Customs, Treasury Department, we are indebted to Myles Ambrose, Commissioner; David C. Ellis, Assistant Commissioner; Robert Battard, Gene McEathron, James Cheatwood, Mario Cozzi, Arthur Settel, and Neil Patton.

We are indebted to Joseph Levine of the FDA Laboratory. From the Fairfax County, Virginia, government we are particularly in-

*Now Retired

debted to Robert F. Horan, Commonwealth Attorney, and Captain James R. Cowden and Lieutenant John W. Zelaska of the Fairfax County Police. From the Metropolitan Police Department, Washington, D.C., we are indebted to Inspector Robert L. Dollard for information requested and for the battering ram photograph, Figure 27.

We are greatly indebted to P. H. Connell, M.D., M.R.C.P., D.P.M., the outstanding British drug abuse expert for assistance in keeping us informed of British writings in this field.

To Gladys M. Harney we owe our greatest debt of gratitude for her inspiration and assistance that made possible the revision of this book.

M.L.H.
J.C.C.

CONTENTS

	Page
Foreword	vii
Preface	ix
Acknowledgments for the First Edition	xiii
Acknowledgments for the Second Edition	xvii

Chapter

1. Introduction 3

    The specialized nature of narcotic investigations—a crime completely underground—an historical resume of the narcotic traffic and addiction in the U.S.A.—Civil War use of drugs—one of the few analgesics in earlier medicine—the Chinese opium smokers—heavy addiction in the early 1900s induces legislative action—long hard fight to contain the narcotic menace—quack remedies proposed—official drug feeding stations (clinics)—the myth of the "British System"—British narcotic experience in Hong Kong—additional "last words" on the "British System"—concern for the worsening of poly-drug abuse during the 1960s in the United Kingdom, the Low Countries, Scandinavia and the United States—the Dangerous Drug Act of 1967 and the opening of special drug treatment centers in the United Kingdom—reappearance of increasing quantities of cocaine, marihuana, barbiturates, amphetamines—hallucinogens such as LSD and many other dangerous substances.

2. Control of Legal Narcotic Drugs 40

    Valuable medicines must be freely available to sick—official channeling of medical drugs from sources to patient—safeguards against diversion, international, federal and state—synthetic opiates controlled—an effective system of great value—psychotropic convention concluded in Vienna in 1971—United States Controlled Substances Act of 1970—summary of jurisdictional changes in federal enforcement of U. S. narcotic and dangerous drug laws.

3. Drugs of Addiction.................................. 46
Addiction defined—the opiates—the opium poppy, the unique source of opium—its growth—control in the U. S.—World Health Organization redefined addiction, 1964—some history and botany of the opium poppy—some fables—forms of opium in the illicit traffic—crude opium—smoking opium—yen shee—powdered opium—tincture of opium—paregoric.

Manufactured opium derivatives—morphine, the chief principle of opium—heroin, the favorite drug of narcotic addiction—some history—heroin as a cure for morphinism—heroin debauchery of the early 1920s—other opiates, codeine, dilaudid, metopon, pantopon, numorphan.

The synthetic opiates, demerol, methadone, levo dromoran, leritine—increasing problems of "methadone maintenance."

Other narcotic drugs—cocaine—cannabis (marihuana, hashish, etc.)—excitant and later a depressant—may induce unpredictable and bizarre conduct—insanity after heavy use—the stepping stone to heroinism in the U. S. A.—subject of prodrug propaganda in polydrug abuse epidemic—history of cannabis research.

Some other dangerous drugs—hallucinogens, LSD, mescaline, psilocybin, morning glory seeds, DMT, STP, MDA, THC (active component of marihuana)—barbiturates and amphetamines.

Tests for opiates, marihuana, amphetamines, barbiturates, tranquilizers, hallucinogens, etc.

Clandestine drug manufacturing laboratories.

4. Narcotic Addiction: Management and Treatment.......... 102
Characteristics of addiction — tolerance — dependence — the desire to enjoy—who becomes addicted—a social vice and disease—usually spread on contact with addicts in underworld—characteristics of some addicts—divergent views of addict personality—methods of treatment—institutional care indicated—withdrawal of drugs—physical and psychological support—community follow-up against relapse—authority required in program—prevention best "cure."

Increasing polydrug abuse—methadone maintenance and its problems—substitution of methadone addiction for heroin addiction—deaths from overdoses of methadone—cyclazocine and naloxone, opiate antagonists, as possible remedies for opiate abuse.

Contents xxi

Present methadone production provides opiate rations for 30,000-40,000 addicts—suggested special therapeutic communities for drug patients.

Methamphetamine abuse epidemic in Sweden.

5. Recognizing an Addict............................. 145
The opiate addict—chemical tests not always feasible or possible—some overt indications of narcotic addiction—possession of drugs or injecting paraphernalia—signs of abstinence or withdrawal illness—admissions and confessions—other signs —experienced officers may recognize from whole picture.

The cocaine user—the marihuana user.

Special vocabulary of narcotic addict, some common argot and terminology.

6. The Addict as a Police Problem....................... 165
Questions frequently asked police—addiction and crimes of violence—sex crimes—other types of crime—quarantine of drug addicts and treatment—post confinement follow-up and Nalline testing—recidivism—predisposition to addiction by ethnic groups unlikely—rather a cultural manifestation.

The parasitic and predatory narcotic addict—will not and can not hold jobs—must supplement income by illegal means—special rackets preferred by addicts—peddlers, thieves, panderers, gamblers, prostitutes—thievery specialties—boosting (shoplifting), pocket picking, burglary, mail box thievery—confidence games—big store and short con games, the "Spanish prisoner" swindle, the "money making" machines, the "Mrs. Murphy" prostitute scheme—other "short con" games—three card monte, the shell game, the "lock" and other "gimmicks" —money changing rackets, "laying the note"—the refund racket—preying on sympathy of bereaved relatives or others.

False pretenses—fraud and deceit in obtaining medical narcotics—simulation of pain and disease—phony prescriptions and other papers.

Addiction an asset in committing some crimes.

Police action in narcotic withdrawal.

7. The Undercover Man............................... 191
Definition—purpose—qualifications for undercover work—disguises—initial contact with suspect—exploitations of contacts—eliciting desired information—surveillance under cover

—maintaining official contacts—auxiliary and supporting surveillance—essential procedures and precautions—pitfalls—avoid entrapment.

8. Surveillance 214
Definition—types—objectives and purposes—desirable qualities for surveillance officers—preparation—funds—surveillance methods—foot surveillance, one man, two man and three man teams—"leap frog" surveillance—combined foot-auto surveillance—foot surveillance problems—detection of foot surveillance—eluding foot surveillance—methods of automobile surveillance—one car, two car and three car surveillance—detection of automobile surveillance—eluding automobile surveillance—surveillance from a fixed point—surveillance of premises—equipment used in surveillance—some general principles—memoranda and reports.

The cameras in surveillance—versatile new photographic equipment available—photographs are persuasive evidence—photography possible under highly adverse condtions—motion pictures effective.

9. The Collection and Preservation of Physical Evidence 242
Procuring and identifying physical evidence—preservation of evidence—processing procedures for specific types of evidence—general considerations—crime scene searches—procedure at crime scene—searching—importance of personal search in narcotic cases—recognizing narcotics found—safe keeping of narcotic drugs—hazards in handling narcotic drugs.

10. Specialized Illegal Activities 262
Criminal groups in narcotic traffic—aberrations of small fractions do not stigmatize whole groups—police can profit by recognizing peculiarities and characteristics.

The Chinese Tongs—primarily an American development—originated as "muscle" groups in intra-Chinese quarrels-later assumed control of criminal rackets among Chinese, gambling, narcotics and prostitution—successful criminal operation aided by segregation, difficult language, race solidarity and police defeatism—tongs a disappearing phenomenon.

The Sicilian Mafia—a persistent criminal group born of generations of oppression in Sicily—original patriots turn criminal—highly effective codes and modus operandi for crime developed—skills transplanted to U. S. with Mafia immigrants—early history in the U. S.—the Kefauver hearings—the Apalachin meeting—the McClellan Committee—a most persistent and dangerous segment of the U. S. narcotic traffic.

11. The Fortified Room................................ 279
Narcotic operations in physically protected premises—types of fortifications—planning the entrance—entrance by ruse—entrance by force—entrance after delay—indirect methods.

12. The Dog as a Narcotic Detector...................... 296
Current interest in canine aids to police—Federal Bureau of Narcotics' experience with dogs in narcotic cases—selection of the animal—dog and man, an inseparable team—training—dogs learn to identify opium and marihuana—successful seizures and cases—dog program abandoned when opium traffic subsided—successful detector dog program of U. S. Customs Bureau.

13. The Informer in Narcotic Cases...................... 306
The informer valuable, often indispensable, in narcotic cases—necessary to point out a hidden traffic—may introduce undercover man to peddler—may purchase evidence—all suspects possible informers—handling informers a fine art—police reputation important in obtaining cooperation—informer should have fair play—should be protected from underworld retaliation.

14. Official Prescriptions for Narcotic Drugs................ 308
Diversions from medical stock now reduced to a small fraction of narcotic traffic—ambulatory treatment of addicts unethical—more experienced and wilier addicts may attempt medical diversions—forged prescriptions, misrepresentations toward doctors to obtain narcotics—official narcotic prescriptions an advantage in eliminating forgeries, reducing other fraud and deceit by addicts and indicating self addiction by a practitioner.

15. Police Cooperation in Narcotic Investigations............ 313
Drug traffic a world wide chain of criminal operation—any narcotic case might provide important clue to larger traffic—complete continuing police cooperation necessary—local cases may develop into international investigations.
Importance of INTERPOL, IACP, and INEOA in international narcotic control—expanded drug abuse training

program of U. S. Bureau of Narcotics and Dangerous Drugs for state and local officers—LEAA and MEG—examples of continued effective cooperation of police officers in various countries in apprehending international narcotic traffickers.

Bibliography 320
Appendix 326
A Federal Source Book: Answers to the Most Frequently Asked Questions About Drug Abuse—general questions—questions about marihuana, hallucinogens, stimulants, sedatives, narcotics, and other substances of abuse—drug glossary.

LIST OF ILLUSTRATIONS

Figure	Page
Frontispiece	ii
1. Addiction graph (opiate), 1900-1966	8
2. Results of opium raid, Newark, New Jersey, August 1927	11
3-4. Conventional attempts at concealment of narcotic drugs by narcotic traffickers	12
5. In Westfield, New Jersey, 7/26/69, 10 kilograms of heroin uncovered in ski poles imported from France	14
6. Buchalter kilo of heroin, part of a shipment of some 150 in baggage in 1937 from Shangai, China	15
7. Seizure of 17,500 ounces of morphine on the S. S. Alesia	16
8. Purchase of an ounce of heroin from a peddler in Atlantic City	18
9. Supervision of legitimate manufacture and distribution of narcotics in the United States	42-43
10. Dolophine, Demerol, morphine solution, heroin capsules and decks or bindles, paregoric, Dilaudid tablets	47
11. Self-regulated experimental addiction to morphine, U. S. Public Health Service Hospital, Lexington, Kentucky	48
12. Peanut oil lamp, container for smoking opium, opium pipe, yen-hock, yen shee gow	49
13. Opium harvest	50
14. Addict's "works"	61
15. Pink pills (heroin)	64
16. Closeup of seed pods of cannabis plant	72
17. Flowering top of cannabis plant	73
18. Special agent examines a marihuana brick	87
19. Lumps of hashish found inside bronze Buddha	89
20. Picture of actual street sale of heroin	237

21. Large haul of Mexican marihuana seized in Illinois	253
22. Vest worn by hitch-hiker en route from Mexico City to Chicago	255
23. Attack on "John Brown's Fort" at Harper's Ferry	287
24. Effect of hand battering ram	290
25. Hand battering ram	291
26. Battering ram, manned	292
27. Battering ram of another type	293
28. Detective dog (Wolf) with seizure of opium	298
29. Albert, German shepherd, on first assignment in Laredo, Texas	301
30. Kishi and Customs dog handler	302
31. Customs dog handler with Scout	304
32. Citroen seized by U. S. Customs at San Juan, Puerto Rico	314

THE NARCOTIC OFFICER'S NOTEBOOK

1
INTRODUCTION

Then Helen, daughter of Zeus, turned to new thoughts. Presently she cast a drug into the wine whereof they drank, a drug to lull all pain and anger, and bring forgetfulness of every sorrow. Whoso should drink a draught thereof, when it is mingled in the bowl, on that day he would let no tear fall down his cheeks, not though his mother and his father died, not though men slew his brother or dear son before his face, and his own eyes beheld it.
Homer, *The Odyssey,* Book IV, as quoted by Fulton in *The Opium Poppy and Other Poppies.*

ESSENTIALLY, OF COURSE, the investigation of all criminal cases is similar. Many underlying principles are common to all types of inquiries regarding crime. But the investigation of narcotic cases has some peculiarities. It is a field sufficiently unique so that the investigator needs special training and special background if he is to be most productive.

Narcotic investigations, let it be said at the outset, represent one of the most difficult and disagreeable forms of crime inquiry. This needs to be said and will be repeated, if for no other purpose than to emphasize the fact that wherever possible, narcotic investigations should be assigned to officers who have no other duties. Often, where the size of the department or the importance of the problem does not warrant the assignment of officers to work exclusively as narcotic specialists, these men may be given duties in other categories as well. When this is the unavoidable situation, the police administrator must realize that the narcotic aspect of the work is likely to suffer. The natural tendency of the officer would be to work more agreeable (cleaner) and more productive phases of his assignments, and the anti-narcotic program will be the loser.

There are many factors which make narcotic investigations a specialized police duty. One of the things which is most obvious about the problem is that the narcotic underworld is a specialized underworld. Narcotic addicts, particularly, are a clannish lot; in fact, they represent a race apart. Most of them feel that they have attained a special status which outsiders do not understand. The narcotic underworld has its own argot, its own lingo. Much of this, with local variations, has persisted over the years. Some of it, however, like other slang, evolves and obsolesces rapidly. A person who left this narcotic underworld twenty years ago might, on re-entering today, find some of his as dated as "23 skidoo," or "Oh you kid."

There is another feature of the narcotic traffic which tends to make this police field unique, and that is the fact that it is completely underground; in conception and operation it is something like an espionage or subversive operation. It is a hidden crime and a hidden way of life in that, broadly speaking, there is seldom any complaint.

If one is attacked in his person or property, he is likely to cry out for the police. The screech of brakes, the sound of crashing and rending steel, and the screams of the injured may bring witnesses to the scene of the crime of the hit-and-run, or the drunken driver. If the beautiful paint and chrome of one's automobile is missing from its customary parking place, the telephone is soon ringing in the police station. When the bank evidences skepticism respecting the art work of one's twenty-dollar bill, there is a half-sheepish visit to the Secret Service, after conscience and prudence have squelched the half-impulse to try to pass it to another victim. The tax-paid beverage dealer screams loudly about the moonshiner. The fellow who can make twice our show on apparently half our income is likely to come to the attention of the tax collector. And "murder will out" is, perhaps, an overly evaluated cliché in the language, but it does express something about most crimes.

So, in very many police crimes, we have the situation where the offense at least is known. Sometimes the suspect is quite obvious. Often, it is merely a matter of finding him and having him identified so that he can be handled in the customary court procedures. Occasionally a narcotic case may develop this simply, but not often. Narcotic business *is* a business. It is a business in which both the buyer and the seller are satisfied. All parties to the illegal traffic reach an end they are trying to accomplish. The clandestine factory operator, the distributing syndicate, the intermediate peddlers, down to the street pushers, all make a profit. It is generally an attractive profit. It is more money than these people can make in any other way known to them. The utter fascination of such a life may be incomprehensible to most of us, but it is well illustrated by this incident:

Years ago, we asked a dealer whom we caught as a second offender why he risked life imprisonment. His succinct answer came without hesitation, "Because I like to live this way."

"Living this way" included food, wine, women—yes, music, and a new Cadillac about every seven or eight months. Everyone connected with this dreadful business, assuming the utter absence of conscience, which is justified by, "If *I* don't sell it to them someone else will," is satisfied. And that satisfaction extends to the miserable addict who, by resorting to the contents of a hypodermic needle four times a day, finds in the result the all and the end-all of existence—finds him completely satisfied to live a shortened lifetime in which all of his waking hours, and perhaps most of his dreams, focus on just one thing—his next shot in the arm.

In its most persistent and characteristic appearance, an endemic occurrence among rather mature criminals, narcotic addiction is not likely to provoke any great public outcry. In this manifestation, narcotic addiction is not like, let us say, alcoholism, which will cover the full spectrum of society and thus attract the knowledgeable attention of responsible elements. It might be expected that narcotic addicts in the underworld would be practically unknown to the other 99.97 percent of us. Occasionally, when addiction breaks this pattern, it can become a matter of grave public concern. This was true back in the early 1900's when addiction was sufficiently rampant through the whole of our society as to attract real notice. This was very much true in 1919, when after World War I, there was an epidemic of heroinism among young people in some of our large cities. This was again true in a period after World War II, beginning about 1947, when there was a spontaneous outburst of heroin addiction among young people in some special areas of a few of our biggest cities. Now that we are threatened with a pandemic of multiple-dependence drug abuse among our young people there is great alarm.

But, even when an acute public interest is aroused, as it is likely to be when our youth are threatened, we nevertheless are not going to receive much detailed information from outsiders on how to develop our narcotic cases, or accurate information as to the problem which must be met. That is underground, and well underground.

From where we sit, we see nothing but a shimmering expanse of dry sand with no intimation or clue whatever as to the underground narcotic streams which may be flowing. We have no magic dowser, no divining rod which will point to the underground current. Typically, we have to locate one of the small capillaries which flows closest to the surface and from that, painstakingly work toward the mainstream of the traffic. This indeed is a job for specialists. On the other hand, all of our police should have much working knowledge of the narcotic traffic. Only in this way can we take full advantage of the great deployment of law enforcement officers in this country. The informed officer will recognize narcotic situations as he encounters them, and small indications or clues may be the beginning of important cases for which specialists should be called in.

Sometimes we may be assisted in the comprehension of details of the police problem by knowing what went on yesterday. It is characteristic of an underground and narrowly held body of information, which the narcotic traffic represents, that "new" features of it are constantly being discovered and rediscovered by amateurs and Johnny-come-latelys. When these people are sincere and earnest, as many of them are, they eventually learn, usually, that the "new concept" is indeed a very old, and perhaps a discredited one. Where the principal motivation of these people is, as too often it seems to be, to catch a headline with a bizarre approach, to peddle a book, or to briefly emerge from scholastic obscurity as Johnny-out-of-step, the results are likely to be unfortunate.

Introduction

It is not our purpose to write a comprehensive book on the narcotic traffic. There are few good ones—but there are a few with which any serious student of this problem should be acquainted. A modern book which is a "must," especially for historical background on United States and world narcotic control efforts is *The Traffic in Narcotics* by Anslinger and Tompkins (Funk & Wagnalls Co.). There is *Narcotics and Narcotic Addiction* by Maurer and Vogel (Charles C Thomas) which is a standard in the field and particularly valuable as to the general medical aspects of the drug problem; *Drug Addiction: Physiological, Psychological and Sociological Aspects* by D. P. Ausubel (Random House). There is an excellent older book, *The Opium Problem* by Terry and Pellens.

A new book, *Addiction and Society* by Nils Bejerot (Charles C Thomas), a Swedish physician, is particularly valuable for the account it gives of drug abuse epidemics in Sweden and elsewhere. Other new and valuable books are *Communication and Drug Abuse* by Wittenborn, Smith, and Wittenborn (Charles C Thomas) and *The Epidemiology of Opiate Addiction in the United States* by Ball and Chambers (Charles C Thomas). There are numerous scientific publications by researchers like Dr. Nathan Eddy of the National Research Council and Dr. Lyndon F. Small, and by the staffs of the U. S. Public Health Service hospitals at Lexington and Fort Worth, including such writers as Treadway, Lowry, Isbell, Himmelsbach, Vogel, and Chapman, which furnish solid background information. There are the official publications of the United Nations Commission on Narcotic Drugs and the annual reports and other official publications of the U. S. Bureau of Narcotics, now the Bureau of Narcotics and Dangerous Drugs, and of the Department of Health, Education, and Welfare. Because these are factual, because they avoid the bizarre, the screwball, and the personal attack, these serious discussions, unfortunately, do not attract the attention they might deserve. For that reason the authors though it wise to preface a discussion of the making of narcotic cases by some reference to the history of the drug addict problem in this country and its nature. Only if we know this can we put the present scene in its right perspective.

The Narcotic Officer's Notebook

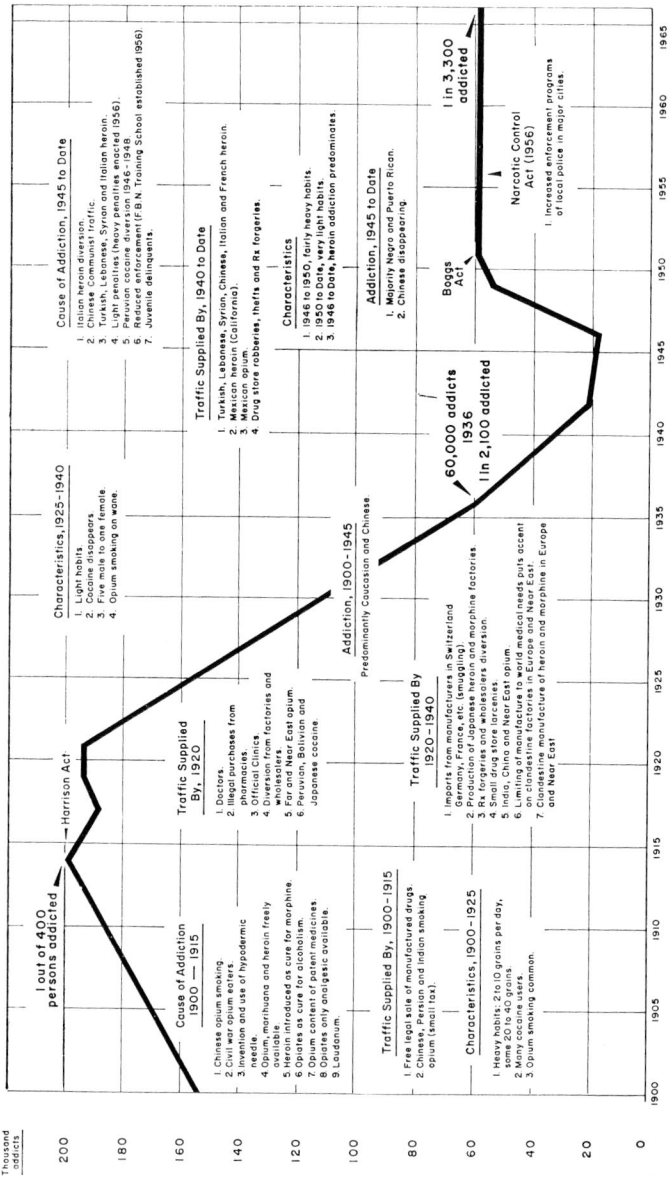

Introduction

One picture is said to be worth a thousand words. We think that the diagram facing this page will disclose, on short inspection, facts about narcotic addiction in this country which volumes of discussion might fail to present as well.

The narcotic officer attempts to enforce the narcotic laws as they are given to him. He should be equipped with efficient, workable tools if his efforts are to contain and suppress the narcotic traffic. Because, as we have pointed out, narcotic addiction and narcotic law enforcement are relatively small and specialized fields, practical acquaintance with these is limited. This situation has given rise to some unreal, unwise, and potentially dangerous suggestions for modification of the country's narcotic control program. Few people, even relatively experienced narcotic officers, have occasion to know how much progress at times has been made in the field of suppressing the abuse of narcotics in this country.

Prior to the enactment of the Harrison Narcotic Law (effective March 1915), most narcotic drugs could be purchased over the counter almost as freely as salt or sugar. When law enforcement

Figure 1. This graph was not continued after 1966, in which year there were marked beginnings of a new style of polydrug abuse. The BNDD counted about 70,000 known active opiate addicts in 1970. Beginning about 1966 and continuing to 1970 there was a relative decline in the proportion in inner city black addicts and a relative rise in white suburban addiction. There was also more addiction among younger persons. Prior to the onset of pandemic drug abuse in this country in the middle 1960's and when opiate addicts constituted more distinctive classes, the Federal Bureau of Narcotics had been able to maintain a counting system which it believed gave a fairly accurate picture of the number of opiate addicts and trends in opiate addiction. (*The Epidemiology of Opiate Addiction in the United States*, by John C. Ball, Ph.D.: Carl D. Chambers, Ph.D. (Ed.). *The Prevalence of Opiate Addiction in the United States*, by John C. Ball, David M. Englander and Carl D. Chambers (Chap. 4). Springfield. Thomas)

With the more explosive and undiscriminating abuse of drugs in the past few years it is more difficult to find an acceptable base for an opiate addict counted about 70,000 known active opiate addicts in 1970. Beginning estimate. As of April 1, 1972 the BNDD had an active opiate addict count of about 85,000. Based on formula estimates, it has suggested that the total number of such addicts might be in the one-half million area. (Since heroin in the street traffic is generally highly diluted most of these might represent light or casual use. Methadone maintenance addicts might be heavily or moderately addicted.)

began, contraband was so plentiful as to be smuggled in, or wheeled out of, the back door of factories by the truckload. Illicit heroin and morphine in the 1920's sold for from $10 to $20 an ounce, where the comparable price today is $500 to $1000.

The dope peddler of those early days is recalled in this story which an addict related to one of the authors (J.C.C.). The "junkie" was crossing the street in New York with five pounds of heroin in a paper bag nonchalantly tucked under his arm. He had just made the safety of the curb when he saw a blue-coated policeman purposefully bearing down on him. He resisted a panicky impulse to throw the stuff away and run. "Buddy," said the policeman to the relieved junkie, "did you know your flour sack was leaking?"

In the four decades preceding the 1960's amounts of narcotics moving in the illicit traffic shrank from tons and hundredweights to a few kilograms. Unfortunately, as we will elaborate later on, this happy trend has been somewhat reversed in the late 1960's.

Ever since the enactment of our first anti-narcotic laws there has been a debate as to methods of control. The same confusion exists today, perhaps compounded by a multiplicity of new actors on the scene. To facilitate his assessment of plausible-sounding expedients it would be well for the law enforcement officer to have some background information of this country's narcotic law enforcement history.

With the hope of enhancing the narcotic officer's general knowledge in this area, there are set out excerpts from a talk made at a Medicolegal Symposium of the American Medical Association at Cleveland in April 1959, by one of the authors (M.L.H.):

"I suppose most people today think of narcotic addiction as something which sprang up about the close of World War II and became widespread, particularly among a quite young class of people. Those of us who long have been around the business know that this is a relatively old condition. It has plagued the human race for centuries. It has been a matter of concern in the U.S.A. for almost a hundred years. It became a very keen and pressing problem about the turn of the century. We had experienced the introduction of the habit of opium smoking into this country by the Chinese, the introduction of the hypodermic needle and the isolation and use of certain of the opium alkaloids. The opiate content of many proprietary medicines was such as to make them addicting. The upshot was a situation in which it has been estimated that one out of every 400 people in our whole population was a narcotic addict.

"This brought about a reaction causing the enactment of the Harrison Law, which became effective in 1915. For a few years this law was left more or less to enforce itself, with partial success, until there was a flare-up of heroin use among young people in 1919 (how reminiscent that sounds!). Then commenced very serious efforts to curb the narcotic traffic in the United States. In

Figure 2. Results of an opium raid, Newark, New Jersey, August 1927. This picture illustrates the changing pattern in narcotic law enforcement. In the early 20th century, opium smoking and Chinese opium users were a characteristic of the narcotic traffic. Within the past two generations, opium smoking, with its more easily detected evidence, was almost completely suppressed. The Chinese narcotic addict—generally a man in a womanless world—has almost disappeared, his end hastened by his addiction. A common weekend feature in the 1920's in many large American cities, it would be impossible to reproduce this picture today. This photo is a graphic reminder that early in the century we imported smoking opium alone in an amount which today would be sufficient to sustain a quarter of a million addicts at the present daily intake of narcotics per addict. And, there were more morphine and heroin addicts then than opium smokers! Photo courtesy U.S. Bureau of Narcotics.

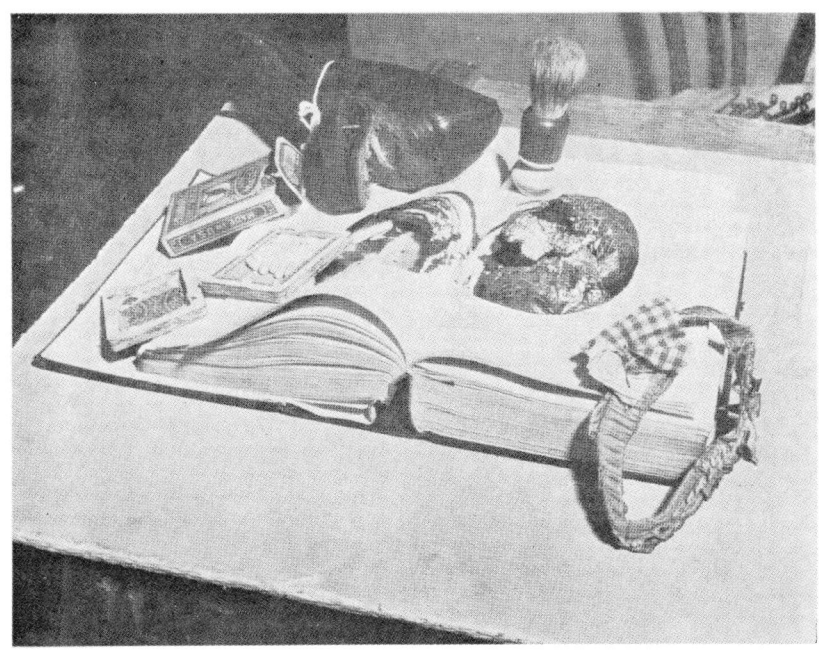

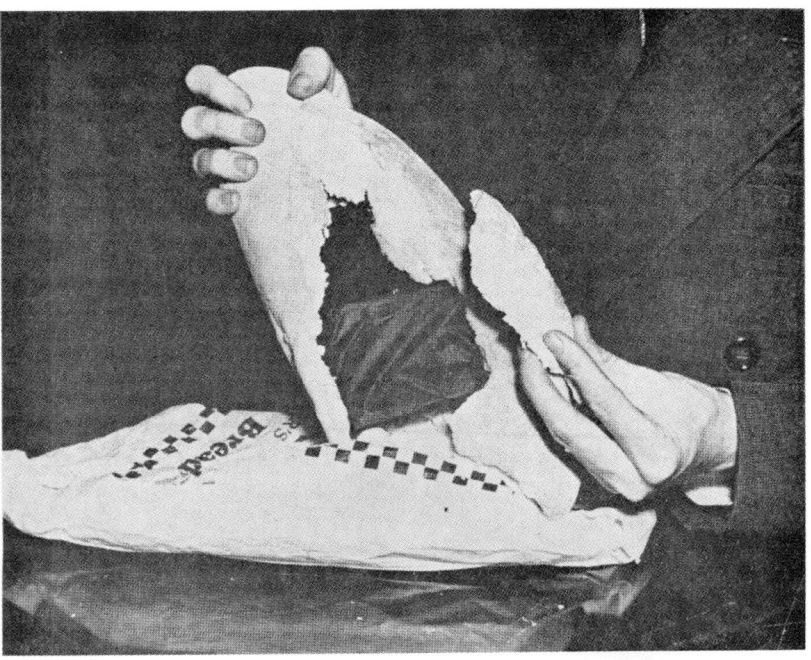

addition to the federal laws, which were changed and strengthened from time to time, most states adopted some variation of the Uniform Narcotic Drug Act.

"In reviewing this history, I hope to support my assertion that any good program of narcotic control must be one of complete containment. We cannot leave any small weak spots. And I think that this history will show that narcotics are narcotics; dope is dope; that 'drugs are the thing'; and this is true whether the addict is able to purchase them freely in a legal, open market; whether they are handed out by a physician or a pharmacist, legally or illegally, to gratify addiction; whether they are acquired by chicanery or theft; whether they are the production of a clandestine, illicit traffic; or given to addicts freely in so-called clinics—all this is beside the point—however come by, the opiates are deadly, ensnaring, enslaving, habit-forming drugs.

"In 1915, in many areas supplies of narcotics were available over the counter in any drugstore, or in a great many department and general merchandise stores, for that matter. Cut off from these, many addicts seem to have quit the habit. The persistent addict population turned to thievery and forging papers, including forged prescriptions. They tried the back door of the pharmacy. They sought out unethical medical practitioners. So promiscuous and indiscriminate were the operations of a few renegades that organized medicine, among others, saw to it that the principle was established—that furnishing narcotic drugs solely for the gratification of addiction was not good medical practice.

"In some cities official clinics, so-called, were opened to feed addicts and were closed when they were shown to spread addiction and to produce scandalous abuses.

"Then the narcotic traffickers went abroad. They smuggled drugs, sometimes by the hundred weight, occasionally by the ton, from chemical manufacturers in Europe. This source of supply

Figures 3 and 4. These represent some of the conventional attempts at concealment by narcotic traffickers. Figure 3 shows the hollowed-out heel, the hollowed-out playing cards, the hollowed-out book, the receptacle in the head of a shaving brush, and the garter. Figure 4 shows a hollowed-out loaf of bread used to conceal heroin. Photos courtesy of U.S. Bureau of Narcotics.

persisted until international action provided that only enough drugs could be manufactured to meet world medical needs. With this accomplished, the traffickers were forced to go to the grass roots, or more accurately, the poppy fields; to diversion of opium at its source and to the subsequent manufacture of morphine and heroin in illegitimate wildcat factories.

"Some wonderful nonsense about our early addiction history has been written and spoken by the amateurs. We have heard it said that addicts in those days didn't know they were addicts. That was undoubtedly true as to a few; let us say a very few. Then it has been stated or implied that addiction was a creation of a couple New York society ladies or of the Hearst Newspapers.

"Let me try to give you a glimpse or two of what the picture really was like near the beginning of this century.

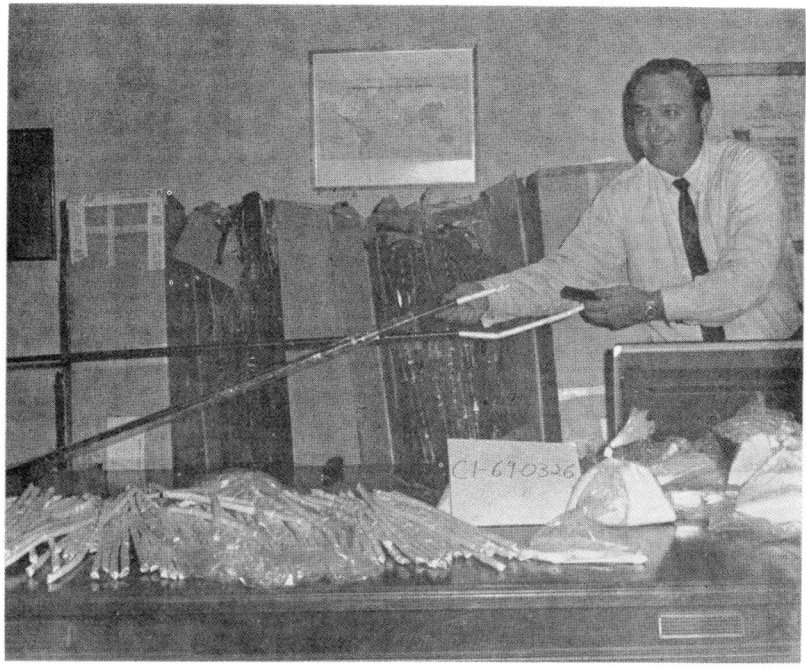

Figure 5. Westfield, New Jersey (7/26/69). BNDD agents in New York and France were led to a suspect in suburban New Jersey. While searching a Westfield beauty salon they uncovered approximately 10 kilograms of heroin concealed in some 200 ski poles which had been imported from France. Photo courtesy U.S. Bureau of Narcotics and Dangerous Drugs.

Introduction

"Looking over some old Treasury files, we find that for the 9-year period 1896 to 1904 with 1900 as a median year, we had a total of 1,927,557 pounds or a yearly average of 143,506 pounds of smoking opium entered through Customs for consumption.

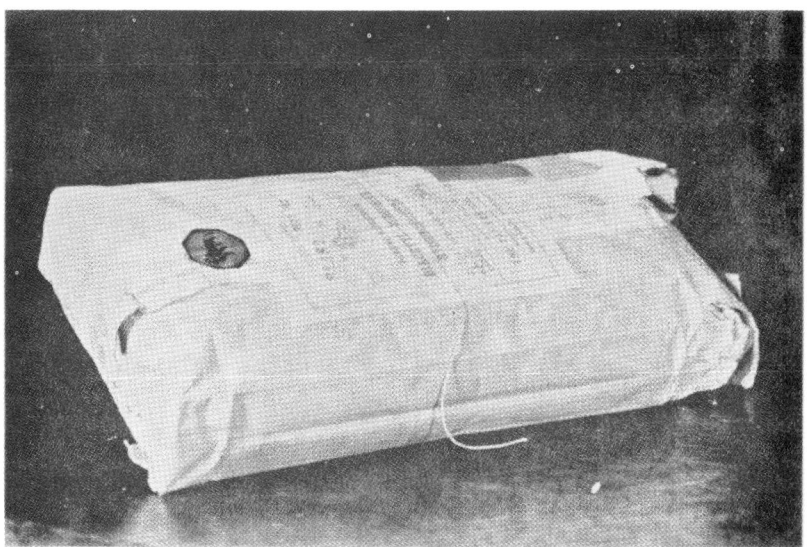

Figure 6. Buchalter kilo. This kilo package of heroin was part of a shipment of approximately 150 in baggage in 1937 from Shanghai. It contributed to the downfall of Louis "Lepke" Buchalter, head of Murder, Inc., and some thirty other conspirators. Buchalter was sentenced to 14 years in a federal penitentiary from which he was subsequently taken to be electrocuted for a murder committed in Brooklyn, N.Y. Photo courtesy U.S. Bureau of Narcotics.

This was not opium for medicinal or manufacturing purposes, but opium so packaged, prepared, and taxed as to be intended for only one purpose—to poison the lungs of human beings. A published study of seized smoking opium samples by Internal Revenue Chemists in 1907 showed this drug to contain approximately 17% of morphine. At 5 grains of morphine per day, this smoking opium alone would have sustained 99,035 addicts. This was when we had a population of only 76 million. If addiction had coincided with population increase, this would mean that today we would have had a smoking opium addict population of approximately ¼ million, or if we express this intake of drugs in terms of today's addiction of perhaps less than 2 grains daily, that import of opium would have accounted for well over ½ million addicts by today's standards [1959].

"The habit of smoking opium, introduced by Chinese, and first prevalent where Chinese colonies existed, had spread to other

Figure 7. S. S. Alesia. The seizure of 17,500 ounces of morphine on the S. S. Alesia is another indication of change in narcotic law enforcement. This was factory-made morphine. Drugs in the illicit traffic today are likely to be of clandestine origin from wildcat laboratories. Courtesy U.S. Bureau of Narcotics.

segments of the population. This was regarded as the most sophisticated and genteel means of taking narcotics. Elaborate smoking rooms were maintained in some of the big cities like San Francisco and New York. To these there repaired, in addition to the well-to-do Chinese, the ne'er-do-well seeking the ultimate thrill. There went also some of the big time gamblers and the elite of the thieves including those selfstyled aristocrats of the underworld, the 'big store' confidence men. To these elegant joints there often went for surcease and sweet oblivion the prosperous madam and the high class harlot. Mingling with these customers was a sprinkling from the entertainment world, show people, some of the vaudeville and burlesque headliners, a few from the legitimate stage and some from the newly burgeoning and incredible area of movie production. These pleasure-mad people had found the seduction of opium only a few short steps down the primrose path. Not all opium joints were elegant. For the ordinary pickpocket, the common thief, for the less well-heeled, the setup tended to be strictly utilitarian. The Chinese dishwasher or the Causasian down and outer smoked his pills in a dingy barracks or a fetid cubby hole. There was no concern here for selected opium carefully prepared by a discerning 'chef' for the right stage of consistency and flavor. His pill or 'pok' was the bitter residue, yen shee, the acrid scrapings from the pipes of more favored smokers, held together with a little putty of fresh opium; the lower on the opium smoking scale the less the percentage of fresh opium and the greater the proportion of yen shee which might be smoked over and over again until the last available fraction of its morphine content was inhaled.

"The argot of the opium smoker became part of the slang of the underworld. Some of it is aptly descriptive. 'Lying on the hip' was the act of smoking opium as that was the posture usually assumed. Even more apt was the phrase for the whole performance, 'kicking the gong around.' For theatrics, atmosphere and some possible use, most of these Chinese joints had gongs hanging on the wall. When a prospective smoker lay down, as a part of adjusting into position, a foot was often raised, almost automatically. That was the kick at the gong. When the opium smoker did not have the time or the opportunity to smoke he usually stayed his craving for the drug by swallowing pellets of opium, an 'opium eater,' or by drinking yen shee suey, a decoction in wine, spirits or water of the still potent scrapings from opium smoking pipes.

"While opium smoking was the most titillating phase of the narcotic traffic, intriguing to the public because of the aura of mystery and sinister machination (mostly phony) ascribed to the Oriental, it was not the mainstay of the wretched business. Most addicts then were users of morphine, a derivative of opium.

"What was then a relatively new drug, heroin, also a derivative of opium, was making great strides among addicts. Discovered in 1874 it was first manufactured in quantity in 1898. Soon it was found that addicts would accept it, nay, greatly prefer it to mor-

Figure 8. Purchase of an ounce of heroin from a peddler in Atlantic City, New Jersey, in 1931. The drug was much more available then than now. Distributing syndicates sometimes pushed "name brands" as this "White Horse" heroin. Sometimes "dishonest" competitors counterfeited this package. This and the assistance which a characteristic package gave to the development of conspiracy cases and the sharply diminishing supply of heroin in the underworld drove such packaging out of business. In this instance the delivery was made on a boardwalk seat by placing the package between the peddler and customer. The peddler was also a fortune teller who did not foresee in his immediate future a man with a badge who would bring disaster. Photo taken after arrest. Courtesy U.S. Bureau of Narcotics.

phine or opium. For a short time it was hailed and vigorously pushed as a cure for the drug habit. Soon there was the disheartening discovery that the cure was worse than the original habit. Heroin was three to five times as potent as morphine, had the most virulent addictive properties and produced sensations in use and effects which made it the preferred drug among addicts. To add to its sinister attributes heroin, most readily among the opiates, could be taken by sniffing as well as by mouth or by hypodermic needle. This simplifies introduction to the drug.

"In this early period more people had become addicted accidentally or innocently than is the case today. In the early 1900's there, of course, had to be much greater reliance on the opiates, in medicine than today. Satisfactory alternative pain relievers were not available. The great reliance on opium was particularly dangerous in self medication. Many proprietary compounds had a high concentration of morphine or some other opiate. The soother in soothing syrups was opium. The patient suffering from a painful accident or disease often had to be treated for long periods with an opiate to relieve his suffering. Today, of course, medicine has many alternative drugs and radically different procedures.

"But even in those early days addiction was mostly, as it is almost entirely today, a vice of the underworld or of delinquency which must be deliberately and voluntarily acquired by a person seeking a new pleasure, a new thrill, a new release, a new experience.

"Opium, and many of its derivatives like heroin, morphine, dilaudid, wonderful medicines in proper application, have several properties which make them most dangerous in non-medical use. While in a few persons some of these drugs may cause some initial discomfort, for most people these narcotics create a profound sense of well-being. There is a sensuous, sometimes orgastic, reaction, an experience which the addict lives to repeat. That would be enough to make the opiates dangerously habit forming. But there are much worse characteristics. Opiates tend to create a tolerance. To maintain the same effect, the drug must be taken in gradually increasing doses. Soon the daily intake can be in amounts which would be lethal to a non-addict. With the establishment of tolerance comes dependence. The physiology of the addict is transformed to a state where to feel 'normal' his system must contain a level of the opiate. When this level drops, he feels distress, and this distress becomes acute suffering if the drug is withheld. Sweating, cramping, vomiting, diarrhea and, in the heavily addicted, even prostration ensue unless the drug can be obtained. A satisfactory dose of the drug straightens out these symptoms as if miraculously. Medical men familiar with narcotics addicts recognize that the distress of withdrawal often is not as bad as it seems. The addict will groan loudest when he thinks it may get him a 'shot' in relief. Addicts live through abrupt withdrawal, in discomfort, but in little danger. In modern withdrawal treatment a morphine-like synthetic 'methadon' is substituted for the drug of addiction and then the addict is 'taken off' methadon. This somewhat prolongs but greatly reduces the severity of withdrawal symptoms.

"While the narcotic user is usually attracted by the euphoria, the sense of well-being, and other agreeably sensuous reactions to the drug when it is at first taken (barring a sick reaction in a few) tolerance and dependence are not attained until many regular doses are received. No person is physically addicted by one dose or overnight. It is a thing which must be worked at and with some diligence.

"Of late, we have seen a rash of publicity from advocates that we take a 'new look' at an old problem. Ever since this country undertook, early in this century, to do something drastic about a growing narcotic menace, there have been some people who thought we should attempt to handle the problem in a less forceful manner.

"First and foremost among these, there has always been the addict himself. He, as all narcotic police know, has what to him is a simple and uncomplicated answer: 'Just give me my drug and let me alone.' In this position the addict has a few allies; some respectable. There are the well-intentioned who are trapped by the logic that the quick way to dispose of illegal acts is to make them legal! Again, there are those who are rightly indignant over the extreme inroads of alcoholism among us and are incensed over the disproportionate public concern with a social problem affecting relatively few. Then there is a strange group, well described by Prentice, writing in *The Journal of the American Medical Association* way back in 1921:

> Public opinion regarding the vice of drug addiction has been deliberately and consistently corrupted through propaganda. Cleverly devised appeals to that universal human instinct whereby the emotions are stirred by abhorrence of human suffering in any form, or by whatever may appear like persecution of helpless human beings; lurid portrayals of alleged "horrible suffering inflicted" on addicts through being deprived of their drug; adroit misrepresentation of fact; plausible reiteration of certain pseudoscientific fallacies designed to confuse the unscientific mind; downright false statement, and insidious innuendoes assiduously propagated are brought to bear on an unsuspecting public to encourage it to feel pity, for the miserable wretches, "whose name is legion" we are told, and whose "sufferings," hysterically exaggerated, are graphically served up to be looked

Introduction

on as if they actually were being made "victims of persecution" by the authorities, who would deprive the wretches of even the drug they crave.

"And he went on to denounce:
The shallow pretense that drug addiction is "a disease" which the specialist must be allowed to "treat," which pretended treatment consists in supplying its victims with the drug that has caused their physical and moral debauchery. . . ."*

"Prentice's observations of nearly four decades ago accurately depict some of the material appearing in current speeches and literature.

"One apologist for the narcotic addict . . . has recently taken up the cudgels with vicious attacks on narcotic law enforcement officers for their inhumanity in forcing addicts to undergo the 'legal tortures' of frequent withdrawals from narcotic drugs. Borrowing a phrase, heretofore used to describe the slow death of narcotic poisoning, this 'expert' has called these withdrawals 'murder on the installment plan.'

"Just recently, I revisited the withdrawal ward of the United States narcotic hospital at Lexington, Kentucky. My escort, a great scientist in the field. commented that the withdrawal pavilion was 'the quietest wing in the hospital.' This was just a dramatic demonstration of what every informed person in the narcotic field knows—since the discovery and use of methadon to substitute for the drug of addiction and the subsequent withdrawal of methadon from the addict, the whole process runs a somewhat prosaic and uneventful course. But our 'expert,' having missed the boat by years, still finds withdrawal 'tortures' a club with which to belabor the narcotic law enforcement authorities.

"In the group described by Prentice are the persons who advocate drug-feeding stations for the addict, with narcotics free or at cost 'to take the profit out of the traffic.' It is they who are assiduously trying to sell the American people on the myth of a non-existent 'British System.'

"It has been alleged that the Bureau of Narcotics, the Department of Justice and the courts drove the medical profession out of the way to turn the nation into a happy hunting ground, stocked with addicts as fair game. It is my pleasant duty to point

*Quoted by permission of the Editor, *The Journal of the American Medical Association.*

out the mistaken direction of this attack. The 'culprit' should have been American medicine, and the truth is that the 'culprit' emerges as the hero.

"In developing that thesis, let me refer you to a series of articles appearing in the November-December, 1957, issues of *The Journal of the American Medical Association,* entitled 'Report on Narcotic Addiction of the Council on Mental Health.' These have been republished in a pamphlet. This is one of the most valuable contributions to the latter day narcotic literature. In my opinion, this job of real scholarship does not quite support some of the mild recommendations made or the reference report. In any event, I suggest that anyone really interested in this subject read the report, and the whole report.

"Let me cite some excerpts from the report:

In 1920 and 1921 the Committee on Narcotic Drugs of the Council on Health and Public Instruction of the American Medical Association made further investigations of the narcotic problem and in June 1921, made a recommendation which appears to have been extremely influential in molding medical opinion. This recommendation reads as follows:

No. 8. Your Committee desires to place on record its firm conviction that any method of treatment for narcotic drug addiction, whether private, institutional, official, or governmental, which permits the addicted person to dose himself with the habit-forming narcotic drugs placed in his hands for self administration is an unsatisfactory treatment of addiction, begets deception, extends the abuse of habit-forming narcotic drugs, and causes an increase in crime. Therefore, your Committee recommends that the American Medical Association *urge both federal and state governments to exert their full powers and authority to put an end to all manner of so-called ambulatory methods of treatment of narcotic drug addiction, whether practiced by the private physician or by so-called 'narcotic clinic' or dispensary.*

At the meeting of the American Medical Association in 1924, this resolution was adopted by the House of Delegates and, therefore, became the official policy of the American Medical Association. In October, 1921, apparently in response to the recommendations contained in this resolution, the Treasury Department issued a leaflet for the information of physicians which contained a statement of policy unqualifiably condemning ambulatory treatment of addiction, and in two years all of the remaining dispensaries were closed.

The Committee on Narcotic Drugs of the Council on Health and Public Instruction of the A.M.A. was charged with visiting the At-

Introduction

torney General and conferring with him as to the practicability of obtaining decisions from the United States Supreme Court which would remove existing uncertainties as to the meaning and applications of the Harrison Narcotic Act with reference to the terms: "in the course of his professional practice only" and "prescription." The committee called on the Attorney General, who agreed to prepare a case by which it was hoped that a definition of medical practice would be reached which would make clear the purpose and intent of the Harrison Act in such a way as not to interfere with the proper use of narcotic drugs in the legitimate practice of medicine, but equally not to permit the supplying of narcotic drugs to addicts even under the guise of medical treatment to cure addiction. In this connection, the committee also called upon the director of the Narcotic Field Force of the Bureau of Internal Revenue, Treasury Department, and transmitted to him the opinion of the Council on Health and Public Instruction to the effect that the medical profession . . . emphatically condemns the practice of distribution of habit-forming narcotic drugs to addicts, in the course of their treatment for addiction, in such a manner that the addicts administer the drugs to themselves. Briefly, the so-called ambulatory treatment of addicts was condemned, whether practiced by the private physician or public institution such as the so-called "narcotic clinic," and the director was urged to make use of the full powers of the Internal Revenue Bureau under the law to put an end to this practice.

It is certainly safe to assume that this visit by the Committee on Narcotic Drugs must have been very influential in causing the Secretary of the Treasury to instruct the Narcotic Field Force to close the clinics. It also appears that the Attorney General brought up the Behrman case before the Supreme Court in order to clarify the intent of the narcotic law. In this case, Dr. Behrman, who had issued prescriptions for large amounts of opiates and cocaine to known addicts, was charged merely with prescribing these drugs without any supervision as to manner or time of taking the drugs, or whether the drugs were ever taken by the addict at all. His good faith in the treatment of addiction was not questioned. The Attorney General asked the court ". . . to hold that, irrespective of the physician's intent or belief, the Act is violated where drugs are placed by him in the sole control and subject to the unrestricted disposal of the drug addict." The Supreme Court sustained the government's position and this decision has since been repeatedly quoted as the basis for the Bureau of Narcotics' regulation that a physician may not prescribe narcotics to an addict merely for the purpose of "gratifying" his addiction.

Why did the Committee on Narcotic Drugs bring in such a strongly worded resolution? Why did it urge the director of the Narcotic

Field Force to close the clinics? Because of the passage of time we, of course, cannot be sure. It certainly is unthinkable that a committee of the American Medical Association was supinely yielding to pressure from law enforcement agencies.*

"Let's go back to that phrase, 'It certainly is unthinkable that a committee of the American Medical Association was supinely yielding to pressure from law enforcement agencies.' That, it seems to me, is the understatement of all understatements. Certainly this positive, well-conceived, and dynamically carried-out program against ambulatory 'treatment' of narcotic addiction must have been founded on the strongest kind of conviction in the medical profession, that not only was something wrong, but something was very, very wrong.

"What was wrong? Here we are in the early 20's with an addict in every 400 of our population. Not only did we have about 8 times as many addicts as we have today, but their intake of narcotic drugs per person was probably 5 to 10 times as great. What was the source of this relative avalanche of drugs? A lot of it was smuggled smoking opium and some of it was eating opium, but the morphine and heroin which the addicts poured into their veins, and the cocaine freely used either by itself or to offset the drowsiness of excess opiates, came in a great measure from diversions from medical sources. Don't misunderstand me; not all of this, by any means, was by the doctor's dispensing or the doctor's prescription. Much of it came direct from the pharmacy and much of it came on stolen and forged papers, but too much of it came from the 'script doctors,' many of whom were addicts themselves. Since about 2% of the physicians then was addicted,** (now much reduced) is it any wonder that the profession which guards its reputation and polices its problems as none other, found it necessary to take all-out, determined action?

"I don't think that all or even most of the doctors who furnished drugs to addicts in the early 1920's and before could be characterized as 'script doctors.' Many doctors furnished drugs to addicts reluctantly or unwillingly, often under implied coercion and because it was an immediate palliation, but no solution of a disagreeable situation. So, the action of the medical profession against

---

*Quoted by permission of the Editor, *The Journal of the American Medical Association*.
**The figure most often seen quoted in 1971 is 1%.

the ambulatory treating of narcotic addiction was not the compliant yielding of the medical profession to the pressures of law enforcement, as has been so libelously alleged against us both. Rather, it was a fine example of organized medicine at its militant best, moving decisively to protect the public and its own standards by prodding the legislatures, courts, and executives into action.

"Let me, with the greatest respect, suggest something more. We have studied opium since the dawn of medicine. In the past 35 years, as in all medicine, these studies have been intensified. Knowledge of the opiates has been extended vertically. However, that has not resulted in any dramatic 'breakthrough' to the cure of narcotic addiction. Again, I don't want it misunderstood, but I think we can agree that the medical profession does not have the extensive contacts in practice with drug addicts that it had 35 years ago. I point that out merely to suggest that we should not reject too lightly the studied conclusions of the profession 35 years ago. I remember what Medical Doctors were thirty-five years ago. I can testify that they were the same wonderful, hardworking, intelligent, compassionate, inquiring people that Doctors are today. It is to the greatest credit of medicine and law enforcement that a drug addict in your office is now a curiosity to many physicians.* At the same time, it is a situation wherein the repetitious clatter of the publicist, turned expert, may get too much attention. Paradoxically, there seems to be an effort to inspire guilt feelings among doctors because they don't divert sufficient time from their healing and life-saving activities to some wily addict who is in the doctor's office for only one purpose— 'self medication'—not on the doctor's prescription, but on the addict's prescription, as he tries to con the doctor.

"But some people seem to be implying that this couldn't happen now. That is for you to judge. Let me put a few facts in evidence. As late as the 1930s we suffered from the outrages of a Ratigan, who, under the guise of practing medicine, sold in one year 400,000 doses in office-administered shots of morphine to addicts in Seattle, several times as much as all the other doctors and all the hospitals in that city dispensed in the same time. Ultimately, of course, he did seven years in the penitentiary. . .

"Some people might recall the Direct Sales Company, Inc., case,

---
*Unfortunately there has been some change for the worse in the last decade.

decided by the United States Supreme Court in 1943. A Buffalo, New York, concern found it profitable to print leaflets which it distributed far and wide among physicians, quoting a direct mail, cutrate price on narcotic drugs. One of the co-defendants, a physician, Dr. Tate, established in a small town in South Carolina, was shown to have made purchases of morphine from this company at the rate of 12,000 normal doses per month for a two-year period.

"Has anything happened in the past few decades which would indicate that the dearly-bought knowledge of the 1920's may be dispensed with? Is opium any different today? Is human nature any different? Have we made advances in medicine that indicate we can safely let a narcotic addict control his dosage? That is the most fantastic allegation. It is a direct contradiction to the very definition of what constitutes a narcotic drug. If there is no chemical or biological specific cure for narcotic addiction, is there anything else in the medical picture which indicates we can take this kind of risk? Where is the information? Where is the evidence? If it exists, it is to date one of the world's best kept secrets. Of course, Doctors, and Lawyers, the evidence is all to the contrary—not the weight of evidence, but all the evidence. As Lincoln once said of Douglas, 'When a man simply keeps repeating that two and two do not make four, then you just can't argue with him.' Most people believe that two and two do make four. That is because most people have a passable acquaintance, at least, with arithmetic. But most people know nothing about narcotic addiction. And I think, of course, that it is a wonderful thing that they do not.* Most people, aside from professionals, who learn any of the facts of narcotic addiction do it the hard way—the very, very hard way. But unfortunately in that atmosphere some people, simply by repeating a myth over and over again in the fashion best attributed to Goebbels, have persuaded many that as far as opiates are concerned, two and two do not make four. This has been in the perpetuation of one of the most curious yarns of modern law enforcement and medicine. I refer to the campaign of misinformation regarding the so-called 'British System.'

"Now, in the first place, it takes either hardihood or ignorance to imply that a side-by-side comparison of single facets of American law enforcement and English law enforcement can be made without

---
*Again, this picture has changed unpleasantly since 1959.

Introduction 27

setting them in the whole context. Great Britain is an insular country with a homogeneous population and with a solid tradition of abiding by the law. Generally, English police don't even carry firearms. The United States has a great continent with a heterogeneous people and a tradition of impatience with legal restraint. The American crime rate exceeds the British crime rate, usually excessively, in every category. Lawyers, certainly criminal lawyers, know that the similarity of American and British criminal procedure often is more apparent than real. Let's just say that while both countries have the same concern for protecting the innocent, the British appear to be a little more practical in convicting the guilty. A 'man from Mars' might conclude that the American system was more concerned with the rules of a game constantly being loaded in favor of the individual, than with the ultimate justice of the end reached. It has not helped that in the past 25 years our Supreme Court has given us a lot of bad ex post facto law in the criminal field—some of it upsetting what we thought had been settled law for 150 years. I would be unappreciative if I did not note that recently we have had some decisions in the other direction.*

" . . .Dilettantes and armchair students of the narcotic problems have long been intrigued with the fact that there is less narcotic addiction in Britian than in the United States. Early they seem to have adopted, as a foregone conclusion, that this was because of differences in our laws. But when these are shown to be fundamentally similar they, nevertheless, continue to insist that the key to the whole problem is an advisory paragraph in the British Dangerous Drug regulations.

"Let's try to lay that 'British System' ghost once and for all. Actually, of course, as has been very thoroughly pointed out, the 'British System' of narcotic law control is not too different from our own. The United Kingdom subscribes to the same international conventions and agreements that we do. Their system of law enforcement doesn't diverge too greatly from that of this country and Canada.

"The English law is:
> In no circumstances may dangerous drugs be used for any other purpose than that of ministering to the strictly medical or dental

---
*And we can hope for some continued progress in the present judicial climate.

needs of his patients. The continued supply of dangerous drugs to a patient solely for the gratification of addiction is not regarded as "medical need."

"As we do, the British make some qualifications to this. They say narcotic drugs can be legally administered as part of a gradual withdrawal. Also, as we do, they say that they can be administered where the shock of withdrawal might be dangerous to an aged or infirm patient, and they add a third qualification:

> Where it has been similarly demonstrated that the patient while capable of leading a useful and relatively normal life when a certain minimum dose is regularly administered, becomes incapable of this when the drug is entirely discontinued.

"Whether there really are such people is certainly a matter for conjecture. If there are such people, their number is so inconsequential that to abandon any elements of our program in that direction would be simply foolish, in my opinion.

"But the story is distorted even further and astoundingly emerges as a flat statement, published over and over, that there is no addiction in England because the doctors there furnish free drugs to addicts!

"These claims of some magic in the 'British System' have been formally debunked by the people best qualified to know. Mr. John H. Walker, Delegate from Great Britain to the United Nations Narcotics Commission, testified before the Canadian Senate in 1955, as follows:

> It is probably the third type of case that has given rise to such misunderstanding of the so-called "British System" and I would invite Honourable Senators to read this condition with particular care and notice how extremely restrictive it is in fact. Here, too, before administration or prescription of the drug is considered permissible, there must have been a prolonged attempt at cure. It must be further demonstrated that the patient is incapable of leading a useful and relatively normal life, and further that he cannot do this without the drug. If these conditions are conscientiously applied in the light of modern medical knowledge, the number and instances where a drug may properly be administered or prescribed in a case of this sort will be very small indeed.

"Following a discussion similar to this at Bethesda last March, Commissioner Anslinger sent a copy of my remarks to the Home Office in London, England, and from Whitehall, in June of 1958, came this reply,

Introduction

> Mr. Harney's remarks seem to make a good deal of sense and I hope that the publication of the record of what he said will help to do some good in your country. As regards the visits of Americans to this country, we are in this difficulty, that it is not possible for us to refuse to have a talk with visiting Americans who ask to be allowed to visit the Home Office to discuss the so-called "British System." However, when we do see these visitors, any remarks which we make are rather in the lines of what Mr. Harney has said, *and we make it clear that there is not in fact any such thing as a "British System," which is an invention of certain Americans who wish to prove a particular point of view.* I usually recommend such visitors to read John Walker's statement to the Canadian Senate Committee of Inquiry of 1955 which is a factual and objective statement of our practice. . . .[Italics supplied.]

"Dr. R. G. E. Richmond, who is described as having for years specialized in psychiatric work in prisons both in Canada and in England, testified as follows in a Canadian Senate Committee hearing in 1955:

> Senator Hodges: I would like to ask the doctor if he can give any reason why there is so little drug addiction in Britain as compared to Canada, considering the huge difference in the population?
>
> Dr. Richmond: I have thought so deeply about this and the answers that I can give I am afraid sound rather vague, but I feel that tradition, cultural standards and perhaps discipline during childhood enter into it to some extent. The tradition that "it just isn't done" in a way I think dies very hard in people.

"Now note very carefully that Dr. Richmond did not say that English addiction was down because of any 'exception' in the dangerous drug rules, as, of course, we know for the very good reason that this exception is inconsequential in our discussion. Neither did he say that addiction was down in England because doctors there feed drugs to addicts, which we know they don't. This man, in a particularly good position to know says there is a tradition that 'it just isn't done.' That's all. It's just that simple—and just that complicated. It just isn't done!

"Despite the usual rigid English conformity to the law, that country recently had its John Bodkin Adams. According to press accounts, Dr. Adams was investigated when deaths among his patients became a public scandal. He was acquitted of murder, perhaps for the very good reason that he may not have been guilty; perhaps again only because there were incomprehensible lapses* in the

---
*(At least it so seems at this distance.)

investigation of his case. In any event, he later pleaded guilty to violations of the Dangerous Drug Laws and was barred from practice. The ironical thing about the 'British System' is that Dr. Adams' narcotic deviations were not discovered until there was a charge of murder. Adams apparently made many heroin addicts, most of whom I would venture to suggest don't appear in the English addiction statistics, but in the mortality tables.

"So, it may well be that the better incidence ratio in the British Isles is not due to any superiority in their system or magic in their medicine. Is it not likely that it is in spite of the small differences in the systems, rather than because of these? Did it ever occur to our friends that people, countries, and cultures differ? In its March 17, 1958, issue, by a masterpiece of mistiming, *Time Magazine* ran a story suggesting that Irish-Americans, like me, were about fifty times more susceptible to becoming drunkards than were Jewish-Americans.*

"Let me try to ventilate the fog surrounding this 'British System' with one more blast of the cold air of common sense. There are more opium-smoking and hashish violations in the United Kingdom than there are in this country [1959]. When we informally query our English contemporaries, this situation is dismissed with the observation, 'Well, this applies only to the colored or Chinese population.' We wish we could dismiss our problem so lightly. Don't misunderstand me; we have a colored characteristic in our problem now, but it's new. Twenty years ago it was white and Chinese.

"Reading the report of the United Nations Commission on Narcotic Drugs for the April-May, 1957, session, one sees such things as reference to 17,697 narcotic arrests in Hong Kong; 12,787 related to heroin. These narcotic arrests loom up to about half as many as for the whole United States. Reports on Singapore are of a similar tenor.

"The report of the 1958 session of the United Nations Commission on Narcotic Drugs states that in Hong Kong the seizures of morphine and diacetylmorphine were the highest ever recorded; in a territory of 400 square miles, the authorities had made three times the seizures reported by the United States. The more recent reports from the Far East present the same picture.

---

*We have been informed that this gap presently may be narrowing, but we do not have a citation.

Introduction 31

"What is the significance of this? Nothing more than the all-important and inescapable fact that these are Crown Colonies of Great Britain (In 1959 the designation of Singapore changed to "State"), governmental entities ruled from Whitehall, and the direct responsibility of the Queen's ministers. The 'British System'! Where do you apply your 'British System'? To whom do you apply your 'British System'? Under what circumstances do you apply your 'British System'? It all depends on the conditions. To the 'British System' we owe the fact that there is a specific type of heroin so common to our West Coast that it is there known as 'cotton heroin' or 'fluffy heroin.' This comes through the Bamboo Curtain to the British Colony of Hong Kong, from whence it is smuggled into this country. In one case, a ring, broken up in 1958, had introduced an aggregate of more than 270 pounds of heroin into the United States over a period of 7 years. In 1957 in California, a Federal Narcotic Officer was killed by a dealer in 'fluffy' Hong Kong heroin which slipped through the 'British System.'

"In passing, Canada has the same rate of addiction as the United States, generally speaking. Dr. Paul Martin, Minister of Health, stated to a Senate Committee that he has been unable to find any difference between the British and Canadian narcotic laws.

"And now let's add a footnote. In *The New York Times* of March 9, 1959, we read that Dr. Granville W. Larimore, Deputy Commissioner of the New York State Health Department and Dr. Henry Brill, Assistant Commissioner of the State Mental Hygiene Department, visited England last fall for an on-the-spot investigation of the 'British System.' According to *The Times*:

> The physicians concluded that the low incidence of addiction in Britain was attributable to habits and customs of the country and not the result of any special methods of handling addicts.
>
> The report said that: "the British narcotics system which appears vastly different than that of the United States on superficial inspection, is found not so dissimilar as is commonly believed upon more careful study of its administrative operation.

'Incidentally, these Doctors have given us a phrase to explain the low narcotic incidence of the United Kingdom. They call it the 'British lack of cultural susceptibility.' Now we may hope that the 'British System' will take its proper place with the Loch Ness Monster.

"If and when British medicine makes a 'break-through' on the opiates, I suggest that we will know about it through medical channels. In the meantime, in my opinion, allegations by non-specialists of any superior approach by the British in the narcotic addiction field are from the standpoint of lawyers mere obfuscation and sophistry, and from a medical standpoint sheer quackery.

"The obsession of our friends in confusing coincidence with cause and effect in the 'British System' reminds me of the story of the suburbanite who went out every evening and sprayed cologne on his lawn. A neighbor stood it as long as his sensibilities and curiosity permitted and then inquired of him why he was using this spray. 'To keep wild elephants off the lawn,' was the reply. 'But,' the astonished neighbor exclaimed. 'There isn't a wild elephant within 5,000 miles.' 'I know it," said the suburbanite—'Pretty powerful stuff, ain't it?'

"The solution of the narcotic problem in this country is primarily one of law enforcement, in the light of our present knowledge. Obviously, we must have help from many other quarters. The Lexington and Fort Worth Institutions have made great contributions. They have done many of the obvious things that a hospital has to do. Their research contributions are beyond all measure, all worth, to the American people. Often their best contribution has been to prove, every once in a while, what isn't so and what we don't know.

"We hear that we are forgetting we have a medical problem. For the sake of argument, let us assume that this is essentially a medical problem. A great many years ago our Public Health people were seriously concerned about Psittacosis, a disease transmittable from parrots to humans. I understand that antibiotics may put us in a relatively improved position today, but that control of Psittacosis is still a serious matter. However, in those earlier days, because we didn't have any better or simpler way of coping with a problem which had to be coped with, the great Treasury of the United States was put in the business of chasing parrots. Customs agents followed parrots from the low countries in Europe to Paris, and by air to Mexico City, and by truck to the Mexican border, and there intercepted birds, not for the sake of revenue, but in the name of medicine! We have no sure cure for addiction as yet—no specific drugs or chemical—as far as I know.* Our hospitals can take credit for

---

*Recently there seems to be some progress in this area.

salvaging many addicts. Despite that, I still insist that the best 'cure' for narcotic addiction is for it not to occur. I think the best medicine is to try to control and stamp out the causative chemicals, illicit opiates. It is sound medicine, I suggest, to contain the addict who spreads the know-how and the way of life in narcotic addiction. Quarantine is one of the oldest and solidest procedures in public health. There can be many variations on the theme of 'Typhoid Mary.'

"I think the truth is that the extended hand of medicine seldom reaches far enough to overcome the blandishments and seduction of opium, until it has law enforcement to remove the all-too-willing victim from the arms of Lady Morphia, and to physically place him within reach, if he is to have the advantage of what modern medicine can do for him. There are exceptions, but let's speak scientifically and generally. To the men of medicine, I say do not let the claque play down law enforcement as if it were something in opposition to, or a substitute for, your work. I think that the most unhealthy situation with which we have to contend today is this drive to make it appear that there is dissension between law enforcement and medicine in the narcotic control field. I suggest that medicine in this field, without the help of law enforcement, would be smothered.

"The record is clear that, despite temporary setbacks, we have made great strides in eliminating the narcotic drug evil in this country. The record is equally clear that much of this we owe to law enforcement, with the support that it has had from so many other quarters.

"To repeat, quarantine and isolation, in my opinion, are elemental concepts in the control of infectious and contagious diseases. We certainly have a sort of transmittable characteristic in the drug addiction phenomenon. Generally, it is the addict who translates to the neophyte, as a great experience, the abuse of a chemical that would otherwise be so much harmless dust. If we want to eliminate this health hazard promptly, we must continue to work for a program where opiates are difficult to get and where we will quickly and surely take the addict out of society, place him in a drug-free environment, and then cautiously let him back into circulation with a string attached. The rehabilitation of the addict is a worthwhile and necessary concern. Marginal and doubtful as he may be, and as he usually is, he is a fellow human being entitled to the best effort we can give him.

"But since the best 'cure' for narcotic addiction is for it never to occur, our chiefest and most practical concern must be for the non-addict contemporary of the addict. To him, we owe the most responsibility. For him, we must have the most rigorous enforcement of the penal laws. For his safety and well being, we must cure or segregate the addict. The mere existence of an aggressive program of this nature has discouraged and will discourage the possible neophyte.

"We keep hearing that we ought to have more research; that we ought to embark on new programs; and, of course, we should. Of course, we ought to keep open minds and look for the fresh approach. But the sort of people who sometimes get into these programs worries me. I think we should carefully guard against a situation where the busy professional leaves too much of the program to some starry-eyed employee who needs, most of all, a few years of real indoctrination as to what this business is all about. Let's make sure our research is solid and not just themepaper stuff. We don't need researching by people who are naively hurt and surprised when they find that narcotic addicts will flock to any new treatment center and that most of them will abruptly discontinue attendance when they find it isn't a source for drugs.

". . . I am disturbed about some present-day tendencies to make out heroinism to be a little on the innocuous side. I'm afraid some of our professionals are doing the country a disservice here. One of the assets of opium as a medicine is that its prolonged use does not directly produce physical lesions.* Some of today's writers

---

*(We have heard a noted medical expert in this field comment that it may be beside the point to stress lack of tissue lesions when the patient is obviously dead of heroin poisoning! Actually the addict runs many physical risks from his addiction. He may take a lethal overdose. He may be infected by unsterile needles, and might acquire transmittable diseases when needles are used by several persons. He may smother or burn to death from a dropped lighted cigarette when he "goes on the nod." Since the addict's only real interest is in his next shot he often is likely to live in a constant state of malnutrition, both as to quantity and proper balance of his diet. He is dehydrated, continually severely constipated, with all his functions under the heavy braking action of the opiates. Symptoms of any disease he may contract are masked until a final disaster. The addict has neither the interest nor the inclination to take care of his physical necessities. The usual cautions, warnings, and pains are all submerged in the false sense of security which narcotics give. And all this contributes to a shortened life.)

like to point out how relatively clean and tractable is the addict compared to the stinking obstreperous drunk. (Addicts don't smell as sweet on the street as they do in the hospital, and they have a passive intractability which can be quite exasperating.) Any comparison of alcohol and opium is dangerously incomplete unless coupled with the warning that whereas many people can use and enjoy alcohol without harm, opium so used will seize on and 'hook' almost any regular experimenter. Also the alcohol user most often is intoxicated only short periods of a day. The essence of opium intoxication is that it is a completely continuous state.

"I think some of our amateur advisors have no comprehension of the evil which they do. Hope springs eternal in the addict's breast. Vancouver, British Columbia,* has by far the highest narcotic addiction incidence in the whole of Canada. I think that it is no accident that this accompanies an almost continuous agitation in that city by what I can only call a lunatic fringe to establish narcotic drug-feeding stations for addicts there. I am most firmly of the opinion that the recently published proposal that we should consider feeding narcotics to all the junkies in New York will encourage many of these poor unfortunates to hold to this way of life, when otherwise they might have been induced to leave it. This is something that the limelight seekers, the sensationalists, and the publicity hunters might well ponder. It could constitute a heavy burden on someone with a conscience.

"Cocteau, following Kublai Khan, has likened the withdrawal of narcotics from an addict to a 'weaning from the milk of paradise." What a shocking proposal it is that we set up this sort of 'milk bar' for our people, including our children. This is not hyperbole. Some have advocated a modest experimental 'poppy juice joint' in Washington. But others recommend that we put the whole addict population in New York on free drug rations.

"What a monstrous proposal it is that we embark on such a program. The contempt of the whole human race is in the epithet 'Dope Peddler.' What difference does it make if you give him a medical degree or if you call him a social worker or a policeman? He is still delivering 'junk' to 'junkies.'

---

*The Washington Post, November 25, 1971, datelined Vancouver, referred to a report that British Columbia has the largest heroin addiction problem in Canada and perhaps in North America.

"Commissioner Anslinger has written that the proposition to stop addiction by feeding addicts dope is so simple that only a simpleton could advance it. However, I am dismayed to see that the superficial plausibility of this idea has appealed to many people certainly as intelligent, if not as well informed, as I think myself to be.

"While Krushchev is trying to substitute buttermilk for vodka, we are urged to open narcotic bars in Washington, D. C., our showcase for the world, to play Russian Roulette with morphine.

"One of the most paradoxical statements we read about narcotic saloons is that they be under 'rigid, legal control.' How could there be any control—rigid, legal or otherwise—if the illicit narcotic traffic is given such an effective screen behind which to work? Any law enforcement officer with 30 days' experience in the business would recognize the utter foolishness of this proposition. You either have control or you don't have control. No enforcement officer with the slightest regard of professional or ethical responsibility should be a party to such a scheme. It might be delusion to its sponsors; it would be dishonesty in the officer who pretended to administer such a law."

* * *

A reflection of the "British System" myth is a White Paper, dated November 11, 1959, laid before the Legislative Council and entitled "The Problem of Narcotic Drugs in Hong Kong." This is indeed a devastating refutation that there is any magic in British law enforcement when it comes to controlling illicit narcotic traffic and addiction. The publication of the White Paper at the time was most opportune. It should have given a final *coup de grâce* to the arguments of well-meaning visionaries, that in some manner American narcotic law enforcement had been missing the boat because it did not adopt the "British System" of narcotic control. The myth of magic in the British narcotic system has been widely repeated and has gained surprising acceptance. In the past, we had attempted to bring a sense of realism into this picture by suggesting that narcotic conditions in Singapore and Hong Kong—British colonies—were bad. From these places, particularly Hong Kong, there comes to this country a steady flow of contraband narcotics. If there were any particular efficacy in the "British System," the British would have invoked it to spare themselves and us this embarrassment. So we have argued.

About 1960 Dr. Lois Higgins of the Illinois Department of Public Safety—one of the world's best known policewomen—was to visit Hong Kong. We suggested to her that this was an opportunity to bring back a personal impression. Her subsequent account of addiction, seen firsthand in Hong Kong, was harrowing indeed. Now it is officially documented in the White Paper, which states that some estimates of drug addiction in Hong Kong place the total addict number as high as 200,000 to 250,000. Conservative estimates, the paper states, are from 150,000 to 180,000. The 1957 estimate of Hong Kong population was 2,600,000. Presumably, it has increased considerably since that time. But, even 150,000 addicts in the small colony of Hong Kong is indeed a desperate situation.*

The White Paper showed that the British had been giving very serious study to their predicament. The British Empire may be shrinking, but it still has some of the finest civil servants in the world. It can be expected that in this study Hong Kong had access to all the wisdom on narcotic control which the United Kingdom could supply. Those of us, then who had been attempting to dispel the ghosts of the "British System" found great satisfaction in the recommendations made in the Hong Kong White Paper. These recommendations were briefly: (1) more stringent law enforcement to curtail the illicit traffic, and (2) compulsory disintoxication and treatment of the narcotic addict.

That program had a completely familiar sound. It was the "Anslinger System." It is the "American System." It, evidently, is the "British System."

Now as might be expected, after a lapse of more than a decade since this was written, there have been additional "last words" on the British System. See Bibliography for publications by P. H. Connell, and Ramon Gardner.

In the early 1960's the United Kingdom became seriously concerned about the administration of its drug laws. A certain amount of looseness and permissiveness which might have been over-

---

*An article, "A Study of Ex-prisoner Female Narcotic Addicts in Hong Kong" by Ding and Chan, *U. N. Bulletin on Narcotics*, April-June, 1970, suggests that "hard drug" addicts in Hong Kong in the late 1960's numbered between 60,000 and 80,000, this in a population of approximately 4,000,000.

looked (and which in the U.S.A. was misunderstood as the British System) no longer could be tolerated in a changing drug scene. The cadre of older addicts (many of whom would have been ignored in American drug law enforcement practices as entitled to continued medical drug doses as medical addicts) were being greatly supplemented by a younger group. Some of these were imports from the U.S.A. and Canada. The American, when identified as such, could be deported, but the Canadians were British and entitled to remain. These people had been lured to England by the erroneous publicity offering a prospect of free drugs, or free access to narcotic drugs. In addition to these outsiders the United Kingdom was rapidly developing its native group of younger English addicts, hedonists, not impressed with the British tradition that abuse of the exotic Eastern drugs "just isn't done, old chap." Some trusting English physicians were no match for this American-style junkie guile. The liberal drug dispensing record of one of these, Lady Frankau, a prominent physician, was especially noted. So, two Interdepartmental Committee recommendations later, Parliament legislated and the Dangerous Drugs Act of 1967 abolished any discretion in narcotic prescribing by private physicians. Special drug treatment centers were opened, effective 1969. British and American drug control operations, long similar in theory, became closer in practice. However, any feeling of satisfaction over this British demonstration that one doesn't control addiction by prescribing addicting drugs is dispelled when we see in this country a rising misuse of methadone in alleged addiction control. On this we shall have more to say later.

As we already have indicated there was a change for the worse in the drug abuse situation in this country in the 1960's. No longer is the hard drug heroin the only focus of our trouble. It is still here and on the increase. It has been rejoined in a small but increasing degree by the long absent, vicious drug cocaine. Marihuana, and more recently the more potent form of cannabis product, hashish, shows an enormous and alarming increase. Added to this recrudescence of our more classic problem, we are seeing a "pandemic contagion of polydrug abuse which has seriously involved hundreds of thousands of young people in major countries throughout the world" (Brill, p. 25). This has included the depressants like the barbituates, the stimulants like the amphetamines, the hallucinogens like LSD, and a wide variety of other substances. No longer is our problem concentrated in the underworld and its fringes nor confined to a few larger cities. As part of an aberrant youth culture it is in almost every nook and cranny of the land. The Low Countries of Europe and the United Kingdom are seeing the change. Sweden and the other Scandinavian countries have had a vicious epidemic of amphetamine-like stimulant drug abuse.

"As in the rest of the world, developments in Sweden are towards mixed addiction. Hashish smoking is spreading like a forest fire among the youth, and just as two years ago with central stimulants, apologists for hashish smoking are now propagating the use of this drug in the popular press and on television. This propaganda comes from just the same circles and there are the same arguments about individual freedom—although no one is so unfree as an addict enslaved by his drug" (Bejerot, p. xvii).

There are ominous reports from other European countries. Japan had a tremendous epidemic of amphetamine-like drug abuse in the 1945-55 decade but seems to have managed to bring it within control.

A perplexing aspect of the new drug dilemma is well summarized by Professor Martin Roth, Dept. of Psychological Medicine, The Royal Victoria Infirmary, Newcastle, England. He says in his foreword to *Addiction and Society* (Bejerot, p. v). "If an expert in the field of drug dependence with knowledge of the international scene had been asked to predict the effects of improved living conditions on the prevalence of drug dependence he would very likely have forecast a decline in parallel with the reduction of poverty and disease and the improvement of living standards. The trends we have witnessed have proved very different. A new population of drug users drawn mainly from the 15-25 year age group and with a social class distribution close to that of the population at large has arisen."

2
CONTROL OF LEGAL NARCOTIC DRUGS

IN THIS COUNTRY we seek to control the legal and illegal distribution of narcotics and dangerous drugs by both federal and state statutes. Recently the federal laws have been amplified and revised in the Controlled Substances Act of 1970, effective May 1, 1971. Many narcotic and dangerous drugs are valuable medicines. It is necessary, then, that they be freely available to the sick. Many of them are dangerously habit-forming and are the commodity in an illicit drug traffic for the maintenance of addiction, which is a grievous affliction. We do not attempt to set out in any detail the provisions of the various narcotic laws, since they are available, in toto, to law enforcement officers. It might be well, however, to very briefly indicate the structure of the narcotic controls on which we depend.

There are international agreements which restrict the world production of manufactured narcotic drugs to medical needs. There have been continuing efforts by many countries to restrict opium poppy plantings—as distinguished from the manufacture of prepared drugs—to world medical needs. These efforts are not yet completely successful. They may bear more fruit in years to come. Neither opium nor coca leaves are produced within the United States. This country's scheme of control is to estimate how much of this raw material is necessary to be imported to meet medical and other legitimate needs, including production of some drugs manufactured for export. Then imports of opium and coca leaves are restricted to a quantity sufficient to produce that amount, automatically limiting manufacture and preventing the accumulation of any dangerous surplus.

Generally, import of manufactured narcotics is prohibited. In the future it might be possible to import finished narcotic drugs during an emergency when domestic supplies are found inadequate or when competition among domestic manufacturers is inadequate and will not be rendered adequate by development of additional domestic manufacture.

The manufacture of narcotic drugs in this country, both from opium and coca leaves, as well as synthetic, is controlled by a quota system gauged to the medical and scientific needs of the country. Narcotics manufactured within the United States may be exported only under a system of export-import certificates, on which the agreement of both the exporting and importing countries is shown. World quotas are established by a supervisory board of the United Nations.

International treaty negotiations called the Psychotropic Convention were concluded in Vienna, Austria, in February 1971, looking toward the more effective control of hallucinogens, stimulants, and depressants; this is pending ratification by countries. The treaty is considered necessary because those existing do not include the effective control of drugs of this type.

The great value of international agreements to narcotic control is not always known or understood. These contributions were graphically described by Mr. H. J. Anslinger, U. S. Commissioner of Narcotics and U. S. Representative on the United Nations Narcotic Commission, in his testimony before a House of Representatives Appropriations Committee in January 1960.

> In the field of limiting the manufacture of narcotic drugs to the medical needs, control of the distribution, the regulation of the trade, the United Nations has been able to drive all of the trafficking in narcotics underground. There is nothing manufactured now in any legitimate factory, and licensed factory, which gets into the [illicit] trade.
>
> There is practically no diversion. There was a time when it all came from licensed factories. There was no such thing as a clandestine laboratory. Today it is all underground. Everything has been driven into the underworld.
>
> There are 65 new synthetic drugs, all dangerous, and we have not had one case yet of illicit traffic in synthetics.
>
> Just imagine what that means. If we did not have the United Nations control limiting the manufacture, control and distribution, we would just be flooded, the world would be flooded with these very dangerous drugs and, as a matter of fact, before we got it under control, for instance, one of these drugs, pethidine, was already

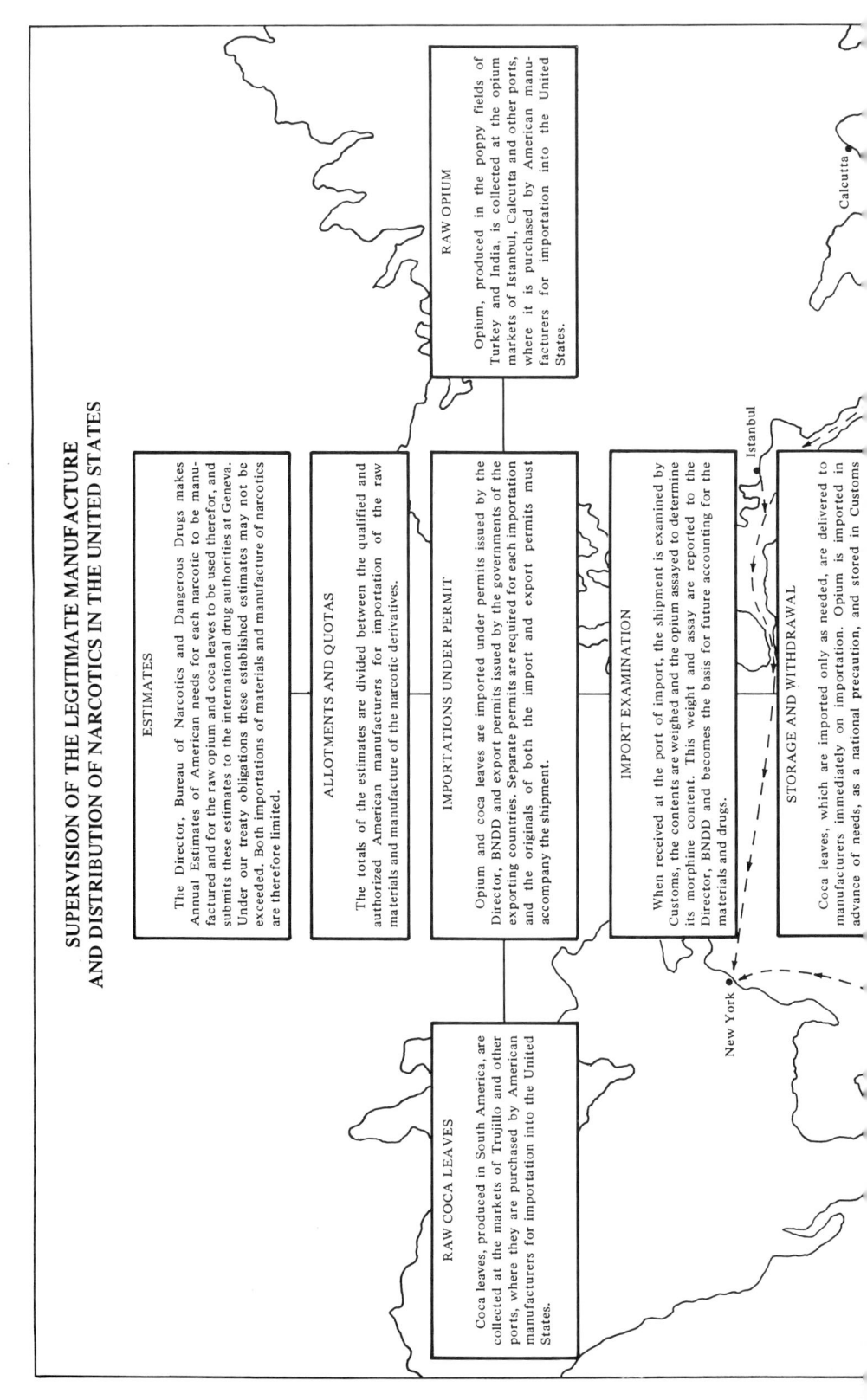

WHOLESALE DISTRIBUTION

Wholesale dealers — who purchase narcotic drugs and preparations in original packages and distribute such packages intact to retail druggists, practitioners and hospitals — render monthly returns accounting in detail for all purchases and sales of such drugs. These returns are audited in the office of the Director and are supplemented by inspections of the wholesale establishments and inventories of their stocks. Wholesalers may also make occasional exports.

MANUFACTURERS OF EXEMPT PREPARATIONS

Persons procuring narcotic drugs for manufacture into preparations of low narcotic content exempted under the narcotic laws, must keep for a period of 2 years, records accounting for the narcotics so received and used and of the exempt preparations sold. These records are subject to inspection at any time by narcotic officers. Those using 1 Kilogram or more of narcotics in a year must obtain procurement quotas and render quarterly returns of their operations.

submit quarterly returns accounting for manufacturing merchandising operations. These returns are audited in the office of the Director, BNDD, and are supplemented by inspections of manufacturing plants and inventories of stocks. Finished products are sold principally to pharmaceutical manufacturers, but sales are also made direct to wholesalers, and other registrants. Some products are exported. Synthetic narcotics, produced from sources other than opium and coca leaves are subject to these same procedures.

NOTE
All sales by one registrant to another must be accomplished by use of special, official order forms issued by BNDD

PHARMACEUTICAL REMANUFACTURE

Pharmaceutical manufacturers who purchase the basic alkaloids for manufacture into pills, tablets, ampoules and other medicines and preparations in forms suitable for use by the patient, render quarterly returns accounting in detail for all manufacturing, packaging and merchandising operations. These returns are audited in the office of the Director and are supplemented by inspections of the plants and inventories of the stocks. The finished products are sold primarily to wholesale dealers, for distribution but sales are also made to retail druggists, practitioners and hospitals. Some products are exported.

RETAIL DEALERS

Retail druggists are not required to render returns but all purchases made by them show up as sales in the returns of manufacturers and wholesalers from whom the drugs are obtained. A copy of each purchase order is also received by the Regional Director, BNDD for the area. Any excessive purchases of narcotics are duly investigated. Sales are made by retail druggists only pursuant to physicians prescriptions and such prescriptions must be kept in a separate file for at least 2 years where they are subject to frequent inspection, as may become necessary by narcotic officers.

PRACTITIONERS

Physicians, dentists, veterinarians and other practitioners are not required to render returns but all purchases made by them show up as sales in the returns of manufacturers and wholesalers from whom the drugs are obtained. A copy of each purchase order is also received by the Regional Director, BNDD for the area. Any excessive purchases of narcotics are duly investigated. Records must be kept of all purchases and dispensing of narcotics, and these must be retained for at least 2 years where they are subject to inspection, as frequently as may be necessary, by narcotic officers.

HOSPITALS, CLINICS, ETC.

Hospitals, sanitaria, clinics, etc., are not required to render returns but all purchases made by them show up as sales in the returns of manufacturers and wholesalers from whom the drugs are obtained. A copy of each order is also received by the Regional Director, BNDD for the area. Excessive purchases of narcotics are investigated. Such institutions are required to keep records of all narcotics purchased and dispensed. These records are required to be retained for at least 2 years where they are subject to inspection, as frequently as may become necessary, by narcotic officers.

EXPORTS

Narcotic drugs are exported under permits issued by the Director. Before any such export permit can be issued the applicant must present an import permit issued by the government of the country to which the drugs are to be exported, and must otherwise comply with the requirements of the international conventions and Title 3, CSA.

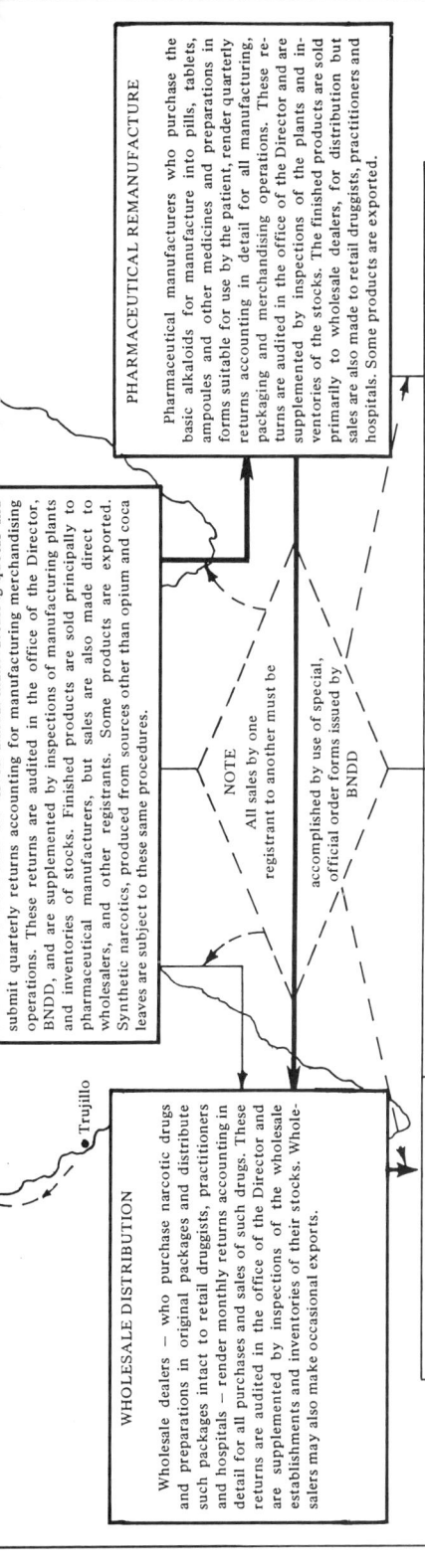

Figure 9. Supervision of the Legitimate manufacture and distribution of narcotics.

being distributed and we grabbed that.

We have not seen in the United Nations any of these synthetic narcotics distributed in the international [illicit] market. That does not mean that some smart chemist is not coming along, but I think we can run him down as we did here. A fellow just got started here and we nailed him. He was with the mob, and since got killed. But with these 65 new drugs, the control is so perfect at this time that I do not think the trafficker is going to be able to get around it. That is all United Nations work.*

Smuggling into the United States is prohibited by severe laws enforced by the Federal Customs. To channel the legal traffic inside the country, and to attack the domestic and worldwide illicit traffic, the Federal Bureau of Narcotics was created. This has been absorbed into the new Federal Bureau of Narcotics and Dangerous Drugs with widely expanded coverage in the dangerous drug and controlled substances field. Because of constitutional limitations imposed on the federal authority, the federal laws must rest on such powers of the federal government as treaty enforcement, control of interstate commerce, or taxation. The Controlled Substances Act of 1970 is now predicated on the power of the federal government to control interstate commerce. Previous tax control statutes have been repealed. Treaty obligations still exist.

Since the operation of Federal laws may not give an entirely comprehensive control, and since it has always regarded the control of dangerous drugs as being a state, as well as a federal responsibility, the federal government has vigorously urged the enactment of uniform state narcotic laws. These, or their equivalent are now in effect in practically every state in the Union. These laws, evidencing the police power reserved to the states, denounce the selling, possessing, transporting, etc., of narcotic drugs directly as an offense, and do not need to rely on the indirection of taxing power or other devices. Taken altogether, world, federal, and state control have exercised a great constricting effect on the narcotic traffic.

One important narcotic drug has some domestic production. That is marihuana, which may be grown in practically any part of the United States. However, the preferred location for produc-

---

*Unfortunately, since Mr. Anslinger made these comments, we began to see in the late 1960's some further indication of the clandestine manufacture of methadone. One substantial laboratory was seized in 1969. There is evidence of further clandestine manufacture of this drug. Increasing maintenance feeding and diversions may inhibit this.

tion of this drug is in Mexico, or other semitropical and arid areas, and the greater part of the supply for the traffic is smuggled. This drug is no longer considered to have any medical use and, unlike the situation respecting opium and coca leaves, there is no importation permitted.

Since jurisdictional changes in the federal enforcement of the narcotics and dangerous drug laws of this country may be a source of puzzlement to the reader, a very sketchy outline of these may be in order.

The first legislation (1909) to prohibit importation of opium except for medical use was a tariff-type control by the Bureau of Customs, with no special effort to enforce its provisions internally.

The Harrison Act to control opium and its derivatives and coca leaves and their derivatives was enacted in 1915 (and reenacted in 1922 with extensive revisions as Narcotic Drugs Import and Export Act) was enforced by the Narcotic Section, Miscellaneous Division, Bureau of Internal Revenue. From January 1920 to April 1926, enforcement was in the Narcotics Division, Prohibition Unit, Internal Revenue Bureau; from April 1926 to June 1930 in Narcotic Unit, Treasury Bureau of Prohibition; from June 1930 to April 1968 in Bureau of Narcotics, Treasury Department. This authority also came to include the enforcement of the Marihuana Tax Act of 1937 and the Opium Poppy Control Act of 1942. Other controls were extended to synthetic narcotic-like drugs.

With the increasing concern over the widespread abuse of three groups of dangerous drugs—depressants, stimulants, and hallucinogens—the Bureau of Drug Control was established February 1, 1966, as part of the Food and Drug Administration, Department of Health, Education, and Welfare.

The present Bureau of Narcotics and Dangerous Drugs in the Department of Justice was established April 8, 1968, when a Presidential order received Congressional approval. It resulted from the merger of the Treasury Department Bureau of Narcotics and HEWs Food and Drug Administration's Bureau of Drug Abuse Control.

Of course, throughout, the Bureau of Customs in the Treasury Department retains very important collateral law enforcement and control responsibilities in all applicable situations.

3

DRUGS OF ADDICTION

Not poppy, nor mandragora
Nor all the drowsy syrups of the world
Shall ever medicine thee to that sweet sleep
Which thou ow'dst yesterday
                    Shakespeare, *Othello*

Opium	*Morphine*	*Heroin*	*Codeine*
Dilaudid®	*Metopon*	*Pantopon*®	*Numorphan*®
Demerol®	*Methadone*	*Levo-Dromoran*®	*Leritine*®

THE ABOVE-MENTIONED drugs are a few of the most common ones in use today. These drugs of addiction will be described in detail in this chapter, but first a word about drug addiction.

Drug addiction is a state in which a person has lost the power of self-control with reference to a drug and abuses the drug to such an extent that the person or society is harmed. A drug that causes addiction is one that is harmful if taken repeatedly over a period of time, and one that the individual is not able to stop taking of his own free will.

1. He becomes emotionally dependent on the drug and desires its effects.

2. He becomes physically dependent on the drug—his body needs it.

3. He becomes ill when he stops taking it. This is called withdrawal illness (the Withdrawal Syndrome).

4. He builds up a tolerance to the drug so that he has to have more and more of it to get the effect he wants.

Drugs that cause addiction should not be confused with habit-forming drugs. Habit-forming drugs are not as strong as addicting drugs and usually are not harmful even if a person takes them for a long period of time, and he can stop taking them if he desires. Tobacco, coffee, tea, chocolate, and cola drinks contain drugs that may be habit-forming, but these drugs are not usually addicting.*

---

*Reprinted from *Facts About Narcotics* by Victor H. Vogel, M.D., and Virginia E. Vogel; copyright 1951 by Science Research Associates, Inc.

Drugs of Addiction

While it would be difficult to convey more or better information in as few words as in the Lexington drug addiction definition (quoted at the outset of this chapter), the concept of drug dependence was elaborated and redefined by the World Health Organization (1964) as "a state arising from repeated administration of a drug on a periodic or continuous basis. Its characteristics will vary with the agent involved and this must be made clear by designating the particular type of drug dependence in each specific case, for example drug dependence of morphine type, of cocaine type, of cannabis type, of barbiturate type, of amphetamine

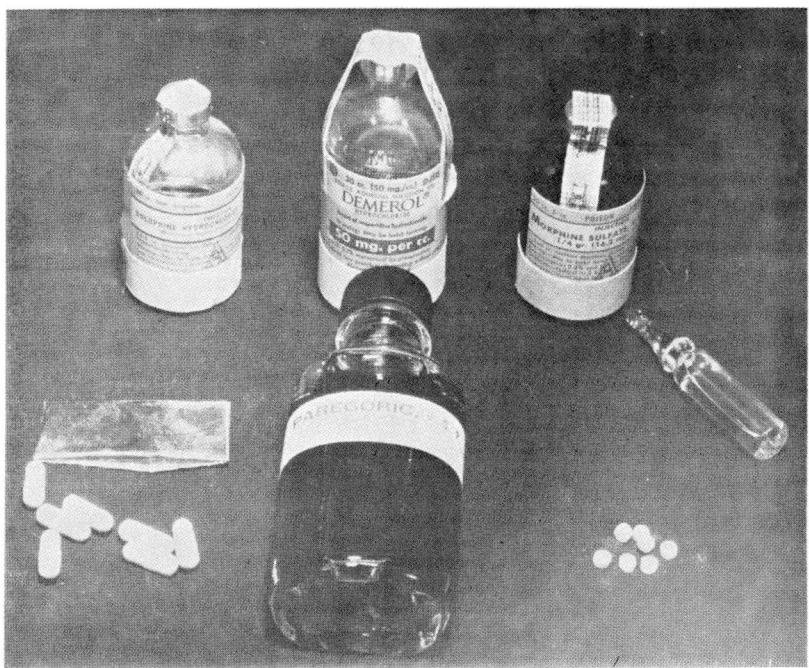

Figure 10. Dolophine, Demerol, morphine solution, heroin capsules and decks or bindles, paregoric, Dilaudid tablets. Reprinted from *Facts About Narcotics* by Victor H. Vogel, M.D., and Virginia E. Vogel; copyright 1951 by Science Research Associates, Inc.

type, etc." These concepts can be the subject of many refinements as Bejerot ably points out in his chapter on "Concepts, Definition, Terminology" *(Addiction and Society)*.

THE OPIATES

Opium is from the opium poppy, *Papaver somniferum*. We have always been intrigued by the old pharmacologists' definition, that

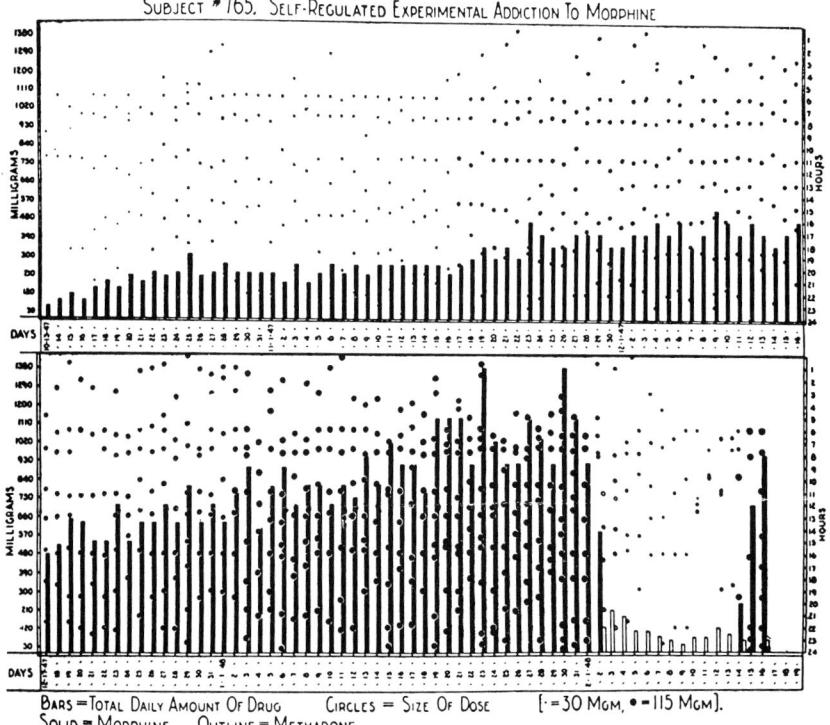

Figure 11. Self-regulated experimental addiction to morphine, as demonstrated at the United States Public Health Hospital at Lexington, Ky. An addict patient was informed he could use any amount of narcotics he chose for an indefinite temporary period. He would be given thirty days notice when he had to quit. In little over three months he built up his daily habit to approx. 20 grains of morphine. When he then was informed he must discontinue taking drugs at the end of thirty days he shifted to methadone to assist him in withdrawal. But near the end of his withdrawal period he abruptly shifted back to morphine in large doses, perhaps for a "last fling" with that drug. This buildup is a dramatic illustration of what most opiate addicts would do if they had free access to narcotics from any source. Chart reproduced by courtesy of Abraham Wikler, M.D. and *Psychiatric Quarterly*.

opium is the "inspissated juice of the opium poppy." "Inspissated" means "concentrated by evaporation." Opium is the dried, or partially dried latex of this one poppy species. As the latex flows from the incised plant, it is milky white. On exposure to air it turns brown, and opium has a dark, molasses brown color. In practice, the milky sap, or latex, is obtained by lightly cutting the unripe seed pods. As Fulton points out *(The Opium Poppy and Other Poppies)*, a similar opium-bearing sap could be obtained from the latex from leaves, stems, or buds, but this would not be a commercially practical operation. The principal narcotic in opium is the alkaloid morphine, and natural opium will contain about 10% or more morphine. Improvements in poppy culture in some

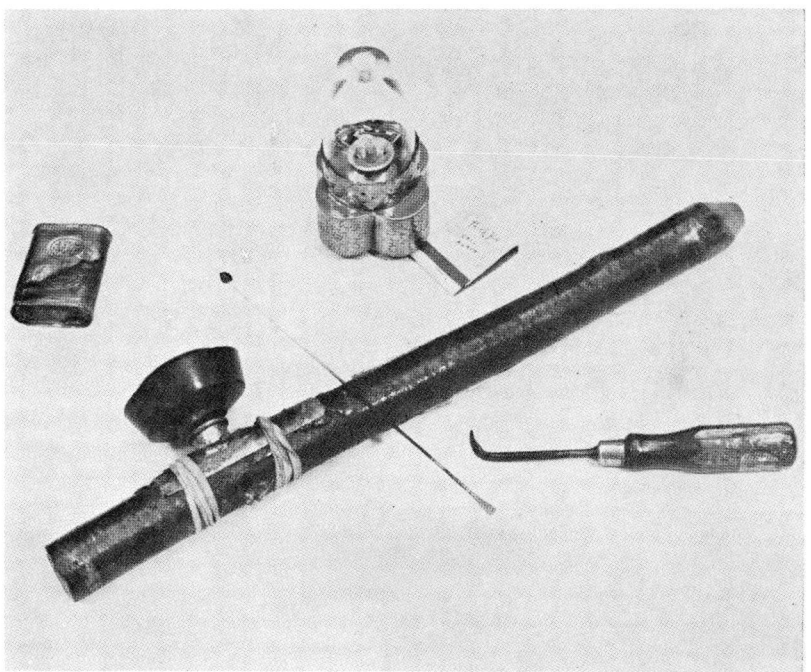

Figure 12. Peanut oil lamp, container for smoking opium, opium pipe, yen-hock (used to hold "pill" of opium for cooking), yen shee gow (used to remove residual opium yen shee from pipe). Courtesy U.S. Bureau of Narcotics.

sections of the world have resulted in production of some opium containing an appreciably higher morphine content, even up to 23 percent. More than twenty other alkaloids appear in opium, but in much smaller amounts than morphine. The opium poppy is the garden poppy which some of our mothers grew at the kitchen door step. It is an annual. It might range through a great variety of color, with flower single or double, petals plain or fringed. The seeds might be light or dark in color. All these changes appear in varieties of the same species. Despite its intriguing name, the perennial oriental poppy, *Papaver orientale,* does *not* produce opium.

Figure 13. The opium harvest. At a stage when the poppy seed capsule is beginning to ripen a circular surface incision, made with a sharp knife, permits a white latex to ooze from the cut. On exposure to air this exudate eventually acquires a dark brown color. When the bleeding is complete the gummy latex is scraped off the pod and collected as with the tool shown or it may be wiped off the capsule with a finger and transferred to a receptacle. This is opium. It is shaped into patties or other suitable forms for sale.

One of the side incidents of World War II was a shortage of edible poppy seed in this country. This seed, which contains no narcotics, is also the product of the opium poppy. (There was no shortage of opium during the war due to the foresight of the Commissioner of Narcotics, H. J. Anslinger, in seeing that this commodity was adequately stockpiled.) Poppy seed had never been produced commercially in the United States. The crop could not compete economically with European production. During the war, when poppy seed soared in price from a few cents a pound to more than a dollar, enterprising people here began to plant the poppy, some in huge acreages. There were a few incidents of diversion, since morphine can be readily obtained from poppy seed capsules or chaff by as simple a process as brewing a tea. This country had no desire to see the establishment of an opium-producing crop in a world in which there already was a surplus four or five times in excess of medical needs, so the Opium Poppy Act of 1942 was passed, permitting the growth of the opium poppy only under license. No such licenses have been issued, nor are they likely to be unless there should occur a world shortage of opium.

It is a curious bit of narcotic law enforcement history that when the necessity arose for restricting a growth of the opium poppy in this country, it had never been definitely determined whether or not this poppy was the unique source of opium or whether it might be obtained from other poppies or even other types of plants. As a matter of fact, there were accounts in the literature indicating that opium might indeed come from other plants such as hops or lettuce. Commissioner Anslinger asked one of us to initiate a study concerned with this possibility. We remembered a brilliant alkaloidal chemist in the Internal Revenue laboratories in St. Paul, Minnesota, and some offhand observations that he had spent afternoons identifying some fifty, or thereabouts, mushrooms as edible. Since a mistake in identifying one of these fungi might have the same result as bad luck in Russian roulette, we concluded that here might be a chemist with more than ordinary botanical background. This proved to be the case. The chemist-botanist Charles C. Fulton made a survey which determined that *Papaver somniferum* was indeed unique as the producer of opium. The summary from his pamphlet, *The Opium Poppy and Other Poppies,* is worth reproducing here.

SUMMARY

[With regard to the poppy covered by the Opium Poppy Control Act.]

1. The Opium Poppy is Papaver somniferum L., an annual,

which is also cultivated for seeds, flowers, capsules, and alkaloids, as well as opium. It can be recognized by the large size of the plant and flowers and its smooth glaucous foliage.

2. Papaver somniferum is a native of the Mediterranean region (southern Europe, Asia Minor), and was first reduced to cultivation, probably for its seeds, in the northeastern corner of the Mediterranean lands (Greece, Anatolia). It has been cultivated in Europe for at least some 4000 years.

3. The "Garden Poppy" of Central Europe is a variety, or an ecological group of varieties, of Papaver somniferum, cultivated for the edible and oil-producing seed. It is not essentially different from the varieties actually used for opium production. It produces the opium alkaloids and if incised will yield opium.

4. The Opium Poppy should not be confused with the Oriental Poppy. That name rightfully belongs to Papaver orientale L., a perennial poppy grown for its flowers. To the flower-gardener only Papaver orientale, its near-relative Papaver bracteatum Lindl., and their hybrids, are "Oriental Poppies."

5. The Opium Poppy should not be confused with the other common annual poppy, Papaver rhoeas L., the "corn poppy" or "field poppy" of Europe, grown in this country for its flowers. Papaver rhoeas is a smaller plant, more hairy and the foliage is a strong green.

6. The Opium Poppy is cultivated in many floral forms and varieties. The flowers may be single, double plain, or double fringed; white, pink, red, mauve, purple, violet, and combinations; the single kinds generally with either a white or a violet spot at the base of each petal. American seedsmen generally listed them as "Tall Annual Poppies" single, "paeony-flowered," "carnation-flowered," and various named varieties. These different forms are still the same poppy.

7. The variations of the Opium Poppy with respect to seed colors, capsule shapes, floral varieties, and agricultural varieties have no significance with regard to its capacity to produce morphine and opium. The seeds may be white, yellow, pink, red, blue, gray, brown, or black. The so-called "Blue Poppy" of Europe is so named from the color of its seeds. There is no basis for the idea that only the white-seeded kind produces opium and that the blue-seeded or some other kind does not.

8. There is only one poppy cultivated now for opium or commercially cultivated for edible seed, although it has sometimes gone under a variety of names. That is Papaver somniferum, the Opium Poppy.

9. The determination of opium poppies will be chemical. Positive proof of the presence of morphine will show that a poppy is an

opium poppy within the meaning of the Opium Poppy Control Act. It need not be proved to belong to the species Papaver somniferum.

Fulton has pointed out some curious bits of folklore which ascribe an opium, or at least a morphine production to other plants than the opium poppy. Over the years some wide circulation was given to the myth that wild lettuce, or even ordinary lettuce had soporific properties due to a morphine content. This idea is completely false. It probably has no sounder basis than that the milky juice of the wild lettuce dries up into a product thought to resemble opium in odor and appearance. The mistaken notion that morphine occurs in hops has a more intricate history. That notion may originally have been folklore arising from the fact that hops have a bitter, alkaloidal taste; also being commonly used in beer-making, it may have been mistakenly deduced that some of the soporific effects of that beverage were due to a morphine content of the hops. However this mistake arose, the perpetuation of the fable resulted in a rather remarkable hoax.

Fulton tells us that in 1885 a chemical house in London (and Brooklyn) announced the "discovery of hopeine," claimed to be a natural alkaloid obtained from hops, and it was put on the market. Actually, hopeine was proved to be a cold-blooded fraud. It was a mixture of morphine and cocaine (the same combination which, in later years, was to acquire much favor in the American narcotic underworld under the term "speedball"). Although the hoax was exposed several times before 1887, "hopeine" died a rather slow death in the literature.

Up to a few decades ago, *all* of the opium alkaloids were produced from opium. However, about 1933, Eastern Europeans perfected a process of extracting morphine and other alkaloids directly from the chaff and straw of the poppy plant; thus, it is possible to bypass the opium stage in producing morphine and other opium alkaloids from the poppy. In this country, however, all medicinal narcotics are produced from opium imported for that purpose. Furthermore, it is very likely that all illicit morphine, heroin, or other true opiates introduced into the country will have been converted or derived from opium.

The production of opium is a costly, hand-labor process. The poppy, as indicated, is an annual crop. Depending on the climate, it may be planted in the fall or early spring. The plant grows in a characteristic, erect fashion. After producing a beautiful flowering display, at the ends of a central and of several side pedicels, it sets a seedpod which on the average may be egg size, but which may run from the size of a walnut to that of a somewhat flattened baseball. When the flower petals fall and the seedpod has attained about a maximum degree of growth, but is still green and sappy, the opium crop is ready for harvest. Skilled workers armed with shallow-bladed, sharp knives proceed down the poppy rows, lightly cutting into the surface of the pod. A white latex oozes from these cuts and dries on the pod surface, gradually turning a dark brown. After a lapse of several hours, depending on the climate—any heavy dew or rain would be fatal to the crop—and when the bleeding of the sap is complete, the poppy harvester returns to the poppy row. With a deft forefinger he wipes the now brown and gummy ooze from the poppy pod and scrapes it into a small container, usually fastened to his belt. The tedious accumulation of these tiny portions is the opium crop. Since most pods, even on the same plant, will ripen unevenly, the opium harvester must rework his poppy rows time and again. Therefore, it is only feasible to produce opium commercially where hand labor is extremely cheap. In some areas a small poppy patch is the chore of old people and children, too old or too young to do heavier labor in the fields.

The field accumulations of opium may be further dried and then pressed into forms or kneaded into shapes of various weights and sizes. Often small stones, leaves, and other debris, as adulterants, are found in this crude opium as an inexpensive way of adding weight.

In the illicit narcotic traffic, opium will be seen in several forms. Perhaps it would be more accurate to say opium *was* seen in many forms, since opium, at present, is a vanishing facet of the narcotic traffic in this country. However, some account of this drug should be of historical interest, and opium, even now, may make an occasional appearance.

Crude Opium

This is the dried latex of the opium poppy as first collected. It will be dark brown in color. It will range in consistency from that of a firmly pressed package of seedless raisins to the texture of plug chewing tobacco. It will come in blocks, molds, or patties, usually in half-pound, or roughly proportional fractions of a kilogram (2.2 pounds). Raw opium often is crudely shaped. We recall that in the early 1920's the Waxey Gordon mob of New York shipped a couple trunkfuls of crude opium to Duluth, Minnesota, designed for the now long defunct illicit market in Minneapolis-St. Paul. The inexperienced officers who accidentally came upon this magnificent haul suspected that they had contraband, but didn't quite know what it was. Over the telephone one of them, from boyhood circus recollections, gave his experienced superior a description which accurately identified it. "Chief," he said, "It looks just like dried elephant droppings." Opium has a characteristic, not unpleasant, musty odor. Crude opium will usually have a morphine content of around 10 percent. Occasionally this will be higher—sometimes twice that amount. Opium used in medicine has a standardized morphine content of 9½ percent to 10½ percent.

Crude opium is seldom consumed in that form although, under some circumstances, it might be eaten, drunk in a decoction, or even, in extreme cases, injected into the vein in a solution. But, in general practice, where it is to be consumed illicitly as opium it is processed into smoking opium.

Smoking Opium

This is a refinement of opium. The crude drug is dissolved in water, the gross debris strained out, and the solution then evaporated down until the opium acquires almost the consistency of caramel or taffy. At this point it may even be subject to a slight "roasting," depending on the idiosyncrasies of the "chef," the title given to the skilled manipulator of the drug. Then a little water is added to bring the finished product to about the flowing consistency of pine tar or thick molasses. In this state, smoking opium is marketed in characteristic containers, one of them being a 5-tael (6 2/3 oz) copper or brass, sealed receptacle, closely resembling in size and shape a Prince Albert tobacco can. This was often embossed with Chinese pictographs and pictures of a tiger, elephant, or rooster, etc., to designate a particular brand. Smaller amounts of smoking opium often were sold in small white glass jars, such as those in which cosmetics are sometimes packaged. Smoking opium also was retailed in small metal containers of the salve box type. Individual rations were sometimes dispensed by being deposited on a folded playing card. In countries where opium smoking is legal or condoned, smoking opium is often marketed in metal tubes somewhat resembling tooth paste containers. Opium sometimes came on the market as stick, or "chopstick" opium, resembling somewhat a long, solid cigar. This was partly refined crude opium, needing only a little working to become smoking opium. The morphine content of smoking opium is relatively high, about 17 percent.

The opium smoker will insist that his method of taking narcotics is by far the most civilized. Since much of our experience with it was inherited from Orientals, particularly the Chinese, there was sometimes ritualism involved, as might be expected. The opium smoker in this country usually used Chinese-type equipment. The main feature was the opium pipe. Near the end of the long, straight stem there was mounted a large, hollow bowl, completely enclosed except for its connection with the stem and a tiny orifice at the top.

The bowl is detachable from the stem to permit of cleaning the inside. When pressed into the stem the union is sealed with a cloth wadding. Opium pipes were sometimes of very expensive, elaborate construction featuring ivory, precious metals, and jewels. In Oriental countries the ornamentation of his opium pipe was sometimes an indication of the wealth and social stature of the opium smoker.

As indicated, the Chinese often brought much ritualism to the process of opium smoking. This smoking is done most comfortably while reclining. The argot is "lying on the hip." For smoking Chinese style, a lighted lamp is required. To insure a non-disagreeable odor, this lamp is usually fueled with peanut oil or some similar vegetable oil. To charge his pipe, the smoker—or an attendant—first dips an instrument like a sharp knitting needle into a container of the molasses-like smoking opium. A twirl of the needle detaches a mass of sticky opium about the size of a large pea. This impaled on the needle is "cooked," heated over the small, peanut oil lamp flame. The opium is just heated sufficiently to drive off some of the water and until the opium pill becomes sticky, about the consistency of well-chewed gum. The process of forming the pill is sometimes facilitated by kneading it on the chimney of the lamp or on the top of the opium bowl.

When it is considered to be of proper consistency, the pill, still skewered on the needle, is placed on the top of the pipe bowl by thrusting the needle through the small orifice thereof. The opium sticks to the pipe and when the needle is removed the pill remains with a small "hole in the doughnut" through which flame can be drawn to consume the opium when the pipe is sucked.

With its pellet of opium atop the bowl, the smoker indulges in two or three lung-filling draughts on the pipe. In doing this, the flame in the peanut oil lamp wick is sucked against the opium and some of it is converted into smoke which is inhaled. Some residue of the opium remains on the top of the bowl, more of it flows inside. All of this residue, or char, is carefully saved by scraping the bowl inside and out, since it still contains a high percentage of morphine. This char is called *yen shee*.

Depending on the size of the pill, two or three pipes of opium would satisfy most smokers and put them in a state of dreamy stupor.

We recall reading, years ago, an article by some Japanese scientists in which they sought to point out that the dimensions and materials of Chinese opium pipes were very carefully calculated to produce a maximum amount of "distillation" and a minimum amount of "incineration" of the opium in the process of smoking.

As the opium smoking operation in this country had become continually more furtive, some addicts reverted to makeshift pipes which might not be readily recognizable as such. One might see a baby's milk bottle with a needle hole as a pipe bowl and rubber tubing used to improvise a pipestem. Doorknobs with a needle hole have been used as makeshift pipe bowls. While the American addict and the American policeman think of opium smoking in terms of the Chinese pipe, much of this drug is consumed in other parts of the world with other apparatus. It is sometimes smoked mixed with tobacco. In some Indo-Chinese areas, it was smoked in an open pipe something like a tobacco pipe. Combustion was assured by packing it with some aromatic tow and a hot coal placed thereon with the tongs to furnish the flame.

As narcotic law enforcement in this country grew increasingly rigid, opium smoking was the first addict practice to disappear. The reasons are apparent. Opium has ten times the bulk of morphine, hence it is more difficult to smuggle and more difficult to conceal. The characteristic odor is a dead giveaway to the educated nose of the narcotic officer. Smoking apparatus requires time to destroy or conceal and its possession is incriminating. So it is natural that the dedicated addict would soon find it expedient to practice his vice in ways less subject to police detection.

Yen Shee

This is a residual ash and debris left when opium is smoked in a pipe. It still contains a substantial proportion of the morphine content of the opium, and is a valuable commodity in the opium smoking traffic. This yen shee, or char, is carefully scraped from opium pipes. It is often mixed with a little fresh opium for resmoking. Often, yen shee is put in a solution with water, wine, or spirits. This the opium smoker or other addict will often use to forestall withdrawal symptoms, the pangs of abstinence, when opportunity or circumstances do not permit him access to his pipe.

Yen shee suey, resembling in appearance a dark, liquid cough medicine or a similar remedy, might be overlooked by the narcotic officer, particularly if the bottle bears an innocent label. We recall the case of an excellent fur thief in Utica, New York. He made a practice of "lifting" expensive fur pieces, placing them in a prepared carton, and almost immediately dropping them in the security of the United States Mail. He came to grief when, suspicious, someone closely examined a bottle labeled as stomach medicine in his effects and it proved to be yen shee suey.

Powdered Opium

Powdered opium is opium dried and reduced to a very fine powder. Powdered opium yields not less than 10% and not more than 10.5% anhydrous morphine. Powdered opium is light brown to moderate yellowish brown. It consists chiefly of yellowish brown to yellow, more or less irregular and granular fragments, varying in size.

Powdered opium is the preferred medical dosage form whenever it is desired to administer opium in the solid state. It is given in doses of 30 to 200 mg. It would seldom be seen in the illicit traffic now except as the incidental proceeds of the burglary of a drug store.

Tincture of Opium

This is also known as laudanum and contains approximately 10% opium. Laudanum is probably the best of opium preparations where the effects of the whole opium are desired. The use of laudanum has greatly decreased since the enactment of the Harrison Narcotic Law. Prior to that time, when there was no control over the sale of opiates, there were many laudanum users in the United States.

Paregoric

This is officially known as camphorated tincture of opium. This contains tincture of opium, benzoic acid, anise oil, camphor, alcohol, and glycerin. There are approximately two grains of opium per ounce. Paregoric is an "exempt narcotic preparation" and can be sold in some jurisdictions over the counter by a pharmacist providing he keeps a record showing the date, name of recipient, preparation, and the amount. Paregoric is sometimes used by addicts when they are unable to obtain their usual narcotic supply. Sometimes this preparation is boiled in order to drive off the alcohol, and the residue is used hypodermically by the addict. Some state laws limit the exempt sale to one person to two ounces in forty-eight hours. The addict may attempt to cheat by going to several drug stores.

Morphine

This in an alkaloid obtained from opium. It is the chief narcotic principle of opium. The morphine alkaloid occurs in the form of colorless, shining crystals, having a bitter taste. Morphine continues to be one of the most important, though most troublesome, drugs in common clinical use. The alkaloid is only sparingly soluble in water and in order to get the maximum desired effect, it is usually given in the form of salts, such as morphine sulphate, morphine hydrochloride, morphine acetate, and morphine tartrate. The most common preparation is morphine sulfate which is sold legally for medicinal use in tablets containing $1/12$, $1/8$, $1/6$, $1/4$, and $1/2$ grain. Morphine sulfate is also combined with atropine sulphate in tablets, usually 1/4 grain of morphine and 1/150 grain of atropine sulphate. This combination is also prepared in sterile solution, usually in 20 cc vials, with 1/4 grain morphine and 1/150 grain atropine sulphate per cc. The morphine and atropine combination counteracts the depressant action of morphine without decreasing the pain-relieving action. Morphine, like all opiates, has a tendency to produce constipation, slows heart action, causes constriction of pupils, and may cause nausea and even vomiting. An average dose of morphine sulphate, 1/8 to 1/4 grain, administered hypodermically in the human, is followed by a prompt drowsiness characterized by muscular relaxation, freedom from anxiety, a rapid flow of ideas, shortening of the sense of time, disappearance of pains, doubts, and inhibitions, and increased ability to discriminate but less ability to concentrate, lessened physical activity, and dimness of vision. Sleep ensues unless the environment prohibts, and dreams may be experienced.

Heroin

Diacetylmorphine hydrochloride is the hydrochloride of an alkaloid base obtained by the action of acetic anhydride on morphine. It is a white, odorless, crystalline powder with a bitter taste. The general physiological action of diacetylmorphine is much like that of morphine. Controlled studies indicate a potency of heroin four or five times greater than that of morphine; a technical study (League of Nations, 1939) of morphine and other addicting agents concluded the therapeutic dose of heroin to be 5 mg against 10 mg for morphine *(Synthetic Substances with Morphine-like Effect,* by Nathan B. Eddy, 1957). Therapeutic dose of heroin is often stated as 5 to 10 mg, even though it has been shown that the pain-threshold-raising dose is only 1 to 2 mg. Duration of effect is shorter for heroin; nausea and vomiting and the milder side effects occur less frequently after heroin than morphine. Heroin is more addicting than morphine and addiction develops more rapidly. Heroin would not have a sufficient preponderance of advantages over dangers to justify retention as a therapeutic drug, and because of the greater danger of addiction following use of the drug, its manufacture or importation into the United States is prohibited. Heroin, which is more potent than most other narcotics, can produce a most vicious addiction. Because of this potency, together with the strong euphoric effects, this drug is always in great demand by addicts, and accordingly it has become the foundation of the illicit traffic. Heroin, when first produced, was sold as a substitute for morphine. It was even claimed to be a cure for morphine addiction. (This was true, only because once a morphine addict started to use heroin he seldom went back to the use of morphine, but preferred the more potent, dangerous drug!)

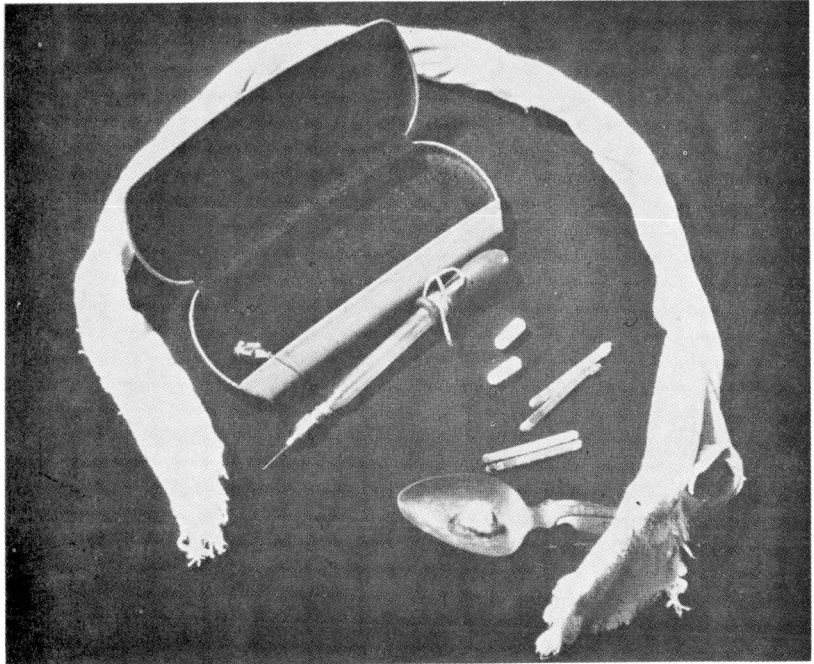

Figure 14. The addict's "works," carried in a spectacle case. His heroin is in the capsule (cap). He empties this into the bent spoon. When it is dissolved in a little water heated with the matches, it is then taken into the medicine dropper syringe through the small cotton pledget (cotton) which serves as a strainer. With a handkerchief, necktie, nylon stocking, or other strong tourniquet, he distends a vein in his arm or other member and injects this vein with the contents of the medicine dropper.

Diacetylmorphine was reported as early as 1874 by C. R. Wright at St. Mary's Hospital in London. At first there was not much interest in the drug which Wright called tetra acetyl morphine. However, in the 1890's Dreser and others studied the physiological effects of diacetylmorphine. Their favorable reports caused the Bayer Company in Germany to start production on a commercial scale. The new compound was marketed by Bayer under the name "Heroin" (probably after German *heroisch,* meaning large, powerful, markedly effective, even in small doses). The drug continues to be best known as heroin. When first introduced, it received a spontaneous and widespread acceptance in the treatment of the then very prevalent tuberculosis and other respiratory diseases. Heroin was first considered to be non-addicting. Although warnings were issued as early as 1899 that the drug might be dangerous, it was a long time before there was appreciation of the full danger of heroin addiction. In the meantime, word of its charms as a dissipating drug quickly spread throughout the drug-using underworld. However, by 1916 the Public Health Service hospitals in the United States had discontinued dispensing heroin. In 1920 the House of Delegates of the American Medical Association adopted a resolution reading in part as follows: "That heroin be eliminated from all medical preparations and that it should not be administered, prescribed, nor dispensed, and that the importation, manufacture, and sale of heroin should be prohibited in the United States." By the 1920's the use of this drug was common in the American underworld, particularly in New York. It was estimated that there were a minimum of 10,000 heroin addicts using a total of 76,000 ounces of heroin annually in New York City alone. Addicts were described as taking as much as 80 grains a day and the intake of the average addict as 15 to 20 grains. *(United Nations Bulletin on Narcotics,* April-June 1953). The amounts of heroin consumed by the individual addict in the 1920's seems almost incredible in the light of the present day situation. Today the addict "shooting" a 5% mixture may take in hardly a grain.

The observation of both physicians and police of that day was that heroin was an extremely dangerous drug contributing to both the physical and moral deterioration of the individual. These contemporary conclusions by astute observers should not be forgotten.

As the result of the disasters experienced with heroin, the Congress in June 1924 passed legislation prohibiting the importation of opium for the manufacture of heroin in the United States. This action outlawed heroin with the exception of residual stocks which might be legitimately in the possession of pharmacists or others. Finally, in 1956 any residual stocks were bought up by the United States Government and the drug completely banned in American medicine.

Heroin, like morphine or other opiates, may be taken by mouth or hypodermically, subcutaneously or intravenously. Addicts may use heroin alone or with cocaine by sniffing it up the nose where it is absorbed through the mucous membrane. Heroin and cocaine are also taken, mixed, by hypodermic needle. This mixture is known as a "speedball." Heroin is in particular favor with peddlers because it can be very readily diluted in sugar of milk or other mixtures. The result is that as it goes from hand to hand in the drug-dealing fraternity, it is cut and cut, each cut representing a large profit. When it finally gets to the street addict, there may be only a trace of the drug remaining in the sugar mixture. Dilutions down to 5 percent are common. Often heroin is sold in as weak as 2% mixtures.

A Chinese practice not yet reported in this country, but which might well be transplanted here, is the method of smoking heroin called "chasing the dragon," or its variant, "playing the mouth organ." In "chasing the dragon" the heroin and any diluting drug are placed on a folded piece of tinfoil. This is heated with a taper and the resulting fumes inhaled through a small tube of bamboo or rolled paper. The fumes move up and down the tinfoil with the movements of the molten powder, resembling the undulating tail of the mythical Chinese dragon. When a matchbox cover instead of a tube is used to assist in inhaling the vapor, that operation is called "playing the mouth organ," which the action suggests. Hong Kong addicts often employ barbiturates as a diluting powder in the smoking of heroin. This brings about a particularly dangerous form of drug addiction.

Thirty-five or forty years ago heroin was commonly smoked, usually with a little tobacco in a small pipe, as a red pill or pink pill. There was no reason for the coloring except as an idiosyncrasy. The pills, somewhat larger than a pea, were rolled from a heroin-sugar mixture, sometimes also including caffeine and strychnine. They were first imported from China. In the middle 1930's, a thriving domestic industry sprang up in Chicago for the manufacture there of pink pills which were distributed throughout the country until raids and arrests finally broke up the business.

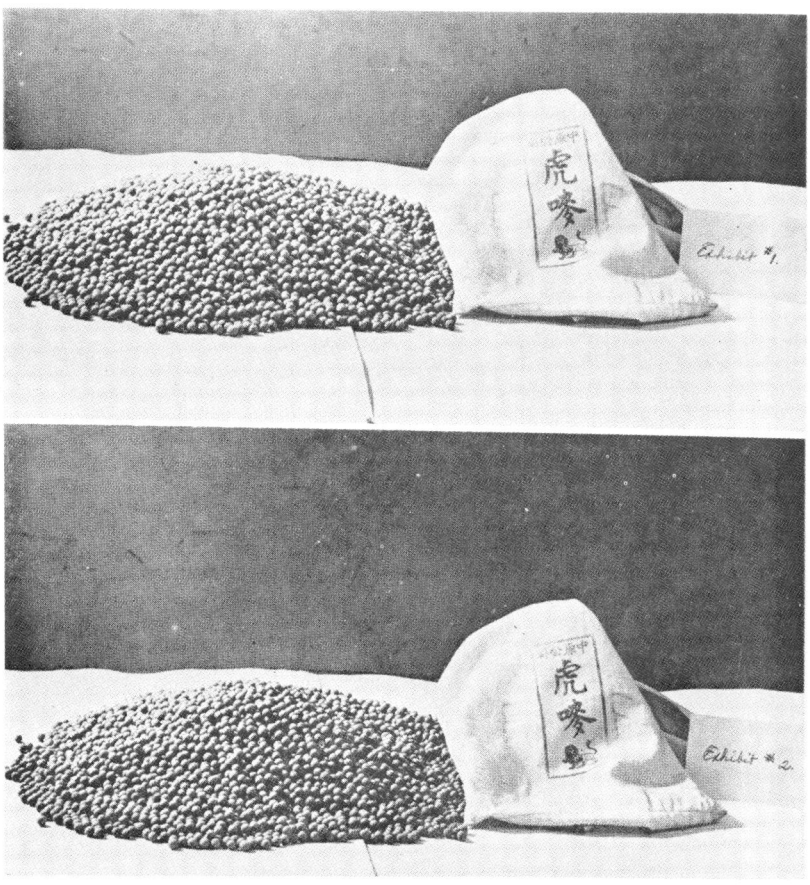

Figure 15. Pink pills (heroin), another part of the changing narcotic traffic. These have not been seen since pre-World War II days. About the size of a pea, these pills contained a mixture of heroin and a sugar paste and were colored pink for no apparent reason. Sometimes the label claimed without justification that they also contained tiger marrow. First manufactured in and imported from China, an extensive manufacture developed among the Chinese in Chicago in the middle 30's. Photo courtesy U.S. Bureau of Narcotics.

Fulton aptly designates heroin as "the most dangerous drug in the world" *("Narcotics" Encyclopedia of Chemistry,* Supplement).

Codeine

This is an alkaloid from opium or prepared from morphine by methylation. Codeine resembles morphine in its general physiological action, although much weaker. Codeine is about one-sixth as strong as morphine and is used for the relief of pain and as a respiratory sedative. As an analgesic it is inferior in power to morphine and scarcely strong enough for acute suffering. It is commonly prescribed in combination with the so-called coal tar analgesics for such pains as those of neuralgia. As a cough sedative, it is probably the most frequently used drug of its class. The great advantage over morphine, which makes codeine the most frequently prescribed opiate in the United States, is the comparatively small danger of giving rise to a drug habit. While codeine addiction is comparatively rare, it is habit-forming. Codeine is capable of alleviating the withdrawal symptoms in the morphine addict, but when the codeine is stopped there is the same type of withdrawal symptoms as seen in morphine addiction. The symptoms of codeine poisoning in man differ considerably from those of morphine. There is usually narcosis, sometimes preceded by a feeling of exhilaration, and followed by convulsions. Codeine is on the market as codeine sulphate and codeine phosphate, in powder and in oral and hypodermic tablet form. There are other codeine preparations on the market in combination with aspirin, phenacetin, and caffeine.

Dilaudid®

This is a proprietary brand of dihydromorphinone hydrochloride, used mainly as a substitute for morphine. It has a much greater analgesic effect, but of shorter duration, than morphine. Dilaudid is about ten times as analgesic as morphine but the duration of analgesia is shorter and is only about four times as somnifacient. It is a fine, white, crystalline powder prepared from morphine and is very popular with addicts who inject it intravenously. As a medicine it is given by mouth, by hypodermic injection, or as a rectal suppository. Dilaudid is in powder form, tablets, suppositories, ampuls, and vials. Tablets are made in different strengths as $1/16$ grain, $1/20$ grain, $1/24$ grain, $1/32$ grain, and $1/64$ grain. There is also a compounding tablet which contains $1/2$ grain Dilaudid. This tablet is known by addicts as a "football."

This tablet is not prescribed but is used by pharmacists in compounding prescriptions. The 1/24 grain tablet is an oral tablet and the others are hypodermic tablets. The suppository contains 1/24 grain of Dilaudid. There is also a Dilaudid cough syrup for use in the relief of harassing non-productive coughs of all types, acute bronchitis, and bronchial irritation.

Metopon

This is a methyl derivative of Dilaudid and was developed in the course of a coordinated program of several agencies seeking to find a non-addicting, pain-relieving drug comparable to morphine. It is a white, crystalline powder produced as a hydrochloride and has a high analgesic effectiveness when administered orally. It does not cause nausea or vomiting, and tolerance and dependence develop slowly. This narcotic is given orally in 6 to 9 mg doses and is used in incurable cancer cases. Metopon is known chemically as methyldi-hydromophinone hydrochloride.

Pantopon

This is a proprietary mixture which contains the total alkaloids of opium as soluble hydrochlorides and can be referred to as a purified opium preparation. This preparation is absorbed more promptly and is free from the nauseant odor and taste of opium. Pantopon is marketed in 1 cc parenteral ampuls, each containing 1/3 grain, in powder form; in 1/3 grain hypodermic tablets; and in 1/6 grain oral tablets. This preparation is used in surgery, in obstetrics, alone or in conjunction with scopolamine, in difficult labor cases. It is less depressing to respiration than the same amount of morphine alone; Pantopon has the same addiction liability as morphine.

Numorphan® (Oxymorphone)

This is a newer morphine-like drug with increased analgesic potency. The addicting properties of this drug are thought to be between morphine and Dilaudid. Since physical dependence is directly proportional to the amount of the administered narcotic, dosage should be kept as low as possible to delay the onset of tolerance. The recommended dosage is 1.5 mg. A dose of Numorphan is equivalent to about ten times the quantity of morphine and to about 1 1/3 times the quantity of Dilaudid.

SYNTHETIC OPIATES

In the last few decades rapidly widening horizons in drug chemistry have produced new drugs, some bringing with them great new values, and some introducing new problems. Among these were synthetic preparations which, although they were not derivatives of opium, have opiate-like characteristics. These drugs were part of the never-ending search for a drug with medical assets of opium without its liabilities, i.e. without its addicting and its tolerance- and dependence-creating properties. At this writing, that drug has not yet been found. Many of these opium-like synthetics are of great value in medicine for their special analgesic properties. Typical of these is Demerol.®

Demerol

This is a brand of meperidine (isonipecaine hydrochloride), a synthetic narcotic used primarily as an analgesic. Its analgesic power ranks between that of codeine and of morphine when effective doses are given. Demerol is now available on the market in nine forms and combinations and is used in the relief of pain as a preanesthetic medication. For parenteral use there are several combinations, such as Demerol hydrochloride 5% solution, 50 mg per cc; new Demerol hydrochloride 10% solution, 100 mg per cc; Demerol with scopolamine; and Demerol with atropine. For oral use the following are available: Demerol hydrochloride tablets; Demerol hydrochloride elixir (50 mg per teaspoon); Demerol powder; and A.P.C. with Demerol tablets (aspirin, phenacetin, and caffeine).

This drug was first synthesized in Germany in 1939. It was introduced into the United States about 1941 or 1942. The drug was announced with some well-deserved fanfare as an analgesic and spasmolytic, and as particularly valuable in obstetrics and gynecology—which it is. However, there was also some sadly mistaken propaganda that the drug was non-addicting. Early in 1942 the U. S. Bureau of Narcotics had received a report by Himmelsbach of the Lexington hospital showing that preliminary studies had indicated Demerol possessed addiction liability. The bureau urged that the descriptive literature on the drug be modified to include addiction liability warnings. Subsequent studies by Himmelsbach at

Lexington confirmed his first findings, that Demerol could be dangerously addicting. In light of the Lexington reports and bureau urgings, the literature on Demerol was revised to indicate that it was an addicting narcotic; however, on the basis of the earlier descriptions, there remained a widespread impression that the drug was harmless. There was soon incontrovertible and pathetic evidence to the contrary in a stream of addicts, many females, some of them nurses, who were seeking relief from addiction. Here is a demonstration of one of the most valuable but unheralded contributions made to medicine by the U. S. Public Health hospitals at Lexington and Fort Worth. In these institutions exact information has been developed on the addicting properties of innumerable new drugs. The experience with Demerol caused it to be brought under federal control by the Act of July 1, 1944. In 1946 a law set up machinery whereby all new opium-like synthetic drugs found to have addicting properties may be quickly classified as "opiates" and placed under federal control.

Perhaps due partially to the circumstances under which Demerol was first put on the market in this country, it is one of the most common drugs of addiction among the few physicians and nurses who become victims of the narcotic habit. Convulsions sometimes seen in users of Demerol are probably due to excessive dosage of the drug. If a person having access to medicinal opiates develops convulsions it is a good tentative conclusion that the patient may have been using Demerol. On the other hand if an addict, not a physician or nurse, develops convulsions within twenty-four to forty-eight hours after drugs are taken away from him, it is likely that this addict has been taking barbiturates in addition to his supply of opiates, as convulsions are often seen in withdrawal from heavy barbiturate use.

Methadone Hydrochloride

This is a synthetic narcotic also known as methadone, Amidone®, Adanon®, and Dolophine®. It was released for sale in 1947. Its effects generally are those of morphine, except that they develop more slowly. Methadone may cause nausea, vomiting, dizziness, faintness, dry mouth, and constricted pupils. Tolerance develops more slowly than with morphine. Single analgesic doses seldom cause euphoria, but large doses in addicts may cause euphoria for one to two days. It may cause drug addiction and it may be used to prevent withdrawal symptoms in morphine addicts. This potent synthetic analgesic drug has certain structural resemblances to both morphine and meperidine. Methadone is used in controlling post-operative pain; in relieving pain in malignancy, renal colic, bladder spasm, and other nonsurgical conditions; as a cough depressant. Methadone is supplied in solution form in 1 cc ampuls containing 10 mg, in 20 cc vials (each cc containing 10 mg), and also in 30 cc vials, in 2.5 mg, 5 mg, and 7½ mg tablets, and a syrup containing 1.67 mg in each teaspoonful.

One of the most interesting uses of methadone is in withdrawing addicts from heroin, morphine, or other opiates. If the person addicted to heroin (or other narcotic drug) has a relatively light habit he might be given a very few doses of the long-acting methadone. With a heavier habit he might require a daily dose of the longer-acting drug for a week or two. This in effect substitutes a methadone addiction for heroin addiction. The addict then can be withdrawn from methadone with less physical discomfort. In the late 1950's when heroin available on the streets was very dilute, "addicts" could be readily withdrawn with the administration only of a sleeping pill or two (see "Narcotic Withdrawal," p. 188).

Now, of course, we are seeing the extensive use of "methadone maintenance" in which the addict is saturated with methadone and kept so for a long or permanent period. This may have alarming implications insofar as a realistic drug control program is concerned. We will discuss this more fully at page 121.

Levo-Dromoran®

This is a synthetic narcotic analgesic similar to morphine. It is particularly useful because of its oral effectiveness and low incidence of constipation. The length of action is somewhat longer than morphine. The addiction liability is equal to that of morphine.

Leritine®

Leritine, also anileridine, is a synthetic narcotic analgesic drug. It is used in all types of pain including angina pectoris, renal colic, and carcinoma. Leritine is used in dental practice, particularly in the field of oral surgery. Leritine is supplied for oral use as tablets and for parenteral use as Injection Leritine in 30 cc vials.

The foregoing list of drugs is necessarily incomplete, but includes, we think, most of the opiate drugs of importance at this time to narcotic law enforcement officers.

Research in the narcotic field may be expected to produce many new drugs. Those of opium-like addicting properties will be legally classed as opiates.

OTHER ABUSED DRUGS

Cocaine

Cocaine is from the coca leaf. The coca plant is grown in the Andean highlands in South America and in the East Indies. The habitual use of cocaine as a narcotic stimulant is a problem of sociological importance. There is a psychic, rather than physiological dependence on the drug. A symptom which is seen in many cases, and which is said to be characteristic of chronic cocaine poisoning, is a sensory hallucination of some foreign body under the skin, or of insects crawling over the person. Some addicts under the influence of cocaine describe police officers entering their room through keyholes and through the cracks of the doors and windows. This was described in the argot as the "Bull horrors." Cocaine is a dangerous drug and a person may develop such strong desires for it that he is unable to stop using it. However, the drug does not cause physical dependence or withdrawal illness.

When the opiates were plentiful, cocaine was used by addicts in combination with morphine, heroin, or opium to counteract the sleep-producing effects of the opiates; conversely, the opiates tended to minimize the sometimes frightening "thrill" of the cocaine. As law enforcement efforts increased, and as Asiatic and South American sources were restricted and as good substitutes were found for the drug in medicine, the abuse of cocaine diminished and in the 1930's it practically disappeared from the illicit market. There was a flare-up about 1947 which subsided rather rapidly. As we said in our preface, this drug has made a reappearance in the drug abuse field in the last few years and now should be a matter of grave concern. The favorite argot for cocaine is "snow," from its white, crystalline appearance.

Cannabis

As with opium and the poppy, only one species of plant produces the active drug principle of marihuana and that is the hemp plant, *Cannabis sativa,* sometimes also known as *Cannabis indica* or *Cannabis mexicana.* In this country the only important appearance of this drug was as marihuana, which is the coarsely pulverized leaves and flowering tops of the cannabis plant. The intoxicating principle occurs throughout the growing plant except in the seeds (however, in the federal definition, and in most states, seeds are included in the definition), but it is most highly concentrated in a sticky resin produced in the flowering tops as the seeds are set. Cannabis may be found in the illicit traffic as marihuana, as the hashish of the Middle East, which is the concentrated resin from the flowering tops, and in various other parts of the world as "kif," "takrouri," "dagga," "bhang," "charas," "manzoul," "maconha," "djamba," and "esrar." While *Cannabis sativa* grows over a wide range of climatic conditions, the intoxicating principle seems to be most highly concentrated when the growth is under hot, semiarid conditions. While there is a considerable domestic supply of marihuana in the United States from plantings which have escaped from hemp cultivation, or which have been developed from the accidental sowing of seeds in birdfeed mixtures, the marihuana crop so produced is relatively impotent and is not sought by traffickers. However, when other sources are unavailable, domestic production of marihuana is utilized. Marihuana is harvested by stripping the leaves and flowering tops of the cannabis plant, allowing them to dry, roughly pulverizing these, and sifting out the twigs and seeds. The resultant product, usually of a texture between tea and smoking tobacco, is smoked as marihuana in this country. It is usually found in a thin, hand-rolled cigarette.

When hashish is produced in Near Eastern and Asiatic countries, the tops of the plants are usually beaten against walls or floors covered with a blanket or other cloth, or leather. The floor or wall covering is then scraped for a sticky deposit and this gummy substance is hashish. It is related that in some very arid countries where the production of cannabis resin on the plants is heavy, it is harvested by workers who walk up and down through the rows in leather coats which accumulate the resin. The sticky resin is then scraped from the coats.

Marihuana does not create the dependence and tolerance of the

Figure 16. Close-up of the seedpods of the cannabis plant from which concentrated hemp resin is obtained. Grown in the United States. Courtesy U.S.P.H.S. (There is little or none of the active principle in the seed itself.)

opiates. That is, it does not do so with the casual use which is characteristic in this hemisphere. There are some indications that

Drugs of Addiction

very heavy use of hashish does produce a dependence. Marihuana though fundamentally a depressant is often primarily used for its initial excitant character. Its effect may be unpredictable. The files of the Federal Bureau of Narcotics contain many well-documented

Figure 17. Flowering top of the cannabis plant grown in the United States. Marihuana. Courtesy U.S.P.H.S.

incidents of bizarre and sometimes senseless crimes committed under its influence. The most severe indictment which can be made of marihuana is that its use in this country has led, with considerable regularity, to the subsequent use of heroin. First initiated to the chemical exhilaration of marihuana, the smoker is readily induced to try heroin for a "bigger kick."

Fortunately, cannabis had never attained the vogue in this country that it has in some areas of the world where it is by far the most outstanding and dangerous drug of addiction. A February 1960 Associated Press dispatch from Cairo, Egypt, quotes the Cairo Institution of Social Research as reporting that in thirty years, 16,000 Egyptians have died from consuming hashish, 35,000 addicts have been admitted to mental institutions, and 110,000 wives have divorced their husbands for using the drug.

The tendency here has been to consider that the casual use of marihuana does not lead to appreciable physical damage to the user. In that connection we might make an observation. In days gone by, when cannabis was still considered to have some therapeutic use, the only way of establishing its potency was by biological tests on an animal. The animals then used for the purpose were dogs. After these dogs had been used in these biological tests, the animals were left so uncoordinated that they had to be destroyed.

A story in *The New York Times,* datelined Rabat, Morocco, April 20, 1960, reports a ban on hashish, or kif, production in Morocco "as the major contributory cause to mental illness in this country. The large majority of the 1850 patients at Morocco's only psychiatric hospital are kif addicts. This is also true of the 565 provincial psychiatric centers." The story further quotes the public health officials that this narcotic "not only affects mental health but is bad for the heart and tends to produce sterility."

* * *

Cannabis might have been thus rather briefly discussed in 1961, but not so today. Within the last few years it has become an important facet of some aspects of the so-called youth rebellion, generation gap, anti-establishment movement or what not. It is now a highly significant segment of the polydrug abuse epidemic. Now it is the subject of the most vociferous pro-drug propaganda ever known in this country.

Dr. Henry Brill, director of Pilgrim State Hospital, West Brentwood, N. Y., and one of this country's foremost authorities on drug abuse, has made a revealing dissection of the pro-marihuana dialectic (Wittenborn, Smith and Wittenborn [Eds.]; Chap. 3).

He says "By dialectic I mean 'a logical term generally used in common parlance in a contemptuous sense for verbal or purely abstract disputation devoid of practical value' or 'argument by critical examination; often used in the sense of destructive argument.' "

Dr. Brill observes "At a moment when the real drug problem is a pandemic contagion of polydrug abuse which has seriously involved hundreds of thousands of young people in major countries throughout the world, we have allowed ourselves to be hopelessly entangled in too much sterile, circular, interminable scholastic discussion about the theoretical significance of 'an occasional marihuana cigarette in a normal person' which distracts attention of the profession as well as the public from the serious drug issues."

Dr. Brill points out that whereas only a few years ago social and hedonic drug use was universally condemned as drug abuse, the situation has changed radically in less than ten years. For the first time in history there is a highly articulate pro-drug movement with informal leadership and a highly developed pro-drug, anti-establishment dialectic. This uses some of the very sophisticated weapons of argumentation which law enforcement officers might sometimes recognize as like the final recourse of the defense lawyer in a bad case. Dr. Brill does a superlative job in pointing out the extensive fallacies of the pro-marihuana dialectic, the "one cigarette" gambit, the phony appeal to science, the incomplete and out of context quotations from surveys and reports, the comparison of marihuana with alcohol, the semantic quibbling, i.e. is marihuana a "narcotic," is it "addictive," aren't some people "dependent" on insulin, and so on. Dr. Brill's presentation could well be read in its entirety by anyone likely to be required to enter on debate. As he says, "This chapter has given some examples of favorite pro-drug arguments and has presented my own views as to what is valid in them and what is invalid, misleading or contrived for the purpose of turning the audience against the speaker."

Complaint has been heard from the pro-cannabis claque that

some of the incidents formerly published by the then Federal Bureau of Narcotics alleging violent conduct by cannabis users were not sufficiently documented. Sometimes the nature of the incident and the opportunity to inquire did not permit of the fullest documentation. Nevertheless these can be cited as a caution to law enforcement people.

As this was being written, there appeared an account in the newspapers of the shooting of two county policemen in connection with a drug and larceny arrest. The case is not further identified, as action is still pending. After the suspect had been arrested and a quantity of alleged marihuana and other suspected contraband drugs had been seized, the prisoner was released on bond. Meanwhile, as it was raining, police officers had taken the suspect's impounded car into a garage for a more thorough search. While so engaged, the released prisoner appeared armed with a pistol, sneaked up behind the busy officers, got the drop on them, disarmed them and then shot two of them, one in the hand and another in the back, and made his escape; to be captured in an eastern city several days later. Unfortunately it may not be scientifically demonstrable that the bizarre acts of the defendant were the result of cannabis intoxication, since presumably he had access to other drugs also, but any intelligent officer will not discount that possibility. As might have been expected, at the trial resulting in his conviction, the defendant claimed that drug use had affected his mind, according to newspaper accounts.

On May 25, 1971 the 21 year-old daughter of a former prominent city official and two young men, 22 and 25 years of age, were arrested on murder charges after the holdup of a savings and loan firm in Washington, D.C. in which a policeman was killed, shot in the back. The alleged robbers and murderers are from backgrounds not ordinarily likely to produce bank robbers. When their alleged domicile was searched several plastic bags of marihuana were found, according to press accounts. On June 10, 1971 the *Washington Star* published a story quoting a Georgetown associate of the suspects as making reference to them as follows: "When it happens to people I have seen and smoked with I begin to wonder where my friends and I are going." (Copyright 1971. *The Washington Star*.) Reprinted by permission.

The Washington, D.C. newspapers recently informed us, (December 16, 1971) that on December 15, 1971, in the District of Columbia Courts the young woman pleaded guilty to first degree murder, armed robbery, robbery and illegal possession of dangerous weapons, and was sentenced forthwith under the generous provisions of the Youth Corrections Act. Her companions have since been convicted.

For those who insist that only laboratory evidence is relevant there is a wonderfully relevant, though unscheduled, demonstration reported by Dr. Abraham Wikler in the *Archives of General Psychiatry,* vol. 23, Oct. 1970, p. 362. "Another subject (of a study at the Lexington Hospital) became disturbed after smoking marihuana cigarettes 'I do not recall how many' in the course of an EEG investigation. . . . Jumping off the bed he seized a heavy instrument (I believe it was a tin shears) held it over my head, threatened to bash it in if I or any of the shop personnel made any move, and accused us of trying to control his mind. . . . Needless to say we did not make any move, but after a few minutes (it seemed like an hour) of verbal persuasion, he allowed himself to be escorted to the disturbed psychotic ward, where he made an uneventful recovery after a day or two."

In the same article Dr. Wikler makes this observation (p. 324): "Is marihuana dangerous to health, personal or public? . . . Apart from the possibility of 'adverse reactions,' I personally would not care to be passenger in a car chauffeured by a driver who could not remember whether or not he had just placed his foot on the brake—or was it the accelerator?"

Coming from a scientist whose hospital and laboratory experience with cannabis would be surpassed by only a very few, if any, this is an impressive indictment of the drug.

Another of the illustrious Lexington scientist coterie, Dr. Harris Isbell, who for many years was director of the Addiction Research Center at Lexington, reported in 1967 that "It has long been known that marihuana and hashish cause psychotic reactions, but usually such reactions were ascribed to individual idiosyncrasies, rather than being usual or common reactions to the drug. The data in these experiments, however, definitely indicate that the psychotomimetric effects of delta 1-THC are dependent on dosage and that sufficiently high dosage can cause psychotic reaction in almost any individual" (Isbell, "Studies of Tetrahydrocannabinol," p. 4844).

The pro-marihuana dialectic insists that there is not enough "scientific information" to disbar marihuana. Such items as the above, plus the recent findings of such researchers as Dr. Vincent dePaul Lynch, Professor of Pharmacy at St. John's University, should be ample warning. In the INEOA Annual Conference Report (1969, pp. 65-66) he states: "Synthetic THC is readily absorbed by animal fetuses across the placential membrane. . . . Our principal endeavors have been in the area of fetal effects—and these studies are very promising—as well as in the area of reproduction and genetically induced abnormalities. The latter opens a whole new world of research, but it perhaps fulfills a prophecy made during a lecture on marihuana in 1949 by Pablo Wolff: 'I repeat my initial warning. There is not, as is the case with the opiates, any reason, any excuse, any indication for its use. It is always an abuse, dangerous to the individual and to the race.' "

With the increased scientific interest aroused by the head-long rush of some of our youth toward marihuana we can expect that there will be much more scientific elaboration on the dangers of cannabis—as if any more were needed. For, of course, all wisdom does not come out of a test tube or through a microscope, although with our training we should be the last to minimize their importance. The oyster had been used as human food for generations before these instruments were dreamed of. We are now reading that this great ape, Homo sapiens, has been around in something very close to his present being for some 40,000 years. In that time he has learned a lot, much of it on primitive empirical observation. Several hundred years ago and perhaps much earlier, he found out there were some bad things about cannabis. Lewis Lewin, described by Bejerot as the "great German toxicologist and polyhistorian" (Bejerot, p. 26) published a remarkable book, *Phantastica,* which first appeared in German in 1924 and was published in an English edition in 1964. In his discussion of Indian hemp—*Cannabis indica*—he relates that in 1374 the Arabic emir Soudoun Sheikhouni, aware of the abuse of cannabis among the poor, sought to end it by destroying all the plants, imprisoning all hemp eaters and pulling the teeth of all convicted hemp eaters. He cites the thirteenth century story of the alleged relationship of the word assassin to Hashishins (herb eaters) and the assumption that this was hemp and that in some sort of dosage it provoked fanatical action and murder. (We are aware that recently more than one lawyer has raised a question on this etymology of "assassin" which has been used on occasion by such authorities as Bejerot, Maurer and Vogel, Anslinger and, we estimate, scores of other experts we have read. The story could be apocryphal. But the point which the recent critics seem to miss is that this tale, fact or fable, persisted in areas where cannabis was well-known as a drug. And the story would not and could not have survived if it had not been associated with the local reputation of the drug described, which of course had to be bad if its use spurred one to assassinations or if the results of its abuse were so obnoxious as to suggest that offenders should be deprived of their teeth.) Lewin cites the abuse of hashish in Egypt. Habitual smokers lost their reason and suffered from delirium and were liable to commit excesses. He cites that in 1800 a Napoleonic general prohibited the drug throughout Egypt. Lewin cites abuse of cannabis in other parts of Africa, Asia Minor, and Asia. His comments on the varying effects of cannabis are often very similar to those we get from informed sources today, which of course follows logic since neither the physiology of the human nor the pharmacology of the tetrahydrocannabinols would have changed. Some of Lewin's observations were as follows: perhaps sexual potency as believed by the user is increased at the outset but it diminishes during the subsequent addiction; anxiety and restlessness are followed by a sense of physical well-being and internal content; there may be an exhibition of gaiety in a childish and stupid manner, convulsive laughter and weeping, and confusion and far-away thoughts; the bonds of time and space are broken; there may be hallucinations and fear, a delirious joy, fear of falling, a torrent of senseless words; dependable servants become unreliable; whole village populations are morally and physically ruined (p. 122).

We have referred thus extensively to a great physician and pharmacologist of an earlier generation simply as a small indication that cannabis long has had a bad reputation. The pro cannabis dialectic assumes that the then U. S. Commissioner of Narcotics, Harry J. Anslinger, in 1937 foisted unwarranted legal controls on a harmless plant. The foregoing is just to suggest that the Commissioner had behind him several centuries of the wisdom of the race that cannabis was bad.

We are reminded that the intoxicant potential of marihuana was noted in a pharmacopeia prepared by the Chinese emperor Shen Nung, dated 2737 B. C. (Lieberman and Lieberman).

Anne Caldwell, M. D., in her delightful and informative book *Origins of Psychopharmacology from CPZ to LSD* Charles C Thomas, Publisher, Springfield, Illinois, 1970, p. 56 reminds us, "psychopharmacology dawned in ancient Greece when drugs were studied by Helen of Troy and drug reports sung by Homer."

Also she reminds us that long before that "the use of such drugs was part of everyday life, blue morning glories covered the entrance to cave man's abode and a bowl or green seeds of ololiuqui might have stood inside. *Amanita muscaria,* the brilliant red mushroom with dots of white grew in shady groves. Yellow-orange fruits of the cactus studded arid plains. Red poppies bent their heads when it rained in the spring. Rauwolfia blossomed pink on tropical Himalaya mountains. Coca grew green and wild in equatorial America and so did cannabis nearly all over the world. Fresh, whole, ground or dried leaves, fruits, roots, bark, stems or seeds were chewed or brewed and sipped, rolled and smoked or somehow ingested to alter mood or state of mind—and this is psychopharmacology." (p. 3).

A related item in the pro cannabis dialectic is that the present contention that in this country there is a progression in drug abuse from cannabis to the opiates is not true. To support this it is solemnly disclosed that while Commissioner Anslinger so testified in 1951 he is on record as saying in 1937 that such progression was not the case. The fact of this contrasting testimony is correct but the conclusion is erroneous and obviously arises out of ignorance of the drug abuse history of this country.

Cannabis is a relatively new drug in our society. It was introduced as marihuana in the 1920's and became increasingly evident in the 1930's, the decade in which Mr. Anslinger is supposed to have brought about the passage of the marihuana control act of

1937 on little or no evidence.* If this were true it would indeed be a remarkable tribute to the capability of one man! A little historical light may be useful here. Mr. Anslinger has been a remarkable public servant. We would rate him as among the top three law enforcement officers of the last half-century. He was an administrator and a diplomatic negotiator of rare ability. Incidentally, he had an unmatched sixth sense to recognize and plug little leaks that unnoticed might have washed away the dikes of narcotic drug containment. Beginning with his employment in the State Department where in World War I he was a sort of one-man OSS in the Low Countries, he became head of a foreign control (of contraband material) office in the Treasury Department in the 1920's and subsequently the first U. S. Commissioner of Narcotics in 1930. He was equipped as few men could have been to know the world picture on the abuse of narcotic drugs. Considering the history of cannabis and its presence at that time in the Near East, Africa, and Asia, one with his knowledge would have been compelled to urge on the Administration and the Congress the legislative course that eventually was taken against cannabis when this dangerous drug was seen to be acquiring a foothold here. However, in 1937 the marihuana underworld in this country was still very small and extremely spotty. It did not then form a wide base for recruitment to opiate addiction. So the Commissioner of Narcotics was factual when in 1937 he so indicated. By 1951 the picture had changed. During the World War II years we had developed a substantial quota of marihuana users, many, in our opinion, anxious to avoid military service. Some of these had shifted from marihuana to cocaine when it made a brief but fleeting appearance here right after World War II. More, and in substantial numbers, went to heroin when it made its post-World War II appearance, as we have pointed out in some detail in this book. We had a part in determining the facts. Intermittently after 1936 we devised questionnaires for our field officers for the interrogation of the opiate addict encountered, as to the route by which he acquired his addiction. Our insistence that the agent report the exact language of the addict yielded information that has supported two propositions respecting opiate addiction: (1) opiate addiction

---

*For a current responsible discussion on this point, see David F. Musto, M.D. The Marihuana Tax Act of 1937. *Archives of General Psychiatry,* 26, February 1972.

is usually preceded by some sort of criminality (it may be that some qualification must now be made in view of the influx of younger people into the drug abuse culture); (2) numerous marihuana users had found a progression to heroin, enough to make it abundantly clear to any narcotic officer that there was a positive association. Our former cannabis users were telling us "I saw them shooting up [heroin] and they seemed to like it so much I thought I'd try it," or "Try this kid, you haven't seen anything yet," or "This is God's medicine."

These arguments have been labored and belabored. But let us repeat a little circumstantial evidence of the sort which most law enforcement officers appreciate when the wordy debate is too prolonged. Maurer and Vogel, with wide experience in the narcotic abuse field, are long-time keen students of underworld argot and they have made profound studies of the argot of narcotic addicts. They point to specialization in the argot of various criminal groups and then state: "Among modern heroin users, however this pattern is changing, since so many of them started with marihuana and consequently carried over into heroin addiction, their earlier argot usage connected with marihuana. In a sense, they have corrupted the argot of the users of hard drugs by needle in something of the same manner that needle addicts 'corrupted' the argot of the old time opium smoker" (Maurer and Vogel, p. 326).

Such evidence as this makes more obvious the obvious, that often there is substantial progression from cannabis to heroin. However, we can expect the pro-marihuana dialectic to continue to beat this dead horse, a practice which now becomes particularly inane in the light of the present developments of what Brill calls a pandemic contagion of polydrug abuse.

One need not be a marihuana user to become a heroin addict. But in our opinion the evidence is irrefutable that it often helps.*

And of course the dialectic insists that cannabis is no worse than alcohol, an observaton which may approach the ultimate in

---

*Reports of progression from marihuana to heroin addiction take on an ad infinitum aspect. As late as November 30, 1971 the *Washington Post* refers to a survey of 225 heroin addicts given exhaustive physical examinations at the District of Columbia narcotic clinic. The average age was 23.1 years. The addicts started smoking marihuana at 18 and switched to heroin at age 19.

faint praise. Bejerot tells us that in Sweden "about 10% of the men and 35% of the women never drink alcohol; 80% of the men consume small quantities of alcohol (moderate quantities only occasionally) while the remaining 10% are heavy drinkers. . . . For heavy drinkers alcohol is a serious problem and about half of them, 5% or somewhat more, of all men in the country suffer from an alcohol dependence of the same severe character and strength which characterizes the classic addiction. Among women, advanced alcohol dependence is far less common and only affects about 1% of the adult women. Alcohol abuse among women, however, has increased rapidly in Sweden since the ration of alcohol was abolished in 1955; the same applies to the abuse of alcohol among the youths" (p. 47).

And Bejerot concludes with this observation: "We 80% who sometimes take a glass and appreciate it and have the situation under control, do our drinking, strictly speaking, at the cost of the 10% who are now or in time will be alcoholics" (p. 50).

There seem to be some rough parallels between the Swedish alcohol problem and ours, and in that light Dr. Bejerot's comment is indeed a sobering one.

Professor Martin Roth, in his foreword to Bejerot's *Addiction and Society,* states (p. ix): "Most of the population of economically advanced countries is largely without social or biological experience of many of the narcotic and stimulant drugs now extending in pandemic fashion. They are therefore in a position analogous to the aboriginal populations who so often appear to have been affected in devastating ways of alcohol."

There has come to our attention a 1970 paper, "Clinical Notes on the Use of Marijuana," by D. Harvey Powelson, M.D., Chief Psychiatrist at the University of California.* The psychiatric clinic sees about 3,000 new students each year and has many other student contacts. On the basis of five years' observation and study, Dr. Powelson, who indicates he was once soft on marihuana, has concluded that "pot smokers can't think straight." Smokers tend toward paranoid attitudes, he observes.

He says, "In summary it is now my judgement on five years

---

*Personal communication to author.

of extensive clinical experience that (1) the use of marihuana leads acutely, and for several hours to days thereafter to a disorder of thinking characterized by a general lack of coherence and exacerbation of pathological thinking processes, (2) that the effects of marihuana are cumulative, (3) that after a period of prolonged use (say 6 months to a year) of marihuana in frequent dosages (on the order of one time daily) that chronic changes occur which are similar to those seen in organic brain disease— islands of lucidity intermixed with areas of loss of function."

As this book goes to the printer we continue to receive evidence of the bad performance of cannabis.

From the September 1971 conference of the International Narcotic Enforcement Officers Association at Albany, N. Y., we have a further report from Dr. Vincent dePaul Lynch who we have indicated is a leader in the field of exploration of cannabis pharmacology. In recent experiments he had administered controlled doses of cannabis to rodents. When these produced progeny there was little evidence of birth abnormalities in the first generation. But in the next, the "grandchild" generation, there have been significant evidences of fetal defects. Dr. Lynch points out that it would not be practical to perform experiments with humans, but findings such as these should help to dispel irresponsible claims for a "harmless" drug.

Also, Mr. Owen H. Stephenson, Assistant Commissioner of Police, Kingston, Jamaica, at the September 1971 conference INEOA at Albany, N. Y., spoke of cannabis, the use of which as bhang (marihuana) was introduced into Jamaica about 200 years ago. Commenting that Jamaican marihuana was regarded as quite potent, he said that no experienced law enforcement officer in those islands would regard it as anything except a very dangerous drug. He said that among its users was a relatively new crop of bank robbers in Jamaica; also its use seemed to be associated with "kill and mutilate" crimes in the islands. He displayed some shocking photographs of what he called "recent bestial crimes" in which marihuana figured.*

---

*Published in Twelfth Annual International Narcotic Conference Report (INEOA) September 1971. Albany, N. Y.

Also in the International Narcotic Report for September 1971 (INEOA), Albany, N. Y., there is a paper by Herbert Berger, M.D.* covering a current study of 343 addicted individuals under the age of twenty over a seven-year period. Dr. Berger reports that the great proportion started drug abuse with marihuana and his breakdown is as follows: marihuana 308, heroin 7, barbiturates 4, LSD 11, amphetamine 13. Dr. Berger's findings on drugs now used are: heroin 290, marihuana 200, amphetamine 39, LSD 12, barbiturates 172, cocaine 4. Dr. Berger explains that the figures total more than 343 because there is multiple use by some addicts and he comments on the significance of graduation from marihuana to heroin.

Recently there has come to our attention a paper, A Toxic Theory Linking Acute Cannabis Intoxication and Regular Use, by Conrad J. Schwarz, M.B., Ch.B.†

Dr. Schwarz cites as his observations that

1. Regular users of cannabis show psychological and physical symptoms similar to those of the acutely intoxicated individual.

2. The effects of cannabis can persist beyond the acute state of intoxication.

3. The symptoms in regular users show marked improvement on discontinuation of cannabis.

4. The major chemically active ingredient of cannabis and its metabolites persist in the human body for quite prolonged periods of time after exposure.

Dr. Schwarz states

Although references used in this paper are almost all from material published in the last two and a half years, like Hollister, I believe that apart from the chemistry and metabolism of cannabis, in terms of the clinical effects of marihuana the recent observations, important as they are, have in general only refined and translated into modern terminology the findings of the older clinicians and researchers. In fact, in some ways the earlier literature is much more informative, particularly in the areas of the physical effects of cannabis and of the general description of the acute experience.

Compulsory Education: A Cause of Drug Addiction, by Herbert Berger, M.D., F.A.C.P., Director of Medicine, Richmond Hospital, Staten Island, New York.

†Consultant Psychiatrist, Student Health Service and Clinical Associate Professor, Department of Psychiatry, University of British Columbia, Vancouver, B.C. Paper read at the Western Institute of Drug Problems. University of Oregon, Portland, Oregon, August 7, 1971. To be published in the proceedings.

From our own rather extensive review we had expected to say something like this in this book. Dr. Schwarz has put it more aptly than we might have, and concludes as follows

> Finally, of course, those who are currently insisting that their regular use of cannabis is not affecting their functioning should be prepared to disprove the hypothesis by submitting themselves to clinical and laboratory examination.

Just received is a copy of a statement by a group of ten leading Canadian doctors* which they recently submitted to the Canadian government and to their medical associates in Canada. It begins with the admonition

> Silence on the harmful effects of marihuana, hashish, and other "soft" drugs must end.

One of the several recommendations is

> That under no circumstances must the government of Canada consider the legalization of marihuana while increasing clinical and scientific evidence points in a contradictory direction. We urge that trafficking be dealt with firmly to prevent further spread of illegal drugs, and that these and other issues be considered and dealt with in recognition of the over-riding need to curb the spread of these substances.

There is included a statement

> The brain and its nervous system is our most precious heritage of evolutionary development. Youth will require the full use of its amazing capacity, unimpaired by drug abuse, to help them deal effectively with life's continuing challenge, both now and for all the adult years ahead of them.**

Rational consideration of the foregoing ought to give pause to those who see no harm in adding another plague to our present alcohol afflictions. As we have said on previous occasions: "What does it profit us if we fill our classrooms, our work shops, our offices, our streets with stoned or half-stoned incompetents? Do we need another intoxicant in the automobile drivers on our highways? Do we really need another hallucinant in our thinking? Do

---

*F. A. Dunsworth, M.D.C.M., Halifax, N. S.; Charles Brown, M.D., Charlottetown, P.E.I.; Austin Delaney, M.D., Moncton, N.B.; M. R. Duguay, M.D., Montreal, Que.; F. W. Lundell, M.D., Montreal, Que.; C. Conway Smith, M.D., Montreal, Que.; Walter Wren, M.D., Windsor, Ont.; Walter L. Percival, M.D.; Windsor, Ont.; J. L. Asselstine, M.D., Winnipeg, Man.; James Carlisle, M.D., Ottawa, Ont.

**The Washington Post, Dec. 12, 1971, carried a story by Alfred Friendly from London that four British doctors writing in The Lancet (Dec. 4, 1971) suggested that prolonged, heavy cannabis smoking might bring about irreversible and serious brain damage.

Drugs of Addiction

we need another deliriant in our drunks? Do we want to add the dry rot of cannabis to the wet rot of alcohol? If I may make a play on the word, the 'stone' of cannabis can cripple the mind, can kill ambition, can destroy the purpose and effectiveness of many lives. To the albatross of booze now hung on our country's neck it would be irrational indeed to add the stone of cannabis suspended in the choking noose of hemp" (Harney, *Wayne Law Review* p. 278-279).

As stated, cannabis in this country will be most often found as marihuana in cigarettes or in bulk, an alfalfa green, roughly pulverized, leafy material. When smoked, marihuana has a characteristic odor which can be recognized. The marihuana user will give some of the indications of the alcohol drunk, but without the alcohol odor. His eyes may be reddened and the pupils may be somewhat dilated. He may laugh or giggle without reason. His ability to judge time and distance is impaired. Because the time interval is distorted, marihuana smoking sometimes was resorted to by musi-

Figure 18. Special Agent Frank Farrell examines a marihuana brick. Forty-six bricks of marihuana, weighing 122 pounds (the equivalent of 122,800 marihuana cigarettes) were found in the door panels, trunk, and under the rear seat of a vehicle in New Jersey bearing California license plates. Photo courtesy U.S. Bureau of Customs, May 1970.

cians, who believed that it improved their performance. Scientific testing has proved that this is like a drunk singing in the shower —it seems sweet only to him.

Hashish

"The leaves and flowering tops of the hemp plant *(Cannabis sativa* and *Cannabis indica)* are covered with a resin that contains the active constituent CANNABIN. (It is the Cannabin in the marihuana plant which produces the physiological effect of the drug.) This resin is collected from the plant by any of several methods (leaching with alcohol, beating, etc.), after which it is compressed. The compressed resin is hashish, which has a euphoric effect on the user ten times greater than marihuana. It takes about 625 pounds of marihuana to yield one pound of hashish.

Hashish is commonly compressed into varying shapes . . . or may be formed into a powder. The hardness or brittleness of the hashish cakes depends on age and exposure to air.

Hashish ranges in color from light brown to brown to dark brown to very dark green to black.

Hashish may be packaged in cloth wrappers . . . plastic bags, wax paper, butcher paper, cellophane, burlap bags, or any combination of these. Hashish cakes have been found concealed behind framed pictures, in table tops, statuary, compartmented handbags, and even manufactured into articles such as decorative plates.

Since Hashish may originate in the Orient, the Middle East, and in Mexico, it may be encountered at any port of entry into the U. S." (Courtesy Bureau of Customs, U. S. Treasury Department).

SOME OTHER DANGEROUS DRUGS

Hallucinogens

Hallucinogens (also called psychedelics) are drugs capable of provoking changes of sensation, thinking, self-awareness, and emotion. Alterations of time and space perception, illusions, hallucinations and delusions may be either minimal or overwhelming depending on the dose. The results are very variable; a "high" or a "bad trip" ("freak-out" or "bummer") may occur in the same person on different occasions.

LSD is the most potent and best-studied hallucinogen. Besides

Drugs of Addiction

Figure 19. Lumps of hashish were found inside this bronze Buddha which arrived in Los Angeles in a false-bottom trunk. Courtesy U.S. Bureau of Customs.

LSD, a large number of synthetic and natural hallucinogens are known. Mescaline from the peyote cactus, psilocybin from the Mexican mushroom, morning glory seeds, DMT, STP, MDA, and dozens of others are known and abused. Along with its active component THC, marihuana is medically classified as an hallucinogen.

For a more detailed discussion of the hallucinogens, stimulants, and sedatives see Appendix.

Barbiturates

Barbiturates have sedative and hypnotic effects. They affect people much like alcohol but leave no odor on the breath. Overconsumption may cause death, since they are not as easily vomited as alcohol. Suspect them as possible cause in connection with intoxication, coma, death, accidents, assaults, wild parties, delinquency.

Typical of the barbiturates are secobarbital sodium, known in the drug industry as Seconal®, phenobarbital sodium, known as Nembutal®; amobarbital sodium known as Amytal®; and secobarbital plus amobarbital, known as Tuinal®. In the illicit traffic these drugs are known as "red birds," "goof balls," "yellow jackets," "blue heavens," etc.

Barbiturates are valuable drugs for legitimate medical purposes but can be very harmful if misused. A person under the influence of barbiturates acts like one who has had enough alcohol to show signs of it. How much it takes to produce the degree of intoxication observed depends mostly on how used to the drug he is. Habitual users keep taking more and more, and in time they get up to amounts that would kill anybody who has not grown accustomed to the drug gradually.

The person who "gets drunk" on barbiturates follows about the same course as the person who takes a drink and keeps on drinking until he "passes out." A small amount makes him feel relaxed, sociable, good-humored, but he is less alert and slower to react. After taking more he becomes sluggish, gloomy, maybe quarrelsome. His tongue gets thick, he staggers about for a while, and then gradually slumps into a deep sleep, or, especially if he has had a lot of the drug, he may suddenly collapse into a coma. If that happens, he may die unless medical attention is prompt. Barbiturates are more dangerous than alcohol at this stage because they are not vomited, and all that is taken will be absorbed unless the stomach is pumped. *Even when there is no sign of life a doctor should be called at once because some cases have been revived.*

Those who become dependent upon the drug must have it to keep from getting sick. Without it they have fits that look like epileptic convulsions and are dangerous. Treatment should be under medical supervision in a place where the patient cannot possibly get any of the drug the doctor does not allow.

Whenever a person acts like he has had a little or a lot to drink but there is no odor of alcohol, it is possible he has been using barbiturates. Sometimes barbiturates and alcohol are taken together. This produces what looks like an ordinary "drunk" but it takes much longer to sober up.

Amphetamines

Amphetamines are stimulants. When improperly used they tend to create reckless behavior and may be a cause in connection with accidents, wild parties, assaults, burglary, and delinquency.

Up into the 1960's, as usually abused in this country, the amphetamines were considered to be less dangerous than the barbiturates. However, there is now seen a worldwide abuse, sometimes epidemic in nature, which presents very serious problems, as described by Professor Martin Roth in his preface to Dr. Nils Bejerot's book *Addiction and Society.*

> In certain respects amphetamine abuse creates a more dangerous form of dependence than that which follows the taking of heroin. Dependence tends to be swiftly established when the intravenous route is used and deterioration of behaviour and social adjustment are rapid.
>
> The most serious social and medical problems are presented by those who escalate from pep pills and marihuana to intravenous heroin or amphetamine-like substances.
>
> Those so affected suffer from a seriously incapacitating form of drug dependence with a high mortality. For psychological and economic reasons they are strongly motivated to convert others to their pattern of drug abuse and, as the intravenous method of administration has also to be learned, the phenomenon spreads in a manner analogous in certain aspects to contagion in an infectious disease.
>
> In 1955 there were more than half a million amphetamine addicts in Japan, about 300,000 of them using the drug intravenously. In

the rigid restriction of the use of amphetamine-like substances that followed they were almost entirely eliminated.

Doctor Bejerot's account of the Swedish epidemic and the lessons he has drawn from it deserve the attention of those concerned with the control of drug abuse all the world over. [pp. vi-vii]

Typical of the amphetamines are amphetamine sulphate and dextroamphetamine sulphate known in the pharmacy trade under such names as Dexedrine®, Dexedrine® Spansule®, and Timcaps. In the underworld amphetamines are often referred to as "bennies."

These drugs have legitimate medical uses but can do great harm if they are used improperly. Their effects are just about the opposite of those from barbiturates; that is, instead of producing relaxation and sleep they make a person more active, and if he keeps taking more he can keep going for hours or even days without sleep or rest. A very few people get sick from a single tablet, but most people are not affected that way.

These drugs are misused by individuals who want to work or play harder or longer than their normal capacity allows, and also by persons who feel that the drugs make them more lively, talkative, and self-confident. The stimulating effect of amphetamines is sometimes relied on by criminals to increase their "nerve." Occasionally they are a cause of reckless behavior by juveniles.

These drugs do not create energy in the body, but whatever is stored up is released by hiding the feeling of tiredness and the need of sleep. They decrease the appetite, and this cuts down the normal supply of energy from food. That, together with the lack of sleep and rest, can ruin health in the long run. Possibly their greatest danger to the individual and society is the effect they may have on automobile drivers. When a lot of any one of these drugs is taken at one time, or if they are used over too long a period without rest and sleep, they may produce hallucinations in which a person thinks he sees something that really isn't there. Or, he may "black out" suddenly while driving at high speed.

TESTS

Heroin and Methadone

There are several tests giving characteristic color reactions which are used for the specific identification of opium and various drugs of the opiate series. These tests are known by the name of the reagent used, that is, Marquis, Nitric Acid, and Ferric Chloride.

Marquis reagent is prepared by adding two or three drops of 40% formaldehyde to 3 cc of pure, concentrated sulfuric acid (H_2SO_4). (Care must be used in handling concentrated sulfuric acid.) Marquis reagent is on the market in small scored ampuls, conveniently packed in small tin boxes. A test set consisting of twelve scored ampuls of Marquis reagent contained in a packet arranged for easy access may be obtained from Ferguson Company, 814 Ridgely Street, Baltimore, Maryland, at a nominal cost.

MARQUIS TEST: Place small amount of suspected powder on white porcelain and add a few drops of Marquis reagent. If heroin is present, a reddish-purple color will appear. The reddish colors are more prominent with heroin than with morphine.

MARQUIS REAGENT

Drug	Results
Morphine	Deep magenta to deep violet
Heroin	Deep magenta to deep violet
Codeine	Blue with violet cast
Opium	A dark purple
Methadone	No reaction
Cocaine	No reaction
Aspirin	Colorless to pink to deep rose
Darvon	Purple to red
Amphetamine	Orange to orange with brown cast/orange to pale red
Miltown	No reaction
Librium	No reaction
A.P.C.	Colorless to pink to deep rose
Tuinal	No reaction
Chloral hydrate	No reaction
Phenobarbital	No reaction
Mescaline	Green, changing rapidly to dark brown, slowly changing to brown with violet cast

FIELD TEST FOR METHADONE (To be done in the absence of a positive Marquis reaction for opium alkaloids): This narcotic drug, known also as Amidone, Dolophine, and *dl*-6-dimethylamino-4, 4-diphenyl-3-heptanone hydrochloride, can be detected in the presence of some other drugs as well as inert diluents by employing the reagent and technique as set forth below. After solution is effected, filtration of the sample is desirable, but not essential to the success of the method, since insoluble substances such as starch and talc are not blue in color.

METHOD

Reagent: Dissolve 1 gram of cobalt acetate, nitrate or chloride and 1.5 grams of potassium thiocyanate in 90 ml of water and 10 ml of glacial acetic acid.
Test: Dissolve the sample in a minimum amount of water. Filter. Add 2 or 3 drops of the reagent to the filtrate. Shake about one minute. A blue precipitate indicates the presence of methadone.

NITRIC ACID TEST: Place a few drops of concentrated nitric acid (HNO_3) on a small amount of suspected powder. If heroin is present it will dissolve with yellow color, which gradually, or immediately on heating, changes into a greenish-blue color and finally becomes yellow. *Note*: Care should be used in handling the strong acid.

Morphine

MARQUIS TEST: Marquis reagent produces an intense purple-red color, changing to violet if morphine is present.

NITRIC ACID TEST: Nitric acid added to suspected powder will produce an orange-red to deep red color, quickly changing to yellow if morphine is present.

FERRIC CHLORIDE TEST: Neutral ferric chloride solution is used. If morphine is present when ferric chloride test solution is added to a small portion of dry suspected powder, a blue color will appear. This is one of the least delicate of the tests for morphine, but is used to differentiate morphine from codeine and heroin, with which morphine might be confused. Heroin and codeine will not produce a blue color with ferric chloride.

Codeine gives a red-violet color with Marquis reagent and a weak red-orange with nitric acid.

Dilaudid gives a red-violet color with Marquis, red-orange with nitric acid, and blue-green with ferric chloride.

An officer should not rely on tests made by him of suspected drugs, unless he is a technician capable of rendering testimony in such matters, but should submit the evidence to a chemist for analysis. If a pharmacist is available he may sometimes be able to give helpful information on the identity of a drug. However, chemical analysis must be the final test.

Marihuana

The microscopic identification of marihuana is perhaps the best test for recognition of this drug. This method requires a high-powered microscope, microscopic slides, and a few chemicals. An officer experienced in handling marihuana is able to detect parts of the plant, such as the seeds, bracts, and leaves.

The procedure to follow in making an examination of a suspected sample of marihuana is to use a magnifying glass, paying particular attention to green leaves covered with white pimples. In a marihuana cigarette or powdered marihuana, there will be found bits of leaves, parts of broken seeds or stems, and sometimes whole seeds will be found. Most of this material is covered with fine hairs, the character of which is not clear under this coarse magnifying glass. The leaves and parts of the seed have their characteristic points. The seeds, for instance, are rather thick-walled and have characteristic markings; the color ranges from green to brown. If one uses a magnification of over a hundred times, many of the more intimate characteristics of the plant can be seen. For examination with a microscope, pieces of the suspected sample are moistened and placed on a microscopic slide and pressed down with a cover glass. There are found the one-celled, more or less curved, non-glandular hairs. Small deposits of calcium carbonate are found at the base of most of these hairs. Deposits of resin are also found on the surface, easily seen through the microscope. Next, place a few drops of concentrated hydrochloric acid under the cover glass. If marihuana is present, an effervescence caused by the breaking up of the calcium carbonate will be seen.

SEEDS: When a sample consists entirely of seeds, their identity alone is not sufficient to bring them within the purview of the law, which requires them to be fertile. To establish their fertility, a number of the seeds should be placed in a suitable container with moist paper pulp or wet vermiculite and placed in a warm, dark place until germination takes place. When reporting a sample containing marihuana seeds alone, their fertility should always be stated. The Federal Bureau of Narcotics and Dangerous Drugs uses the following chemical test for marihuana, among others:

DUQUENOIS-LEVINE TEST (MODIFIED): Extract 30 to 100 mg of the sample with 15 to 20 ml petroleum ether. Filter and evaporate the filtrate in a white porcelain dish. Add 2 ml Duquenois' reagent and stir to bring the residue into solution. Add 2 ml concentrated hydrochloric acid, stir and let stand for 10 minutes. A color develops. Transfer this colored solution to a test tube and shake with 1 to 2 ml of chloroform. If marihuana is present in the sample, a violet color will be transferred to the chloroform layer.

RAPID DUQUENOIS-LEVINE TEST (MODIFIED): Place 25 to 60 mg of dry crushed marihuana in a test tube and shake with 2 ml Duquenois' reagent for 1 minute. Add an equal volume of concentrated hydrochloric acid and observe the color changes to a final violet shade. Shake the mixture with 1 to 2 ml chloroform. If marihuana is present in the sample, the violet shade will be transferred to the chloroform layer. (The foregoing is the procedure most likely to be employed in a chemical field test.)

DUQUENOIS' REAGENT: Dissolve 5 drops of acetaldehyde and 0.4 grams of vanillin in 20 ml of 95% alcohol. (This reagent may be kept for some time in glass-stoppered bottles in a cool dark place. It should be discarded after assuming a deep yellow color.)

Amphetamines

This field test for identifying amphetamines is useful in screening out caffeine, vitamins, saccharin or other substitutes proffered as amphetamines.

TEST MATERIAL: The test material consists of two or three drops of Marquis reagent (2 drops of 37 percent formaldehyde in 3 ml of concentrated sulfuric acid) in a small glass ampul.

TEST PROCEDURE: Break the ampul at the scored center and place one or two drops of the reagent on the sample. This should be done on a glass ash tray, inverted tumbler, etc.

Amphetamines react with the reagent to give a red-orange color, turning to reddish and then dark brown within one or two minutes. The reagent gives this characteristic color reaction when applied to white, pink, yellow, peach, or green amphetamine tablets. The speed with which the color is formed appears to depend upon the hardness of the tablet. The red-orange color forms immediately on some tablets while with others it appears in 10 or 20 seconds. *Therefore, the critical period of color differentiation for amphetamines is within the first 20 seconds.* The peach-colored caffeine tablets give a color which might cause some confusion. The difference between the color formed by this tablet and that formed by a peach-colored amphetamine tablet seems to be more obvious if the tablets are crushed before the reagent is applied. Once the difference is seen, there should be no trouble in distinquishing one from the other.

As indicated by the table below, the only materials which give the same color change as amphetamine are the phenyl tertiary butylamine HC1 tablets and the Wyamine® sulfate tablets. Both are similar chemically to the amphetamines.

Amphetamine powder and tablets	Red-orange onset to reddish brown to dark brown within a couple of minutes
Caffeine powder and tablets	No color
Methamphetamine	Red-orange to reddish brown and then to dark brown in one or two minutes
Phenyl tertiary butylamine HC1	Same color change as amphetamine
Wyamine sulfate	Same color change as amphetamine

Barbiturates

For the tentative identification of the barbiturates, the Zwikker test is used.

ZWIKKER TEST: An anhydrous methanol solution of the barbiturate upon the addition of several drops of cobalt chloride in methanol solution gives a bluish color which changes to dark blue upon being alkalized with 5% isopropylamine in methanol. A compact kit which utilizes the Zwikker test is manufactured by the Atkinson Laboratory, 3031 Fierro Street, Los Angeles, California.

TEST MATERIALS: The Zwikker Test Kit consists of a small plastic box containing three solutions in plastic dropping bottles and a small porcelain spot plate.
Solution 1: Anhydrous methanol.
Solution 2: Cobalt chloride dissolved in methanol.
Solution 3: 5% isopropylamine in methanol.
Caution: The above solutions are volatile and inflammable. They should be kept closed.
TEST PROCEDURE

1. Place part of sample into spot-tester (enough to cover letter "O" on typewriter key).

2. Put two drops of Solution 1 on sample in spot-tester. (Sample should dissolve.)

3. Add two drops of Solution 2. (This may produce violet or blue color.)

4. Add two drops of Solution 3. If color deepens to a darker violet or blue, this indicates presumptive presence of barbiturate.

Caution: Do not let dropper bottle touch the sample, as the solution will become contaminated. Wash and dry spot-test plate after use.

Identifying the Dangerous Drugs

It should be emphasized that the field testing of suspected contraband drugs by officers is for information and probable cause and should not be relied upon in any way to establish identity for criminal prosecution. Drug identification calls for a highly qualified, specialized expert. Much sophisticated equipment often is available to assist in the determination. Sometimes the defense may produce very sophisticated testimony and cross-examination to try to counter the expert prosecution witness. It is desirable that a valid analysis of the drug be completed in a minimum time after an arrest or seizure.

A legal identification of barbiturates, amphetamines, tranquilizers, hallucinogens and the like must, of course, be left to the chemist. When these drugs, as often is the case, are of commercial manufacture and have characteristic shapes, forms, and colors, a working identification may not be too difficult, except for the vast number of such products now on the market. The officer experienced in the drug abuse field becomes familiar with a great many of the abused chemicals. Tentative recognition may be facilitated by consulting such publications as the *Physicians' Desk Reference,* Section 4, Product Identification Section, published by Medical Economics, Inc., Oradell, N. J. This gives actual size photographs in color of many products which may be subject to abuse. Some law enforcement supply houses stock similar publications. A doctor is likely to have one in his office, and the pharmacist may be able to assist in an emergency. We have noted *300 Most Abused Drugs; A Pictorial Handbook* by Edward Bludworth, P.O. Box 2350, Tampa, Fla. 33601.

The officer who has to deal with "dangerous drugs" of clandestine origin is in a more difficult area as to identification and needs, when possible, the closest backing of the chemist. Enforcement organizations in the drug abuse field may be expected to stock specialized field kits and similar devices to facilitate tentative recognition of illegal drugs.

THE CLANDESTINE DRUG MANUFACTURING LABORATORY

An area where the immediate and continuing backing of the enforcement officer by the chemist is vital is in the increasingly serious problem of the clandestine drug laboratory. Prior to the 1960's we infrequently saw wildcat laboratories. Antedating World War II these were occasionally set up when circumstances were such that a smuggler could obtain opium or sometimes morphine base but not finished heroin abroad, and would convert that opium to heroin in this country. As the French and Italians, among others, acquired more expertise in the illegal laboratory area, opium tended to be processed into heroin abroad because of the obvious advantage of very much reducing the bulk (to 1/10th) of the contraband to be smuggled. During World War II, when significant opiate sources were very much confined to Mexico and to thefts and robberies from drug houses in this country, the laboratory again appeared here to convert Mexican opium to heroin, and stolen morphine or other opiate derivatives to this most favored form. Again, as operators close to the source of opium supply gained laboratory expertise the conversion to heroin began to take place there. "Mexican brown" heroin appeared and continued in the traffic, especially on our west coast and in the Canadian West.

The clandestine heroin laboratory in this country was small and quickly set up, operated, and dismantled. In one instance an operator "borrowed" the large kitchened apartment of an unsuspecting friend for a weekend for such a venture. The chemistry of these operations was not too involved and the modus, equipment, essential components, diluents and other accessories not too difficult to come by. Despite the problems of hitting such a mobile target we were successful in seizing a number. A few others were discovered when accidents in handling some of the volatile processing material caused fires. The success of the Bureau of Narcotics in capturing these laboratories was due in part to resourceful and ingenious collaboration of narcotic agents and chemists in developing and utilizing tracer chemicals and other procedures in connection with some of the raw materials and diluents used in the laboratory operation (acetic anhydride, quinine, etc.).

One methadone laboratory was seized in this country as early as 1953. Here was an ominous harbinger of possible trouble, but one which could not be properly evaluated in the happier narcotic law enforcement picture of that time. It may now serve a valuable purpose in demonstrating the real menace of methadone, and help to correct in a small way the flood of pernicious propaganda that makes out this opiate, which can be destructive and deadly, to be an innocuous "cure" for heroin addiction. In the more recent past, 1969, a methadone laboratory was seized, the substantial output of which was distributed by a well-organized mob and was eagerly accepted in the illicit heroin market as was that of the 1953 laboratory. There now is increasing evidence of the production of clandestine methadone which, with the cover of increasing promiscuous individual prescribing by doctors and the loose operation of official methadone "clinics," may be fraught with disastrous consequences as we will discuss later.

Becoming apparent in the late 1960's, there has been a proliferation of clandestine laboratories manufacturing LSD, mescaline, other hallucinogens, and the stimulants like the amphetamines, and these are now believed to number several score. As with methadone, the chemistry of these is more involved than that of heroin production but it is no insurmountable problem in this age of many sophisticated chemists, and with the "help from friends" who peddle "psychedelic cookbooks." What we see may be just the beginning if we are not able to impose effective curbs. The *Washington Post,* Sept. 24, 1970, reported a Los Angeles psychiatrist as predicting to a physicians' meeting at Los Angeles that within five years society will be faced with the problem of dealing with dozens of new drugs with new mind-altering capabilities.

We may have to rely increasingly on our chemists "in the white hats." Even now it is imperative that the chemists be on the scene of the seizure of the clandestine laboratory so that there may be an "on the spot" scientific appraisal of what has been going on, in order to recognize ingredients and end products and help safeguard the seizing party against dangers inherent in highly explosive, incendiary, or toxic substances.

4
NARCOTIC ADDICTION: MANAGEMENT AND TREATMENT

> *How came any reasonable being to subject himself to such a yoke of misery, voluntarily to incur a captivity so servile and knowingly to fetter himself with a seven-fold chain?*
> Thomas DeQuincey, *Confessions of an English Opium Eater*

AT THE ONSET of Chapter 3 we gave definitions of drug addiction and drug dependence. Herein we will discuss particularly opiate addiction. Who and what are opiate addicts?

Abraham Wikler, experimental neuropsychiatrist at Lexington, says in his book *Opiate Addiction* that for clinical purposes, drug addiction in general may be defined as the *compulsive* use of chemical agents which are harmful to the individual, to society, or both. Implicit in his definition is the rather ill-defined concept of "emotional" or "psychological" dependence on drugs. In the United States the drugs which are used most commonly by addicts include such opiates as morphine, heroin, Dilaudid®, and Pantopon®, and the opiate-like synthetic analgesic compounds such as Demerol® and methadone.

One of the characteristics of opiate addiction is *tolerance,* which—and again we are quoting Wikler—"refers to the progressive diminution in the intensity of the effect of the same dose of the drug in question during continuous, regular use." To put it another way, it takes more of the drug to bring about the same effect. Then we have *dependence*. "Physical or psychological dependence," says, Wikler, "refers to the fact that after a period of such drug use, the abrupt withdrawl of the agent is followed by the development of an 'abstinence syndrome,' which is associated with measurable physiological changes and which is apparently reduced in intensity by administration of sufficient amounts of the drug in question or its analogues." Translating a bit, this means that an animal accustomed to a regular, continuous, heavy dose of opiates will become very ill if suddenly deprived of the drug. The intensity and time course of this syndrome vary considerably with the nature and amount of the drug used, as well as the duration of addiction and individual factors which are difficult to define. To borrow a phrase which our medical men like to use, this withdrawal syndrome is a self-limiting illness. Wikler gives us this excellent summary. "Opiate addiction is therefore characterized by three principal phenomena—'emotional' dependence, tolerance, and 'physical' dependence. To these may be added a fourth—the tendency to relapse to the use of the drug after repeated 'cures.' "

To discuss emotional dependence a little further, this may mean merely that the addict reports that he is, or behaves as if he feels discontented, anxious, or unhappy unless he is under the influence of an opiate. Obviously, in an attempt to explain this we might get very profound and actually come to no more valuable conclusion than if we tried to state it simply with the hypothesis that the opiates relieve "anxiety" and produce a feeling of "euphoria," that is, a sense of exalted well-being which the individual seeks to experience repeatedly by continued use of the drug.

Tolerance and physical dependence are usually considered together. As Wikler says, "Most, but not all of the evidence indicates that the processes underlying tolerance and physiological dependence are closely related, if not identical." There has been a tremendous amount of work done and very much speculation to develop a hypothesis for the tolerance and dependence phenomenon. The complete story is unknown. One of the most reasonable views is that morphine depresses the autonomic nervous system and that, after repeated injections of the drug, counter-adaptations develop which are held in check by the depressant effects of each dose of the opiate. When injections of the drug are discontinued, the counter-adaptations are released and manifest themselves in the autonomic changes which characterize the morphine abstinence syndrome. We have heard Lexington physicians explain it rather graphically this way. The opiates generally exert a suppressing, depressing effect on all bodily functions. When under the effect of an opiate, these functions adjust themselves to work against this smothering restraint.

If this restraint is suddenly lifted, by cutting off the opiate, it is like suddenly releasing the brake on an automobile with the accelerator already pressed to the floor, or like the outburst when a flywheel drops off a motor. So much for a few generalizations.

Some writers who feel very sorry for the addict, as we all do, in stressing the tolerance phenomenon and the abstinence syndrome are completely misled by it as to the real facts of narcotic addiction. These writers see the poor addict as being caught up in a treadmill in which he must have more and more of the drug to keep him "normal." Let's put some very large quotation marks around that "normal." Obviously, no rational animal would stay with a habit which made such senseless demands on him. There is more to addiction than a mere feeling of "normality." Listen to Wikler. "These (tolerance and abstinence) changes are accompanied by a strong 'craving' for the drug and, when the latter is administered, the relief of these symptoms is intensely pleasurable. Many addicts have stated that they prefer to space their injections of morphine in such a way that mild abstinence changes do occur before each injection, and that under such conditions, the desirable effects of each dose are enhanced. Frequently, they compare this experience with that of hunger." So says Wikler.

One of us (J.C.C.) likes to recall a revealing incident seen when we were working incognito, associating with a group of addicted peddlers to gather evidence. We were accepted by the group to the extent that some of them injected narcotics in our presence. We had the opportunity to see first hand how one of these gradually "built up his habit." When preparing his "shot" (i.e. injection) the addict would measure out his usual ration of narcotics, then he would add a little more to the dose in the spoon turning his head away quickly, at the same time giving a little shrug of his shoulders as if to convey "Well, I didn't see it, what can I do about it now?" The next day or so the dose measure was a little larger, and it too received a shrug of the shoulders. This procedure was followed by the addict until he was taking twenty-five grains per day of a narcotic, of which any more than a two grain dose might be lethal to a normal person.

Let us summarize by paraphrasing Newton and setting down a "First Law of Addiction": A person in the condition of opiate addiction, with free access to opiates, will continue in that condition at an accelerated rate of consumption unless the course of addiction is deterred by some extraneous force.

Addicts liken the effect of a shot of heroin to a sexual crisis. Actually, the total effect of opiate taking may result in one of the most profound and seductive pleasures known to man. Jean Cocteau, the French writer was an opium smoker for ten years. He described withdrawal from opium as a "weaning from the milk of paradise." Again, Cocteau puts it, "Trying to persuade a drug addict to give up his poison is like urging Tristan to slay his Isolde on the plea that he will feel so much better afterwards."

Now, who becomes addicted? Here again, we must make generalizations, and we will find these generalizations valid even if some of them seem to be mutually contradictory. However, there is one statement which we may regard as axiomatic. Only persons having access to opiates become opiate addicts. This may provoke a smile as primer stuff, but we can assure the reader that this is a fact most often overlooked by a vociferous group of self-constituted experts in the narcotic addiction field. We must immediately make some reservations. All persons exposed to continuous administration of opiates do not become addicted to a similar degree, or even in a similar pattern. Some of the medical textbooks stress that the person addicted to opiates through treatment for pain, even though he may build up a physical tolerance and dependence, may often not demonstrate any emotional liking for addiction and, when he is withdrawn from the drugs, after some discomfort, that is the end of it. On the other hand, we have before us what often happens even with addicts produced through the treatment of pain. Alex King and Bill Stern were highly publicized examples that addiction acquired through treatment for pain may also completely take over the personality and require firm measures before it can be cured. King was a narcotic addict for many years and, after several trips to Lexington, discontinued drug use. To this, many factors seem to have contributed.

Alex King was of course, a wise-cracker, who made startling statements for effect. He did this cleverly enough so that it helped make him a fine living. In his very readable book, *Mine Enemy Grows Older,* he said some things about drug addiction which to us are of particular interest. This is due, in part, to an impression we got from the book that although this was a "cured" addict of great intelligence, there is still some nostalgic longing for a habit put aside. Here is the aging Romeo's recollection of an illicit romance. She was not good for him—nor he for her . . . that is agreed. But it was wonderful while it lasted, and regret is all but submerged in fond recollection!

I originally became addicted through the help of regular medical practitioners who prescribed morphine to relieve my kidney pains.

I must say I liked morphine from the start. It performed a sort of minor miracle for me. It made me graciously tolerant of every form of human imbecility, including my own. It lifted from my mind every worry, every heartache, and every form of urgency. I never had any bodily pains, and for nine years I didn't have a single cold. Drug addiction is, in all probability, the secret cure for the common cold. Although it is a drastic cure, I can testify that it works.

You have no hangover after drugs, you just have to have more drugs. An addict can do beautifully without women. He is not necessarily impotent, he just doesn't need them. His euphoria is so complete he can do fine without seductive titivations. He has only one anxiety—that he will run short of his poison.

Otherwise he is abreast of any contingency. Suppose the phone bill is overdue, the rent unpaid, and his wife threatens to leave him. The addict can liquidate such difficulties with a smile of sweet understanding.

So what is wrong with drug addiction? First of all, it is illegal. It is safer for you to renege on your income tax than to get mixed up with drugs. Uncle Sam is bound to get you sooner or later and then there is heaven and hell to pay. Geography, too, is against you. You can be an addict in Bangkok in perfect safety, but the U.S.A. is definitely out. So, if you can make a living in Siam, go ahead and move into your tropical snowstorm with Santa Claus!

The second reason why addiction is taboo is that it makes you absolutely uncompetitive. You can't survive without cheating or stealing because you're certainly not going to work. Let's face it, we are living in a world which is not only highly competitive, but which admires strenuousness for its own sake. So you can't afford to tune out. If you want to lie down blissfully on a wet cement floor and pass your time just thinking about lovely things, you'll have to get yourself a transfer to Thailand. And you'd better go in a hurry, before some United Nations sub-committee on narcotics catches up with that shady corner. (I'm sure their consulate will solemnly assert that you can't get drugs there even now, but they are most thoroughly misinformed.)

"Let's agree, then, that narcotics are definitely un-American. It must be obvious by now that the nine years of my addiction must have had certain nightmarish overtones. I certainly had to tell lies from the very beginning, since no doctor would prescribe my constantly increasing dosages. So I went to twenty doctors for my needed prescriptions, which is illegal even if you are sick. Fortunately, I ran into a few practitioners who charged me ten to fifteen dollars a visit and gave me two prescriptions a week, knowing perfectly well that I was hooked." (From *Mine Enemy Grows Older* by Alexander King, Copyright© 1959 by Alexander King by permission of Simon and Schuster, Inc.)

Now, let us go back and take a further look at Alexander King. According to his own statements, he became addicted to narcotic drugs in 1949. His first arrest for a narcotic drug violation was September 13, 1950. His offense involved the writing and passing of forged narcotic prescriptions. He stole prescription blanks from a physician's office and forged the doctor's name. The United States Attorney released King on his own recognizance on condition that he enter the hospital at Lexington, Kentucky, for treatment. King failed to abide by this agreement and continued to issue forged narcotic prescriptions until he was arrested again on April 3, 1951. Those of us who have read his second book will recall that King states he also used admission papers to the Lexington hospital to get drugs from doctors. He would display these asking for drugs to carry him to the hospital. He did not go there but, according to King, used these papers until they were worn out. At this time, the officers located 87 prescriptions which he had forged and on which he had obtained 1,560 tablets of Dilaudid. On his person were found nine forged prescriptions. King was then placed on probation for a period of three years. Upon his plea of guilty in federal court, one condition of his probation was treatment at the hospital at Lexington, Kentucky. In 1954, evidence was obtained that King had again violated his probation, and federal narcotic agents attempted to locate him. On November 12, 1954, narcotic agents located the apartment of his wife. King was not in the apartment, but was found hiding in a hallway closet of the same building. In November 1954, King was sentenced in federal court to a term of eight months for violation of his probation. According to his book, he served six and a half months of this term.

Now, Mr. King has very generally ridiculed the psychiatrists.

He very specifically, and with unfair reflection on the great mass of practitioners, ascribes his continuation on narcotics partly to the greed of doctors. In his first book, he had a kind word to say for the narcotic agent. In his second book, he refers most disparagingly to the Commissioner of Narcotics.

As we read his books, King gave his wife, and himself mostly, credit for his cure. Mrs. King was the attractive and wholesome-looking person whom we saw playing the drums on the Jack Paar program. But let us bear in mind that King had her when he unwillingly was taken out of that hallway closet. What made his last cure stick as long as it did? Who can say? Perhaps King least of all. Maybe it was because he had become a little older. If we had to make a guess, we would say perhaps one of the most significant factors might have been his forced separation from the drug for a substantial period, for some six and a half months. For whatever reason, it seems to us that this is pretty good evidence that if it had not been for the operation of the coercive features of the federal narcotic laws, King would have been a broken bum, or a long dead derelict, instead of the author of best sellers.

Although King displayed a tendency to bite the hand which had lifted him from the gutter, those of us who have had anything to do with the administration of the country's narcotic program can find some satisfaction in that he was one of many who have been rescued from oblivion by the understanding and compassionate administration of the present program. King's case also is to us a dramatic illustration of the many pitfalls which would be encountered were there any weakening in the present concept of complete containment of narcotic drugs.

Just in passing, let us observe that if New York had a law like the California and Illinois narcotic laws requiring the audit of official prescriptions for narcotic drugs, King's addiction very likely would have been dealt with much more speedily.

It is likely that any primate regularly receiving opiate dosage will become addicted. Tolerance and dependence are easily demonstrated in monkeys. Chimpanzees can become addicted. Tolerance and dependence have been demonstrated in a spinal man—this is, in a human being whose brain was accidentally so badly damaged as to make this title descriptive.

We can make another generalization. Drug addiction is a social vice—a social disease. It spreads from person to person. While sometimes addiction can be the calculated contrivance of a pusher, most often it spreads like any vice—from the example of and the acceptance of the practices and standards of one's contemporaries. People learn to take opiates as they learn to smoke tobacco or drink alcohol. Usually this is not in innocence or ignorance. It usually arises from too complete acquaintance with the causative chemical; with knowledge that there is some danger, but either with a "don't give a damn" attitude or with the all too human opinion that "I can go so far and stop," or that "It can't happen to me."

To Dr. Marie Nyswander, in her book *The Drug Addict as a Patient* (Grune & Stratton) we are indebted for a note of warning. She reports that at the Lexington Narcotic Hospital, when staff members are occasionally used as controls in testing reactions to drugs there is a long spacing between doses as a precautionary measure. This is for the very good reason that some staff members, whose reaction to initial doses of morphine was negative or adverse, found that when doses were repeated they were enjoying euphoric effects, finding the drug attractive. Dr. Nyswander concludes that it is fallacious and dangerous to assume that there is an "addiction-safe" personality.

Against these generalizations, let's see who does become addicted. As of no consequence numerically, but of the greatest significance to validate our availability hypothesis, a few of the finest people in the community become addicts. These are in one narrow highly specialized category. These are the only substantial people in our present society who have pretty much of a free access to narcotics. They are doctors and nurses. Within the last year some readers may have seen news articles indicating that about one percent of the medical profession was addicted. We think this figure is too high; but the fact remains that, of people of high education and good economic status, medical doctors are, practically speaking, the only addicts.* (Incidentally, more than 90% of these doctors can probably be cured.) Again, the incidence

---

*This may now be modified by the affluent youth addict.

of narcotic drug addiction among nurses, as small as it is, is very much greater than is addiction among school teachers or stenographers. But, as we said, as far as the totals go, the number of such persons who are addicted is an almost insignificant one. Also, the number of persons who become addicted through medical treatment, and who remain problems, is relatively very, very small. For most practical intents and purposes, when we consider narcotic addiction today we are considering an urban underworld vice and disease.*

And now, who becomes addicted in the underworld? When emphasis is put on the medical approach to narcotic addiction control we talk about mental health. Because the standards of what is mental health are so variable, this can include a lot of territory. But, here we can make some worthwhile generalizations. Very few narcotic addicts are psychotic; that is, very few of them are out of touch with reality to the extent that we would call them "crazy." The opiate addict undergoing withdrawal might give rise to some such impression, but he is more disturbed physically than mentally. However, we often refer to the people who become addicted as 'inadequate personalities." That, again, is a term which can be defined and redefined, and for which we all may have our own definition. We hear such phrases as "the addiction-prone personality." There is the type of person who, in simple English, we might refer to as "an inadequate weakling." On the other hand, there is the hedonistic hell-raiser. Then there is the venturer who has missed in the development of discretion. He isn't too far away from the admirable character who ate the first oyster, or the young fellow who will strap on a pair of skis and make the first run down a new slide to test whether the mathematics of the slope square with the law of gravity.

Not all inadequate personalities become narcotic addicts. There are accidents of geography, of neighborhood, of social situations, of accessibility to drugs, all complicating the picture. Personality deficiencies can only be a part of the explanation for a problem which, in a generation, has changed in incidence from a rather general, country-wide distribution among Caucasians, men and

---

*It is now making some inroads in delinquent affluent suburbia.

women, and among Chinese men, to what is now a phenomenon of Negro (and some Puerto Rican and Mexican) neighborhoods of a few large cities (and here very much among younger males), and to an occurrence which follows neighborhood and sometimes even block lines in cities. We sometimes find that the practice is taken up as casually as more accepted vices, like drinking alcohol or smoking. Such an occurrence, in our opinion, does not necessarily need to have an invariable connotation of psychopathy.

In the last few years we have seen opiate addiction become a spin-off of a segment of so-called youth rebellion and to have become more generally diffused throughout our society.

Well . . . is there any classification or group into which the typical addict will fall? Is he a moron? An intellectual subnormal? Not at all! Prior to the early 1960's we would have said that he might be above average in intelligence in criminal groups and that he usually appeared as a criminal. We would have said that this was not only because he might have to be a criminal to continue as an addict, but also, by its very nature, American addiction then found good recruiting in delinquency or crime areas. Because of today's wider spread of drug abuse to include a more complete representation of all segments of our society, the incidence of criminality may not be as high. But the existence of delinquency or criminal conduct antedating addiction is probably still true. The natural tendency of young criminals to straighten out as they acquire maturity and a sense of responsibility is defeated by addiction.

Some characteristics of the narcotic addict are very well summarized in the testimony before a Canadian Senate committee in 1955 by Dr. R. G. E. Richmond. Dr. Richmond, a psychiatrist, has had long experience in both English and Canadian prisons and borstals.

> Some super-added manifestations following addiction are increased dependence of the individual on other people and marked aversion to work, which seems to be shown by many.
>
> There seems to be a cancerous invasion of the moral structures, specifically related to the addiction, with absence of ethics, scruples, and even the minimum demand of human decency in the attempt to obtain drugs. I would like to emphasize here, sir, that it is specifically related to the drug taking, and not a general observation as to their character.

There is entire lack of control in relation to the urge for drugs. There is a very close link between addicts. There is an inability to face situations, a flight and escapism. In many there is a gross egocentricity, which is perhaps not solely the feature of addicted delinquents. It may be shown by others as seriously delinquent but not addicted. There appears to be a lack of trust in counsellors, with a strong tendency to use them as a means towards some generous alleviation of their [the addict's] plight. When compulsorily away from drugs, many addicted delinquents express a desire for treatment, but not when they are speaking as a group.

Many addicts show some benign qualities in their personality with sometimes a remarkable degree of understanding and insight concerning general situations, in marked contrast to their inadequacy to curb their overwhelming impulse. In the Witness's experience, the addicted delinquent needs rigid limits imposed on his many indulgences as evidenced during imprisonment, more especially in the way of lack of acceptance, by authority, of excuses tendered to avoid work and other discomforts.

Whatever is offered to many addicted delinquents in the form of attention is regarded mainly as a means to obtain more. As far as sedation, of any type, is concerned, it has to be almost eliminated, otherwise the addicted delinquent becomes even more disturbed, craving and pleading for more and more. The addicted delinquent seems to prosper under firmness and appreciates it.

In a report to the sheriff of Santa Clara County, California, by Drs. Norman Nomoff and Joseph Fischer, these physicians offer this summary on the personality of the addict.

The average addict, (as analyzed by psychiatrists) is infantile in his personality development. He is self-centered, unable to relate to others in an adult fashion, and is hostile (because of his deep insecurity). He lacks self-esteem and is easily depressed by reality. Narcotics, particularly heroin, give him a measure of immediate gratification which is a meaningful substitute for the sense of frustration experienced by him due to his inability to obtain satisfaction from the usual actvities of society. From our day to day contact with addicts, we are in agreement with this analytic personality description. The heroin addict, as we see him, is an immature and inadequate individual. He has never achieved success in any phase of social or economic endeavor. He has been in trouble with the law since early in his teens. He has had a mediocre record of performance in school, and has seldom held a responsible job. He knows no trade. It is noteworthy that he is frequently not married and has usually been a failure when he has attempted marriage. His ties to the community are primarily with the members of his own clique (fellow addicts and others with little or no visible means of support). He has a very low tolerance for pain and emotional stress. His outward facade of toughness is easily penetrated when he is not in contact with his cronies, and he reveals a loneliness and a strong sense of dependency. Since most of his social development has been an attempt to evade or avoid social responsibility, he is hostile and suspicious of those whom he considers part of the legitimate world. To him, they are "squares" and he bolsters his own ego against admission of his own loneliness and insecurity by believing that he is smarter and better off in his little world than those in the community around him. His associations with fellow addicts is one of his real social needs.

We do not believe that the narcotic addict is basically different from other immature and insecure individuals. The heroin addict, unlike the user of marijuana, or other non-narcotic using criminals, manifests behavior which is dictated by the economic and physiological properties of heroin. To the user of heroin, the drug gives a complete solution to life. The effect that he seeks and finds in heroin is one of relief from responsibility and release from tension. Heroin is more desired than sexual intercourse, close personal friendship, success in business, or social status. It is in a real sense a substitute for all of these.

Drs. Harris Isbell and H. F. Fraser are among the world's outstanding authorities on narcotic addiction and the following is quoted from their article "Addiction to Analgesics and Barbiturates."

The treatment of drug addiction can be carried out successfully only in institutions. Attempts at treatment in the home practically never succeed and, in fact, complete withdrawal of drugs is seldom accomplished under such circumstances. It follows that a certain degree of coercion is usually desirable and necessary in the treatment of drug addiction. Coercion may take the form of pressure from relatives, friends, or law enforcement officers. In many instances the only solution is to arrest the addict and have him sentenced for violating the narcotic laws.

Time is an important element in the treatment of drug addiction. The optimum period of time varies in individual cases, but, in general, several months are required before maximum benefit from treatment is reached.

After drugs have been withdrawn, any curable physical disease which the addict may have should receive appropriate medical or surgical treatment. In patients suffering with chronic diseases which are not curable, the treatment should be designed to achieve the maximal amount of physical benefit possible and to teach the patient to live with and manage his disease without resorting to narcotics.

Occupational therapy forms an exceedingly important part of treatment of drug addiction. All patients who are able to work should be provided with an opportunity to engage in a useful, productive occupation of a nature which will maintain and add to any existing skills. Patients with chronic diseases should not be allowed to vegetate in infirmary wards but should, within the limits imposed by their disease, be given some type of useful activity to pursue and, if possible, should be trained in some occupation which they can carry on despite their infirmity and which will enable them to support themselves when discharged. Occupational therapy should be reinforced by a program of recreational therapy including a program of athletics, motion pictures, music, and other amusements, and an ample supply of reading material.

The psychotherapeutic treatment of drug addiction is essentially not different from the psychotherapeutic treatment of non-addicted individuals who suffer from neuroses or character disorders. It is, therefore, a very broad subject which cannot be adequately covered in this review. Psychotherapy always has to be individualized and is dependent both upon the training, orientation and skill of the therapist and on the nature of the psychiatric problem. The first decision which must be reached in any given case is whether psychotherapy should be offered at all. Many addicts with intense infantile fixations obtain very little benefit from psychotherapy and, in such instances, the best procedure is to provide a short period of intensive institutional supervision, followed by a long period of supervision of the patient in his home environment. Other patients who develop a higher level of emotional maturity prior to becoming addicted should be offered intensive individualized psychotherapy. There are, unfortunately, not enough psychiatrists to administer psychotherapy to all the patients who need and will accept it. This deficiency in psychiatric facilities can perhaps be partially bridged by organizing group psychotherapeutic sessions.

Many addicts appear to derive great benefits from participation in the inspirational approach of the group known as Alcoholics Anonymous, or the more recently organized Addicts Anonymous. These groups also provide a continuing stimulus to remain abstinent from drugs after the patient is discharged.

Whenever possible, treatment should be continued after the patient is discharged from the institution. Prior to discharge, the patient should have a definite plan of life. He should have a job and a place to live. Arrangements should be made for continuing supervision of the addict by his family physician, parole officer, minister or friends. The addict should not be returned to an environment where frequent contact with other addicts is unavoidable. Resources of an efficient, well-organized, social-service department are invaluable in assisting the patient to make proper plans for post-institutional treatment.*

Now let us listen to another view. Dr. Marie Nyswander is a psychiatrist who has had considerable experience with narcotic addicts. She has many views respecting these, with which we are not in sympathy.

Some time ago, she was concerned with a so-called "voluntary rehabilitation" project in New York City. The project started out with some 30 professionally trained psychotherapists, 7 psychiatrists, 11 psychologists, and 12 social workers, and with about 70 narcotic addicts. After a lapse of 12 months or so, the project apparently had the same 60 official personnel. The number of addict patients had evaporated to 13. The rest were lost sight of, and the prognosis for some of those 13 was not too good. *(American Journal of Orthopsychiatry,* October 1958.)

Nevertheless, Dr. Nyswander expresses a view which should be carefully considered. She thinks, according to some of her writings, that we make too elaborate a process out of "curing" narctoic addicts. In an interview published in the October 1, 1957, issue of *Modern Medicine,* this colloquy takes place:

> Q. "Of course, as a psychiatrist, you are skilled in such matters. However, can the general physician in private practice achieve such a relationship with addicts?
>
> A. "Probably 80% of the addicts who have stopped taking drugs have done so without psychiatric treatment and with the help of general physicians. They just need firm authority, encouragement, some sleeping pills for rest at night, and a little support and interest for the four-day withdrawl period that is so difficult. After all, for years, drug addicts have been cured without benefit of psychiatrists. A few addicts will avail themselves of psychiatrists, but I think addiction is primarily a pharmacologic problem. Anyone can become addicted; as far as we can see, there's no specific addiction personality."**

Dr. Nyswander may be confusing us by thinking primarily in terms of the person who has been addicted through bonafide medical treatment. Few authorities would agree with her that any attempt should be made to separate a real addict from drugs except

---
*Quoted by permission of H. F. Fraser, M.D., Harris Isbell, M.D., and the *Journal of Pharmacology and Experimental Therapeutics.*
**Quoted by permission of Marie Nyswander, M.D., and *Modern Medicine.*

through a considerable period of forced abstinence. The minimum would be about 90 days. Of course, good results might be obtained with shorter periods with the superficially addicted people we see so frequently today.

Another psychiatrist who has probably had more direct experience with narcotic addicts than most physicians outside of Lexington is Dr. James G. Terry, who for many years was the medical director of the Santa Rita Rehabilitation Center, Alameda County, California. Dr. Terry, in a ten-year report (1949-1959) makes this comment:

> The problem of rehabilitation of the addict is quite different than that encountered with the alcoholic. Law enforcement, not the practice of medicine, is the chief weapon. In- or out-patient psychiatry has accomplished so little. Unless the addict is stimulated by the narcotic officer directly or indirectly to undertake treatment, no treatment is received. Doctors can easily treat withdrawal symptoms. Psychiatry is usually offered to the narcotic user. The addict in return customarily contributes only superficial participation. As narcotic addiction is found in the community and not in institutions, emphasis on follow-up, following discharge from whatever type of hospital or jail, is mandatory. The Nalline test, when performed by a physician in an out-patient basis surrounded by necessity with narcotic, parole, and probation officers, can come up with findings of value. The doctor, in a practical sense, is totally dependent on the narcotic officer and simply supplements the officer's activity.
>
> About 35% of our inmates are involved with narcotics to some degree. As a group they are far more involved in crime than the alcoholic. The average addict was first a criminal and then added narcotics just to complicate things. The addicts we have are of the lowly motivated type. They are motivated little, if at all, to abstain from narcotics in or out of an institution. We hardly ever see overt withdrawal symptoms. The last time we had to treat an addict with morphine because of the severeness of withdrawal symptoms was a little over two years ago. The heroin nearly all addicts use is so dilute and of such poor quality that a moderate to heavy addiction is nearly impossible. This is indeed a triumph for narcotic law enforcement.

Dr. James A. Hamilton, Associate Clinical Professor of Psychiatry, Stanford University School of Medicine, has stated, "General psychiatric experience indicates that various psychiatric syndromes which comprise the vast majority of addicts have in common the fact that they are remarkably unresponsive to any form of treatment. Irrespective of whether or not they are addicted, these individuals characteristically get into all kinds of difficulties. When rescued from one problem they are almost magnetically attracted to another." Recently Dr. Hamilton has written:*

It is my belief that a great deal of what is written and said about all forms of narcotics, misses the point.

Among the statements often made in defense of marihuana are the following: (1) it does not cause lung cancer; (2) it does not cause emphysema; (3) it does not injure the liver; and (4) it does not excite some sort of strange physical demand which automatically impels a young man to seek heroin.

All of these statements are true, but they have little or nothing to with the drug problem.

From my studies of cases of polydrug abuse, I am of the opinion that the problem is largely a psychological one, and only in the last heroin stage is there a physical demand which deserves the term addiction. However, most of the cases I have studied which have ended in heroin addiction, demonstrate the progression of a very simple sequence of psychological events.

Here is the sequence:

Stage 1. The youth says, "I am mad at my Mommie and my Daddie. I don't like to be ruled by laws, and I am angry at government in general and the President in particular. To demonstrate my independence from all of these oppressive influences, I will smoke pot."

Stage 2. Marihuana produces a sort of dreamy intoxication. The smoker is usually quite relaxed, and often reports that "nothing seems to matter." The effects seem to disappear in a few hours. However, when marihuana is smoked frequently, another very subtle development is likely to occur. This is a a gradual decrease in ambition, drive, or what used to be called stick-to-itiveness. Concurrently, judgment is impaired. In most cases, neither the smoker nor his associates notice any change at first. However, if there are indices of his productivity, these are likely to fall off. In college, the grade point may fall off, but concurrently the habitual smoker retains his optimism, often until he is dismissed from college. I have had several patients who have gone through this phase, but who have eventually given up all drugs. I have tried to get their colleges to accept them for another chance, but it is remarkable how austere deans can become under these circumstances.

---

*Personal communication to author (MLH) August 3, 1971. Dr. Hamilton is now a psychiatrist in private practice in San Francisco, California, and Associate Clinical Professor of Psychiatry at Stanford University School of Medicine.

The diminution in ambition or drive is a phenomenon which has been observed by others who are clinicians working with individual patients. However, I know of no psychological test which is capable of measuring it. The conflict between clinicians who *see* the phenomenon and psychologists who fail to test it, may account for some differences in opinion regarding the matter.

Stage 3. The next stage, the movement from marihuana to LSD or excessive use of amphetamines, occurs almost entirely as a result of social pressure. Marihuana smoking is often a group activity, and in any event the procurement of marihuana involves social contacts of a quiet surreptitious or secret quality. Among the social contacts there emerge individuals who are regarded as leaders, experienced users, wise men, or "good heads." When one of these leaders says "you really haven't been with it until you have dropped acid," this is effective social pressure. The marihuana smoker progresses to LSD.

Amphetamines are started by the same social pressure, either before or after LSD. When the respected leader suggests that the neophyte "try speed," he is introduced, not only to the use of amphetamines in toxic doses, but he is introduced to the needle.

Stage 4. The effects of LSD or of amphetamines by needle can only be described as toxic psychoses. With LSD, the hallucinations and delusions and distortion of reality resemble schizophrenia, while with the amphetamines, the hyperactivity, pressure and agitation have more of the quality of mania. The effects vary from a preponderance of schizophrenic symptoms to a preponderance of manic symptoms, but their reality as psychoses is hard to question. Usually the effects are over within a day or so. Sometimes, a "bad trip" hangs on indefinitely. I have treated persistent, severe symptoms two years after a single dose of LSD.

Stage 5. Use of LSD and/or intravenous amphetamines prepares the way for the last act. As before, the leader, or wise man, plays a critical role. He now deprecates the other drugs and says "There is nothing like heroin, especially to 'come down' from acid or speed."

And, in truth, the immediate effect of heroin is massive relaxation. But the soporific effect wears off in a few hours and relaxation is replaced by agitation. More heroin grants another short respite of relaxation, but actually stimulates the agitation which follows. Within a short time the youth is an addict.

In summary, the problem of polydrug abuse in the young often arises from rebellion against parents, authority and law. The youth acts out his rebellion first by smoking marihuana. In doing this, he enters a social system which is dominated by elders, who in this case are experienced drug users or peddlers. The neophyte, led by these leaders, progresses from marihuana to LSD and/or intravenous amphetamines. He experiences toxic psychoses with these drugs. Social pressure from the leaders moves him eventually into heroin addiction. The progression from marihuana to heroin is a straight-line course, directed by social pressure from dominant personalities in the polydrug environment. The neophyte is a sucker, led by predatory persons. Once in the heroin orbit, he becomes physically dependent, or addicted. The whole course of his pilgrims progress, from marihuana to heroin, is an exercise in stupidity.

The position could be taken that the population which I have seen, and from which I draw my conclusions, is one which is subject to special selection. This is true, and I must agree that all of my patients have gone the full course, including heroin addiction and/or persisting drug-induced psychoses.

It could be claimed, and correctly, that the clinical psychiatrist might have no experience whatsoever with the person who smokes marihuana without ill effects, without trouble of any kind, and without progression to more noxious drugs. I would agree that this is true. However, since we do know that progression from one drug to another occurs in the cases which eventually become serious psychiatric problems, I believe that we should be slow in adopting a permissive attitude toward marihuana. I would think that any contrary position should be supported by a workable method for distinguishing persons who can smoke marihuana with reasonable safety, and those who cannot do so. I do not believe that anybody is close to achieving such a differentiation.

We think that Dr. Hamilton makes an excellent point respecting the addict who becomes such because he is mad at Mommie and Daddie and the President—what we might call the "brat syndrome." We think this is a sound concept and paradoxically one which might give some hope since many of us may think we have successfully outgrown being bratty.

In view of what we have to say about this drug later, here may be the place to observe that serious as may be the offense of dishonoring father and mother it should not deserve a life sentence of the child to enslavement to the opiate methadone, as some now seem to advocate.

Now . . . what have we? We have a vice and disease for which there is no specific chemical cure. There is no wonder drug. We have a situation where there is much speculation as to the worth, or need for psychiatric processes. Certainly the psychiatrists have been successful in many cases—but where psychiatry is indicated, the patient must be available to the psychiatrist and vice versa.

But, even if the necessity for psychiatric treatment were more obvious in more cases than has been demonstrated, there are just not enough psychiatrists available to scratch the surface. Then, should we abandon the medical approach? Of course not! Who knows what tomorrow may bring? Although, personally, we do not expect that new tomorrow to come very soon. In the meantime, let us do the most we can with what we have. And let us continue to follow good medical principles. Quarantine and isolation are among the oldest and soundest concepts in medicine.

Remember what we said about the large percentage of cures in physician addicts. California has reported curing 92 percent. Our experience in the Federal Bureau of Narcotics and in Illinois convinces us this is a realistic figure.

How do we cure an addict doctor? We say to him, "Surrender your privilege to write prescriptions and to order narcotics, and put yourself under the care of another physician. Get yourself into a hospital and be disintoxicated." The doctor also realizes what we do not need to tell him: "If you don't do these things, you may be disgraced professionally and socially, prosecuted criminally, and your identity as a doctor destroyed by the revocation of your medical license." These are heavy sanctions. This is harsh medicine. But it works. Do these physicians require or undergo intensive psychiatric treatment? Not in most cases of which we are aware. Of course, they are a far cry, in our opinion, from the typical addict personality described by Nomoff and Fischer.

As we have said, let's follow good medical precepts. Let's isolate the causative chemical by law enforcement. Let's reduce its virulence by diluting it as we have to a 2% mixture of heroin in sugar of milk. Let's quarantine and dry out the addict. And let's cautiously let him back into society with a line on him through our parole or probation process, or civil commitment procedures.

This is not a simple job. Here, generally, we have a person who probably had dubious assets socially, even before he was addicted, and that is the person we are asked to "wean from the milk of paradise." Let us remember that when we read of visionary dreams to have addicts voluntarily accept followup, out-patient treatment. Follow-up treatment is perhaps the most important feature of the whole addict salvage program. In our opinion, most of this is a worthless concept if there is no authority in the program. In our sympathy for the addict as a down-trodden person, in recalling what he faces in his rat race against withdrawal symptoms, we forget that the addict generally is completely satisfied with his lot. We have never heard what we consider a sincere expression of regret, or a wish for a change, from an opiate addict who had access to drugs.

METHADONE MAINTENANCE—MIRACLE OR MIRAGE

It was rather casually that we discussed methadone in 1961 in our first edition. Over the years we had acquired some familiarity with this drug in what was then the Federal Bureau of Narcotics, and later when we were in charge of the Illinois Division of Narcotic Control. As we have said, its use in somewhat gradually withdrawing an opiate addict, be it to heroin, morphine, Dilaudid, Demerol, Pantopon or the like, by the interim substitution of methadone had made "the withdrawal ward the quietest wing in the hospital" at Lexington. We knew street addicts would use it. In the late 1950's our narcotic prescription form audits in the Illinois Division of Narcotic Control showed a small abuse of methadone. But it was not well-known to addicts or for that matter to many physicians and pharmacists. However, we learned of cases where the wily addict facing arrest would manage to take a methadone tablet before going to jail and perhaps smuggle in a tablet or two despite a casual search and thus avoid the onset of withdrawal symptoms. We knew of addicts who carried methadone until they got to Lexington USPHS Narcotic Hospital or "found another connection." It was a trite observation supported by the mute testimony of worn out hospital admission papers that they hoped it would be the "other connection" which was reached first.

We knew what is made such a point of by advocates of a "methadone maintenance program," that methadone is not likely to be the drug of choice in situations like that confronting an addicted doctor or nurse who might have a free choice among many drugs. These people would select morphine, Dilaudid, Demerol, etc., rather than methadone. This is sometimes cited to give methadone a certain aura of respectability. But what is not stressed is that given a situation where methadone is "the only drug in town" it will be eagerly seized upon and used, not with any idea of alleviating withdrawal symptoms only, but to continue to enjoy an opiate-type addiction of a somewhat less attractive nature. This might be quickly abandoned when better stuff like heroin, morphine, Dilaudid, or Demerol became available.

In the interest of historical accuracy it must be stated that the degree of heroin addiction at the time and place (Chicago, Ill., 1958-60) based on the available 3% to 5% street drugs supported only what could be described as a "needle habit." These people showed no marked withdrawal symptoms, and any withdrawal medication was usually an aspirin or other sedative. As a matter of fact many were abandoning opiate use spontaneously as "no good, just crap."

* * *

At this writing, the most discussed chemical in the drug abuse control field is methadone.

"The pharmacological actions of methadone are identical with those of morphine. The outstanding properties of methadone are its effective analgesic activity, its efficacy by the oral route, and its extended duration of action in physically dependent individuals. The drug also causes sedation and respiratory depression and exhibits effect on smooth muscle and the cardiovascular system similar to those of morphine. . . . The principal danger of over dosage is diminished pulmonary ventilation." (From Goodman and Gilman, *The Pharmacological Basis of Therapeutics*, pp. 260-261.)

Paraphrasing Jerome H. Jaffe, M.D. *(ibid.)*, methadone meets the classic tests for an opiate or opioid in that (1) it suppresses the opioid withdrawal syndrome when tested on subjects dependent on morphine; (2) it produces morphine-like physical dependence when given chronically, (3) post-addicts consistently identify it as dope (morphine-like) and repeatedly request it when offered the opportunity to do so.

Dr. Victor H. Vogel, M.P.H., M.D., for many years medical officer in charge of the U.S. Public Health Hospital, Lexington, Ky., and chairman of the California Narcotic Addict Evaluation Authority, states: "Methadone is attractive to the addict and supports opiate addiction. Addicts taking it experimentally often identify it as either heroin or morphine."

"Proposals that methadone be given addicts after discharge from an institution as a non-addicting, continuing substitute for heroin can only lead to disaster, repeating the tragic introduction of heroin as a non-addictive substitute for morphine. To whatever extent it may be synthesized illegally or diverted from legal channels it will appear in contraband trade. Methadone is under control of the Federal narcotic laws" (Maurer and Vogel, p. 77).

The present campaign for a methadone maintenance dole as an alleged cure for opiate addiction verges on the bizarre, as is perhaps the whole idea of curing one opiate addiction with another opiate addiction. As first promoted, the proposition was not that bald. Sometimes it was represented to be a tapering-off sort of thing, an idea which of course would enlist support because of methadone's good reputation in stepping down the severity of withdrawal symptoms from heroin. But now it is being advanced that total withdrawal is not the objective. The patient is to be maintained on methadone in perpetuity, on the highly questionable theory that he will stop stealing and will thenceforth be a useful citizen. During much of the early promotion of methadone there was seldom, if any, mention that methadone is a dangerous opiate which very quickly establishes a tolerance and dependence; something which a sophisticated person would expect from the employment of a morphine-like drug. The news media seldom mentioned this, from lack of fuller information in methadone promotion. Instead of pointing out the fact of a cross-tolerance between heroin and methadone we began to hear that methadone "blocked" the craving for heroin.

"Once burned, twice shy" is a good basis for the scientific approach. We suppose that we have acquired an inbuilt suspicion of an "instant" chemical or other simple cure for opiate addiction, although we have not hesitated to devoutly hope for that eventuality in what we say and write. But our narcotic history so far has been that of hope sadly deferred. We have been among those who early pointed this out. Now we have much support in knowledgeable writers and we will sketch but a few reminders.

Sometimes we refer to the interest, in the mid-nineteenth century, in the perfection of the hypodermic needle with the hope that parenteral administration would avoid the "oral appetite" for morphine.

Then there were the adventures with cocaine of the great Sigmund Freud who, in addition to giving an assist to its development as a local anesthetic, became concerned with it as a cure for morphinism. He had read in some American literature that it was such. In 1885 he was writing that it was a specific antidote, that the morphinist could be cured without the attendance of a physician if he dosed himself with cocaine when he felt withdrawal symptoms. Eventually Freud came safely through his own game of Russian roulette with cocaine, and in 1887 he was writing that treatment of morphinism with cocaine resulted in the substitution of a worse addiction; it was "driving out the devil with Beelzebub" (see Becker; also Freud).

We have quoted Fulton on the use of such patent frauds as hopeine as a morphine cure. We have also described at some length the rather long acceptance of heroin as a cure for morphinism when the underworld knew better, and the early action of the U.S. Public Health Service and the medical profession to outlaw this dangerous opiate. We have recited the Demerol story, the great discovery to alleviate the pains of womankind and the rest of the human race—and non-addicting, so it was alleged. It took very prompt and emphatic action by the U.S. Public Health Service and the Commissioner of Narcotics to demonstrate what we quickly had from street experience that this wonderful drug was addicting to a most remarkable degree. It is amazing that this myth of non-addictiveness still persists in some degree respecting Demerol.

There is some irony, we suppose, in the fact that methadone did not slide into medicine under false pretenses. The Lexington scientists were now operating in top form. As Samuel Levine, former director of the Division of Drug Control, Department of Health, Commonwealth of Pennsylvania, and long-time federal narcotic officer and administrator, reminds us, "As a narcotic agent I could recall the many drug addicts who came back from Lexington during the time that the original research was being done and who proclaimed the wonders of this new drug which was then only known by the identifying number 10-8-20" (INEOA Conference Report, Sept. 1969). So prior to its introduction into our medicine, methadone was well identified and completely described by the country's top opium alkaloid scientists as a dangerous and addicting chemical (Isbell *et al.*, 1947).

What seems to us to be particularly repugnant is the hard sell in the methadone promotion. We might liken some aspects to the old-time patent medicine pitch. There is the euphemistic approach, the invention and employment of a disarming jargon to advance an addicting and killing drug. Many other valuable drugs are addicting and are killers, but they usually are so labeled, and it would be unethical and illegal not to do so. Certainly this would be true in the usual well-organized medical campaign. But in the total impression given by the methadone hard sell, these hard facts seldom emerge. True, recently the news media more frequently mention that this is an addicting synthetic narcotic, but the fact that even now this is relatively infrequent and relatively new only indicates how successful a campaign of equivocation and avoidance has been in the promotion of this opiate. But just as often we will see as in a state of New York official release, "methadone is a synthetic drug which, when properly administered, eliminates the craving for heroin and eliminates its euphoric effect." Or, as reads a recently received federal magazine which we highly respect, "methadone is a synthetic drug, the Center points out, which, when properly administered, blocks the destructive efforts of heroin." One really can not blame the editors. This is the accepted jargon. Apparently one of the first effects of methadone maintenance propaganda is to "block" reference to the drug as narcotic and addicting.

There is a well-designed mumbo jumbo which substitutes the healthful and wholesome phrase "blocks heroin addiction" for the plain truth that it substitutes a methadone addiction for heroin addiction. We are told by inference by the clinic operators and directly by the addicts in clinic medicine shows on television that he is a man who has been "cured" of his addiction by something almost as innocent and innocuous as orange juice. Certainly the truth is that our patient must be addicted and well addicted to the new drug. As a matter of fact his skin is filled to the ultimate effective milligram. If he stops using it he has withdrawal symptoms, not as intense as with heroin but of longer duration. There is, of course, something more, much more. Otherwise he would throw away this crutch and would walk on his own two feet like a man. If he did not have a very strong psychologic addiction he would not be deterred from this by the possibility of a fortnight, more or less of possible influenza-like symptoms.

The methadone hard sell has many aspects which influence the very great preponderance of good people who are inclined toward accepting the policy of methadone maintenance by the desperate need for an opiate cure on the one side and the almost instant relief pictured in the methadone mirage. These good people are taken in by such statements as "methadone to an addict is like insulin to a diabetic." Let us remember that this analogy originated with or has been adopted by the principal promoters of methadone maintenance. We have heard this phrase defended on the ground that the public needs to hear something dramatic. What the public needs to hear, of course, is the simple truth. And the simple test of the insulin analogy is "what happens to the seriously afflicted diabetic when you forcibly separate him from his insulin?" The answer is, we suppose, that he may lapse into a coma which might prove to be fatal. "What happens to the methadone addict if you take away his opiate and deny him access to it for a few weeks?" The answer is, of course, that depending on the drug of addiction and the intensity of his habit he would go through a short period of withdrawal, a few days or a couple of weeks. Then in good surroundings he would develop an increased appetite, would generally gain weight and strength, would become more clear-eyed and alert, and all in all would be healthier than he ever had been since he took his first addicting dose of an opiate.

The methadone promoters do not fail to use other adjuncts of hard sell. We would call them "con" and "muscle." This description may startle the professionals in the programs, but they should be made to see what it could look like from the other side of the television tube. Often the format is the professional who comes on, earnest, sober, dedicated, and in dire need of public funds right now. Substantial funds, that is. He may be accompanied by a good cluster of patients who solemnly avow that now that they are on methadone they are "cured" of heroin addiction. They are not likely to refer to their drug as methadone. It is more likely to take on the euphemism of "orange juice" or "juice." Earlier in this book we have referred to opiate addiction as apparently enhancing the art of the confidence man. Recently we saw an article by Albert A. Kurland, M.D., director of the Maryland Psychiatric Research Center, Baltimore, Md., who says "Prominent among the facets of the personality projected by the image of the narcotic abuser is one of deception." And Dr. Kurland goes on to demonstrate what law enforcement officers in this field discovered early, that the addict can be full of self-serving "con." Dealing with amateurs, of which there seem to be many in the methadone maintenance management, he could have a field day (Wittenborn et al., (Eds.), p. 265 et seq.).

To our view, and we have seen so much of this, the methadone addict panel seems to represent the con man in his finest flower. No reference is made to the fact that he is still firmly "hooked" on another drug. There are only sketchy references to useful employment which might turn out to be "made work" and often no work, and no mention that he may live in a world where drug-free urine samples and fake employment records are for sale. One can hardly criticize this narcotic addict for taking full advantage of administrative naivete which sometimes permits for months the operation of so-called clinics without the elemental precaution of the establishment of a central identification register!

And just in case "con" doesn't seem to be the convincer, we hear this "muscle" persuader, "If you don't give us our free methadone we will have to take to the streets to gun you down, or knock you down to rob and steal to get money for heroin." We are approaching the bicentennial anniversary of our country. Even though we may seem to have become far removed from some of the principles that made our nation great it might be well to try to recapture a little of the spirit that was voiced by Charles Cotesworth Pinckney when he was our Ambassador to France in 1796: "Millions for defense, not a damned penny for tribute."

Another of the disturbing facets that sometimes appear in the operation of the methadone maintenance scheme is the tendency to reject the help that the police might render. We have commented elsewhere on the value of police cooperation in narcotic disintoxication programs. Several excuses are given for excluding the police, such as invasion of privacy, harassment, and the like. This is not completely novel in drug abuse treatment programs, but is seldom seen where the medical personnel are informed and the people in charge are competent. These people come to realize that the police may be just as human and just as interested as anyone else in getting the addict back to be a useful member of society. The claim of invasion of privacy is somewhat unrealistic. Next to doctors and clergymen we suppose the police successfully carry more secrets than most any other segment of society. As for privacy, many of the people involved appear on television. The treatment facilities seem to be so handled that the fact of addiction is within the knowledge of a great many people, not all of the best character. Some methadone addicts take part in public demonstrations.

It is distressing to hear the issue of harassment. Some of these representations seem designed to put the methadone addict in a privileged criminal class. A well-conceived program, convinced that its results would equal its representations, should in our opinion welcome the fullest assistance of the police who might contribute much to the accuracy of reported results and to the conservation of public funds.

There is a tragic irony in establishing this wide base of opiate addiction in this country. For years we have been personally involved in programs to reduce the available amounts of manufactured drugs which might be diverted to addicts, and in this we had some great success. Years of effort to reduce the amount of opium produced over and above medical needs of the world were not as fruitful, although they probably very much minimized the production which otherwise might have resulted. In this country and through world-wide agreement we are still making a strong effort to reduce opium plantings in such countries as Turkey. Turkey, of course, has its own historic, economic, traditionalistic, and nationalistic reasons for producing opium. These are hard for even the best intentioned administrations to overcome. In some quarters it has been suggested that we get very tough with a country which may be our soundest ally in its part of the world. The irony is that on the one hand we should push around the Turks on the theory of suppressing opiates while on the other hand we are licensing additional outlets for the American pharmaceutical industry to produce an opiate, methadone, to drug our people.*

Of course it should be a fervent hope that the persistent and well-considered efforts now under way will reduce the Turkish poppy plantings without encouraging a shift to other geographical areas where they would be under even less control.

We suggest that it may be a great regression when we go back to the practice of the rare but distressing slattern whom we sometimes saw in our boyhood days. Unable or unwilling to control her squalling infant, she would feed it paregoric.

There is much drum beating about alleged reduction in the crime rate. We have not seen what we would consider a single valid study which would demonstrate this. Methadone proponents are quick to seize on situations where there has been a reduction in the rate of crime which might coincide with a methadone maintenance program even though at the same time the effective police force might also have been increased by a considerable fraction. In any event there must come a time when the rate of crime increase must decelerate somewhat lest eventually we have a society of more felons than honest citizens. We suppose a good case could be made for the proposition that a methadone-using felon might be a little more efficient than a heroin-using felon if for no other reason than that he could accommodate to a more flexible time schedule.

Combined with the threat of the cost of crime and as part of the semantic mumbo jumbo is the claim of the contrasting small cost of the daily dose of methadone which is described as "pennies a day." This is one of those things which our idiom calls a halftruth, but in which the fraction of truth is certainly less than onehalf. A competent observer informs us that about two years ago he took a casual look at costs of some methadone maintenance projects and stopped counting when the figures disclosed at least

---

*In 1968, for medical and scientific purposes, the United States imported 122,974 kilos of opium—74,992 kilos from India and 47,981 from Turkey. Much of this was used in the manufacture of codeine here. (*A Resume on the Abolition of Opium* by John T. Maher), files of the U. S. Bureau of Narcotics and Dangerous Drugs.) For the year 1970 this country imported a total of 204,004 kilograms of raw opium, 172,965 kilos from India and 31,039 from Turkey. With the 1971 fall planting Turkey may be growing its last crop of opium poppies. We can hope for some benefit from this. That hope must be tempered by the danger that illicit opium production may be dispersed to less obvious and even less manageable areas.

7000 dollars per patient per year. This does not quite agree with the inflated cost of criminal depredation we usually read about, but it is not "pennies a day."

Speaking of criminal predators, of whom we have known many, we have consistently urged, as we do elsewhere in this book, that one of the best ways to reduce thievery is to put drug addicts in jail. Our premise is not that all thieves are addicts. Certainly we are among the few writers who knew that up to recent years, at least, 75 percent or more of the people arrested in the narcotic traffic had had other criminal records first. Our rationale is simply that if you have an addicted burglar you have two potential handles by which to seize him: one as a burglar, the other as a narcotic offender. Again we are in the area of half-truth, although we will concede that the methadone proponents here perhaps just don't know. But we should inform them that we have many, many non-addicted criminals and that the non-addicted burglar, for instance, is likely to be more efficient than his addicted counterpart.

Also we should correct the impression that money for "dope" is the only objective of thievery. As we have also pointed out in this book there are many other more conventional objectives. It may cost more money to underwrite one expensive playboy thief than could be accumulated by scores of addicts.

Recently we have read *Are You Safe from Burglars?* by a self-styled professional burglar, Robert Earl Barnes. We have a little more than casual knowledge of Mr. Barnes and have been assured that he is not, and very likely never has been, a narcotic addict. The catalogue of his "take" is amazing and it would require the operation of a great number of junkie thieves to approach it; in fact most of his exploits would be beyond their capabilities.

One of the most successful burglar gangs recently captured in this country, (Fairfax, Va.), called the Beltway Burglars, were non-addicts. They eventually built up to a substantial scale of depredation and a corresponding imposing scale of high living before their careers were interrupted by the Fairfax County police and prosecutors.

Again in the half-truth category is the claim that methadone, in the oral administration designed package with orange juice,

Tang, etc., is not injectable. Certainly methadone maintenance administrators ought to know that in fact young people have been successfully injecting these mixtures.

Up to very recently in this country there is a general acceptance that drug abuse was bad, especially opiate abuse. An even stronger attitude of that sort saved the British from much opiate addiction, as we have pointed out at great length. Now, are we to say to the susceptible, or the unthinking, that an addicting opiate is so innocent and so desirable that we can give away one of our strongest protections against drug abuse, an almost unanimous social disapproval?

The methadone maintenance program also fails to recognize the indispensable element of a containment program; that containment should be a practical possibility. One shouldn't pretend that he can carry much water in a wicker basket! It is in this area that the real amateurism is so glaringly apparent in methadone maintenance. We hear of people being given three-day supplies, five-day supplies, two-week supplies of a take-home medicine. We later hear that some of it has killed little children and adolescents and young adults. How little the people who permit this seem to know about the diversion and other misuse of drugs by addicts! The ingenuity of the user in this respect is classical. He often has seen fit to resort to cough medicine, paregoric, barbiturates and what not. Any heroin user might be delighted to find methadone of medicinal quality to supplant his badly diluted street heroin. So there is now being loosed a flood of a legal drug which will seep out or pour out through the dispensaries and from the methadone addicts. The street heroin addict will go to the best source.

Robert F. Horan, Jr., Commonwealth Attorney for Fairfax Co., Va., which is adjacent to Washington, D. C., and suffers from a spillover from some of the methadone maintenance ventures there, said in testimony before the U. S. House of Representatives Select Committee on Crime, April 28, 1971: "Methadone addiction appears to be growing at a faster rate than heroin addiction. Our drug treatment program over the past year found it necessary to engage in medical detoxification of thirty-nine patients—thirteen of these were detoxified for a heroin habit and twenty-six were detoxified for a methadone habit. A large majority of those detoxified were below age twenty. . . . In the past eighteen months we have had five provable methadone overdose deaths and at least two suspected methadone overdose deaths. Each of the deceased was below age nineteen. In the same period of time, my jurisdiction had one heroin overdose death."*

From another adjoining county—Prince Georges, Md.—Charles F. Colao, M.D., referring to the District of Columbia program, writes in part (Washington, D.C. *Evening Star,* May 2, 1971): "A massive, poorly controlled, substitute narcotic program has been instituted with gay abandon. We are now begining to see methadone babies and the junior high schools are filled with narcotized, nodding students."

Should present trends continue, methadone might well become the drug of choice in a freely available underworld drug market. In addition to diversions, we can expect the small clandestine methadone production to mushroom. The detection and suppression of this underground trade will be immeasurably handicapped by cover afforded by the free-flowing legal maintenance drug. And in the present wonderland of methadone the worst these people might expect when caught up with would be that they would be transformed into lifelong addiction to a supersaturation of methadone. What will the end be? How many methadone-loaded human creatures do we expect to accumulate?

Of course this is too good an opportunity for the smarter confidence man addict to overlook. We have seen some good results from the employment of ex-addicts in detoxification programs. But as we understand the Dole-Nyswander concept, detoxification is immaterial or undesirable. Sharp operators attracted by loose government money or generous charity funds seem to be moving in and may have a field day in the fringes of these programs. Addict "con" is likely to cost the public and the sick addict dearly.

One of the most objectionable features of this objectionable philosophy is the claim that not only is methadone a good anti-

---

*More recently, in a television news documentary—Methadone in the Capital: Does it Really Work - WTOP, Washington, D.C., Oct. 26, 1971, Mr. Horan disclosed that in the last 24 months in Fairfax Co. (Va.) there was one heroin overdose death. In the same months there were ten methadone overdose deaths. Seven of these were within the last twelve months. Of these seven, three were sixteen years of age.

drug-abuse program but that it is the only one. This entirely disregards the fact that for some decades in this country we did reasonably well in controlling opiate addiction. As a matter of hard coincidence, and only that, an opiate abuse rise has accompanied the methadone maintenance push.

Earlier in this chapter we quoted Dr. Marie Nyswander on opiate withdrawal. "They [addicts] just need firm authority, encouragement, some sleeping pills for rest at night, and a little support and interest for the four-day withdrawal period that is so difficult." We partially agreed but commented to the effect that she made it a little too simple. Of course Dr. Nyswander wrote this in 1957, before she became celebrated as a member of the husband and wife team of Dole and Nyswander. How has the nature of narcotic addiction changed since 1957? Would she now sentence people of this type to a permanent methadone dole?

We have referred herein to the addicted physician, who, although he is a rarity, does illustrate that axiom which is so constantly overlooked: one must have access to opiates to become an opiate addict. Medicine is the only profession of great stature in which a distinctive incidence of opiate addiction can be recognized. Why? Of course because he has free access to narcotics. On the other side of the coin it was our proud claim that we helped free from their addiction and salvaged and preserved as useful instruments for healing in our society as many as 90 percent of these physicians. What should we now do with the addicted physician? Sentence him to methadone? From their writings we would be inclined to think that Dole and Nyswander would have no compunctions about allowing a methadone addict to practice medicine. Perhaps such people are now practicing in some clinics. To us it is not a reassuring thought.

Currently we see a situation where smaller suburban communities are suffering from the overflow of methadone maintenance programs in the urban centers. As a part of this, a new version of the notorious script doctors of the early 1920's has appeared. These are very few in number but their impact in tragic methadone overdose killings has been enough to keep this a lively item of news. Recently, and apparently as promptly as the legal situation permitted, we have seen some medical societies take steps to crack down on these methadone script doctors. This is only a small indication of the many troubles that will plague opiate drug control with the opening of the Pandora's box of methadone maintenance. When the suburbs ask the city to control its methadone spillover, the reply sometimes is "Start your own methadone maintenance clinic," which we would translate to mean "put your own 17-year-olds on methadone for the rest of their lives."

It should be emphasized that we see value in methadone as a substitute addicting drug incident to complete withdrawal from opiates in order to minimize withdrawal symptoms. At the same time we should repeat what we have already pointed out, that when heroin is greatly diluted, withdrawal symptoms will be so minimal that the intervening steps of methadone addiction may not be necessary in most cases. A prolonged administration of the substitute methadone and the building up of a huge tolerance for this drug might mean only the establishment of a real opiate addiction for what was only a "needle habit" in the low-grade heroin user.

Perpetual methadone maintenance addiction as now recommended as a substitute for cure of heroin abusers should be rejected for many reasons. To summarize only a few: (1) it has been foisted on the public as a cure for an addiction, whereas it is in fact an addiction to another dangerous opiate; (2) this maintenance concept gives social acceptance to opiate addiction as an element in our culture, thus contributing to its rapid increase among our people; (3) it makes it much more difficult to control other dangerous drugs which may be no more harmful than this one; (4) the perpetual methadone addiction program makes it impossible to physically control the drug and is so subject to abuse as to make restrictions relatively meaningless; (5) it will result in addiction of many people, particularly youths, who will graduate to it from relatively trivial abuse of other drugs; (6) its presence and advertisement as an alleged miracle drug-abuse cure will delay the development of possible worthwhile controls of drug abuse; (7) we should not allow ourselves to be bullied into free opiate rationing by the threat of street crime. There are more honorable answers to extortion than to submit to it.

In the field of criminology, methadone maintenance is a novel and disturbing concept. We might suggest that it is immoral and unethical if these terms are still permissible. There invariably comes to mind the television program where the zoo master goes out to capture a wild animal and shoots it into tractability with a dope gun. Our methadone captive will rather have been baited by "orange juice" and perhaps thereafter confined by the invisible bars of a methadone zoo for the rest of his life. The acceptance of this philosophy might make one believe Orwell's "1984" is closer than we think.*

As would be expected, methadone can be lethal. Gardner and Connell (p. 455) report that when oral methadone was prescribed in the dose range of 10 to 20 mg daily, a patient received a prescription for 100 mg which he was able to double within hours by obtaining the next day's supply shortly after midnight. This led to a death from inadvertent overdose.

Bejerot (p. 218) reports a death from methadone poisoning at Gothenburg, Sweden, in which the prescribing doctor was subsequently convicted of manslaughter.

As we have pointed out, methadone deaths are becoming commonplace in this country, especially among the young. Some of the methadone deaths now being too frequently reported in the press appear to be from drugs obtained on prescription issued by what we might call "script doctors." Since the criminal law may be in an ambiguous position to deal with these cases we suggest that in instances where minors are involved in a methadone death (or for that matter where an addiction is originated or perpetuated by loose prescribing practice for a minor) the parents might be well advised to seek civil damages from the physician. This could aid the medical profession in preventing a repetition of the calamity of the 1920's when "script writing" practitioners were a great source of opiate addiction.

Recently we had a note from an M.D. friend, a great expert in the narcotic field and a wit. He resents, as we do, the employment of the inaccurate analogy that methadone to the addict is like insulin to the diabetic. He observed, "Perhaps what these people are trying to say is that halitosis is better than no breath." We ap-

---

*Another unfortunate spin-off from what we think is an unfortunate undertaking is that some radicals, both black and white—with some appearance of logic—have seized on the methadone maintenance program to belabor "the establishment" for employing maintenance as a device to control the lives of the black and the poor. (*National Observer*, May 19, 1972.)

preciated his quip and perhaps this is a more exact figure of speech than the one employed in the methadone push. But we get a macabre reaction. It brings to mind those pictures in living color of drug-connected deaths which the pathologists show at our conferences. The doctors are likely to point out the characteristic pink frothy exudate from the breathing apparatus of the victim, which indicates respiratory failure. The deceased smothered, died from lack of oxygen. So our friend's quip about methadone, a respiratory depressant, can really suggest "no breath" and the odor of death.

The obvious, to us, fallacies of methadone maintenance should not discourage the search for other chemical remedies for opiate abuse. It is unfortunate if the overblown claims for methadone have diminished this quest. Drugs like cyclazocine and naloxone which are opiate antagonists, but non-addicting, are under investigation. The Select Committee on Crime, U.S. House of Representatives, recently (4-29-71) heard testimony on a new drug, which allegedly can eliminate a heroin addict's craving for his drug in a week and is non-addictive. If there is to be a chemical cure for opiate addiction it seems that hope lies in this area.

In International Narcotic Report (INEOA) Albany, N. Y., for October 1971, is an account of the discussion in the U. S. House of Representatives on September 21, 1971 by William R. Anderson, MC, on the newly discovered proposed opiate addiction cure known as the carbon dioxide rapid coma technique.

On September 14, 1971 the Washington, D. C. newspapers carried the story of an incident which we fear will become all too typical of methadone in polydrug abuse. The District of Columbia medical examiner is said to report that a young powerfully built man, arrested for possession of marihuana had been found dead in his jail cell after suffering acute secobarbital, methadone and morphine poisoning. The medical examiner is quoted as saying that there was only a small amount of morphine in the deceased's body but the amount of methadone and seconal found was not compatible with life. The deceased is reported to have been employed in a methadone maintenance project, which perhaps could have guaranteed the potency of this drug. Since heroin in the body is often reported in terms of morphine it may be that weak street heroin was the source of the small morphine finding. If so, we may have here in a capsule a synopsis of the drug abuse street scene.

Recently the newspapers in Washington, D. C. quoted a speaker at a convention of psychologists as deploring the "animalistic" concept apparently held by many practitioners who seem to ignore the moral or ethical qualities sometimes considered to be peculiar to the human species.

Operators of the methadone maintenance program are of course entitled to their own individual notions. But we wonder if what seems to be an animalistic bias does not incline some of them to ignore what others might consider very precious human rights. The offering to a drug addict patient a choice between a drug free environment and the opiate environment of methadone is not really a free choice. Anyone with the slightest familiarity with the opiate addict knows that "weaning from the milk of Paradise" is generally a distressing emotional process. As Bejerot (1970) quotes Rado, "the patient does not suffer from his illness, he enjoys it." And as the WHO (World Health Organization) definition has it, he has the "compulsion to continue taking the drug at any price." "Multimodality" is now a popular word in describing approaches to drug abuse rehabilitation. But can it be argued seriously that there is much true multimodality which offers to the addict a choice of remaining on an opiate drug? Or is this not indeed very unfair competition to any program with a drug free objective? Do we not, in truth, see much of the weight of "rehabilitative" effort in effect taking advantage of the addict's lack of will power to force him into the rut of methadone addiction? Here often surrounded by "technical assistants," themselves often addicted and on methadone maintenance (who "never had it so good" salary wise) the luckless addict has little motive or opportunity ever to escape a life of thralldom to methadone. Is it decent to present this lopsided choice to seventeen-year-olds?

Minor aspects of some methadone maintenance programs seem to reflect a callousness toward human values. At the September 1971 conference of the INEOA at Albany, N. Y. a methadone maintenance expert casually dismissed questions as to what to do with the young girl addict who is pregnant. It was stated that usually it was very late term and there was not time to consider withdrawal. But even if the matter came to attention earlier it was really not a matter of consequence or concern. "We know how to manage these cases routinely, we do not need to consider detoxification." It took another question to determine that the baby had to be detoxified. We have read that maternal narcotic addiction damages both fetus and the newborn infant. In some methadone maintenance situations the narcotic dosage of the mother may be better regulated. However, we would think that with the massive dosages of methadone maintenance the opiate intake of the mother usually would be much the heavier. In any event, we take it, any narcotic addiction would be bad for the fetus and the newborn child.* Equally disturbing was an observation that because of the maintenance on methadone of a husband or wife, it might be well to put the other spouse on methadone also to make a more congenial family. Few persons, we suppose, are as familiar as we are with the tragedy of intrafamily addiction; the addiction which sometimes spreads from husband to wife and even to children. We know of wholesome women who "married the man to reform him" and wound up "hooked." We have seen the doctor's wife follow him into addiction. So we are repelled by the seeming nonchalance which would call on the spouse's loyalty to have her descend into methadone opiate addiction with her husband, an unsettling version of Ruthian devotion: (*Holy Bible* - The Book of Ruth).

It is not surprising then that after hearing much discussion the INEOA membership at its annual conference at Albany, N. Y., August-September, 1971, passed by overwhelming vote a resolution decrying reliance on methadone maintenance in treating drug addiction. (International Narcotic Report, INEOA, Albany, N. Y. Oct. 1971).

The associate director of a methadone maintenance clinic on the eastern seaboard was recently quoted in a magazine of national circulation to the effect that methadone maintenance must be given a full trial with the definite implication that if results were not satisfactory he would wish to legalize heroin to destroy the traffic by making heroin cheap or free. He is apparently ignorant of the fact that the most intensive abuse of heroin in this country occurred when this product was very, very cheap. Furthermore, he sharply criticized a prosecutor for recommending that efforts be made to

---

*Zelson, C. Rubio, E., and Wasserman, E.: Neonatal narcotic addiction: ten-year observation. *Pediatrics, 48*:178-189, (August) 1971.

wean young people away from opiates before committing them to a methadone maintenance program. Such attitudes of people of responsibility in the methadone program are alarming.

At the September 1971 conference of INEOA we had occasion to interview separately two persons from diverse fields who had recently been in West Germany, the area where methadone had been synthesized during the World War II years. These were Sheriff Ralph E. Kreiger of Cuyahoga County, Cleveland, Ohio, who had made a government sponsored visit there, and Dr. Howard B. Lee, Research Associate and Drug Consultant, University of Wuerzburg, Germany. Independently, both these men expressed the idea that West German drug abuse enforcement officialdom were amazed at any American reliance on methadone as a cure for drug problems and were wondering when we would wake up to its dangers.

One of the common trade names for methadone is Dolophine®. There is a long current story that this was derived from the "Adolph" of Adolph Hitler, the ruler of Germany in World War II when methadone hydrochloride was synthesized to produce a narcotic which would relieve Germany from dependence on the opium poppy for a pain killer. However, this seems to be apocryphal and the name may have a chemical origin. Nevertheless, it now could be that—in a way he had no reason to think of—Dolophine, in burgeoning rise to maintain opiate addiction in this country may prove to be a posthumous "Hitler's Revenge" on the American people.

Another account of the genesis of the name Dolophine is that it derives from the Latin "dolor," meaning grief or pain, and "finis" meaning end, which described the analgesic properties of this drug. Dolophine, as we have indicated, is a good medicine in assisting the complete withdrawal of the heavily addicted heroin addict. When the manufacture of Dolophine began in this country in 1947 we rejoiced as members of the Federal Bureau of Narcotics, charged with responsibilities for stockpiling opium against war shortages. We recognized that this synthetic would reduce our dependence on imported opium. But Dolophine, in our opinion, is not ending the pain of our opiate drug addiction epidemic. Rather it is bound to greatly intensify this social "headache."

Sometimes we are asked "Isn't it better to have a methadone addict on the streets rather than a heroin addict?" While we might demonstrate that there are two sides to this argument the proposition in fact begs the real question. It is not a choice between one methadone addict or the same person as a heroin addict. The real proposition is whether goals are, on the one hand, government sponsored and promoted opiate addiction or, on the other hand, no opiate addiction; whether we want a *free drug society* or a *drug free socity*. There is nothing more axiomatic about drug addiction than that drugs and addicts create drug addicts.

Our production of methadone has increased from 80 kilograms in 1965 to 1,221 kilograms in 1970, mostly to provide rations for about 25,000 opiate addicts. For 1972 the estimated production of methadone is about 2,600 kilos to provide opiate rations for 30,000 to 40,000 addicts.

Despite the fact that one-third of the confirmed addicts in this country may now be on methadone rations, we have not been able to discover any credible indications that this program has contributed anything to the reduction of opiate addiction. The contrary seems increasingly apparent to us.

As this goes to the printer we read an article by William H. Dobbs, M.D. *JAMA, 218(10)*:1536-1541, (December, 6), 1971. entitled Methadone Treatment of Heroin Addicts, Early Results Provide More Questions Than Answers. This is a study of a random sample of 100 clinic patients receiving methadone maintenance treatment in the Narcotics Treatment Administration of the District of Columbia government. To us this is a disturbing but not surprising report. It indicates that a majority of the patients are still using heroin. The conclusion which the sophisticated reader must draw is that a proportion of the heroin addict population is using the methadone maintenance program as a convenient backstop to continue the maintenance of heroin addiction.

Dr. Dobbs postulates, and his reviewer (p.1565 *ibid*) implies that some of the weaknesses disclosed by Dr. Dobbs may be due to abuses resulting from apparent understaffing, inexperience, ignorance and mismanagement in the clinic (our language). But we think the dismal results indicated primarily are because the whole concept of methadone maintenance to reduce opiate addiction is fallacious and foredoomed to spiral upward opiate addiction in this country. Dr. Dobbs suggests that the original Dole theory of a methadone "blockade" of heroin rests on a shaky foundation and included only a small group of but seven patients. He appears to agree with what we have previously set out, that the term "blockade" is a misleading, unfortunate and obscuring euphemism. He speculates on what we think is now common knowledge among many narcotic law enforcement officers, that many methadone maintenance clinic patients are able to enjoy heroin habits supported wholly or in part by sale of "medicinal" methadone supplied to them by clinics on a takeout basis.

In his recent book Dr. Nils Bejerot proposes some elaborate measures for reclaiming drug abusers.

> Hardly any psychiatric condition is more difficult to treat than a well established addiction. This is partly because the addict generally does not suffer from his disease, he enjoys it, as Rado so tellingly described it. The drug effects take on the strength of libidinal desires and outweigh all mental, physical, social and economic complications arising from the abuse. . . . If the patients are to receive permanent help they must, with few exceptions, be forced out of their addiction environment and kept free from drugs for a long period, with or against their will. Systematic investigations show clearly that compulsory treatment has better results than voluntary treatment and probation gives a far better prognosis than ordinary medical after-care. [p. xvii]

Dr. Bejerot suggests special therapeutic communities, in more or less isolated villages, on islands, or in depopulated areas, perhaps taking over old buildings. The patients, under the guidance of a small well-qualified therapeutic and management staff, would run their own villages, work in craft shops, etc., and would be paid ordinary wages. Dr. Bejerot even suggests an island for the more intransigent addicts and that these addicts might be kept drugged. We would agree with the island concept, but certainly there would be no purpose, in our opinion, in keeping them there on drugs. We have seen many dedicated addicts who had been kept forcibly separated from their drugs, often for many years, and can unequivocally say that, generally, they never looked healthier!

Sweden, to its great good fortune, has had little experience with opiate addiction, but it recently has had a devastating epidemic of methamphetamine drug abuse, mostly by hypodermic injection, and among younger people. So it is helpful to get this fresh view. What we especially value in Dr. Bejerot's contribution is his insistence that there must be compulsion in these programs when necessary and evaluation follow-ups and checks on the patient's performance.

"Now and then this person [Preludin addict] under arrest may show great interest in seeking treatment, but in a very shallow and opportunistic way, as for instance when faced with a risk of prison sentence. . . . After care must also involve a certain amount of pressure on the individual." (Bejerot, pp. 247 and 275)

Dr. Bejerot suggests countermeasures against the "serious illness" toxicomania, produced when susceptible individuals are confronted with dangerous agents, the toxicomania-producing drugs.

1. Attack the agent itself.

2. Try to control the paths by which the dangerous agents are spread.

3. Prophylactic measures. "These problems are so complicated, however, that the information to the public must largely take the form of indoctrination ('Thou shalt not abuse drugs')."

4. Isolation and long-term care of the highly contagious cases.

One of us (M.L.H.) recalls that as a young officer he was the victim of what we later learned was the favorite gambit of a smart old morphine addict. "Do you really want to know how to clean up dope addiction?" he asked. We were all ears and said so. "Well," he said, "you will have to round up all us junkies." "Yes," we said. "Then you will have to get us an island in the South Pacific. We would like that mild climate." "Go on," we urged. "There might be a little wine around, but we are not interested; some women, but we're not interested; some music, but we're not too interested. Then fill us up with all the junk [drugs] we can use. We're interested, that's heaven, and then . . ." he paused. "What then?" we asked. "Well, then you blow the island to hell," and he roared with laughter at his own punch line.

Specialists in the behavioral sciences have commented profoundly on this old chestnut. It is a sample of the macabre humor of the opiate addict; it may reflect the addict's entire identification with his habit, his entire opposition to the cure, a self-destructive suicidal stance, etc. And of course he was having fun pulling the leg of a young greenhorn. But part of this apocrypha may have some use.

We will say here, as we have elsewhere, that many addicts can be cured. Without going into a discussion that could be interminable we might observe that we have never seen an adequately devised civil commitment addict control program, and this includes some we have tried to set up. The usual fault is paradoxical—the program is generally too expensive, too complex, and too involved. Still it is not complete enough. We have never seen any real recognition that a medical epidemic is involved which requires the full use of civil commitment policy against all the addicts. How this concept can be ignored in the acknowledged epidemic of today is puzzling. But the general bent is to try to take charge of the addict only when he comes rather willingly, seeking escape from the rigors of prosecution for a felony.

We have experience going back to the depression days for organizing idle people. We have decades of experience with the mechanics of civil commitment of the ill person who is a danger to the community. Why not try simple work therapy? Why not clean our rivers, our roadsides, and preserve our forests? This might serve to take some of the "romance" out of the drug culture and in some cases perhaps substitute the satisfaction of a job accomplished for the hedonism of drug abuse.

Samuel Taylor Coleridge, in a letter to a friend, said of his own addiction: "In short, conceive whatever is most wretched, helpless and hopeless and you will form as tolerable a notion of my state as is possible for a good man to have." For most modern addicts the picture is not as dark as Coleridge painted. Today's addict finds drugs so dilute, so expensive, so hard to come by that many of his fraternity find it impossible to inject enough narcotics to maintain a pronounced habit.* Coleridge had little but his own sapped willpower to protect himself from drugs. Today's victim has a substantial armament from law and medicine. The result is that many

---

*The increasing availability of methadone may destroy this happy situation.

do recover from addiction and remain abstinent. Nevertheless, the nature of the addiction experience and the lack of a specific dependable cure is a clear indication that the best of the methods for "treating" is to see that it does not occur.

And if I drink oblivion of a day
So shorten I the stature of my soul.
George Meredith
Modern Love

5
RECOGNIZING AN ADDICT

THERE MAY BE TOO much of a tendency to conclude that certain chemical tests are the only means of recognizing and proving opiate addiction.

There has been the discovery and wide use of Nalline®,* a drug which is an antagonist and antidote for heroin, morphine, and similar opiates and which, when subcutaneously administered, quickly precipitates the onset of the withdrawal syndrome. One of the first indications of withdrawal reaction is the enlargement of the pupil of the eye. Within 15 to 30 minutes after the injection of Nalline, this manifestation will disclose that the subject has an opiate in his system. Methods for the analysis of urine, the classic reliance, have been perfected and the operation much shortened.

However, in practice such tests may be impractical or impossible. Recognition and proof of opiate addiction may depend on some of the numerous other indications.

The following list, abstracted and modified from Maurer and Vogel on *Narcotics and Narcotic Addiction,* may be a helpful guide:

"The most significant signs which may (when supplemented by further objective evidence) indicate [opiate] addiction are:

"A statement by the individual that he is an addict.

"The possession of addicting drugs (either medical or contraband) without adequate medical explanation.

"A tendency on the part of the suspect to hide or conceal these drugs.

"The presence of needle-marks in the form of black or blue spots

---

*Nalorphine (N-allynormorphine hydrochloride).

resembling tattooing; these may indicate skin-shooting, and will usually appear in the arms and legs, or even on the backs of the hands and also on the feet. Fresh needle punctures, sometimes topped by minute scabs or crusts, are especially significant.*

"The presence of elongated scars (frequently of tattooed appearance) over the veins, especially those of the forearms, the insteps, or the lower legs; however, these may have a medical explanation unrelated to addiction.

"The presence of boil-like abscesses over the veins or near the sites where veins approach the surface.

"An appearance of drowsiness, sleepiness, or lethargy ('on the nod'), especially if accompanied by a tendency to scratch the body as if itching. This sometimes indicates a slight overdose of opiates or their synthetic equivalents.

"The tendency to develop withdrawal symptoms if isolated completely and observed constantly for a period of 12 to 24 hours. Beginning with yawning, sneezing, sweating and progressing into stomach and muscle cramping—sometimes to acute prostration, etc.

"Wide fluctuations in the size of the pupils of the eyes, with the pupil reaching a maximum of constriction immediately after the suspect may have taken an injection. Sometimes the whites of the eyes are discolored.

"The possession of equipment for smoking opium, unless, of course, this equipment has only a curiosity value, or is owned by a collector. If it is freshly or currently used, the odor will be characteristic.

"The possession of hypodermic equipment, excepting those persons with a legitimate need for such equipment, such as diabetics who must take regular injections of insulin, or medical addicts. However, the legitimate user will invariably possess a standard medical syringe and needle, while the addict usually (but not always) tends to prefer the home made syringes.

---

*The great significance of the needle mark (tracks) as a means of identifying the opiate addict may be diminished somewhat in the newer world of polydrug abuse. Needle marks may be the result of amphetamine injection, for instance. A rising tide of methadone addicts may confine themselves to some degree to oral intake of the drug. But the needle mark will remain of great importance.

"Tending to wear long sleeves or other concealing clothing even in hot weather to cover needle marks. Sometimes tattoos made over injection sites for concealment. Small blood spots on shirt sleeves or other clothing from skin punctures.

"A tendency for the individual to sit looking off into space, known to young addicts as 'goofing,' this may indicate the use of heroin or barbiturates, or both.

"The possession of a cooking spoon with handle characteristically bent backward, or a cooker made from a metal bottle cap with a wire handle; small glass vials are also sometimes used. They are all characteristically blackened from being held over a lighted match.

"A knowledge of the argot of the underworld narcotic addict. While some addicts who secure their drugs exclusively from medical sources never learn any of the argot, these addicts are decidedly in the minority; most addicts will know and respond to terms from the argot of the underworld addict, and especially to terms employed predominantly by users of the type of drug which the addict takes.

"A tendency for the suspect to isolate himself at regular intervals (about four or five hours apart) in order to take hypodermic injections.

"An obvious discrepancy between the amount of money the suspect earns, and the amount he spends for the necessities of life; if he makes $100 a week and is always broke, with no obvious expenditures for necessities, he may be supporting a drug habit.*

"The tendency for a person who has previously been reliable to resort to thievery, embezzlement, forgery, prostitution, etc. This may indicate that he or she needs the large amounts of money to support a drug habit."

As stated, the fact that a suspect is an opiate user may be further demonstrated by tests such as the Nalline test, and tests of body fluids such as urine.

Sometimes the question of the recency or chronology of needle marks on the suspected addict may become important. Dr. Harris Isbell, former director of the Addiction Research Center at the

---

*Allowing for inflation!

U. S. Public Health Service Hospital, Lexington, Kentucky, has given us these comments.

"About ten years ago [circa 1950] for reasons which I have forgotten, I made some observations on addicts receiving morphine intravenously. As I recall I watched three men, all of whom were white. I circled the site of the venipuncture with a skin pencil and examined the site twice daily for a week. The needlemarks were still discernible after a week but of course many changes had occurred.

"During the first half-day about all one can see is a tiny hole in the skin without any surrounding area of inflammatory reaction, and which contains a tiny plug of clotted blood or serum which does not protrude above the surface and which is quite easily removed.

"By 24 hours a definite scab (crust) has formed which projects above the surface. On careful inspection, a tiny ring of inflammatory reaction is seen surrounding the venipuncture. The crust at this time is soft and easily removable by light stroking with a cotton applicator and usually has a definite reddish-brown color.

"By the second day, the inflammatory reaction surrounding the puncture (if sterile) has disappeared, the crust has taken on a more brownish appearance, requires moderate pressure to remove, and leaves an oozing base which will recrust.

"In 72 hours the crust is firmer and even harder to remove.

"For about five days, if the crust is removed, one finds an area of light-reddish tissue underneath, and ordinarily no new crust will form.

"By the seventh day the crust starts drying up and is easily removed. The red area is still seen under it, and gradually fades over a period of about a month, after which either nothing can be seen, or a very tiny round whitish scar."

As to the scabbing or crusting of injection sites, Dr. James G. Terry states:

"I learn as much or more [contrasted to visual inspection] by lightly feeling the area in question. The crusting gives a sandpaper-like sensation."

There may be occasions when the officer might wish to bring this information to the attention of an examining physician.

As experienced officers well know, narcotic addicts have a real genius for recognizing one another. This recognition often seems to come about from a combination of indications and circumstances intangible and ephemeral to the uninitiated. Therefore, one addict may lead to others.

One of the surest ways to determine narcotic use or addiction is for the addict to be questioned by the *informed narcotic officer.* Very often, when an addict realizes that he is talking with such an officer, he will readily admit addiction. At the same time, he might strenuously deny the fact to someone with little or no knowledge of narcotic addiction.

It is important that narcotic officers see and talk with many addicts. In that way, knowledge will be obtained leading to accurate recognition, and usually prompt admission by the addict that he is a user.

THE COCAINE USER

The cocaine user will be infrequently seen nowadays. However, his number is showing some increase. He may give the appearance and have the actions of being intoxicated, i.e. "high" without the odor of alcohol. His pupils may be widely dilated. His nose may be reddened from sniffing cocaine. Formerly, in heavy users, we sometimes saw tissue damage in the nose. If and when heroin is very plentiful we might expect him to inject a mixture of cocaine and heroin as a "speed-ball."

The heavy user, as we have said, may have hallucinations. He may have a frightening impression of being taken to a great height with risk of falling. He may imagine police coming in through the key-hole of the door to his room, or experience similar illusions. The cocaine user often experiences acute sensations of insects "crawling" on his skin. He may think these insects are burrowing under his skin or fingernails. On superficial observations he might be confused with the methamphetamine "mainliner."

THE MARIHUANA USER

Like the cocaine user, the marihuana smoker may be exhilarated without the odor of alcohol. If he is in a closed room or a closed car, there may be about him a smoke which has the odor of burning grass. In his reactions, he usually is not as violent as a cocaine user, but may be unpredictable and dangerous and have very disturbing hallucinations. He does not have the constricted pupils of some phases of opiate use. He may be laughing and giggling without apparent reason. The marihuana user is likely to be a social creature who congregates with others to take his drug.

ARGOT OF THE DRUG CULTURE

Since the argot of the opiate addict or the marihuana user is one of the surest hallmarks, we reproduce here a few of the most commonly used words of the narcotic trade. The newer polydrug abuse culture also is developing its own vocabulary and some of this is included.

This list is necessarily limited and includes mostly words going to the essence of drug abuse or traffic. The criminal investigator will, of course, need to have a much wider vocabulary. For this we refer him to such special publications as *Narcotics, Lingo and Lore* by Schmidt (Charles C Thomas); *Dictionary of the American Underworld Lingo* by Lipsius; the glossary in *The Narcotic Traffic* by Anslinger and Tompkins (Funk & Wagnalls Co.) or that in *Narcotics and Narcotic Addiction* by Maurer and Vogel (Charles C Thomas).

Narcotic officers must be thoroughly familiar with the peculiar language of narcotic peddlers and narcotic addicts. For undercover work, particularly, wide and ready knowledge is indispensable.

Verbatim reports of negotiations leading to the purchase of narcotic drugs in which argot is reproduced, may tend to refute a defense of entrapment since this will show the seller to be conversant with the criminal narcotic underworld.

The foregoing presents a situation which requires two precautions.

1. Drug abuse officers should not fall into the practice of substituting argot for good conversation in talk with nonunderworld people. Such a course may cheapen and degrade the officer with respectable people.

2. In testifying in court, the officer should carefully separate his assumed identity and talk from his official position and diction.

The argot of the old time opium addict sometimes was crude and coarse, but much of it showed imagination, subtlety and indirection.

For the phenomenon of narcotic dependence the addict's expression that he is "hooked" is a terse but complete description of his condition. But we like the more involved figure "monkey on my back." The roundabout story on this is: Many carnival workers were addicts. In the old days they worked in proximity to dog and pony shows. In these there was always an act in which a monkey rode on the back of a dog, usually a shaggy collie. As the dog went through its evolutions the monkey clung to his back for dear life with all four "hands" and a tail. Small wonder that the addicted "carney" likened this unshakable rider to his habit!

A little more earthy but with the same roundabout and the "you must be in the know" quality is this one: The opiates tend to dry up normal body secretions and consequently most narcotic addicts have difficulty with constipation through the formation of a very hard, difficult to pass, stool. Yen Shee, the char from smoked opium, still has a potent morphine content and is smoked with fresh opium or drunk in a decoction to satisfy narcotic craving. Therefore it very logically follows that an addict, having had a long and difficult time at stool, will eventually report that he had a "Yen Shee baby."

The following is from a booklet, *Glossary of Terms in the Drug Culture,* prepared by the Laboratory Operations Division, Bureau of Narcotics and Dangerous Drugs, U.S. Department of Justice, and is reproduced by courtesy of the Bureau.

A Boot: Under influence of drugs.
Ace: Marihuana cigarettes.
Acid: LSD or other hallucinogens.
Acid Head: LSD user.
Ad: Addict.
All Lit Up: Under the influence.
Angel Dust: Phencyclidine on parsley.
Apple: Non-addict.
Apples: Fellow addicts.
Are You Anywhere?: Do you smoke marijuana cigarettes?
Around The Turn: Gone through withdrawal period.
Artillery: Equipment for injecting drugs.
Bag: A container of drugs (usually a one-ounce package).
Bag Man: Supplier.
Bambita: Desoxyn or amphetamine derivative.

Bammies: Poor quality of marihuana.
Bang: To inject drugs; one injection of a narcotic.
Banging: Under influence of drugs.
Barbs: Barbiturates.
Barrels: LSD tablets.
Batted Out: Arrested.
Beat the Gong: Smoke opium.
Bedbugs: Fellow addicts.
Behind the Iron House: In jail.
Belongs: On the habit.
Belted: Under the influence of drugs.
Bending and Bowing. Under the influence.
Bennies: Benzedrine (amphetamine sulfate).
Bernice: Cocaine.
Bernies Flake: Cocaine.
Bhang: Marihuana.
Big Bloke: Cocaine.
Big John: Police.
Big Man: Supplier.
Big O: Opium.
Bindle: Small package of narcotics (usually an ounce package).
Bingle: Supplier.
Bingler: Seller of narcotics.
Bingo: To inject drugs.
Biz: Equipment for injecting drugs.
Black Beauties: Amphetamines.
Black Stuff: Opium.
Blanks: Poor quality merchandise.
Blasted: Under influence of drugs.
Blow: Miss the vein in injecting.
Blow: Leave a place.
(A Joint, Pot, Grass, Stick, Hay, Tea): Smoke marihuana.
Blow Charlie or Snow: Sniff cocaine.
Blow Horse: Sniff heroin.
Blue Birds: Amytal (amobarbital sodium).
Blue Devils: Amytal (amobarbital sodium).
Blue Heaven: LSD.
Blue Heavens: Amytal (amobarbital sodium).

Blue Velvet: Pyribenzamine (an antihistamine).
Blues: Amytal (amobarbital sodium).
Bobo Bush: Marihuana.
Bombido: Injectable amphetamine.
Boost: Rob.
Boss: Real good.
Boxed: In jail.
Bread: Money.
Broker: Dope peddler to addicts.
Browns: Long-acting amphetamine sulfate (capsules, many colors).
Bull: Police.
Bummer: Habit; a bad trip.
Burned: Received phony narcotics.
Burned Out: Sclerotic blood vessel from too many injections.
Busted: Arrested.
Buy: Make a purchase of drugs.
Buzz: Moderate euphoric reactions to drug.
"C": Cocaine.
"C" Joint: Place where cocaine is sold.
Cadet: New addict.
California Sunshine: LSD.
Can: 1 or 2 oz tin of marihuana for cigarettes.
Candy: Barbiturates.
Cap: Container of drugs (usually a one-ounce package).
Caps: Capsule of drugs.
Carmabis: Marihuana.
Carrie: Cocaine.
Cartwheels: Amphetamine sulfate (round, white, double-scored tablet).
Catch Up: Withdrawal process.
Caught in a Snowstorm: Drugged with Cocaine.
Cecil: Cocaine.
Charged Up: Under the influence of drugs.
Chicken Powder: Amphetamine powder.
Chip: Taking occasional small injections.
Chipping: Irregular drug habit.
Chocolate Chips: LSD.
Cholley: Cocaine.

Cleared Up: Withdrawal process.
Clipped: Arrested.
Co-pilots: Amphetamines.
Coast to Coasts: Long-acting amphetamine sulfate (capsules, many colors.
Coasting: Under influence of drugs.
Coffee Habit: Novice in use of narcotics.
Coke: Cocaine.
Cokie: Cocaine user.
Cold Turkey: Sudden withdrawal without drugs to alleviate symptoms.
Coming Down: Effect wearing off.
Connect: Make a purchase.
Connection: Supplier.
Cooker: Bottle cap for heating heroin and water.
Cop: To obtain drugs.
Cop a Deuceway: Purchase of $2 pack of narcotics.
Cop a Sneak: Leave a place.
Cop-man: Supplier.
Cop Out: To alibi; to confess.
Corinne: Cocaine.
Cotton Shot: Water added to cotton to get whatever heroin is left.
Crank: Methamphetamine.
Crink: Methamphetamine.
Cris: Methamphetamine.
Cristina: Methamphetamine.
Croaker: Doctor.
Croaker Joint: Hospital.
Crusher: Policeman.
Crystal: Methamphetamine.
Cube Juice: Morphine.
Cube (The): LSD.
Cut: To adulterate with quinine, milk, sugar.
Cut Out: Leave a place.
"D": LSD.
Dabble: Irregular drug habit.
Dead on Arrival: Phencyclidine base.

Dealer: Supplier.
Deck: A container of drugs or narcotics (usually a one-ounce package).
Dexies: Dexedrine (dextroamphetamine) (orange-colored, heart-shaped tablet).
"Dime Bag": Ten-dollar purchase.
Do a Bit: In jail.
Do Righters: Non-addict.
D.O.A.: Phencyclidine base.
Domes: LSD tablets.
Domino: Make a purchase.
Double Trouble: Tuinal (amobarbital sodium and secobarbital sodium).
Down: After-effects of marihuana.
Down It: Swallow.
Downers: Sedatives.
Dream: Cocaine:
Dripper: Eye dropper.
Drop Out: Leave a place.
Dropped: Taken orally.
Dujie: Heroin.
Dummy: Poor quality merchandise.
Dust: Heroin; Cocaine.
Dust of Angels: Phencyclidine base.
Dynamite: Heroin and cocaine taken together; strong drug.
Eighth: One-eighth of a teaspoon.
Emsel: Morphine.
Eye Openers: Amphetamines.
Factory: Equipment for injecting drugs.
Fall: Arrested.
Fallout: Addict nods or sleeps after injection.
Feds: Federal agents.
Fine Stuff: Finely cut marihuana (manicured).
Fix: To inject drugs.
Fixed: Under influence of drugs.
Flake Off: Leave a place.
Flash: Euphoric reaction.
Flats: LSD tablets.

Flea Powder: Poor quality merchandise.
Floating: Under influence of drugs.
Flying: Under influence of drugs.
Fold Up: Withdrawal process.
Folding Stuff: Money.
Foolish Powder: Heroin.
Footballs: Amphetamine sulfate (oval-shaped tablets).
Freeze: Turn down a sale.
Fresh and Sweet: Out of jail.
Front the Bread: Put the money up first.
Fu: Marihuana.
Fuzz: Police.
Fuzzy Tail: Police.
G Man: Federal agent.
Gage: Marihuana.
Garbage: Poor quality merchandise.
Gazer: Federal agent.
Gear: Drugs in general.
Gee Head: Paregoric user.
Geetis: Money.
Geezer: Needle shot of any narcotic.
Geezer: To inject drugs.
Get a Gift: Acquire narcotics.
Get Off: To inject drugs.
Get the Wind: Leave a place.
Gimmick: Equipment for injecting drugs.
Girl: Cocaine.
Glass Eyes: Narcotic addict.
Glued: Arrested.
Go in Sewer: Inject into vein.
Go Over the Hill: Leave a place.
Gold Dust: Cocaine.
Good Go: Fair amount of narcotics for money spent.
Goods: Drugs or narcotics in general.
Goof Balls: Barbiturates.
Got Beat: Bought a bag containing no heroin.
Gow Head: Addict.
Grape Parfait: LSD.

Grass: Marihuana.
Greenies: Amphetamine sulfate (oval-shaped tablets).
Griefo: Marihuana.
Gun: Equipment for injecting drugs, eye dropper.
"H": Heroin.
Hack: Doctor.
Hairy: Heroin:
Hand-to-hand: Delivery at time of payment.
Hang Up: Withdrawal process.
Happy Dust: Cocaine.
Hard Stuff: Morphine.
Harness Bull: Police.
Harry: Heroin.
Hassle: Ritual of buying drugs, preparing it, taking injection.
Hawaiian Sunshine: LSD.
Hay: Marihuana.
Hearts: Dexedrine (dextroamphetamine) (orange-colored, heart-shaped tablet).
Heat: Gun or police.
Heavy Man: One who has narcotics.
Hemp: Marihuana.
Hit: Make a purchase.
Hitting the Pipe: Smoking opium.
Hitting the Steam: Smoking opium.
Hitting the Stuff: Under influence of drugs.
Hitting Up: Injecting drugs.
Hocus: Morphine:
Hooked: Addicted.
Hop: Opium.
Hop Head: Person who smokes opium; addict.
Hoppie: Narcotic addict.
Horner: Sniffer of narcotics.
Horse: Heroin.
Hot: Wanted by police.
Hot Shot: Load of pure heroin, strychnine, potassium cyanide sufficient to cause death.
Hot Sticks: Marihuana cigarettes.
Hustle: To prostitute.

Hype: Addict.
Ice Cream Habit: Irregular drug habit.
Iced: In jail.
I'm Beat: Needs marihuana lift.
I'm Holding: Has drugs.
I'm Way Down: Needs marihuana cigarette.
In a Jam: Wanted by police.
In High: Under influence of drugs.
Indian Bay: Marihuana.
Indian Hay: Marihuana.
Jab: Hypodermic shot; to inject drugs.
Jive: Marihuana.
Jive Sticks: Marihuana.
Joint: Syringe and needle; one stick of marihuana; opium smoker's den.
Jones: Habit.
Joy-pop: A shot in the muscle of the arm rather than in the vein.
Joy Popping: Irregular drug habit.
Joy Powder: Cocaine.
Jump Skid: Leave a place.
Junk: Narcotics.
Junker: Addict.
Junkie: Addict.
Kee: One kilo.
Kick: Get rid of the habit.
Kicking: Withdrawal process.
Kicking the Gong: To spend time around place where narcotics are sold.
Kilo: 2.2 pounds.
Knocking on Door: Addict attempting to stay away from other addicts; attempting to break the habit.
L.A. Turnabouts: Long-acting amphetamine sulfate (capsules, many colors).
Laying on the Hip: Smoking opium.
Laying the Hypo: Taking a shot of narcotics.
Lay Out: Equipment for injecting drugs; opium smoker's outfit.
Leaper: Cocaine user.
Leaping: Under influence of drugs.

Lemonade: Poor quality merchandise.
Lettuce: Money.
Lid Poppers: Amphetamines.
Lie Down: Smoke opium.
Light Artillery: Hypodermic addict.
Lipton Tea: Poor quality merchandise.
Lit Up: Under influence of drugs.
Load: 25 bags of heroin.
Loco Weed: Marihuana.
Log: Marihuana cigarette.
Long Green: Money.
Love Weed: Marihuana.
"M": Morphine.
Machinery: Equipment for injecting drugs.
Mainliner: One who injects directly into the vein.
Make a Croaker: Deceive a doctor into giving narcotics.
Make a Meet: Make a purchase.
Make a Reader: Have a doctor write a prescription.
Make the Turn: Withdrawal process.
Man (The): Police.
Mary Jane: Marihuana.
Mary Warner: Marihuana.
Merchandise: Drugs or narcotics in general.
Mexican Horse: Mexican (brown) heroin.
Mezz: Marihuana.
Mickey: Chloral hydrate.
Mickey Finn: Chloral hydrate.
Micro Dots: LSD
Miss Emma: Morphine.
Monkey: Drug habit with physical dependence.
Mootos: Marihuana cigarettes.
Mor A Grifa: Marihuana.
Morph: Morphine.
Morphie: Morphine.
Morpho: Morphine.
Mouth Worker: Narcotic addict who swallows drugs.
Mr. Whiskers: Federal agents.
Muggles: Marihuana.

Mule: Supplier.
Mutah: Marihuana.
Nail: Needle.
Nailed: Arrested.
Narc, Narcos: Narcotic agent.
Nats: Possible code for barbiturates.
Needle Freak: One who enjoys using the needle.
"Nickle Bag": Five-dollar purchase.
Nimbies: Nembutal (pentobarbital sodium).
Nimby: Nembutal (pentobarbital sodium).
Noise: Heroin.
Nose Candy: Cocaine.
O.D.: Overdose, death.
On Ice: In jail.
On the Beam: Feeling fine.
On the Bricks: Out of jail.
On the Ground: Out of jail.
On the Nod: Under influence of drugs.
On the Street: Out of jail.
Oranges: Dexedrine (dextroamphetamine) (orange-colored, heart-shaped tablet).
Orange Wedges: LSD.
Out Of It: Non-addict.
Over the Hump: Completion of withdrawal.
Owsley's Acid: LSD.
P.G.: Paregoric.
P.O.: Paregoric.
PCPA: p-Chlorophenylalanine.
Pee: Heroin powder.
Panic Man: Addict whose source of supply has been terminated.
Paper: A container of drugs (usually a one-ounce package); prescription.
Peace: LSD tablets.
Peace Pill: Phencyclidine HCl.
Peace Tablet: LSD tablets.
Peaches: Benzedrine (amphetamine sulfate) (rose-colored, heart-shaped tablets).
Peanuts: Barbiturates.

Peddler: Supplier.
Pep Pills: Amphetamines.
Pepsi-Cola Habit: Small habit.
Peter: Chloral hydrate.
Pickup: Make a purchase of drugs.
Piece: A container of drugs (usually a one-ounce package); ounce of heroin.
Piki: Opium smoker.
Pill head: One who takes pills or capsules.
Pillows: Heat sealed, black polyethylene bags containing amphetamines or barbiturates.
Pinks: Seconal (secobarbital sodium).
Pin Yen: Opium.
Pipe: To look; opium device.
Plant: Hiding place for drugs.
Play Around: Irregular drug habit.
Pod: Marihuana.
Pop: To inject drugs, usually beneath the skin.
Pot: Marihuana.
Pot Head: Marihuana user.
Product IV: PCP-LSD combination capsules.
Purple Barrels: LSD.
Purple Haze: LSD
Purple Ozoline: LSD.
Pusher: Supplier.
Push Shorts: Cheating, selling "short" amounts.
Race Horse Charlie: Old morphine user.
Rainbows: Tuinal (amobarbital sodium and secobarbital sodium).
Rap: To talk.
Reader: Prescription.
Reader with Tail: Forged prescription.
Red and Blues: Tuinal (amobarbital sodium and secobarbital sodium).
Red Birds: Seconal (secobarbital sodium).
Red Devils: Seconal (secobarbital sodium).
Reds: Seconal (secobarbital sodium).
Reefer: Marihuana cigarette.
Riding the Wave: Under narcotic influence.

Roaches: Butts of marihuana cigarettes.
Rope: Marihuana.
Roses: Benzedrine (amphetamine sulfate) (rose-colored, heart-shaped tablets).
Rush: Intense, orgasm-like euphoria experienced immediately after drug injection.
Sam: Federal agent.
Sativa: Marihuana.
Scag: Heroin.
Scene: Place where drugs are sold.
Schmeck: Heroin.
Score: Make a purchase.
Scrap Iron: A bootleg drink made with alcohol, mothballs, and a hypochlorite solution.
Script: Money.
Scratch: Prescription.
Script Writer: Sympathetic physician; one who forges prescription.
Seccy: Seconal (secobarbital sodium).
Seggy: Seconal (secobarbital sodium).
Sewer: Vein.
Sharps: Needles.
Shit: Drugs in general.
Shoot Up: To inject drugs.
Shooting Gallery: Places where addicts can purchase narcotics and use needle.
Short Go: Take a small amount of narcotics.
Shot Down: Under influence of drugs.
Sizzling: Wanted by police.
Skee: Opium.
Skid: Heroin, leave a place.
Skin Pop: Intradermal or subcutaneous injection.
Slammed: In jail.
Sleeping Pills: Barbiturates.
Sleigh Ride: Under influence of cocaine.
Smack: Heroin.
Smears: LSD.
Sniffer: Narcotic addict who consumes dope through the nose.
Snort: Inhale drugs.

Recognizing an Addict 163

Snorter: One who sniffs up nose.
Snow: Cocaine.
Snowbird: Cocaine addict.
Sound: Benactyzine HCI.
Speed: Methamphetamine, usually, but may be any stimulant.
Speedball: Heroin and cocaine mixture; also Percodan and Methedrine mixture.
Speed Freak: Use habituated to methamphetamine.
Spike: Needle.
Splash: Amphetamine powder.
Splim: Marihuana.
Split: Leave a place.
Splivins: Amphetamine powder.
Square: Non-addict.
Squirrels: LSD.
Star Dust: Cocaine:
Stash: Hidden supply of drugs.
Station Worker: Narcotic addict who injects dope in arms or legs.
Stick: Marihuana.
Stinking: Under influence of drugs.
Stoned: Under influence of drugs.
Stoppers: Barbiturates.
Straight: Feels well, no withdrawal.
Strawberry Field: LSD.
Strung Out: Heavily addicted; regular user.
Stuff: General term for drugs or narcotics.
Sweet Lucy: Marihuana.
Swing Man: Supplier.
T-man: Federal agent.
Take a Powder: Leave a place.
Take the Wind: Leave a place.
Taking a Main: Injecting in vein.
Tar: Gum opium.
Taste: Small quantity of narcotic.
Tea: Marihuana.
Teed Up: Full of dope; intoxicated.
Texas Tea: Marihuana.
Thing: Capsule of heroin, cocaine, etc.

Three-day Habit: Irregular drug habit.
TNT: Heroin.
To Be Off: Withdrawal process.
Tools: Equipment for injecting drugs.
Toye: Small tin of opium.
Trey: Three-dollar purchase.
Truck Drivers: Amphetamines.
Turkey: No narcotics or drugs present.
Turkey Trots: Marks and scars from use of hypodermic needle.
Turn On: Introduce one to taking drugs.
Turn Up: To feel the influence.
Turned Off: Withdrawal process.
Turned On: Under influence of drugs.
Twisted: Severe sedation from drug.
Uncle Sam: Federal agents.
Unkie: Morphine.
Uppers: Stimulants.
Viper's Weed: Marihuana.
Wake Ups: Amphetamines.
Washed Up: Withdrawal process.
Wasted: Under influence of drugs.
Wedges: LSD tablets.
Weed: Marihuana; to take more than one's share of the loot.
Week-end Habit: Irregular drug habit.
Wen-shee: Gum opium.
Whickers: Federal agents.
White Junk: Heroin.
White Lightening: LSD.
White Merchandise: Morphine.
White Stuff: Morphine.
Whites: Amphetamine sulfate tablets.
Whiz Bang: Mixture of cocaine and morphine or cocaine and heroin used by old addicts.
Work the Leather: Leave a place.
Works: Equipment for injecting drugs.
Yellow Dimples: LSD.
Yellow Jackets: Nembutal (pentobarbital sodium).
Yellows: Nembutal (pentobarbital sodium).
Yen Shee: Ashes of opium.

6

THE ADDICT AS A POLICE PROBLEM

THE WIDE SCOPE of the narcotic addiction problem is well demonstrated in the many questions presented to us. Some time ago, one of the authors (M.L.H.) assembled some of these and published them with answers in the *Chicago Police Digest* (August 1959). We think that this dialogue portrays some very significant aspects of the narcotic problem. Hardly a principle can be stated to which there is not some qualification.

"Q. Is there a correlation between narcotic addiction and crimes of a violent nature?"

"A. By narcotic addiction I suppose we mean opiate addiction. If it is possible to give a bad dog a bad name, it may be that in earlier years the lumping of cocaine and cannabis use with opiate narcotic addiction may have placed too much onus on the opiates. In later years, writers, whose only acquaintance with the subject is theoretical, have tended to swing the pendulum far too far in the other direction. Too, a differentiation must be made between the actions of the addict when he has enough narcotics in his circulation to put him near equilibrium, as contrasted to what might be more desperate actions when he is undergoing withdrawal. However, apologists for the addicts have taken this theme to the ridiculous extreme. There comes a time in withdrawal when the addict is too sick to do any harm and a long time when he is weak as a kitten.

"During World War II, because of lack of other supplies, addicts were sticking up drugstores. I followed up a series of cases in Chicago. In many of these, the addict had recently had a shot; in some of the cases he had an old supply of drugs on his person. Some of the prohibition era "torpedoes" (professional assassins) were opium addicts. Phillip Chadwick, one of the country's very succesful bank robbers, was a narcotic addict. His mistake was to turn to sticking up narcotic wholesale houses. The last murder of a narcotic agent, which one of us had the sad duty to investigate, was committed by a Chinese narcotic addict, between 30 minutes and an hour after the addict had smoked the second of two morning pipes of opium.

"One doesn't need to say this to medical men, but others should realize that the action of these drugs is very complex, and just what the addict's reaction is might depend on the exact interval of time and amount of an injection. Let's not forget either that the property of opium which lets us contemplate the surgeon's knife with some composure might also take some of the quiver out of the front sight of the gunman's pistol. We recall a holdup crew—all addicts—who never went out on a job without giving themselves a slight nip of heroin before taking off.

"The amateur criminologist generalizes that the addict is mostly in non-violent crimes. Of course he is. There are so many more non-violent crimes committed, that it is simply pointless to make such an observation. There might be 20 times as many.

"We recall once sending to Dr. Kenneth Chapman (1951) the information that the Minister at Bangkok was closing all the licensed opium dens between Midnight and 4 a.m. because they were being used as headquarters for robber gangs.

"An addict recently told us: 'Why should I face that stick-up rap, when I can coast along picking stuff off store counters with a price mark of $49.95 or under?" [Then the upper limit for petty larceny.]

"Commissioner Anslinger cites a case. For years, he had looked for the case of an addict who would be entitled to a legal ration of morphine. Finally, there came the case of the wife of a North Carolina doctor, addicted for 20 years, and having had 12 cures. The Commissioner called in what he considered the greatest expert. This doctor rejected the idea the woman needed morphine—her supply of drugs was discontinued—she returned to society—and took part in civic affairs with great credit. About a year later, during an emotional upset, she managed to obtain a morphine prescription. After an argument with her husband, under the influence of drugs, she attacked him with a hatchet; whereupon, he shot and killed her. He was exonerated.

The Addict as a Police Problem

"Perhaps there is some shading to less violent criminal pursuits by the opiate addict, but one should not bet his life on it. He could lose."*

"Q. It has been said that narcotic addiction and sexual crimes have direct relationship. It this true?"

"A. Here, again, there may have been too much confusion between the opiates and such drugs as cocaine and hashish (cannabis). The opiates may have received some unwarranted blame in specific cases. But, again, we are the victims of over-generalization by the apologists for the opiates. It is well known that narcotic addiction inhibits sexual activity. This is true both physically and psychologically. The addict needs no wife or sweetheart, other than Lady Morphia. But the opiates are a great menace in this field. For instance, we all know of the common situation in which the procurer, the panderer, finds his commercial operation is simplified if the prostitutes he employs are addicted. This contributes to good discipline. They are less likely to listen to a better financial proposition or stray to a handsomer master, if they are dependent upon the procurer for a steady supply of narcotics. Most important, of course, in connection with sex crimes, is the fact that the woman who is an opiate addict is likely to be completely promiscuous, whether commercially or otherwise. Every experienced narcotic officer will have personal knowledge of instances in which apparently fine and personable women have become veritable 'bums,' and this in only a few months' time.

"Jean Cocteau is a dubious authority. But he was an opium addict for some time, and he translates poetically. He says, 'With a man the drug does not put his heart to sleep, but his sexuality. With a woman it arouses her sexuality and puts her heart to sleep.' Actually, I do not subscribe to that observation. It is simply the fact that the degradation of opium wipes out every fine principle of woman-hood.

"In discussing narcotics and sex crimes, let's not forget that incident to the casual use of these drugs, to 'joy popping' and

---

*As did two fine investigators of the Post Office Inspection Service who were murdered in Chicago, Illinois, on March 14. 1960, by three scheming narcotic addicts who hoaxed the investigators into a defenseless situation and then shot them to death.

'week-ending,' one of the primary reasons for the drug use may be sex, and specifically, the seduction of uninitiated females."*

"Q. Is it possible to treat heroin addiction successfully? Can other narcotics, such as morphine, be used as a substitute in treating the heroin addict?"

"A. Use of a narcotic, such as morphine, would only be the substitution of a very hot frying pan for fire. Physical heroin addiction can be treated successfully by the very simple process of separating the addict from his drug. Convincing the addict that he should continue to live without the drug in a free environment is something else again. The best indications are that a good minority of lightly addicted heroin addicts—as many as 20%—may never revert after an arrest or a hospitalization.

"The synthetic drug methadon is useful in temporarily substituting in withdrawing from heroin and morphine."

"Q. Does heroin contribute more to violent crimes, sexual offenses, or prostitution than other forms of narcotic addiction?"

"A. I don't know of any solid evidence to sustain a position in any direction here. Most experienced narcotic officers will agree that heroin is by far the drug of choice of narcotic addicts because of its exceptional impact. Occasionally, an addict will brag that he uses only morphine, but we will generally find that that assertion is made to preserve his snob status of obtaining drugs from medical sources. Given free choice, the addict usually overwhelmingly prefers heroin. It is no hardship that these days he has little other choice because (1) the peddler, for his own reasons, prefers to sell heroin, and (2) because of the care exercised by the professions entrusted with morphine, this drug is more difficult to come by.

---

*The consensus of the medical experts regarding the suppression of the sex instinct by the opiates makes such a loud chorus that in modern narcotic literature it has completely drowned out the small voice of experience. Older narcotic officers recall the Chinese association of smoking a casual, weekend pipe or two of opium coincidental with a night out with the girls. Like a voice from the past is the current testimonial of the late, great "sexpert" Errol Flynn. In *My Wicked, Wicked Ways* (1959), Flynn says, "She introduced me to a completely new experience—opium smoking. . . . When I took Ting Ling to another room, I had never known I was capable of such feats."
"Today I'm told that the effects of opiates remove physical desire in the man in adverse ratio to the female who becomes more excited. Dr. Flynn can tell us that such is not the case." (From *My Wicked, Wicked Ways* by Errol Flynn. Copyright © 1959 by G. P. Putnam's Sons, and reprinted by their permission.)

The Addict as a Police Problem

"Heroin has a tremendously seductive appeal for people who are introduced to it. It represents an additional hazard to the proselyte in that one can be introduced to its joys by the casual act of sniffing."

"Q. Would it be feasible to treat addicts in the same way that victims of leprosy have been treated, that is by isolating them in colonies?"

"A. Here is the principle of what I think is the most sensible way of handling the narcotic addiction problem. The addict must be segregated, not only from the drug which is his disease, but to prevent him from contaminating others. His situation, of course, is more hopeful than was that of the oldtime leper (I don't know what the immediate picture is on Hansen's disease). The disintoxicated, treated addict can be released into society rather promptly, with a string attached. We have been doing too much talking about feeding addicts, supporting the degradation of addiction in the community, and pursuing 'British System' myths when long ago public opinion should have been mustered—in the few communities necessary—for the erection of simple confinement and treatment stations, where the addict could be disintoxicated, and to which he would be promptly returned if he would not remain abstinent. Eventually, with such an institution, we might acquire a small, hard core of 'lifers' who would be humanely held there, to a great profit of society and their own health. But with a well-developed testing program and specialized parole supervision which would quickly disclose relapses on the part of the addict (who now has much incentive to return to addiction and little reason to avoid it), we would salvage many people. More important, we would so diminish the fad or 'cat' status of addiction that recruiting would be diminished greatly, in my opinion.

"It is a real pity that the bizarre and sometimes superficially plausible solutions agitated for by the amateurs distract so much from profitable and constructive discussion. I think there is a pilot program pretty well developed in this country which all of us who have problems should observe very closely. This was evolved by a group including the Chief of Police of Oakland, California, the prosecuting attorney and Sheriff of Alameda County, California, and a Physician, a Psychiatrist, Dr. James G. Terry, who is the medical officer in charge at Santa Rita, a rehabilitation center of Alameda County, California.

"Realizing the extreme importance of prompt detection of relapse on the part of disintoxicated addicts, these gentlemen and others formed a plan to utilize the drug, Nalline, the properties of which, as an opiate antagonist, have been one of the many fine demonstrations of the Lexington hospital.

"Briefly, an injection of Nalline will very promptly bring on withdrawal symptoms in a person dependent on most of the opiates. In summary, the addict goes to Santa Rita, for disintoxication. Theoretically, this could be either on a criminal charge or as a civil commitment. For practical purposes, weaknesses in the civil commitment procedures limit the treatment to criminal commitments at the present time.

"The criminal population at Santa Rita consists of all types of short-termers. Only 20% or so of the population are addicts. No attempt is made to segregate them, either as to residence or treatment. They get such medical attention, including psychiatric treatment, as appears proper, individually and generally. When the disintoxicated and treated addict is released, either on probation or parole, he is required to submit to tests with Nalline.

"As to the misdemeanant addict, these are carried out by Dr. Terry in a medical annex to the county jail. The addict is tested rather promptly after release; sometimes within a day or two. Those of us who know addicts will appreciate the wisdom of this. The addict continues to receive surprise tests, usually at lengthening intervals.

"A vital part of the program—it may be the most vital part—is that the released addict is under rather intense parole or probation supervision; that is, the parole officers handling these addicts have relatively light caseloads. Critically important, in my opinion, is the fact that they are narcotic specialists. They have no other case responsibilities. This is a situation, of course, where one hand washes the other because Nalline testing tends to simplify the probation officer's responsibility.

"This program has been in effect for some three years. About 7000 addicts have been given the Nalline test by Dr. Terry. The enforcement officers and prosecutors in Alameda County are enthusiastic about the result. They claim a great reduction in addiction. Furthermore, if an addict does relapse, the program permits of prompt detection of that fact. The addict can be recommitted for further treatment before he has an opportunity to reestablish a heavy habit. The professional thief is back in custody before his depredations grow too large.

"Santa Rita is an open-type institution, converted from an abandoned Army installation."

"Q. In contrast to compulsory hospitalization for mental illness, the majority of compulsory hospitalization statutes for drug addicts have a one year maximum. Is this due to the belief that if the condition can be successfully treated, a cure will result during this period, or is the period a criminal penalty with the place of detention changed from a prison to a hospital?"

"A. There is no question that it takes time, even if only to effect disintoxication and to rebuild the physical man. The period of treatment, if stated as a period not to exceed one year, in my opinion, is not intended as a criminal penalty."

"Q. There have been some recent studies on out-patient treatment of drug addicts. Do you know the rate of recidivism of such patients as contrasted to drug addicts who have been imprisoned without treatment and as contrasted with those who are involuntarily hospitalized and treated?"

"A. I know of no worthwhile information in this field. As a matter of fact, I have been suggesting, with some impatience, that someone should undertake even a Roper- or Kinsey-like survey to see what information can be developed.

"Obtaining valid figures respecting results from different types of procedures in handling addicts would, in any case, be difficult. Let's take Lexington. You might expect better results from the voluntaries who stayed the prescribed period at Lexington, as compared to sentenced prisoners who also stayed the optimum period. This would be on the guess that the voluntaries were better motivated. On the other hand, Lexington accomplishments with voluntaries would be minimized if we counted people who left against medical advice. In Illinois, I would expect our results with civil commitments to be superior to the results with criminal commitments, for the simple reason that the civil commitments will represent a group, the individuals of which present better prospects for rehabilitation.

"If the inquirer means out-patient reductive ambulatory treatment, it would appear we could safely say, from past experience, that recidivism would be practically one hundred percent or, perhaps more accurately, there were not even reasonably temporary cures obtained by this method."

"Q. At least one state permits the superintendent of a hospital for drug addicts to release an addict he believes incurable with a certificate allowing him to obtain a prescription from a health department approved druggist. What are the advantages and disadvantages to the community under this approach to the drug addiction problem?

"A. If this means releasing an addict with a perpetual prescription for drugs to gratify his addiction, there is no advantage, whatever, to the community. The disadvantages are to preserve the know-how and way-of-life of addiction, to present a constant threat of addiction to every person with whom the addict comes in close relationship, and to furnish a cover for illicit drug traffic.

"It would mean putting the addict in the state described by the late Pope Pius XII as 'permanent abolition or considerable and durable diminution of his freedom, that is, of his human personality in its typical and characteristic function. Such an act degrades a man to the level of a being reacting only to acquired reflexes or to a living automaton. The moral law does not allow such a reversal of values.' "*

The Federal Bureau's attention has not been called to any actual instance of such a "permissive" rationing of an addict. They believe such a practice would be unlawful, as tested by the Federal law and decisions. It might be mentioned in this connection that if an alleged drug addict were committed for treatment, and the physician at the institution found that the addict was suffering from a disease such as cancer, where some dosage of narcotic drugs was medically indicated, the patient might be discharged and a letter might be sent to his attending physician, stating the diagnosis of the physician at the institution."

"Q. What, if any, heredity factors play a role in addiction?

---

*September 14, 1952, Address by His Holiness Pope Pius XII to the First International Congress on the Histopathology of the Nervous System, With Reference to Psychoanalysis. Reprint of an article from *L'Osservatore Romano*.

The Addict as a Police Problem

"A. I have never seen anything persuasive on this point. The susceptibility seems to be cultural rather than hereditary. When white addiction was common, there was a proportionate representation of people of Irish extraction. But they tell us there are only 5 opiate addicts in the whole Irish free state. Jews, in this country at least, are notably resistant to alcoholism but, again, in the past I saw many Jewish narcotic addicts. Today, of course, the big addiction problem in this country is with the Negro, but 30 years ago our problem was with Caucasians and Chinese, and Negro addiction was almost a curiosity. I do not recall ever having seen or read anything which would lead me to believe that any race or nationality was immune from, or highly resistant to, narcotic addiction."

"Q. Why is the narcotic problem substantially greater in the United States than in Europe?"*

"A. One could write an essay on this. Off hand, the biggest single difference may be that we had the invasion of Chinese, who brought the opium smoking culture with them in the late 1800's.

"Another point is the American impatience with restraint. We choose not to endure the restrictions of the more complete law enforcement in many European countries. The free-wheeling American atmosphere develops us in every direction, including in crime and dissipation. With narcotic drugs in relatively scarce supply, the American underworld is the only one which has the time and money to support narcotic addiction.

"When I was in England a few years ago, one of my British contemporaries said, 'Thank God for the Yankee dollar, which sucks this heroin right past our little island.'"

"There is a lack of cultural susceptibility in England and some other European countries. Also some of the facts of addiction may be swept under the rug. Some other peoples do not have our capacity for public breast beating. In a few European countries there is not the same social consciousness as in ours. Recently I saw a news story, how reliable I don't know, that a Nazi occupation crackdown reduced cocaine use in France!"

"Q. Are many new immigrants to this country subject to addiction?"

---

*The addiction picture has worsened in Europe since 1961. Scandinavia, the United Kingdom, the Low Countries, France, and others are seeing increasing problems.

"A. I have never seen anything to indicate that. The only migratory correlation I have noted is in connection with a few young rural Southern Negroes when they come to the big city ghettos. This may be primarily due to the dislocation from rural to urban setting."

"Q. Realizing that the solution to the addiction problem must be both preventative as well as curative, do you feel that enough emphasis is being placed on the preventive phase?"

"A. Since narcotic addiction re-appeared among us in the late 1940's, we have been rebuilding our preventive defenses. Federal forces have been increased. Specialized police squads have been re-established and expanded, and penalties have been made more severe. It is always difficult to know how much enforcement should be deployed on any project. Usually there is only so much police money available. Emphasis in one direction usually means de-emphasis in another. Let's say that it would appear that there was enough preventive effort in every state of the Union except New York, Illinois, California, and Michigan, and it may be that we have established downward trends in most of these. Speaking for Illinois, that is moderately true."

"Q. What effect will the opening of the St. Lawrence Seaway have on the smuggling of narcotics into this country?"

"A. The opening of the St. Lawrence Seaway will, of course, give smugglers a great many more options as to where they might introduce drugs. However, since the most effective way of attacking smuggling combines is through intelligence operations to involve principals, this is no insurmountable handicap."

"Q. It has been said that we do not have enough Federal agents to cope with the smuggling of narcotics into this country. Has additional help or additional men been requested? If so, when and how many additional men did we ask for?

"A. I do not think we have enough Federal narcotic officers. This is one of the few situations in which I would disagree with Commissioner Anslinger. The present contingent of approximately 290 is, I believe, pretty close to what he has asked Congress for. The Commissioner has a firm conviction in which, of course, there is much wisdom—the police problems should be left to the states as much as possible. He has been quite wary of a situation where he would attempt to build up a force of a few hundred up into one large enough to assume the principal responsibility for narcotic law enforcement in the United States, to a degree where more than a quarter of a million police might abandon what he thinks are their responsibilities. It is a question of judgment. My own opinion is that another hundred Anslinger-trained officers would get us more results than any other anti-narcotic dollar and would not upset any Federal-State balance." (As applying to a 1961 situation.).

Wherever narcotic addicts appear, they are a serious police problem. Almost invariably they are found to be engaged in crime. Much has been written in the argument as to whether the criminality came first or was preceded by the drug addiction. Some surveys by non-police groups have claimed to show that addiction preceded criminality. Those by police organizations usually indicate the contrary. It is our observation from nearly four decades of close association with narcotic addicts that the addict was delinquent, anti-social, or criminal before he undertook addiction. This is usually quite patent with the person who becomes addicted in the very late teens or subsequently. For the younger person, although he may have represented a severe control problem before addiction, time and circumstance may not have established a documented criminal record.* It is important that law enforcement and rehabilitation officers know this and have an appreciation that the problem before them may represent much more than narcotic addiction alone. The subject could very likely be a person who long before his addiction decided that "only chumps work for a living."

The addict is a police problem because he is parasitic and predatory. These are harsh terms to apply to any human being and particularly toward a person who is given much attention as a "sick" individual. But these are terms of realism. Police cannot afford the luxury of being anything except realistic.

The addict is parasitic because, generally speaking, he will not work; he cannot work efficiently. On this point we can muster testimony from Alexander King on down to the lowliest junkie bum.

---

*As addicts become younger the percentage of prior criminal records might diminish.

The addict is predatory because the drugs which he needs to satisfy his addiction are so expensive due to their scarcity that ordinarily he can't derive sufficient income from legitimate sources to buy them. It is often stated and assumed, perhaps without too much factual foundation, that the addict thief needs to steal more than the non-addict thief because of the necessity for satisfying his addiction. This may not be too valid a conception.

On empirical observation, most police would say that whereas the addict spends the entire take from his thievery on drugs and nothing else, the non-addicted thief might spend his on alcohol, slow horses, fast women, sports cars, and other weaknesses of the flesh.

One essential point of difference must be made. The non-addicted thief with increasing maturity, new associations, or for numerous other considerations, might decide to discontinue a life of crime. The opiate user, hooked to his habit, does not have as much freedom of choice.

To the law enforcement officer then, the narcotic addict must be far more than someone who is interesting as a difficult medical problem. He is a problem who, in the great preponderance of cases, must be persuaded by the law before he will consent to become a medical patient. The addict is a difficult social problem. He is a very difficult criminal problem, indeed.

As we have indicated, he may run the whole spectrum of crime. He will be in the narcotic racket as a peddler. Usually he will be a small operator, which is not too surprising or remarkable since there are so many of them in proportion to the large-scale operators. However, this is a truism of wholesale and retail merchandising which escapes many otherwise intelligent people when they seek to comment on narcotic law enforcement: "So many little peddlers are arrested and so few big ones." The big-shot narcotic trafficker is not likely to be an addict, though we know of many who were, proving only that they were human and could succumb to the propinquity of narcotic drugs despite a daily experience which should have strongly conditioned them against the use of narcotics.

As we have said, we knew killers of the gangland mobs who were addicts. Some professional robbers and stick-up men are.

Addicts can be found in the gambling rackets, e.g. numbers and policy. Males may be pimps and panderers. A great proportion of women addicts are prostitutes. Usually this observation is followed by the statement that this is the only way the unfortunate woman can get money to supply her habit. We suspect that any penetrating examination of individual cases will disclose that most such women were trollops first, addicts second. We have known of many tragic exceptions, however. As we have pointed out, opium seems to quickly destroy the finer sensibilities of womanhood.

In the "white slave traffic," there are some advantages in having the women addicted. Perhaps these are overstressed. Since opiates inhibit the normal body secretions, the menses are suppressed and the woman's working schedule is not interrupted. In the medical literature we find some indications that opiate addiction does not entirely prevent conception. Addicted women have given birth to children. Conception may have taken place when the woman was abstinent or only lightly addicted. In this instance, of course, the infant is an addict since it has shared its mother's blood and is born with a dependence on narcotics. The mother's condition must be recognized by her medical attendants and the baby given diminishing doses of an opiate to prevent it from developing dangerous withdrawal symptoms. This was usually in the form of paregoric. In later years we are informed that chlorpromazine, a non-narcotic, has been used with great success.* From the standpoint of people who traffic in women, the principal advantage in having a victim addicted is that she is more tractable and likely to be dependent on her "managers" for a source of narcotic supply.

Women and men shoplifters are often addicted. Many of these, especially the males, like to work with a "booster box," i.e. a merchandise box wrapped and marked to indicate that it is goods which have just been purchased. One side of the box is hinged and fastened with a snap lock. Into this, merchandise "lifted" off counters or racks can be slipped. Women prefer to walk out of the store with pilfered goods hidden in voluminous bloomers or similar devices. A variation of this was worked by William (Big Bill)

---

*Zelson, C., Rubio, E., and Wasserman, E.: Neonatal narcotic addiction: ten-year observation. *Pediatrics, 48*:178-189, (August) 1971.

Hildebrandt, who is referred to elsewhere in this book. This erstwhile king of the Twin Cities underworld, after serving most of a twenty-year sentence for narcotic trafficking, was released from penitentiary and fell on evil days. A partner, concluding that twenty years might be all of a man's lifetime, had long ago absconded with the nest egg that Big Bill had entrusted to him when he "went away." So Bill had to revert to the skills of his youth which had included "boosting." Bill, a giant of a man, converted his size, which could have been a handicap, into an asset. Under his tentlike top coat he draped a huge "booster bag." With this he proceeded to systematically reduce some of the choicest inventory of stores in the Twin Cities and vicinity. Federal narcotic agents, checking up on his post-prison-release behavior, saw activity they recognized as unusual. Cooperating local police arrested Bill in flagrante delicto and discovered a veritable warehouse of stolen merchandise.

Addicts who "boost" stores often work in pairs, one to divert the clerk while the other purloins merchandise. There is often great artistry in this team work. "Turn the man around" is a phrase often heard. A good confederate, engrossing the clerk with his patter, ingratiating personality, and well-timed requests for service, can literally turn a clerk around and keep him from looking at the man who is stealing the merchandise.

During the period of heavy narcotic traffic in this country a very large proportion of the pickpockets, then a highly professional group of thieves, were addicted. Some decades ago the late Joseph M. Bransky, a district supervisor in the Federal Bureau of Narcotics, made a close study of the pickpocket addicted to narcotics. To Joe Bransky, an early 16 mm amateur photographer hobbyist, we are indebted for the first action pictures we ever saw of a pickpocket mob in operation, including the selection of the "mark," the attention-diverting "jostling," and the smooth finesse of "lifting the poke" from the "pratt pocket" of the unsuspecting victim. We can speculate on reasons for addiction among pocket pickers. They were a highly gregarious group with a great pride of craftsmanship. Since "addicts make addicts" is the most obvious truism, it may be that the factor of association was important. If a few became addicted it would spread. Again pocket picking is an art which

The Addict as a Police Problem 179

requires a certain amount of aplomb, coolness, and lack of self-consciousness. These opiates would furnish.

Addicts will be in all sorts of burglary. They may be weekend supermarket thieves who expect a "score" running into the thousands of dollars for breaking through a building roof and leisurely opening a safe containing Saturday's receipts. Or the thief may be the small-time house prowler. We may have the merchandise counter "booster" who is sometimes a man of discretion, as we have pointed out. The mailbox thief and check forger is often addicted.

But the addict seems to come into full flower as a confidence man. In this area there is certainly a long tradition, or affliction, of addiction. As we have noted elsewhere, the big-time confidence man of the more unsophisticated era of the early 1900's was often an addict. Usually he was the genteel opium smoker, as befitted his criminal stature and his means.

The "Big Store" confidence racket was directed against a sucker who was usually a well-heeled business man. The con men liked to pick out someone whom they learned had sold out a business and retired and thus might have ready, liquid assets. The mob "built into" this prospect through many stereotyped devices which were often adhered to as rigidly as the script of a drama. Sometimes it was the "pigeon-drop." A purse or billfold containing a considerable amount of money was dropped. The "sucker" was allowed to find it right along with a member of the mob. When the two honest finders took it to the owner whose identity was indicated by other contents in the billfold, that grateful person insisted on cutting them in on a large future reward. The usual representation was made that in some way, such as through a confidential employee in a brokerage house, through a tap on a wire, or in some other manner, the con man had inside information on how to make a financial killing. This might be in some business deal, in the stock market, or at the race track. Because of his fine action the sucker was to be allowed to come into the supposed venture where the big killing was to be made. On the fateful day things went as expected and now they were all rich. However, to show good faith, it became necessary that the venturers produce funds which would have been the appropriate ante if the thing had been a legitimate business proposition. Unless this ante were shown there would be no payoff. After weeks of an hypnotic buildup we now find the sucker wiring to his banker for from five thousand to one hundred thousand dollars (whatever the traffic would bear). That money would be taken to a hotel room, delivered to a third party to be held "in escrow." Then the sucker would be distracted long enough to permit the escrow man and the money to disappear. Sometimes the sucker would be so firmly convinced that he could be "re-loaded," i.e. again victimized. He would be told that something had gone wrong, perhaps that the confidential employee who had leaked the valuable information had been disclosed; but that now there was another chance to make an even bigger "score" if the sucker could dig up some more money.

A confidence racket which operates on a classic pattern is the "Spanish Prisoner" swindle. The sucker receives a communication addressed to him which starts out with some variation of "I am a prisoner in a Mexican (or some similar place) jail. A reliable party has given me your name. I have, hidden away, a considerable sum of money (or buried gold or diamonds or valuable securities, etc.). These I am unable to recover because I am imprisoned and do not have the immediate funds available to recover the buried treasure. If you are interested in sharing a large reward for helping me please write to so and so," etc. If the sucker shows interest he receives appropriate follow-up letters and finally delivers or sends money to the swindlers. Sometimes, if the sucker is young enough (under seventy) the swindlers may send as emissary "my beautiful daughter Juanita" who walks away with the "investment" of the victim.

The addiction tradition also went to the smaller fry, the "short con" operators and it persists to this day. We have always found the manipulations of these people to be highly interesting, sometimes fascinating. The exponents of judo and its variations continually stress "make use of the energy of your opponent to destroy him." Likewise the con man tries to use the latent cupidity, the venality, the "larceny in the heart" of the sucker to ensnare him.

The addict really relishes the confidence game. He, of course, has no conscience to mollify—the junk in his veins has taken care of that—but he gets the kick, that all confidence thieves do, in outsmarting a sucker when the sucker himself has "larceny in his heart." So the Secret Service will rarely have a complaint from a victim who has been sold a "money-making machine," a small portable gimmick which the sucker has seen (he thinks) turn out money identical with that produced by the great presses of the United States Bureau of Engraving and Printing. All that the chump has really seen, of course, is a demonstration that the hand is quicker than the eye, and that the eye is likely to be less quick when influenced by wishful cupidity.

Innumerable are the variations which the addict con man plays on human weakness. Let's let Monty, long-time thief and con man who became addicted at some point in his criminal career and now supports a $25-a-day habit*, tell us about one of the interesting variations, which in some con circles is called the "Mrs. Murphy" racket. Here lust rather than larceny contributes to the sucker's downfall.

"I hang around cocktail bars to spot a prosperous sucker who is out on the town and who might be looking for girls. I strike up an acquaintance and, after a drink or two (and here Monty apologizes for drinking alcohol, which junkies seldom do—"But this is business"), I suggest that if he is looking for women "Mrs. Murphy" has some good ones. I usually throw in some vivid descriptive details about a Chinese girl and a Japanese girl in the harem. When the sucker is interested, I walk him up the street to "Mrs. Murphy's" which may be just an apartment house or something like that where I have a friendly understanding. During the conversation I have let the sucker know that "Mrs. Murphy's" place is just one in a chain run by the Syndicate; that we are very anxious to keep good will and to have our clients satisfied. When we get to the foyer of the apartment house I tell the sucker that I want to go to see "Mrs. Murphy" to see if things are ready. I cut away from him, come back in a minute or two, tell him there will be a slight delay and add, 'By the way, there is never any way in which we can be completely sure about what goes on upstairs. My people want to be very careful nobody loses any money in our operation—and people have been rolled and robbed even in the best places—so we have a safe deposit service here.' Then I whip out a business-like envelope to persuade the sucker to turn over all his money, except so much for the girl and so much for the room upstairs.

*(1958).

"I carefully count the rest of his roll, which sometimes may be one, two, three hundred dollars; put it in the envelope, note the contents on a receipt stub and start to seal the envelope. Then, if I notice the sucker has a good watch, I say 'Oh, by the way! You probably want your watch safeguarded' . . . and 'Oh, that ring!' . . . or 'that pin!' if he should happen to be wearing a valuable one. The money and belongings are then sealed in the envelope and I hand over a receipt. I start the ardent sucker upstairs to cold and empty halls, and I take out the back way with the envelope full of loot!"

Sometimes the sucker really has a leathery conscience. Not long ago the United States Tax Court had to consider the plea of a poor taxpayer who had been swindled out of $15,000, in what he thought was a scheme to duplicate $100 bills and for which the con man assured him the return would be $45,000. According to the con man's pitch, the money-making process involved bleaching out $1 bills and transferring the excess ink from $100 bills onto the bleached dollar bills. The sucker solemnly assured the court that after watching the con man "demonstrate" his duplication process he invested $15,000. The following day "petitioner discovered that the $15,000 was missing"—And how!

The tax court had to tell the sucker that the $15,000 was not deductible as a business expense, that there is a "sharply defined public policy against counterfeiting obligations of the United States."

There are "short con" games which are classics, usually operated around carnivals, or where people foregather in a sporting atmosphere for recreation. These games rely on the victim's eagerness to capitalize on a "sure thing." The old shell game, depending on sleight of hand, had the victim eagerly taking advantage of a supposed slip by the operator to make a "sure thing" bet on which walnut shell covered the pea. In his case the judgment of the sucker often was reinforced by a member of the audience who "tipped off" the victim. This fellow was, of course, a confederate, a shill, for the con man.

Three card monte, a game in which the sucker thinks he can make a certain selection of which one of three cards is black or red, also is a classic with many little embellishments. The victim thinks he sees a distinctive marker or "lug" on the appropriate card. A "friend" who is a confederate of the con man confirms this opinion. However, when he selects a card, the "lug" has been shifted and the victim picks the wrong card.

Carnival hangers-on work innumerable variations of the "lock." This is a cigar cutter, knife or similar piece of hardware. The con man opens it, shuts it and says "I will bet you ten dollars you can't open it before I count to ten." The "lock" gets passed around. In the crowd a confederate asks the victim if he has seen one of these. The confederate says "To open it all you need to know is to turn it up-side down" and demonstrates. So the sucker bets his ten dollars. In the meantime the con man has palmed the lock and has substituted for it another one which is jammed and cannot possibly be opened. The victim frantically pries at it while ten is counted off. After he has lost his ten dollars the confederate sometimes will recover the working lock and again demonstrate it to the victim saying "You did not have it *straight* up and down. See, here is how it opens."

Carnival men often use boards on which marbles are rolled down into slots to make a count on which rewards are paid for certain numbers. Here the gimmick is sometimes only a fast count. The con man will over-count in the victim's favor until he has pyramided quite a score, then fast-counts against him and forfeits his stake.

As we have said, narcotics have no conscience. In many addicts, of course, they are in the veins of a psychopath who had little or no conscience to begin with. Naturally the addict con man, following the number one precept of con men everywhere, prefers to work rackets where the victim, the "sucker" or "mark" in addict vocabulary, has himself "larceny in his heart." But this being absent in the prospective victim does not make the addict hesitate to exploit other emotions beside the baser ones of larceny or lust. He may even capitalize on one of the noblest emotions of them all—sweet charity. Some time ago in Washington, D. C., an addict approached a ninety-year-old woman known for her generosity and fondness for children. He had, he said, a fifteen-month-old son who needed a brain operation costing $1500. After receiving the $1500 the con man returned a few days later to get an additional $600 for "expenses" from the benefactress. When suspicious neighbors of the good Samaritan asked the police to inquire they soon found the "sick child" non-existent, merely a figment of imagination to embroider a con man's tale. When the police went to break the news to the good woman they found she had been in church praying for the recovery of the "child." Any discomfiture at being victimized, she said, was tempered by the knowledge that there was no child suffering. Meantime the con man had been laying the ground work for an attempt to extract $2000 more from the victim.

Con men will watch the obituary columns and try to deliver merchandise at an exhorbitant price which they will claim the "deceased has just contracted for." Or a swindler may misrepresent that the deceased has made some investments in Mexico or elsewhere, and if the family will give him $1000 he will complete the affair and get "clearance and title to the property."

The addict confidence man also likes to ply a reverse of the short change racket, which is sometimes called "laying the note." This depends on no special motivation on the part of the victim. It is carried out in the usual routine of merchandising. Essentially the con man depends on a confusing patter and quick hands to mislead the merchant and to cause him to overpay the con man when making change for a purchase. Often this is worked by a pair of confidence operators. When the con man presents a ten-dollar bill he expects to beat the shopkeeper out of five dollars; if it is a twenty, his take is ten dollars. When the storekeeper starts to count out change, the con man or his confederate suddenly decides he has a smaller bill, tenders that and in the ensuing confusion he manages to pick up his original tender plus the change for it. As stated, the operation depends on obfuscation. Note layers are notably hard to prosecute since the complainant often has difficulty in giving a lucid story of just what took place. Sometime ago a couple of addict slickers imposed on the cashier of a big restaurant. One of the pair produced a fifty-dollar bill. There was some hocuspocus about change. When the pair had driven away, the cashier found herself twenty dollars short. About all the bemused girl could remember was that they were a couple of very handsome boys with nice southern accents.

Because of the note-laying racket and similar trickery, many merchants are now carefully schooling their cashiers in the handling of cases where there is any request for the return of a bill. The cashier presses a bell that calls the manager who can cut through any fog of conversation to see that sound arithmetic is followed in giving the customer his change.

Another swindle racket directed against merchants in the normal course of business is the refund racket. The refund racket means that the thief will visit a store and pick up some merchandise. Later on, a confederate will call at the adjustment counter to return the goods for cash. The advantage of this racket is, of course, that the thief gets the full retail value for the merchandise which he has stolen. The disadvantage is that merchants are getting more circumspect and blasé. They will usually insist that a copy of the sales slip or some similar evidence be produced. To defeat such cynicism, the thief will sometimes put on a really artistic histrionic performance. One addict specialized in stealing Bibles. He would go into the book department and select and make off with a beautiful Bible worth about twenty-five dollars. After a suitable lapse of time he would return the Bible and ask for a refund. His story was a heart rending one: he bought this beautiful Bible for has favorite kid sister who was lying ill in the hospital, and when he took it out, he was met in the corridor by a nurse who broke the news that his sister had just died. Having seen her decently put away and now able to somewhat control his grief, he thought maybe the store would take back the Bible. It represented a financial outlay which he could poorly afford. His sentiments respecting his sister would preclude him from giving the book to anyone else. The performance usually winds up with the store people shedding a few tears in sympathy and refunding the cash value of the book he had stolen.

As might be expected, it is in "promoting" narcotics for his addiction that the con man comes into the full flower of his art. In histrionic ability he reaches the apogee. He can recite and display the symptoms of renal colic to textbook perfection. A jab of a needle in his finger or elsewhere and he has the means to fake blood in a freshly voided urine specimen. With a little pressure on his softened gums and a racking cough that comes from his toes, he can produce the bloody sputum of a victim in the last ravages of tuberculosis. Sometimes he will carry as a "property" an amputee or a cancer-riddled accomplice good for a prescription at the many doctors' offices as he can canvass in a day. With a smelly sore, sometimes induced by plastering a copper coin to a scratch until it festers, he will invade a doctor's office with the suggestion that morphine is the only medicine which will do him any good and the physician's judgment might be influenced by a desire to get this odoriferous specimen out of his waiting room.

However, the addict usually does not need to be so dramatic to be just as effective. Like some other con men, an occasional addict will have an affinity for a "kit" or "work papers." In conning narcotics from doctors this will sometimes consist of an alleged hospital discharge with an indication of some chronic pathology requiring the administration of narcotic drugs. When such a paper wears out from over use, it is often copied, usually suffering in the typing and spelling in the process. Some documents which have been accepted by practitioners as authentic reflect a low professional opinion of the literacy of hospital administrative offices. A careful physician, of course, would never accept any document in lieu of his own diagnosis in prescribing narcotic drugs; however, these papers accompanied by the beguiling patter of the addict are often effective in producing narcotic supplies. A rather effective paper "gimmick" is the "Lexington Admission Paper." Addicts will write to the Lexington Narcotic Hospital for admission and receive a favorable reply. Armed with this, the addict who probably has no intention of going to Lexington unless somebody like the law furnishes him with a real incentive, will go from doctor to doctor, showing the hospital papers and indicate that he needs some narcotics to stave off withdrawal "until he can get to the hospital."

The adept addict develops many effective little nuances. Some do not ask the doctor for morphine outright. That might be a patent indication of addiction. Instead, he has a bit of folded paper on which is crudely written, and perhaps misspelled, something like the word "Dilaudid." This very potent drug the addict enjoys as much as any except perhaps heroin, and he is as familiar with it as he is with his own name. But when he gingerly mispronounces it, as if it were strange to him, indicating that that is what Dr. Blank gave him when his pains became unbearable, the physician-victim is disarmed into thinking that this is a man who knows nothing improper about narcotics.

Some very successful addict con men use a great deal of selectivity in picking a physician to victimize for narcotics. They like to find an aged and infirm doctor who, for one reason or another, maintains some practice. He may have little left of the faculties which once made him a wonderful doctor—except compassion. And he now has an excess of that. When such a doctor is discovered, addicts may literally beat a pathway to the doorstep of the unfortunate man.

It is the more intelligent addict, the more wily and astute one, who is likely to attempt to victimize physicians. This is usually not attempted by the younger addicts. The problem can be successfully dealt with quite simply, as it is in California and Illinois, where an official prescription blank in triplicate is required for the prescribing of the more potent narcotic drugs. A central machine audit of the triplicate soon trips up the addict who goes from doctor to doctor using subterfuge, fraud, and deceit. Likewise, it quickly frustrates the addict who substitutes himself for the doctor and forges prescriptions for narcotics. With some addicts, narcotic prescription forgery is a highly developed art. This statement would not be complete if we did not say, "including the very bad handwriting."

There are other types of addicts who prey on medical narcotic stocks. One is the automobile thief. He may hang around hospital parking lots, or just take notice whenever he sees a parked car identified with the caduceus, or other insigne, of the medical profession. If the doctor has left his bag on the seat or the floor it is soon in the thief's hands. He may only take the few grains of narcotics which was the doctor's bag supply. The expensive bag and the much more expensive equipment may be discarded in a trash can or down a sewer. A careful doctor will never leave a bag in sight in a parked car.

There is another addict-thief of the "booster" category who specializes in pilfering narcotics from drug stores. These usually operate in pairs, sometimes with women. While one distracts the attention of the pharmacist, the other, often on a pretense of fitting some intimate equipment, will get near the drug supply and quickly disappear with it.

Larger jobber, wholesale, and manufacturer's concentrations of medical narcotics are usually carefully guarded. The protective requirements of the Federal Bureau of Narcotics and Dangerous Drugs are high and must be met before these businesses are registered to handle narcotic drugs. During World War II, when supplies to the illicit traffic were extremely scarce, there were many burglaries and hold-ups of these establishments by professional criminals. These seldom occur now.

By now it should be apparent that there is something in heroin, morphine and similar opiates which gives the addict the insouciance, the imperturbable calm, the indestructible aplomb, the smoothly masked brassiness which is of tremendous value in the perpetration of certain types of larcenies, in all variations of confidence games and in many other types of crime.

Where addicts are found crime will increase. A most effective method of diminishing the incidence of crime is to reduce the street addict population. Perhaps the cheapest thievery insurance which the community can buy is the effort to put the addict in custody and to cure him. Many addicts, of course, are dedicated criminals before addiction, and would not refrain from depredation upon being cured. But the prospect that they might is enhanced when they abstain from narcotics. And the addict cannot steal when he is in custody.

NARCOTIC WITHDRAWAL

The narcotic officer or police custodian is sometimes confronted with problems arising from the just arrested or just sentenced addict who is experiencing distress from the withdrawal of narcotic drugs. Most addicts in the situation obtaining at this writing will not show any keen distress from withdrawal. Most of the heroin available to today's addict is so dilute that he does not have enough intake of real narcotics to establish much of a tolerance and dependence. The result is that he can be abruptly separated from his drug source without incurring any serious physical distress. At the most, he may show some yawning, watery eyes and a runny nose as if from the onset of a cold. He may perspire somewhat, be uneasy and anxious and have difficulty in sleeping. Usually no special handling is here indicated and the situation will improve in several hours. However, there occasionally will be seen a more severely addicted person who will exhibit the classic withdrawal syndrome. After being deprived of drugs for approximately eight hours or more he will begin to show the symptoms above indicated, but these will become progressively severe. The addict will develop muscular cramping, vomiting, diarrhea, indicate acute suffering and distress and usually will plead for narcotic drugs. Barring some organic physical defect, the addict will go through a period of acute distress, which may last several days, without danger. However, medical opinion seems to be unanimous that this suffering serves no purpose toward a cure of the addict. Humanitarian consideration, then, requires that he be treated, which means that the police surgeon or other physician be called in.* In late years medicine has developed excellent methods for diminishing the rigors of withdrawal. Through the courtesy of the authors and the publisher we reproduce below an excerpt from an article on the subject by H. F. Fraser, M.D., and James M. Grider, Jr., M.D., which was published in the *American Journal of Medicine,* May 1953.

WITHDRAWAL OF DRUGS

Opiates. Although a great many withdrawal procedures have been published, the best method of withdrawing heroin, morphine or similar drugs from addicted patients involves substitution of methadone for whatever opiate or synthetic analgesic the patient has been using, followed by reduction of the dosage of methadone over a period of about ten days. This method of treatment is based on the facts that methadone will prevent the appearance of signs of abstinence from any known analgesic drug and that abstinence from methadone is milder than abstinence from any of the other commonly used analgesics. One milligram of methadone can be substituted for 4

---

*In sum, we have found little or no support for the belief that withdrawal from narcotics is a dangerous and often fatal process. Indeed, our study has shown that opiate withdrawal is an extremely uncommon cause of death among addicts. To date, we have been unable to find a single documented case in which opiate withdrawal was the sufficient cause of death. We conclude that death due to withdrawal of narcotics may not occur. (Glaser and Ball, p. 287.)

mg. of morphine, 2 mg. of heroin, 1 mg. of dilaudid, or 20 to 30 mg. of either meperidine (demerol) or codeine.

The speed with which withdrawal is completed is dependent on the physical condition of the patient and the extent to which he is dependent on narcotics. Addicted patients with serious organic disease should not be subjected to the strain of relatively rapid withdrawal. In such cases it is best to treat the organic disease before attempting to treat the addiction. When in the judgment of the physician, the organic disease has improved to the point where mild abstinence carries no danger, withdrawal is cautiously begun and, depending on the patient's response, withdrawal is completed in fourteen to thirty days. In the experience at the Lexington Hospital less than ½ of 1 per cent of narcotic addicts require such special treatment.

The first decision which must be reached before withdrawal begins is the degree of dependence on narcotics. The patient's history is of little use in this connection since addicts frequently exaggerate the quantities of drugs taken in the hope of receiving large amounts of narcotics in the first part of withdrawal. Furthermore, illegal drugs, especially heroin, are adulterated and the narcotic concentration may vary enormously. Hence the patient, unless he has had considerable experience with various narcotics, is unable to estimate the quantity of narcotics used.

The degree of dependence is best estimated by the physical examination, which will disclose whether the patient is intoxicated with narcotics or is exhibiting symptoms of abstinence. If a patient shows morphine-like intoxication, or if he displays no signs of abstinence, narcotics should not be administered until definite symptoms of abstinence appear. When symptoms of abstinence are present on admission or develop shortly afterward, it is usually possible to estimate the addiction dosage, especially if the physical findings are considered in conjunction with the addiction history. Information regarding the specific drug and the number of hours which have elapsed since the last dose of self-administered narcotics is very helpful in this connection.

In milder cases, a tranquilizer or a grain of codeine orally may be all that need be prescribed. Sometimes lightly addicted persons will simulate great distress in the hope of getting "shots" of opiates. Of course, the methadone maintenance addict, heavily saturated with the drug, requires some time for detoxification if it is attempted.

7

THE UNDERCOVER MAN

In our discussions of such subjects as undercover work and surveillance we have relied heavily on the lecture outlines developed at the Federal Bureau of Narcotics Police Training School. Over the years we have had much to do with the preparation of these outlines. This material has been presented to hundreds of law enforcement officers of every degree of experience. These outlines have been furnished to many other law enforcement groups and thus have had the most searching evaluation. While the discussion of these subjects might be extended at great length, we think that the views expressed represent the consensus of the best professionals in the field.

Incognito investigation, undercover work, as understood by law enforcement people is one investigative method of learning what crimes are being committed, by whom, where, and when. The object is to compile police intelligence data on the hidden activities of criminals and to afford the best opportunity to trap the crook in flagrante delicto—to "catch him with the goods"—or more exactly, to obtain evidence which is admissible in court and will assist in convicting the guilty.

Crooks naturally try to avoid the sight or knowledge of the law enforcement arm and of law abiding people. They try to conceal their work. Sometimes this is by the dark of night, by mask or turned-up coat collar. More often the criminal may depend on the quick stroke and the confusion and terror of possible witnesses. The "business man" racketeer, the big and little gangster, puts on the appearance of respectability. His overt moves have the semblance of legitimacy or look innocuous. His illicit moves and contacts are in a highly specialized world where the self-interest of those having knowledge tends to prevent them from giving willing testimony of illegal acts. This is the situation which applies in most narcotic offenses. Even if the violator is well-known as a drug dealer, this traffic is ideal for secretive operations. The valuable contraband is so compact as to be easily concealable. It is completely inconspicuous. It can be easily passed off as innocent material. It can be destroyed on a moment's notice. It can be passed hand to hand on the most casual contact.

In the field of federal law enforcement the restrictions on enforcement officers on obtaining admissible evidence are severe. In the past three decades, the Supreme Court majority has, with few exceptions, constricted the right of law enforcement officers to act in cases presented, and these have been quite numerous. In the matter of search and seizure, after-arrest admissions and confessions, in the application of the conspiracy statute and in many other areas, more and more artificial hurdles have been erected. Many of the state courts have felt inclined to follow the federal court lead. While the result has been a lessening of effectiveness of all law enforcement officers in every field of crime suppression, these obstacles naturally loom highest in front of officers attempting to combat a traffic like that in narcotics, which is almost completely underground and covert.

Thus, it is good tactics to support other police measures with undercover operations against a crime where evidence is seldom obvious.

As the language implies, the undercover officer abandons the appearance of his official identity and approaches the criminal in an assumed role. By pretext, dissembling, and disguise he presents himself in the criminal underworld as a fellow criminal or in such a way as to be accepted as part of the criminal "scenery." Rarely is the disguise physical, although small changes in dress, eyeglasses, deportment, and speech may be most valuable in avoiding casual identification. The traditional false whiskers are usually confined to the acquisition or abandonment of a real mustache.*

One of the first essential elements of an undercover disguise must, of course, be that the prospective undercover man not be well-known as "the law" in the area where he is to work. Very im-

---

*Of course these comments might be modified in the light of the hairy appearance and special dress proclivities of today's "underground."

The Undercover Man

portant is an introduction, a cover story which will be accepted by the prospective criminal quarry as validating the assumed identity of the undercover man.

Much stress, often too much, is put on the appearance and other physical qualifications of the undercover man. Any officer possessed of intelligence, resourcefulness, and with initiative, energy, and courage can do undercover work. If he does not have these talents in good measure, he is in the wrong profession. While physical attributes can be real assets, as we will point out, they are rarely indispensable. Too much attention to them has prevented many investigators from developing full potential, and administratively it results in a loss of manpower and in bottlenecks in investigative programs.

Important are such intangibles as self-confidence. This often can be acquired and instilled through an apprentice training program in which the neophyte works with a skilled undercover man. Keeping his eyes and ears open and his mouth shut he usually will be quickly imbued with the spirit of this great game of wits. We expect our man to have good judgment and to keep mentally alert. He cannot miss too many cues. He should be resourceful in meeting unexpected emergencies. This will be a natural result if he has spent time in study of the nature of his assignment.

There are special individual factors which the undercover man may possess or acquire which will facilitate his work. It might be an initial handicap if he happens to come in a large size, to "look like a cop." What does a "cop" look like? When we go to a police convention the officers in mufti look like salesmen or bankers. A convention of crooks might be hard to distinguish in general appearance from one of school men. There is no easily definable criminal type, or police type.

One of the biggest crooks we ever prosecuted was William (Big Bill) Hildebrandt. He was notorious as overlord of the Twin Cities underworld. He was big physically, weighing about 260 pounds and about six feet five inches in height, almost as tall sitting as a small man standing. When he put on his courtroom decorum he had the demeanor and the air of the solid respectability of your favorite banker. "Big Bill" suggests that often the large undercover man can make an asset of his size by adopting a "monicker" which will catch the fancy of his thief associates. He can be "Biggy" or "Tiny" or "Moose" or "Mouse." If his size is more apparent in his members he can be "Footsie" or "Satchel" or "Schnozzle," or just frankly "Big Nose Charley."

George White, a district supervisor of the Federal Bureau of Narcotics, who, among other abilities, was one of the great undercover men of Treasury law enforcement, belied the big man handicap. George is not very tall, but with little effort or simply by abandoning effort, he can soon acquire the proportions of Mr. Five by Five. Like Nero Wolfe he demonstrates that the fat man can be a great detective. Like Archie Moore he can take off weight in a hurry. This metamorphosis, not recommended for all, can contribute to an effective disguise.

While over-average size may suggest some initial but disposable handicap to the undercover man, the smaller than usual individual has no such problem, but an asset. Lightweights and under do not suggest "law" to a crook.

It is a strange chauvinistic myth of our people, all of whom are immigrants or descendants of immigrants, that much of American crime is committed by "foreigners." This myth is cheerfully believed by the underworld. So often it is an asset to have a foreign accent, real or acquired. If acquired, it had better be correct. Knowledge of a foreign language may be of assistance. Perhaps just as valuable is the second generation knowledge or understanding of some vocabularly with ability to speak a few catch words. In a reverse twist, there sometimes are great possibilities in a situation where the undercover man, with knowledge of a foreign language and working with people who exploit it, pretends to understand only English. Before World War II, for example, it was well accepted among Chinese that no "Westerner" understood the language. That was true enough to be taken as an axiom. Consequently, a Caucasian customs agent who had been reared in China in a missionary family, literally had information forced on him by Chinese who freely discussed criminal enterprises before him. This is no spot for one who is self-conscious.

At times race can be important in undercover operations. In the Federal Bureau of Narcotics we recruited Chinese as narcotic agents whenever possible. These officers worked against Chinese drug peddlers, of course. They were just as valuable among non-Chinese violators who were sure that no Chinese was a law enforcement officer. Formerly this generalization applied almost equally as well to Negroes who might be quickly accepted in the underworld as not suspect as police. However, the present wide employment of Negroes in police work tempered this somewhat.

Since the villains in our dramas often have had a saturnine aspect it is also in line with our chauvinistic prejudices if the undercover man be of swarthy complexion and Mediterranean origin. This real asset rests mostly on folklore. Sometimes it has a real basis. In the Federal Bureau of Narcotics we found it most useful to recruit agents who had some Sicilian background to work on Mafia narcotic traffickers. (One natural result was an unusual proportion of Sicilian names of officers in top echelons of the Bureau.) If a principal suspect does have a background which is foreign or of some minority race we might exploit that by picking an appropriate undercover man who at the proper time could exemplify the right variation of the theme "We Arabs must stick together" or "Why let these outsiders in on this good thing?" Sometimes this tactic has helped an undercover man to detour around intermediaries and reach for the top.

The narcotic undercover man must have acquired a good knowledge of the narcotic traffic. That is self-evident. This includes information of the nature of the traffic, a good knowledge of narcotic addicts, and perhaps of other crime. It calls for the acquisition of a specialized vocabulary, an argot which must be used accurately to the occasion. Generally, the more readily the undercover man comprehends crime from the criminal's standpoint, the better. After all, he is now a figure in the world of crime, or so he pretends. As a young narcotic agent, one of us (J.C.C.) had an opportunity to make a close study of confidence games practiced by narcotic addicts and other thieves. As a cover to investigate the diversion of narcotics from drugstores, somewhat common in those early days, Cross joined a carnival. This brought about the successful completion of the indicated investigation. It led to other larger cases. Most important, the experience with the carnival roustabouts, thieves, and con men of those days gave us a knowledge of that underworld which in subsequent years was to provide an open sesame for admission to the underworld in innumerable undercover projects. Thieves everywhere recognized the vocabulary, knowledge, and techniques and had no difficulty in assuming the correct answer to "Are you with it?" For example, in one case it appeared that newly found narcotic dealer acquaintances needed some assurance they were dealing with a bona fide thief customer. We maneuvered these peddlers into a position where they saw us go into a store to make a small purchase. We left the neighborhood hurriedly, and "accidentally" showed change in such denominations that our sophisticated audience was convinced that we had "laid a note," i.e. had worked the "solo short change racket" on the store clerk.

Opportunities to learn underworld activity and thinking continually present themselves to the undercover man and they are sometimes overlooked. Because of the wide criminal background of many narcotic addicts and peddlers, narcotic officers should make these people the object of unceasing study. Most of them are glad to talk, to brag about exploits, and to discuss ways and means of committing crime. Here can be acquired a vast background of criminal lore and practice which is invaluable in undercover work and in many other aspects of criminal investigation.

It is puzzling that this aspect of the work is so often overlooked by otherwise astute and dedicated officers. As Patrick O'Carroll, then director of the Treasury law enforcement schools liked to point out, the radio, television, and other drama media often exploit the offbeat character as of great human interest. Certainly one of the most fascinating aspects of the narcotic investigator's job can be the acquisition of knowledge by direct contact with underworld characters and their exploitation for direct and background knowledge of the criminal world.

Having determined that the undercover approach is necessary or desirable in an investigation we must pay some attention to details. How much and what efforts are to be made will depend on each case and the facilities available. If an officer can be introduced to the mob and vouched for by an informer, that may very much simplify the job. It may be that we can find some third party who will unwittingly vouch for our assumed identity. Failing that, we may have a long, hard row to hoe, a task that we will undertake only in a case of sufficient importance to warrant the expenditure of time, effort, and funds. In any event, we will usually encounter the same elements of operation, to be varied in emphasis as the occasion requires.

A first step, naturally, is to abandon one's official identity. Badge and credentials and any items of official clothing or equipment which might arouse suspicion should be removed. Cards, papers, notebooks and all other such material not consistent with the assumed status should be stored. Having abandoned his true identity the officer then adopts a new one. This must be compatible with the objective of the inquiry and suspects in prospect. In a really comprehensive undercover project, particularly where for long periods of time the officer loses his own identity and assumes another, he is likely to be very much on his own. Primarily, the greatest demand for the job is imagination, and quick intelligence must substitute for many of the protections the usual policeman has. In many undercover assignments it would be extremely foolish to go armed, even though there is a great deal of physical risk. But the risk of disclosure through the finding, by his associates, that he was carrying a concealed weapon, usually would be fatal to the success of the investigation. There is, of course, the exception, when the carrying of weapons might come naturally. If so, the undercover man might well disclose the fact first, before the weapon is "accidentally" discovered. However, in these days of Sullivan Acts and general, stringent concealed weapon laws, the thinking hoodlum does not usually go equipped with "hardware" except at the crux of the job. And while this is drawing it pretty fine, we have found that with the possession of the weapon as an "out," the less experienced undercover man, falling for a bluff and too quickly conceding that his identity is exposed, may reach for the weapon to reinforce his revelation, "I am the Law," when, without this escape hatch, he might very well have relied on his intelligence to talk himself really solidly into the mob.

The possibilities should be reviewed and choices made. For background we might select a remote city familiar to the officer but possibly not known to the suspect. Even better might be a selection of a remote city with which the officer and suspect were familiar, but where the suspect's knowledge was not as current as that of the undercover man. This makes for convincing answers to questions of the "Who do you know?" type. The background story should be reasonably detailed to indicate that it rests on fact. Coached and cooperating informers in the background town may be relied on for corroboration or a situation arranged where a third party might unwittingly vouch for the officer's assumed identity. In our early days of investigation in the Twin Cities such a person was referred to as an "unconscious" informer.

The cover story, while as plausible as possible, should tend to avoid features which can be easily disproved. Corroborating persons are best found among bartenders, waiters, hotel clerks, and similar non-suspect callings. Or they might be gamblers, narcotic dealers, confidence men or other thieves of one sort or another. These latter will most likely be people who unwittingly have accepted our undercover pose. Often, even with astute criminals, it requires little except good acting to put over a good cover story. It is highly important that the actions and reactions of the officer be consistent with his pose. The smallest incident, if it seems in character, may solidify the success of the undercover man's job.

On an undercover project often it is necessary to extemporize, to feel one's way. The cover story may not quite hold up, or there may be entirely unforeseen or unexpected developments. The thing to do then is not to panic, but to stay in the contest and try to "rock the case along." Sometimes there is so little background to go on that the officer must simply decide to make a start somewhere and then hope to "play it by ear."

Consider the case of the "Cake with the Cocoanut Frosting." Many years ago there was a heavy narcotic traffic in Asheville, North Carolina. Ernest Gentry, then a district supervisor of the Federal Narcotic Bureau, and one of us (J.C.C.) as federal narcotic agents were assigned to work undercover to obtain evidence to disrupt this traffic. After associating with narcotic addicts in Asheville for a short time we learned that one substantial narcotic peddler for the area was a certain Guy Robertson. He lived in a small town near Asheville, we were told. We went to that village to reconnoiter and in due course visited a restaurant and struck up an acquaintance with a waitress. We asked her if she knew Guy Robertson and where he could be found. She responded, "Why, he is serving time in a road camp for shooting a deputy sheriff." About that time a customer entered the restaurant and the waitress said, "There comes Guy's brother-in-law. Maybe he can help you fellows." She called the man over, told him we were friends of Guy's and had not known about his trouble. The brother-in-law took us outside, told us that his sister was married to Guy Robertson and that Guy's brother, Porter Robertson had taken over the business since Guy's trouble. He went on to say that his sister, Guy's wife, would be along on the next bus.

We waited a short time and, when the bus arrived, a woman got off and came over toward the filling station. The man said; "Sis, come here. I want you to meet a couple of Federal men." At this remark the woman started running toward the filling station and it took some persuasion on the part of her brother to bring her back, telling her that he was just kidding her, as we were friends of Guy's and wanted to get some narcotics.

She agreed to take us to Porter Robertson and introduce us. This she did and through Porter we were able to make several "buys" of heroin there in Asheville. Later Porter took us to a small town near Fayetteville, North Carolina, and introduced us to a big narcotic peddler, Charlie Herndon.

As time went on we continued to associate with Porter and his sister-in-law, and through them we were meeting other narcotic dealers. Once they had a party and invited us and a large number of people. At this party the word got around that we were users of narcotics. Several tried to get us to take a drink. When we refused they stated that they understood why. (Most narcotic addicts have no use for alcohol.) During our travels with Porter he kept asking questions about our friendship with Guy and several times made inquiry as to the place Guy made his deliveries to us. We told him that it was always out of town. He stated he knew this was true as Guy would never make a delivery in Asheville.

On a Tuesday afternoon Porter informed us that Sunday was visiting day at the road camp and told us that we would all take a trip to visit Guy that weekend. The road camp was located approximately sixty miles from Asheville. Arrangements were made, said Porter. We should pick him up early Sunday morning at his mother's home. This posed a problem. We knew we could not visit Guy with Porter as we had never seen Guy Robertson!

This development called for some fast footwork on our part. We got in touch with our friends in the North Carolina Prison Administration and outlined the problem. They came up with a quick and simple solution: Guy Robertson was soon to be transferred to the main prison in Raleigh. They would just step up the schedule and do it right away.

So, with our confidence well restored, early Sunday morning we drove to Porter's mother's home. Porter came out carrying a number of packages and requested us to open the trunk of the automobile. Porter's mother also came out of the house with a large cake with a mountain of cocoanut frosting. This cake was also carefully placed in the trunk. We all drove to the road camp and as we entered, carrying the cake in our arms, we told the guard that we were relatives of Guy Robertson and wanted to visit him. The guard thumbed through some books and turned to us and said, "I am sorry; Guy has been transferred to Raleigh." In Porter's presence we indignantly protested to the guard the procedure of transferring a man without notifying his relatives so that we had made a long trip for nothing. The guard accepted our remarks philosophically.

After we got outside Porter remarked, "You boys sure told that guard a few things."

We were now in a position where we could suggest making a trip to Raleigh to see Guy. We knew very well that under quarantine regulations he would not be allowed to have visitors, having been there such a short time. This made a strong impression on Porter, and there was never any doubt in his mind after that about us being friends of his brother.

We went on to make many more cases in North Carolina, and Guy was still in prison when they were finished.

Sometimes the undercover man can develop small incidents to overcome the suspicions of a wary dope peddler. When one of the authors (J.C.C.) was working undercover with a carnival we found a narcotic peddler, who went by the name of Goo Goo, to be somewhat reserved and not inclined to talk narcotic business. One day we knew that a couple of our associates in the carnival would be coming by our room to pick us up on some errand, and that Goo Goo would be with them. When they arrived and knocked at the door we delayed for an appreciable time before answering, then opened the door and pretended great relief, saying we had not recognized the knock, that it did not sound right. Being in the act of taking a "fix" (i.e. injection of narcotics) we had thrown the "outfit" out of the window. We pointed it out to Goo Goo in the areaway below and asked him to keep an eye on it until we went down and retrieved it. We then examined the package containing an addict's "works" (i.e. injection paraphernalia) in Goo Goo's presence to see if anything was broken. This was the "convincer." Goo Goo was completely sold on our pose of addiction, accepted us wholeheartedly and soon was selling us his heroin.

Narcotic agent Ben Moore did not have what we sometimes think of as the natural physical appearance of a good undercover man. Big, broad shouldered, sinewy, with large and capable hands and ample underpinning, he looked as if he might have been a good football tackle or, what he had been for most of his life, a cop. In his earlier years he had been a deputy sheriff in his native Nevada, and then had become a Treasury agent to work in the Narcotic Bureau. Ben's distinctive appearance was further enhanced by the particularly upright manner in which he carried his head. This was not an idiosyncrasy, but somewhat of a necessity because his neck muscles had been damaged when he had been shot by a narcotic peddler in New Orleans.

Ben Moore had a keen mind, personality, and plausibility, and when he went to work on a hoodlum any initial reservations quickly wore off.

So successful was Moore as an undercover operator that his accomplishments were frequently cited to officers who hesitated to undertake undercover work because of some assumption that their personal appearance might militate against them. But, in the case we like to tell about Ben Moore, he needed a special and unintended incident, a peculiar break, to make a beautiful case.

Ben was working in the Omaha territory. In those days, there was substantial traffic in that city supplied both from Chicago and from Big Bill Hildebrandt, who had been king of the Twin Cities underworld. With Hildebrandt's arrest, Moore, then resident agent at Omaha, concentrated on breaking up the Chicago connections and, through some hard work and good luck, he managed to make a case on an elderly ex-convict we will call Tracy.

Tracy had a reputation for being rough, tough, and astute, and for being a "stand-up guy." Moore, of course, talked to him about

Tracy's connection," but got nothing. Moore noticed that Tracy seemed to be in physical distress; this, Tracy minimized. But Moore insisted that a doctor be called. It then developed that Tracy had had some chronic heart trouble. The next day, after Tracy had made bond, Moore was surprised to see him come into the office. Tracy wasted no words. "I have never talked to a cop in my life, but I'm going to now. Maybe I won't have to die in the can. I know what you are going to tell me—You won't give me any promises. But whatever happens, I'm going to lay it on the line. I'm going to tell you something which will surprise you. Did you ever hear of Tommy Nelson of St. Paul?" And Moore said, "No."

Tracy said, "I didn't think you would have; he has never been in this racket. He is an ex-counterfeiter who married an oldtime madam in St. Paul. They have a bakery business on Snelling Avenue. When Big Bill Hildebrandt went to the penitentiary, he arranged for Tommy to handle a few choice, out-of-town accounts. I was one of them."

When the Minneapolis office verified the bakery, and the fact of an apparent close friendship between Hildebrandt and Tommy Nelson, an attack on Tommy was in order. But Tracy said he had gone as far as he could go to assist. After some persuasion, he consented to go one step further.

"I will give you a set-in; but it must be the kind I can back away from. I will vouch for you, but only as a good customer I have known for just a few months and whom I want taken care of because I am quitting the racket and going in the hospital."

When surveillance indicated that Nelson was fishing in upstate Minnesota, several telephone calls were made to his bakery office in St. Paul from Omaha, seeking to locate him. Finally, Tracy "managed" to reach him. "I've been trying all over the state to get you for a couple of days. I've got a little panic on my hands and I'm sending somebody up to see you."

Nelson exploded furiously. "You aren't sending anybody! I won't see anybody!"

Tracy: "But we've been trying to get hold of you, and the man is already on his way."

Nelson said, "I won't see anybody," and slammed down the receiver.

The Undercover Man

In that atmosphere, a few hours later, Ben Moore walked into the bakery in St. Paul and, on information furnished by Tracy, found his way into a little cubbyhole off the working part of the establishment where Nelson was ensconced among some flour barrels.

Moore's reception was frosty, as he had anticipated. But, acting as if he assumed that he was as welcome as the flowers in May, he proceeded to introduce himself and went into his pitch as a new customer. Nelson listened with the cold-eyed impassivity of the old con. Finally, he raised a hand to stop Moore. "I don't know what you're talking about. The only business I know anything about is the bakery business. You talk about dough—the only dough I'm interested in now is what we make from this," slapping a flour barrel.

Sensing a losing battle, but game to the last and unable to resist a cliché, Moore whipped from his pocket a wad of bills and, pitching it down under Nelson's nose, he said, "Well, here's *dough, right on the barrelhead."

Nelson, unmoving, stared silently. Moore slowly picked up and pocketed his money and walked through the door of the office, when Nelson said, "Hey! Come back here. How much can you take?"

Weeks later, after several similar transactions, carefully corroborated, had taken place, the bakery and Nelson's house were raided. A small fortune in heroin was found. Ruefully discussing the case later with District Supervisor Joseph Bell, Nelson said, ". . . I had positively decided to handle only a few of Big Bill's customers and, under no circumstances, to do business with anyone else. Before Moore picked up his money off that barrelhead, I knew I would have no part of him. But then I noticed that the wad was made up with a crapshooter's crimp.* And, as Moore walked away, I said to myself, 'Well, of course, this fellow is a thief, and

---

*In Moore's native Nevada, and in many other areas where gambling is done in shirt sleeves and currency is thrown on the table, as in craps or blackjack, the dealer's pile of bills almost inevitably gets high. To store this temporarily out of sight, he slides it in a side pants pocket. However, before doing this, he is likely to fold a fourth or fifth segment of the pile of bills tightly back on itself. When this is thrust, fold first, into the side pocket, the fold expands outward and the roll is fish-hooked in the pocket against easy dislodgement.

why should I let that money walk out of this place,' and so I sold him the stuff."

Moore had adopted a practice from the evening diversions of his early youth, and this unwittingly, but most fortunately, salvaged a big case.

Thieves generally and addicts particularly are a superstitious lot. A good undercover role may be undermined if one is not aware of this. It is reinforced if the proper rites are observed. Often a stranger is not accepted as a "right guy" if he persists in throwing his hat on the bed, walks under ladders, fails to detour around black cats and does not observe the long catalogue of "don'ts" which help to make a thief's life interesting. A close study of the superstitious reactions of the mob and quick adaptation to them will be part of the undercover man's protective coloration.

As has been indicated, addicts usually do not use much alcohol. When they do it is likely to be a sweet wine. They are usually fairly light eaters, with no great interest in food. Most will prefer coffee with plenty of sugar. An undercover man posing as an addict might raise serious doubts if he is seen to be an earnest trencherman. One of us (J.C.C.) recalls a case where an addict associate became positively ill when we ordered brains and eggs and we had to pretend that it made us sick, too!

The great attraction of undercover work is that it gives the fullest play to the imagination, ingenuity and intelligence of the officer. Infinite in number have been the devices and stratagems of the undercover man. In New York it was most important that short contacts with a big narcotic dealer be corroborated. This character, with the underworld's frank cruelty, was known as "Pip the Blind" because of a defect in one eye, but he was not defective in resource and cunning. He talked to only one man at a time and that with the secrecy insured by the walls of his hideout. The problem was to bring him out in the open. It was solved by the story of an "automobile accident." The undercover man with a "broken leg," heavily burdened with a plaster cast, appeared in Pip's neighborhood. It would be impossible, he sent word, to make it up the stairs on crutches. Would Pip come down to the automobile? He did, to be photographed and recorded, and later to be convicted and imprisoned.

Small details may threaten to trip the undercover man. District Supervisor Irwin Greenfield*, who was one of the Federal Bureau of Narcotic's experts in this field, told of an incident in which a very small item nearly defeated his project. His principal objective was a very rough, uncouth character who was wholesaling narcotics in Detroit. Greenie tried to play it on the thug's own level. All went smoothly until one afternoon when the character dropped in at Greenie's room. Anticipating such a happening, Greenie was "clean," or thought he was. But he was an omnivorous reader. Through automatic habit he had picked up, on the way to his diggings, a magazine he favored, and it lay on the dresser. The periodical was slightly on the egghead order. Soon Mr. Thug spied it and picked it up. "Say," he said, "what's a lug like youse doing wid dis?" Fortunately Greenie had looked at the magazine enough to know its contents. By sheer good fortune these included a scholarly treatise on something like "The Horse and Man." The resourceful Greenie was able to pull out of the air an excuse that he thought it had something to do with the improvement of the breed and now wanted his money back. The hood was convinced, but thereafter Greenie restrained his penchant for serious reading until the investigation was concluded.

It is sometimes helpful—but it can also backfire—to simulate infirmities. Appearance of poor eyesight or of deafness may convey the idea that the undercover man is not the "law"; and in a subtle way that he is not dangerous. The employment of a cane or a display of some other assumed disability may lessen the caution of the suspect.

Naturally the undercover man will dress the part. His garb will be what the "boys" wear if the boys are following any particular mode and will be appropriate as to quality, price, age, fit, and cleanliness. Clothing labels and laundry marks must be consistent with the cover story or should be removed.

Most people are expected to have some sort of occupation or racket. Our cover story should allow for that. If we claim a trade or profession or business we should know something of it. Sometimes carrying the tools or equipment of a trade or profession is a most persuasive silent argument for an assumed identity. But they should not be brand new.

---
*Now deceased.

Any officer seriously taking on extended undercover work should have appropriate assumed credentials, such as identification card, letters addressed to his fictitious identity and the like. Here is another great field for the resourcefulness of the undercover man. Newspaper clippings may be faked. Police files can sometimes be padded for the purpose. The extent of preparation in this field of assumed credentials will depend somewhat on the importance of the case.

Some time ago American narcotic agents were working undercover in Mexico, collaborating with Mexican officials. They were in protracted negotiations to purchase several kilos of heroin from the mob of Mexican producers who were exceedingly skeptical, and little progress was being made. Seeing them in association with shady characters, the local Mexican gendarmerie decided to pick up the Americans on suspicion. The agents stood pat, and managed by prearranged methods to communicate their plight to the Mexican narcotic agents. These, after being satisfied that the actions of the local police were bona fide, decided to make a virtue of adversity. To make it "look real good" the American agents were held in durance for fourteen hours and this in an institution not highly noted for sanitation, comfort, or food. But when they were released, all reserve of the Mexican peddlers had evaporated, and negotiations for the purchase and delivery of the heroin were promptly concluded and arrests made.

The establishing of the initial contact with the suspect is, of course, most important. As we have said, the quickest and best is often through an introduction by an informer or similar agent. When this is attempted, the informer and officer will, of course, thoroughly agree on a background story, "We were in Lexington together," etc. Sometimes the employment of an intermediary for an introduction is not possible. Then our job may really become slow and difficult. We may try living in a locality where the suspect or his friends will be encountered, where we may strike up an acquaintance with him or his associates. We may be able to carry out a course of conduct and plant enough "information" which, coming to the attention of the suspect, will bring him to us as a business prospect. This is a happy eventuality. Many good narcotic officers have enjoyed being pursued by narcotic peddlers who wanted to sell them merchandise, the officers maintaining just enough reserve and distance to make it the peddler's chief concern that he might lose a good prospect!

One of the greatest of the great undercover men produced by the Federal Bureau of Narcotics—and that institution developed more than its share of these—was the late Benedict Pocoroba. Benny, through a tortuous procedure, had infiltrated a Mafia-type mob engaged in smuggling opium from Mexico into California for consignment to New York. One of the mob principals was Charles Lagaipa, widely and in law enforcement circles unfavorably known as Big Nose Charlie, for a very apparent reason. Benny, who was masquerading under the impeccable credentials of lamster Joe Ricci of Philadelphia, had noticed that Charlie was absent from the usual afternoon foregatherings of the mob. When Benny asked them to drop in to his seaside cabin for chicken with sherry (for the preparation of which he had already established a terrific reputation with the mob), Benny took occasion to press his inquiries about Charlie a little. The noncommittal response he got sounded a warning bell. But time was short. Benny became a little insistent, without getting any answers. Finally, one of the gang who had a particular affinity for chicken with sherry, and with whom Benny had established some real rapport, took an opportunity when the rest of the people were diverted. With an arm around Benny's shoulders he made a startling statement. The best approximate translation from the poetic Italian is, "Joe, my friend, you have been asking questions. Have you stopped to consider that it might be unwise to persist in making inquiries about an absent one, who may already have gone to a grave prepared for him long in advance?" From that shocked moment, Benny realized that Big Nose Charlie had been the subject of organization discipline. Today, after the passage of some twenty-five years, there is no indication that Big Nose Charlie Lagaipa ever has been seen alive or his body found. And it is not likely to be. About two weeks after this conversation, we found Charlie's automobile abandoned in a parking lot on the Oakland mole. The laboratory reported the debris on the roof, windshield, and seat to be blood, urine, and brain tissue.

Later, in the same investigation, Pocoroba was to have another touching and disturbing demonstration of just how well he had built himself into the confidence of this Mafia mob. Not only was there internecine warfare, subsequently demonstrated by proof of Big Nose Charlie's disappearance, but the mob apparently was very uneasy about the bona fide character of certain customers with whom they were dealing in opium. And mutual suspicion developed to a point where the transaction of business was likely to stop, unless an honest intermediary could be found to act as escrow agent for the money to be paid and for opium to be received. Naturally, Benny, as Joe Ricci the Philadelphia lamster, was not completely privy to these discussions. But from hints and scraps of information he could deduce what was going on. Nevertheless, he was a bit flabbergasted when he learned just who the warring factions finally selected as the "honest intermediary"—Benny himself! The undercover man's predicament was heightened by the fact that neither side was exactly taking any chances. Both sets of hoodlums subsequently had him under one kind of surveillance or another; he was completely shut off from any means of communication. His contacts on the outside did not dare to make any untoward moves which might jeopardize a beautiful set-in.

So, there came a dark night when Benny, in his lonely seaside cabin, found himself the uncomfortable possessor of $25,000 in good United States currency, the property of the mob, and the possession of which made him worth exactly $25,000 more dead than alive to some hoodlums who might decide to try to hoist that bundle. After an anxious wait of a few hours, Benny was relieved to be able to count over, in accordance with his escrow instructions, this rather warm $25,000, and to immediately find himself in possession of a much hotter potato—a suitcase full of 5-tael cans of smoking opium.

From about midnight to the small hours of the morning, Benny babysat with this dubious cargo, helpless to communicate with the outside world without arousing suspicion because of the watch on him, and his isolation. Finally, when the consignees for the opium arrived and Benny had to sit futilely and watch this precious cargo go out the door, out of his possession, out of sight and control, it was indeed a painful moment. And this painful moment was to stretch into many tense hours.

Fortunately, through listening and checking over the weeks and through such other surveillance as we had been able to establish, we had a good line on the identity of the opium carriers and on their likely route of transportation. After a while, we were relieved to locate a couple of them on a transcontinental train. To preserve Benny's incognito, we waited until they were between trains in Chicago to relieve the passengers of some heavy cargo and substitute a heavy load of guilt for transporting narcotic drugs.

In gaining and maintaining working relationships with suspects, the good undercover man, by instinct and design, attempts to act in a natural manner, without revealing strain or showing artificiality. He strives neither to overplay nor underplay his part. Remembering that the smartest thieves are reticent, he avoids making too many statements or too many explanations on which he accidentally might be tripped. He will not bluff more than is necessary. A good rule is that too much talk is dangerous and likely to lead to unconscious revelation of inconsistencies. On the other hand, a well-thought-out conversational line can be used to divert a suspect when he becomes too inquisitive. One of the authors (J.C.C.) has found it most useful, when confronted with a too nosy subject, to carry on what amounts to a monologue. The suspect manages to get in very few questions and if sufficiently diverted and entertained sometimes just stops asking.

The undercover man will not give out unnecessarily statements which might be refuted. He will be cautious not to be seen observing the suspect or his operations too closely. He will not be seen taking notes or doing mysterious writing.

The undercover man will not ask for trouble by getting too friendly with the suspect's wife or women friends. That is not the road to mutual confidence. An exception might be small courtesies to the suspect's mother or children. It is just good generalization that women are apt to be poison in an investigation. Countless writers have stressed the fact that women are keenly interested in people as people. Their observations on personalities are likely to be intense and actue. If the woman's "intuition" does not stymie the investigaton and it is brought to a successful conclusion, the undercover man may nevertheless be taken down a peg when an arrest is made by hearing something like this from the mobster's distaff connection. "See, I told you this might happen. I knew that guy was phony. I told you not to have anything to do with him."

Sometimes the suspect becomes very aggressive in demanding that the undercover man satisfy him as to his bona fides. Under these conditions it is often possible to reverse the picture, and shift the burden. The officer can simulate anger and disgust and make counter demands for the suspect's identity and good faith.

If the undercover man can contrive to have the word leak out that he is indeed a very tough and dangerous hombre, that may often open doors for him, since most all thieves respect hard characters. But this can backfire.

The undercover man must be patient. Particularly in narcotic cases there is no timetable. Procrastination is resorted to, time and again, as a test or for other reasons. In another case in Detroit, District Supervisor Greenfeld was successfully working undercover when a combination of circumstances threw suspicion on him, and negotiations to sell him narcotics stopped. Greenfeld voiced the appropriate indignation of a solid hoodlum wrongfully subjected to the horrible suspicion that he might be "the law." He persisted with this pose and waited while weeks went by. Finally the suspect came to him to suggest they resume business. "I know you are not 'the man,' (i.e. an officer). If you were you would have done something before this." Greenfield "grudgingly" agreed and soon the dealer and his mob were in the toils.

Often a speaking acquaintance with the suspect is accomplished but with no basis for talking narcotics. Here it sometimes may be best to discuss crimes other than the drug traffic and to let narcotics be a subject for later natural development. Careful listening and the observing of the suspect's operations may give clues as to how to advance the undercover purpose. Questions that are too much to the point should be avoided until there is a firm basis of understanding. Anything resembling "nosing" for information may immediately arouse distrust. Since crooks are primarily interested in easy money, effort should be made to convey discreetly that the undercover man has money, or access to it. This impression might be reinforced by carrying some evidence of money transfers or deposits. This is usually much better than a reputation for being continually in possession of large sums in cash. This could get the undercover man assaulted or killed.

The Undercover Man

Usually it is a mistake to attempt to make undercover contacts by free spending. Important narcotic dealers may spend much money in good living, but usually they do not throw it around. Such a dealer, looking for an outlet, is on the alert for a business man and may not "cotton" to what seems to be a free-wheeling lush who might be indiscreet and do something foolish and dangerous to the group.

An indication to the suspect to look out for "government money" is the urge to pay the asking price for narcotics when the undercover man senses a deal. This is contrary to the rules of the dope business which extracts all the traffic will bear. A quick agreement to pay the first price suggested may promptly freeze the transaction. The peddler might well conclude that such generosity could only be backed by the United States Treasury. The undercover man, embarking on a buying project, will be fully briefed as to the prevailing market prices for drugs of given purity and will carefully avoid suggestions or offers which are out of line.

Since the primary objective of narcotic investigation is the major traffic, the cover story should generally provide room to grow; i.e. there should be a natural reason for the buyer to wish to acquire larger amounts and to reach more important people in the traffic. In accomplishing this he should keep in mind the self-interest of the peddler. He should not be allowed to think that he will be cut out as the undercover man goes to a higher echelon in the traffic, but must be assured of a profit either from the undercover man or from the higher "connection" which he makes for the officer.

In all his contacts with underworld suspects the undercover man must avoid "entrapment," which is a good legal defense for the suspect and, more important, is ethically and morally wrong and indefensible. A criminal in the unconscionable narcotic traffic, or in any other criminal racket, may be given an opportunity to complete a sale of contraband to the officer for the purpose of exposing evidence, and it is the right and duty of the officer to afford him this opportunity, when advisable in obtaining evidence. But no officer, by word or deed, should lure into a wrongful act a person who, on his own initiative, had no intent to commit a crime. Brutal frankness should suggest that if anyone is to "do time" under these circumstances it should be the officer. An important detail, then, of an undercover narcotic investigation, particularly where drugs are being purchased, is to note and place in the files all direct and circumstantial information indicating that the suspect is in the business of selling narcotics. Under such conditions a plea of entrapment will be a foolish and dangerous defense, since this claim on the part of the defendant then makes the matter of his reputation a relevant issue in the prosecution.

Sometimes the undercover man will become so imbued with his job, so dedicated to an artistic performance, that he may find himself in situations where he has gone above and beyond the call of duty.

Narcotic agent Joseph Define had some great natural gifts as an undercover operator. An American born in French Algeria, he had a trace of an accent. A swarthy skin and fine, hawk-like features let him assume any type of a Mediterranean background. We have pointed out that it is part of unfounded but real American chauvinism, that a person having these attributes might well be in criminal rackets, particularly lucrative ones. Perhaps this is, in part, due to some atavistic recollection of the European gypsy.

Joe Define was working in Kansas City. This was at a time when there was a substantial morphine traffic in Oklahoma. Joe had managed to come to Kansas City with a pretty good background as a well-vouched-for narcotic dealer looking to tie up with the big Kansas City Syndicate connection. Joe proceeded to build himself in with a nightclub owner who, we were told, would lead him to the big connection, if he played his cards right.

The deal seemed to be progressing smoothly. The nightclub owner made some inquiries to which he apparently got the right answers; he wanted to be satisfied that Joe had the money, which he did have.

The nightclub man then suggested to Joe that he go to his hotel and await a call. As Joe entered his hotel room, he sensed that he was being closely followed, and before he closed the room door, two quick-moving hoodlums pushed in with pistols and a peremptory, "Hand over your money."

When Joe produced a small billfold there was a curt demand, "Come on, dig it up. We know you've got it," which might have been revealing, even to a person of less than Joe's keen discernment. He produced a substantial roll of Government "buy" money and watched the pair, now carefully registered in the Define photographic memory, depart.

Joe then went down to the nightclub. In a deadly, matter-of-fact tone, he told what had happened, ending with, "As far as I'm concerned, you are the only person who could have engineered this heist." For a minute the impresario and Joe were engaged in a contest to outstare each other. Then the nightclub man suddenly broke into a smile. "Well, we just wanted to know if you were on the level. Go back to the hotel. Your stuff (morphine) will be be there in half an hour." It was.

8

SURVEILLANCE

IN THE TREASURY Law Enforcement Officer Training Schools we defined surveillance as the secretive and continuous watching of persons, vehicles, places, or objects to obtain information concerning the activities and identities of individuals. We sometimes attempt to break down this activity into types: moving surveillance when the investigator follows a subject on foot or in a vehicle, or stationary surveillance when the observation is carried out from a fixed point of vantage or concealment.

Surveillance is one of the oldest and most obvious of investigative tools. It is one of the first and last resorts of both the tyro and the old pro in the business of gathering evidence. Its universal application attests to its efficacy.

The objectives of surveillance are as varied and as broad as the object of the investigation itself. We establish a surveillance in an attempt to see or find evidence of a crime. More narrowly we may be trying to locate a person, defendant or witness by watching his haunts or his associates. We may wish to obtain detailed information about the subject's activities.

The possession of such knowledge, even though it actually may be fragmentary, may subsequently prove invaluable. It may greatly simplify questioning when suspects or witnesses are interrogated. The subject may have been seen moving in a roundabout manner and observing many practices and precautions consistent only with a desire to conceal. Realization that the investigator knows of some of his activities in some detail may cause a suspect to conclude that we know all of them, and he will make admissions and confessions which would not otherwise be forthcoming.

Surveillance is a valuable check on the reliability of informants and in disclosing any ulterior purposes these may have. It may lead to the location of hidden property or contraband.

In the narcotic field surveillance is particularly valuable in obtaining information as to the identity of persons in the higher echelons of the traffic, and in obtaining the basis of probable cause for the issuance of search warrants. It is employed for corroboration purposes in conducting investigations through informers or through unwilling or reluctant third parties. Knowledge that there is such surveillance serves to prevent double-dealing by persons in an extra-official capacity and to get a fuller measure of assistance from these. It may serve to protect the persons of undercover agents or special employees in case of personal attack, assaults, or the rigging of false defenses. It will furnish corroboration of the testimony of an undercover man operating singly, and will serve to explode phony alibis.

Surveillance may be used to prevent the commission of a criminal act or to catch a criminal in such an act. Against the narcotic traffic, surveillance is a proved method which sometimes discloses whether certain suspects are active in the traffic and whether there is narcotic traffic in the community. Surveillance is one means of establishing that a witness will be available when needed, or that a prospective defendant can be picked up at the time most advantageous for the breaking of a case.

Any person who can pass the physical examination as a law enforcement officer should make a good surveillance agent—not to exclude many who could not. Certain physical qualifications would be helpful, but usually these are over-stressed. Outstanding physical characteristics which may attract attention to the officer are a liability. The best appearance is, of course, an "ordinary" appearance. Most of us might qualify in this regard though we would not like to admit it. Most valuable is the ability to act naturally under prevailing circumstances. This is a talent which comes easily to some. With others it must be acquired by application. The best way to perfect this ability is through actual operations or trial runs in the field. It is a strange commentary on police training that while practice is a requirement in many other specialty fields, very seldom are officers given the opportunity to try out their abilities in surveillance or undercover work under test conditions. We suppose part of the reason is that there is so much real work to be done that practice is relegated to the background. In our opinion, some measure of it would produce excellent dividends in the development of techniques, and in the acquisition of assurance and aplomb on the part of the surveillance or undercover man.

The surveillance agent should have the assets and the approach we would like to see in any officer. He should be alert and be able to stay alert. Sometimes that takes some doing. We have seen long hours of intensive surveillance work go by the boards, wasted and worse, because an officer on a dull observation post figured it was safe to "duck out a minute for coffee" during just the wrong five minutes. Like the alert automobile driver the investigator should learn to "think ahead," to anticipate moves and to meet them with a good degree of resource. We expect our agent to have good powers of observation and memory. If these do not seem to be present they usually can be acquired. It is remarkable in how short a time, for instance, the ability to remember automobile license numbers can be developed, simply by working at it.

The investigator on surveillance must be patient and enduring. There is little room in law enforcement for the man who does not have these underlying qualities. In the narcotic traffic, especially, one of the first recognitions is that as far as the trafficker is concerned, nothing occurs on schedule. Actually there is a good rationalization behind such seeming anarchy. The smart peddler often stays off schedule because he wants to keep the "law" off balance. By his erratic observation of time he tries to do what the baseball pitcher does with a good change of pace. Patience and endurance are then more than academic words. The seat cushions of an automobile may seem to be wearing thin but the officer still must sit. And often his post is not the relative luxury of the modern automobile. It may sometimes be the unyielding contours of a coal pile, an unheated house in mid-winter in Minnesota, a mosquito-infested swamp under a blazing summer sun. Some years ago in Chicago, narcotic agents acquired an excellent surveillance post in a vacant apartment. Unexpectedly, and altogether by chance, narcotic dealers moved in their line of access and egress. To use it would have meant disclosure. The officers did have access to some stale bread. With this and refreshment from the water taps they were "treed" for about seventy-two hours. But they made the case. (The incident occurred most opportunely at a time we were trying to demonstrate

Surveillance 217

to a Congressional committee that narcotic agents often were required to work unplanned overtime!)

It is perhaps trite to stress preparation in a surveillance case, but it must be stressed, as too often it is neglected or incomplete. The files often contain valuable information which is sometimes overlooked in the haste to get out on the job. If the dossiers are extensive, the surveillance officer will almost immediately sense the continuity of activity if the criminals are "working."

From the files may come names and aliases, with perhaps invaluable nicknames. They may supply photographs and descriptions in one degree of detail or another. They may disclose characteristics and mannerisms of the suspect, sometimes more valuable in covering him than mere personal description. We may find information on the identity of some of his associates and personal contacts, his hangouts, his habits, his routines, his modus operandi.

The files in our own or other enforcement agencies may give us a hint as to whether a surveillance project will be easy or difficult, and may indicate what special measures, if any, should be taken to avoid his countermeasures and suspicions. We will wish to know what we can do about the neighborhood where we are to operate. What the files don't disclose we should try to acquire. Do we have trusted sources of information in the vicinity? If so, these should be consulted. What is the area like? Are strangers likely to be accepted or is every regular inhabitant part of a society closed against the law? What appearance and dress and actions would most likely allow us to operate without undue notice? Any individuality of the neighborhood as to race, color, language, or nationality might be important.

The files in our own or other agencies may give us specific addresses of meeting places, hideouts, caches or "plants." Usually very important is knowledge of the identity of the automobile used by the criminal. We would like to know his driving habits, the streets or routes he generally uses, the parking place or garage and repair facilities of his cars. It is desirable that we identify cars by more than license numbers, which may often be shifted among several cars.

To fill gaps in the file information, or where this is lacking, there should be preliminary reconnaissance of the probable scene of the operation. If not already known to the surveillance officers, the suspects should be pointed out to them, if possible, by someone who knows them, or they might be identified by photos or other information. There should be a physical survey, if possible, to establish acquaintance with the geography of the area. The astute officer will profit from the example of the astute thief who does not make an important move against a premises without the preliminary examination which he calls "casing the joint." This physical survey will be used to evaluate the information in the files, to supplement it, and to establish the working conditions. What is the nature of the neighborhood? Are vantage points available? What pretext and cover might be acceptable? What are the traffic conditions? Are there one-way and dead-end streets? Are there essential arterial routes to the neighborhood which must be used and on which a suspect might be "spotted" for trailing at a place somewhat remote from his neighborhood?

After these preliminary inquiries plus discussions with informants, and the consulting of other sources of information, the surveillance officer will be in a good position to know his best method of approach. He will observe some general principles, one being that he will avoid anything in the way of dress, equipment, vehicles, etc., which will be conspicuous. By force of habit or custom some officers, without realizing it, may wear distinctive articles of clothing or jewelry which will almost immediately identify them. These must be discarded. Obviously if weapons are carried there should be no conspicuous bulges. The means of a quick superficial change in appearance might be carried. This is fairly simple if the officer is in an automobile. Changing or donning a pair of glasses—not sunglasses in a dark cafe unless he is "beatnik" or "Hollywood"— may make a good change in superficial appearance. In an automobile hats, caps, shirts, etc., can be shifted quickly. Obviously the surveillance officer will try to have an automobile which is not known and which is not too distinctive. The officer will avoid using license plates which can be identified with an official series. Officers will try to obtain numbers which are not recalled easily. We will remember that suspects may be able to identify automobiles by other than license numbers. Besides frequent changes of these and the use of popular makes of cars, an occasional change of paint jobs and the avoiding of the use of identifying external gadgets on the car are desirable.

In his personal preparation the officer should not overlook equipping himself with a sufficient supply of pocket money for anticipated needs. It has proved embarrassing for some officers to be caught without sufficient taxi fare when unexpectedly it was necessary to use a cab on a long trail across town. An adequate supply of funds will eliminate the necessity for the officer to identify himself to obtain cash. If the officer came in from a distant town for an extended stay it may be important that the Federal Reserve designation on his money agree with the neighborhood from which he claims to be.

As with so many of the techniques of police work, only guidelines and suggestions can be advanced. The first development in a case may show that a planned course must be completely revised. The officer will then "play it by ear" until he can get in touch with his associates and superiors to determine on new tactics. Sometimes instruction can be taken too literally. District Supervisor Irwin Greenfeld of the Federal Bureau of Narcotics, who often lectured on this subject at the Treasury law enforcement schools, said that this story, which we suspected was apocryphal is true: In World War II many of the regular narcotic agents went into armed services. Manpower was short and recruiting to fill vacancies difficult, and many applicants were of doubtful capacity. To try out one of these, "Greenie" gave him a problem. "Go up to Whatsis Cafe in midtown. It is a hangout for narcotic peddler Joe Doaks whom you can identify from this photo. Don't take any police action. Just buy yourself some apple pie and coffee, sit there, watch whom Doaks meets this afternoon, and then come back and give me a report." In a too-short thirty minutes the applicant was back in Greenfeld's office. "So soon?" asked Greenie. "What did you see happen that you came back so soon?" "Nothing," replied the applicant. "I didn't see anything happen. They were all out of apple pie."

If the type of case warrants, it may be desirable to establish observation or listening posts in a neighborhood. Here visual observation combined with radio may facilitate the surveillance project with reasonable security from detection or interruption. Such observation posts must be obtained discreetly, of course. Sometimes the local precinct may have sources which can be relied on in renting a room or apartment or obtaining access to a vacant lot or store. Friendly real estate people may be able to accommodate the investigators. Sometimes it may be necessary to rent a premises incognito and to depend on circumspection not to arouse unduly the curiosity of the landlord or neighbors.

The officer should be alert to recognize and exploit the aid of janitors and building employees who are honest and sympathetic to law enforcement. These persons if handled skillfully can become walking observation posts. Their value and potential could be of incalculable worth particularly where officers would find it impossible to attempt surveillance.

If there is to be more than one officer on a surveillance project, someone should be in charge. There should be at least a general understanding of tactics and plans for handling of the problem as it then appears. Signals and other methods of communication should be devised. These should minimize the necessity for personal contacts between officers. If one of the group should be suspected, or "burned up," that contamination should not be spread to the others. If the job is a long one, and it is likely to be, suitable arrangements should be made for relief. Substitutions, however, should be minimized. In most cases the surveillance will be more successful if the same officers stay on it to the extent of their physical ability. In a surveillance, officers may not be freely interchangeable. One may have seen many things which did not seem significant at the time and were not recorded or passed on. However, he has these details in his mind. Then comes a development which makes his individual knowledge highly significant and which would be altogether lost on a replacement. Again the officer thoroughly familiar with the persons and pattern in the surveillance is likely to react more effectively to situations as they arise.

There should be a central coordination point to enable officers to keep in touch with one another and, if possible, a means of quick contact when plans go awry or there are new developments. There should be a sure means of communicating with headquarters or superiors. The officer should be diligent in making ample notes whenever possible. He should not try to rely too extensively and too long on memory, however good. Current reports may have great value for quick association with other information.

The investigator should anticipate that under certain circumstances he may be accosted by the suspect or others with a request to explain his presence in a particular place at a particular time. Rather than to rely on Fifth Amendment tactics, or on his badge, the officer should have some excuse, the more reasonable and more plausible the better. We know a handsome Latin type who was always believed in the most awkard places when he implied that a lady had something to do with his presence there. Naturally it would be more than stupid to try to identify the "lady" with any special person. In any event, the story should be better than "waiting for a streetcar." If possible, it should be fully convincing. Lacking that, it should allow for doubt whether or not the officer is "the law."

SURVEILLANCE METHODS

Certain classic patterns have been evolved for surveillance. Any pattern must be based on a commonsense appreciation of human habits, capabilities and reactions. Practice and experience will demonstrate to the officer the efficiency of various tactics. Tactics which work splendidly for an experienced officer or team may be found useless for the unsure, self-conscious neophyte. Officers who have become accustomed to working together learn to blend their activities into smooth teamwork. Both individual techniques and team operations must be developed by actual experience. One can learn much about how to swim or how to play football from books and diagrams. But one does not become a swimmer unless he gets into the water, or football player except on the gridiron.

It is a common fault of law enforcement texts and lectures that we presuppose ideal situations as to manpower, equipment, and time. Often these ideal conditions are lacking. Sometimes we are called on for a one-man foot surveillance. This is a difficult job. Often the requirements of the investigation, and almost always the success of the trailing, require that the subject be kept in view at all times. Hence the trailing will be very close, and somewhat dependent on traffic, both foot and vehicular, and on the physical layout of the territory. If on the opposite side of the street the officer will keep abreast of his quarry. In built-up downtown areas the trail must be quite close to note when the subject enters buildings, turns corners or makes other quick routine or distracting moves.

The two-man surveillance team is much better suited to do a successful trailing job. On busy streets both officers normally stay on the same side of the street with the subject, one officer fairly close to him and the other at an interval behind. On less crowded streets the second officer might cross the street and walk on the opposite side nearly abreast of the subject. Shifts in assignments between the two officers will lessen the risk of recognition of the trail.

A more ideal surveillance method involves at least three officers on a foot surveillance in the so-called ABC pattern. In normal city traffic, officer A, on the same side of the street keeps a reasonably close distance behind the suspect. B follows A at an interval. He keeps A in view, and the suspect if possible. He is also alert for any countersurveillance by an associate of the suspect. Officer C, the third member of the team, walks on the opposite side of the street, not quite abreast of the suspect. Where there is little or no traffic it may be wise to put two of these officers on the opposite side of the street or to have one in front of the subject. In very crowded streets all three officers might be on the same side as the subject, the leading officer very close to the quarry to observe his actions if he turns corners or enters doorways. The officers should constantly rotate assignments to minimize detection.

In normal street traffic C across the street should lead the subject to a street intersection. Pausing at the corner, or crossing the street—a maneuver sometimes dependent on traffic signals—officer C is in a position to observe and to signal to A and B the actions of the suspect if he disappears from their sight by turning a corner. If the suspect delays on the corner, either through traffic control or otherwise, the A and B officers, or one of them, may find it desirable to precede him, relying on signals from C. If the subject stops after turning the corner, A may cross the street. Turning can be the occasion for rotating the assignment of the trailing officers.

Where direct and continuous trailing is considered too dangerous, or the suspect so wily that he is lost by the trailers, the "leap frog" or step-by-step technique may be successful. In this the suspect is taken to a certain point and then dropped or lost. The method presupposes that the subject makes the same trip at frequent intervals and follows the same route. Obviously there is a weakness if he does not fulfill these requirements. But if we have some reason to think that this is the pattern, on the first trip the suspect is taken to the break-off point. Observation the next day or on the next trip is resumed at the break-off point, and the suspect taken to a second break-off point. On the third attempt he is taken from the second break-off point and so on until the cache, hideout, confederates, or whatever the objective of the surveillance, is disclosed.

The advantage of the step-by-step technique with a wily suspect is that once trailed away from his home base he may be less alert. He is usually most sensitive when leaving a premises with which he can be identified, and may take many precautionary methods, like circling the block several times, before taking off for his objective. Near home base he may have the observations of confederates to detect a trail. Often there is great benefit in appropriate coverage when a suspect is seen away from his home base. District Supervisor Greenfield told of a case. He and his squad were observing a narcotic peddler in a New York neighborhood. They broke off the surveillance when they sensed he had recognized he was being followed. Hours later and far uptown, entirely by accident, they saw the peddler again, trailed him closely, saw a narcotic transaction and made an arrest. "I made you fellows downtown this morning," said the astonished and chagrined peddler. "How in the world did you manage to tail me all this time and away up here?" Greenfeld made the appropriate answer: "Oh, we have a system."

Often it is of advantage to combine foot surveillance with automobile support, with one or two officers in the vehicle. This assures the foot officers of replacement, facilitates radio communication, and supplies a ready means of transportation if the suspect should get into an automobile or board a taxi or other motorized transport. The method has a disadvantage in that a slow-moving automobile may be conspicuous.

SPECIAL FOOT SURVEILLANCE PROBLEMS

No attempt will be made to cover all contingencies which may arise. We point out only some of the most common with the admonition that this is a job which calls for no cessation of a state of keen alertness and for constant "thinking ahead."

If the suspect enters a building, at least one officer would normally follow; that is, unless the nature of the building is such that this move would expose the officer. Usually the officer would not find it possible to accompany the quarry into a private house, a small shop or some enclosure on a premises where his presence might be particularly noted and perhaps challenged.

If the building is a large public establishment, then all the trailing officers might enter the building. Depending on the problem and the number in the trailing force, one officer might remain in the building lobby, and others cover other exits in case the subject is lost. If the subject enters an elevator the trailing officer might accompany him. If it is known that the subject is going to a big, active office the officer might get off at the same floor. For a smaller office it might be wiser to get off one floor higher or lower and walk down or up. If so, however, the officer should consider whether he is likely to debouch through a fire door directly into the suspect's "lap." Sometimes with a cautious suspect it may be best not to get on an elevator with him, but to watch the stop indicator or listen for his order to the operator and to take the next elevator to the floor where he might stop. Meanwhile, other officers in the lobby will keep alert, as the subject may be using the elevator merely for the purpose of "shaking the tail," i.e. eluding possible trailers.

If the suspect enters a restaurant at least one officer should enter after him. When the suspect's actions indicate that he is ordering food the trailer should do likewise—whether or not they have apple pie! The officer should try to sit near the suspect and attempt to hear any conversation. Such eavesdropping provided a pivotal piece of evidence in an important narcotic conspiracy prosecution. Officers inside, or on the outside observing through a window, should be careful to note any contacts which the subject may have with other persons in the restaurant. In the narcotic traffic quick and fleeting meetings may be all-important. Sometimes the officer will be able to pay his check and leave just ahead of the subject. He should be careful not to be caught in a delay or traffic jam in paying his bill. A helpful practice is to have ready an ample supply of change so that, if necessary, the bill plus tip can be paid to the waiter in the exact amount indicated. If it is necessary to pay the cashier direct the officer can speed his departure by putting down exact change.

Should the suspect board a streetcar, bus, or subway, at least one officer should accompany him, sitting, if possible, behind him on the same side. If he thinks that frantic efforts to get on the common carrier might attract attention, the officer may decide to follow in an automobile or taxi for the full distance or to use such a vehicle to overtake the common carrier and board it at an appropriate stop.

A combination of automobile surveillance and accompanying foot officers is likely to be very effective. If the subject takes a taxicab it may be possible to follow in an automobile or in another taxicab. If no such transportation is in sight the officer should make a note of the identifying number of the taxicab and the time and place. Taxicabs, especially those of the larger companies, keep good records of their vehicles, and the destination of a fare can usually be determined by checking records.

If the quarry enters a telephone booth it may be possible to listen from an adjoining one. In such a situation the officer should go through the motions of dialing a number, or other natural actions. If the booth is isolated he might pretend to check a number in the directory. However, this may expose him to scrutiny by a cautious suspect.

If the person being followed takes a plane, train, bus, or boat, whether the officer will accompany him will depend on the understanding of the plan of operation and instructions from his superior. Often such a suspect will be picked up for surveillance by a local crew at a distant point. "Out of town" surveillance is likely to be most productive. Often the caution of a criminal seems to diminish as he gets a long way from home base. Here he figures the chance of being recognized as a crook is reduced. Not only is he likely to move less cautiously, but he sometimes talks more freely.

The destination of the suspect boarding out of town transportation can sometimes be determined when he is buying a ticket or from the records of the transportation company, from the ticket agent, or the conductor of a train. The suspect's baggage may give a clue to his destination and purpose.

If the quarry should enter a race track, amusement park, theatre, ball park or similar place, the officer should normally follow the subject. Regular admission charges should be paid, and credentials used for obtaining admission only when it is well-established and accepted routine which will arouse no suspicion. Here the subject will be followed closely so that he will not be lost in the crowd. In a darkened theatre the surveillance officer may have an opportunity to get close to the subject and perhaps hear messages to a confederate or observe transfer of contraband.

When the subject meets a "contact" the trailing officer will get the best possible description as well as noting the time and place of the meeting. A photograph might help to preserve this evidence or information. If the conversation can be overheard, it might quickly resolve whether this is a "business" associate or someone who may not be likely to prove of consequence in the investigation. Along this line, the attitude of the subject toward the contact can be observed. Is he giving or taking orders? Is this a serious or frivolous meeting?

Sometimes a subject registers in a hotel. Here he has the advantage of cover from outside view. But the competent officer often can exploit this situation. If the hotel is a first class establishment, its personnel usually will cooperate fully with the officers. However, some minor employees might be inclined to sabotage an investigation with the hope of personal advantage. Furthermore, the cooperation of the hotel will be more wholehearted if the management is assured that care will be taken to avoid unfavorable publicity for the institution. The room assigned to the suspect can be determined from the room clerk, house officer, assistant manager, or appropriate personnel. If this inquiry is not considered advisable, the quarry can be followed to his room or its number ascertained by overhearing inquiries of the bellman for keys, mail, etc.

Sometimes an adjoining room or rooms can be obtained to assist in keeping track of the subject. The telephone numbers called from a hotel room are generally recorded at the switchboard and usually may be obtained by subpoena or otherwise for leads to the suspect's activities. The contents of wastebaskets and other trash left by a suspect may give clues to his criminal operations.

Sometimes, even with the best-laid plans and operation, the quarry is lost to the trackers. Usually this calls for immediate notification of the officer in charge. Known hangouts will be put under observation. Any previously demonstrated pattern of activity will be exploited in an attempt to pick up the trail. An officer may be left where the suspect was last seen for his possible reappearance there. Telephone calls on pretext to his friends or associates may disclose something worthwhile.

If an officer is discovered by the subject to be a surveillance agent, it is usually wise to have that officer relieved. If the case is particularly "touchy," all surveillance activity may be discontinued for a time to let the "heat" subside. On the other hand, many surveillance officers are likely to be unduly sensitive to the possibility of recognition. The officer should try to be reasonably sure that it is not he, rather than the subject, who is seeing shadows.

Expert criminals may resort to special stratagems or normally pursue a course of conduct designed to detect surveillance operations. These are as diverse as the ingenuity of man can contrive. An astute criminal may never reveal the fact that he knows he is being followed, but will simply carry out evolutions designed to lose his pursuers. Sometimes the quarry, suspecting a surveillance, may go through with a dummy operation, resembling a transaction in narcotics, hoping to bring confirmation that he is being observed, or reassurance if he is not. Often knowledge that the trailers have been "made," i.e. recognized by the quarry, is apparent from the ease and simplicity with which a "cooperative" subject manages to keep himself in sight of his pursuers, until he chooses otherwise.

A common method of testing for foot surveillance is to stop abruptly and look for people behind. Often the suspect will look around with the appearance of great casualness. He may reverse his course. He may board a street car or bus and quickly alight before it starts, or after a block or two. He may make a last-second dash for public transportation to try to determine who also is dashing. He may circle a block or neighborhood in a taxi or private automobile, often several times, to see what unorthodox movements he may stimulate in others in the vicinity. He may enter a building simply for the purpose of leaving by another exit. He may turn a corner, abruptly about-face and wait for a hurrying trailer to figuratively, and sometimes literally, fall into his arms. He may employ a convoy, a counter-observer of his own. He will watch reflections in show windows. He will alternate a slow and rapid pace. He will drop paper or similar material to see if it is retrieved by a person following him. He will use the old dodge of appearing to fix a shoe, carefully observing everything within sight at the time. He may have observation posts where confederates check for any possible hostile interest in his movements. This might be done by friendly store operators on his beat, or through long-range observation by field glasses from an observation point. He may use the mirrors in hotel lobbies, bars, or other public places to observe any covert action by others, such as persons peering around or over newspapers, showing undue interest in arrivals and departures from a room, and the like. He may make a quick start to leave a hotel lobby or waiting room and then stop to note if his action has prompted similar moves by others. In a hotel room he may look for wires or listening equipment. He may listen for the door of an adjoining room to be opened, quickly pop out into the hall and take a quick look to determine the character of the occupants of the room next door. He may pretend to leave a hotel room by opening and shutting a door and then wait to see if that prompts anyone in the room next door to come out into the hall to look. The subject may pretend to leave his hotel room but remain there quietly, listening for any movement or sound next door.

Many suspects, even when not "hot," i.e. when not alerted to a real possibility of active surveillance, will nevertheless pursue certain routine precautions against being followed afoot. If the suspect is alarmed or alerted he may intensify precautionary operations. These might be such as jumping on or off a bus or streetcar or subway as the doors are about to close, taking the only taxi in sight, especially if he can hail one across the street in a position to make a U turn. He may leave buildings by side or service exits. He may try to lose himself in a crowd, or cross the street just as the traffic light changes. He may enter a theatre and immediately leave by another door, but most crooks hate to spend the money. He might contrive to have the surveillance officer accosted by a patrolman to explain his actions. Sometimes the suspect may resort to a change in clothing, eyeglasses, and the like to escape superficial scrutiny.

AUTOMOBILE SURVEILLANCE

In surveillance from an automobile the principles and many of the practices of foot surveillance may apply. If only one automobile is available, its position usually will be behind the subject's car. The distance and procedure will vary with traffic conditions and other situations. Generally in congested city driving it is unwise to allow more than two vehicles to interpose between the quarry and the trailing officers. If further back the subject is too easily lost from sight. Should he turn a corner he may get away completely before the surveillance car reaches the intersection. A favorable trailing position is to the right of the suspect, out of easy view in the rear vision mirror. Of course, if the trailer is once spotted in this position by the subject and continues obstinately in this course, contrary to normal driving habits, the precaution in itself may be a dead giveaway. In rural areas the subject is usually allowed a good lead, where possible, with another car in between. Where intersections are known to be infrequent the subject may be allowed to take a considerable lead. The pursuing car will usually drive with headlights on low beam and all other lights not required for traffic operation should be extinguished. Automobiles used for surveillance should be checked for characteristics which might make them easy to spot in a trailing situation, such as uneven headlights. Careful officers often take the precaution of turning off the dome and other inside car lights which often come on automatically when a door is opened. On the other hand, the failure of the suspect to do that may make his identification certain as he enters or leaves the car. There was a prisoner, serving a life term as a narcotic repeater, who was considered to be one of the most clever and wily peddlers in Illinois. Positive identifications under his interior car lights contributed strong evidence leading to his conviction.

Two or more surveillance cars usually will be found to be much better than one for quicker and safer completion of a trailing job. In a city, during daylight hours, both cars will usually be behind the subject's automobile. Sometimes one car may be operated on a parallel route. It will be driven to arrive at intersections just before the subject car so that route changes in direction and pace can be noted. Where the traffic situation and other factors make this method feasible it is an excellent device, attracting no attention from the subject. It is a good system to use at night and in suburban and rural areas where parallel roads make it possible.

A three-car surveillance team makes for good coverage of a subject. Use can be made of any parallel routes. Changes in the position of the cars make identification by the quarry less likely. Sometimes one car can be put in the lead, ahead of the subject, to observe his movements in the rear vision mirror. Such a team can more readily detect any countersurveillance moves by the subject, such as the use of a convoy car.

Sometimes due to lack of manpower or equipment, or because of the caution of suspects, it may be necessary to resort to so-called "leap-frog" surveillance. Official cars are stationed along a probable route of the quarry. As his car is seen to pass, a trailing car falls in behind, passing the subject at sufficient speed to take up a new post where the process is repeated. Where several official cars are employed, the subject can be followed pretty closely without the appearance of a car trailing him. Flaws in this technique may be in the failure of the quarry to take an anticipated route. High-speed driving by the suspect may make the maneuver difficult, but it is usually a good method where time is not pressing. It may result in the location of criminal hideouts, "fences," narcotic caches, stills, counterfeit plants, and the like. Criminals, like the rest of us, are creatures of habit and are often likely to follow the same driving routes and schedules. Sometimes by taking advantage of this a lone trailer can successfully run to ground even a subject quite wary of a following car. The suspect is picked up and cautiously trailed for a period and then dropped. Next day or next trip he is picked up at the point where dropped, taken a distance further, again dropped, and the process renewed each day or each trip at a further point until the ultimate destination is reached. This requires time and patience.

One of us (M.L.H.), as a young officer, had a lasting lesson in a demonstration of the art of trailing by, of all persons, a burglar. "The Ghost" as we came to call him, a good professional burglar, forsook the orthodox practice of his art in the early days of prohibition to become a hijacker, or more exactly, a thief of contraband liquor. Apparently the business had its rewards. There was no longer the danger of complaint to the law since the losers were in no position to "holler copper." The Ghost did run the danger of more summary justice from the bootleg mob's muscle men and torpedoes. This he sought to checkmate by a most crafty modus operandi involving all the patience of the most competent hunter and tracker. To find liquor to steal, The Ghost started with the obvious. From a sugar warehouse or other source of fermentable material in Minneapolis or St. Paul he would trail loaded trucks to a distillery, usually carefully hidden on a secluded farm many miles out in the country. Since these sugar trucks were often convoyed and he operated strictly as a lone wolf, The Ghost sometimes was able to track the truck only a short distance at a time. But day after day he picked it up further and further along, and finally would be satisfied that he had located the distillery.

At this point, where an officer's objective would have been all but accomplished, The Ghost was only half through. It would have been too dangerous to attack a well-manned whiskey making plant. Even if he did that successfully, it would close down. The Ghost had no desire to kill the goose that laid the golden egg. So now he had the job of picking up the trucks or automobiles which were hauling moonshine from the distillery, and to trail them back to a cache in town. Since most of the return route was usually different from the sugar trail, here was another surveillance job, sometimes to be accomplished bit by bit, until the whiskey "drop" in the Twin Cities was located. Often this was in private garages or sheds, the operators depending on unobtrusive operation and frequent shifts for protection from the law and predators. The plant being finally located in a garage or warehouse, The Ghost would carefully "case" the area. At a time when his observations convinced him the coast was clear he would use his considerable burglar skills to enter the building and cart away a load of whiskey.

The usual result of such a foray was some consternation among the moonshiners, a tightening of their internal security measures, some undeserved suspicion on the "kids" who drove the cars and trucks for the mob, and the shifting of the liquor drop to a new spot. It would never occur to the mob that the plant had been located by such a roundabout and devious procedure. So the still usually continued in operation. The Ghost returned to the still area, picked up the departing whiskey cars and soon located for himself a new moonshine or alcohol drop. The Ghost was no hog. But after a lapse of suitable time there would be another burglary and these were continued at such intervals as he thought the traffic would bear. In due course The Ghost met with some misfortune at the hands of the law. It was then that we were able to put some of his ability to the use of the Government.

As a thinker he was way ahead of his time, a testimonial to the virtues of capitalistic incentive. His trailing car was a most inconspicuous-looking vehicle. While it didn't look as if it would make the next hill, the mechanism ran like a watch. Inconspicuous, under the dash board, was a rheostat which altered the brightness of the headlights, running lights and tail lights over a wide range. Every so often The Ghost personally gave his "Q" car a new coat of paint—not an uncommon do-it-yourself job in those days, from which it emerged changed, but still drab and not eye-catching. Several sets of license plates, a spare set of bumpers, an easily removable side rear vision mirror, were only part of the equipment of this remarkable character.

Equally remarkable was his operation on foot which we had the opportunity to observe. When a choice was possible, The Ghost worked in the dark of the moon. He took special care about his clothing and wore dark colors. In the Minnesota climate, when called for, he wore a topcoat or overcoat as long as was appropriate without attracting attention. He avoided any appurtenances which in any way reflected light. Most effective was his use of almost complete immobility. The sniper, the sharpshooter, the skirmisher, all military men know that movement may destroy the most effective concealment and camouflage. Law enforcement officers know it too, but sometimes forget what an essential principle this is. We still recall the almost uncanny ability of The Ghost to merge with the scene, to melt away in darkness. In a misty predawn one might be almost upon him when he appeared as a wraith suddenly become material. The Ghost was an artist and a perfectionist. We were pleased when, after a not-too-long stint in a correctional institution, he took the straight and narrow path of honesty and respectability. Some of his accumulated wisdom, freely offered, we have passed on to innumerable young officers to bring about, we hope, some added effectiveness in their surveillance and undercover operations.

The problem of trailing an automobile may be simplified if it is realized that though Detroit's production is in millions yearly, any one car is likely to be just a little different. If in no other way, it will have its own bumps and scratches. Tail lights, as standard as the assembly line can make them, may nevertheless show their own peculiarities. A car, closely studied, may often be recognized at some distance at night from just a minor variation in its running lights. Sometimes if access to a subject's car is possible, it may be feasible to alter a tail light without interfering with its functions by a strip of Scotch tape or even with grease or a wad of chewing gum to produce enough individuality to permit some assistance to recognition at night.

In radio equipment the modern policeman of course has splendid tools to assist in car surveillance. (He should not overlook the possibility that criminals sometimes make use of this facility.) Radio helps in the employment of the parallel route technique in trailing, in the interchange of positions, and in giving notice of unexpected changes in the actions of the subject. Inside and out, trailing cars should present the appearance of normal passenger pleasure cars. Sometimes small trucks can be used effectively. Oversize antennae or other noticeable equipment should be avoided. The use of the car radio can be further extended by the employment of walkie-talkie or other personally portable radios. This equipment must be kept in the best possible operating condition.

The suspect who fears he may be subjected to an automobile surveillance will resort to many devices to establish the fact. He may alternate fast and slow driving. He may run stop signs. He will try to hit traffic lights as they change to Stop, even running the red light. He may make frequent U turns, or even drive against traffic on a one-way street. He may park frequently to try to assay the situation. He may drive into a dead-end street. He will pull in and out of a filling station, or drive through a parking lot. He may go around a corner or over the sharp rise of a hill and quickly slow down. Temporarily out of sight, the principal may leave the vehicle with a driver to continue on as decoy.

FIXED POINT SURVEILLANCE

Sometimes all or part of the surveillance is conducted from a fixed point where adequate observation and concealment are present. Appropriate care must be employed in acquiring the lookout facility and in its operation. Peering through curtains, particularly if they are moved, is likely to be easily noticed from the outside. If not out of place, a venetian blind is a good device for safe observation. Sometimes it is possible to lower the roller of the conventional blind an inch or so below the top of the window frame. This leaves a space through which observations can be made unobtrusively. Avoid peering and peeping around window frames, curtains and shades. Proper placing of lights at night is all-important if observations are to be made out of a window after nightfall. The careful officer will go out to "take a look" to see how his observation post looks from the outside. Usually a high-up observation post is more secure from outside detection. People seldom look up. The post should be equipped with the necessary accessories. Binoculars or other glasses assist in the positive identifying of persons, the accurate reading of license numbers, and other vital matters. Cameras with telephoto lenses may be valuable. There are available police devices using infrared light on the sniperscope principle. Presently these are effective only at moderate ranges but might be expected to improve.

As in almost every investigative enterprise the officer should make careful and full notes, including descriptions of persons entering the suspected premises, their automobiles, if any, and other pertinent equipment. Jack Webb, as "Sergeant Friday," has made the chronological police record a matter of household knowledge. It is nonetheless most valuable. Often the investigator will find the meticulous time record to be his greatest support in court for backing up the information acquired on a surveillance or other investigation. Those chronological notes may serve to destroy faked alibis and to refute trumped up and phony defenses. They add to the air of solid veracity of the officer's testimony.

When it is desirable to put a premises under surveillance and no room or other observation post is available in the vicinity, it may sometimes be possible to put observers in the area on one pretext or another. Street repair crews, canvassers, salesmen, utility men, and the like may be simulated. Obviously these devices may be limited as to time and in effectiveness. The officer should not become so engrossed in the cover operation as to miss the real objective. In Instanbul, Turkey, Narcotic Supervisor George White was working undercover, an American narcotic agent collaborating with the Turkish police. It became necessary to give him secret cover and protection in a big heroin purchase he was negotiating. The resourceful Turkish police moved into the area as a street repair crew. However, the sale did not go off as scheduled. There was a long delay. The "street crew" became so engrossed in tearing up the cobblestones that when the signal to close in finally came, it was missed. An anxious and very much on-the-spot Agent White finally had to throw a chair through a window to attract attention.

Mechanical aids can be of great assistance on a surveillance. We already have noted the use of radio. Microphones, where proper and legal, may be a great asset. Fluorescent powders or other chemicals may be used to show that the criminal handled "hot money," or was at the scene of the crime. Sometimes a hidden cache of narcotics can be located by the tell-tale marks of a tracing chemical. Sun-glasses equipped with a reflector can be used to unobtrusively observe people behind the officers. In surveillance by automobile, the front or side rear view mirrors often furnish a means of observing a suspect without giving any indication of interest in him. Sometimes the small, low-flying aeroplane or a helicopter is effective on a trailing job. With these as with other devices, appropriate caution should be used. Unusual and unlikely as it was, a narcotic suspect in New York a few years ago properly deduced that a helicopter was being used to trail him. Fortunately, he confided his suspicions to the wrong person!

The minimum standard for surveillance automobiles is that they should be inconspicuous, although some forces successfully use marked squad cars under optimum conditions. The car generally should have a two-man crew, one to drive and observe and the other to observe and take notes. The second officer is available for foot surveillance if necessary. It is our experience that more than two men in a car are noticeable and likely to attract attention. The driver should maintain a constant state of alertness, thinking ahead at all times. Any accident, however trivial, might defeat a very expensive surveillance project. The officers should change seats from time to time. Sometimes it is effective to carry a woman's hat or scarf for disguise, particularly if the car is to be parked for observation purposes. If the surveillance is continued for any length of time, it is well to change license plates from time to time. It is useful to have the car so wired that the quality of the lights can be altered by a switch. On embarking on an automobile surveillance project the officers will see that they have an adequate supply of gasoline in the tank. It may be necessary sometimes to have a reserve supply. Occasionally it may be advisable to carry food, raincoats, tire chains, and the like. Under certain conditions the officers might equip themselves with a marking device of some sort to be fastened under the suspect's car which will leak powder or liquid to leave a trail. Under certain rare circumstances it is possible to track a suspect's vehicle to which there has been surreptitiously attached an electronic device which may be trailed using "homing" instruments.

If a search of the premises is made in the absence of the suspect and no police action is to be taken, see that the contents of the premises are left in the original condition.

"Think ahead," using natural subterfuges if the suspect seems to be noticing the trail. Use opportunities to surreptitiously check mileages on the suspect's automobile. This may help to locate "plants" or headquarters. Decoy communications, such as telephone calls on pretext, may be used to determine occupancy of a premises.

Some general admonitions should be repeated here. The fundamental attitude of the successful undercover or surveillance officer is that he acts naturally. With some this quality seemingly is present always. With others it is acquired after experience. Try to avoid exaggerated reactions for the artificial situation. Do not "slink" or "peep" or "peer." If the officer feels that he is "uncovered," that the suspect has "made" him, he should try to avoid confirming that suspicion in the subject. He should not go directly home or to his office, but should first try to throw the suspect off the scent. The officer should always have a story to explain his presence and actions, should stick to it, and unless he decides to make an arrest he should seldom give the suspicious subject the satisfaction of confirming the fact that the trailer is an officer.

PHOTOGRAPHIC AIDS TO NARCOTIC INVESTIGATIONS

In recent years photography has played an increasingly important role in criminal investigation. The purpose of this material is to indicate the many ways in which photography can be used in the investigation of narcotic offenses, particularly as an aid to surveillance. No attempt will be made to cover the principles of photography or to go into detail on photographic techniques. It will be assumed that most criminal investigators have at least a basic knowledge of photography, i.e. the ability to handle a camera so as to provide satisfactory results.

Surveillance Photography

With the advent of small cameras that can be concealed easily, the development of fast lenses, and the introduction of new

Figure 20. A "working photo." Picture of an actual street sale of heroin. Narcotic agent and employee purchase drugs from peddler, left foreground. Photo from hotel window about 50 yards distant. Courtesy U.S. Bureau of Narcotics.

types of high-speed film, photography during surveillances is now not only possible but practical under a wide range of lighting conditions.

Before considering this use of photography, we should probably discuss the types of equipment and material now available which might be adaptable for this use. Consideration should be given as to whether your departmental budget will allow for the purchase of several pieces of photographic equipment for specialized use, or perhaps like many small organizations one camera is required to serve all purposes. In the latter of the events, it has been our experience that a good 35 mm single lens reflex is probably the best suited for police use. This type of camera has the advantage of being suitable for almost all types of photography, including "mug" shots and copying. This camera should be equipped with a fast lens, at f/1.2 at least, and a telephoto lens of at least 135 mm. We have had considerable success using a 300 or 500 mm telephoto lens in daytime operations. However, most of the long focal length lenses are not fast enough for photography under dim lighting conditions.

Since the development of high-speed film emulsions, such as Tri-X® and Royal-X Pan®, and Eastman Kodak Company's introduction of high-speed infrared film, photographs can now be taken under a variety of conditions previously considered impossible. With such materials and a fast lens, it is now quite possible to take useful pictures at very low levels of illumination.

Before attempting available light surveillance photography, you must realize that these pictures will not be of the same quality as those taken under ideal conditions. By the nature of the film and processing, these pictures may be grainy, and they may often be fuzzy due to the manner in which the camera is held and the slow shutter speeds utilized. However, bear in mind that the purpose of these photographs is identification, i.e. placing a person or persons at a given place at a given time, and therefore they do not require "salon" quality.. Confronted with a photograph in which only his mother might recognize him, a suspect is often moved to admit or confess.

Before attempting this type of photography on an actual case, the investigator should expose several rolls of film by the trial and error method. By doing this, he should be able to estimate within reasonable limits the exposure required for any given picture and thus determine whether a useful picture is possible.

In exposing your first roll of test film, we would like to suggest that you set the camera at the largest lens opening (f/1.2), the shutter at 1/30th, and develop your negatives in Kodak D-76® for about twice normal development time. After printing these negatives on the most contrasty paper available, we are sure that you will agree that this type of photography is a valuable investigative aid.

Infrared Photography for Surveillances

With the development of Kodak High-Speed Infrared® film, surveillance photography can now be accomplished where little or no visible light exists. There are many and varied uses for infrared photography in criminal investigation, however, we shall discuss only the use of this material during surveillance photography when the photographer may have no control over the available light. Many types of electric signs and older-type street lighting equipment have a high level of infrared radiation. At night we recommend using this infrared film without a filter, thus gaining the advantage of exposure by visible light in addition to infrared light.

Since infrared light and visible light do not focus on exactly the same plane, some focusing compensation should be made when taking pictures by infrared. If there is no red auxiliary focusing mark on your camera, a rule of thumb for test purposes is, after focusing for visible light, to shift the focus setting to a nearer distance by about the space between the infinity and the 50-foot mark on your lens.

If the lens opening used is f/8 or smaller, there will probably not be any need to make a focusing correction since the depth of the field at this aperture will probably be sufficient to insure a well-focused image of the subject. However, during nighttime surveillance photography, a larger lens opening will normally be required. Therefore, it is recommended that test exposures be made to determine proper focus.

In determining exposure, the trial and error method must again be used. Several test exposures should be made and careful notes made. Using a shutter speed as slow as possible for conditions, bracketing exposures should be made under varied conditions that might be encountered. In a "stake out" type surveillance, thought should be given to the possibility of illuminating the area with supplemental infrared radiation if this could be accomplished without detection. In the event this is feasible, test exposures could be made and the proper exposure arrived at prior to the taking of actual evidence photographs.

Motion Pictures

In the field of narcotic enforcement, the motion picture camera can be used for best results. For instance, there is always the chance that the subject may bend down or turn in another direction just at the moment that a still picture is taken, thus obscuring his features and hindering identification. The use of a 16 mm movie camera equipped with a telephoto lens avoids this by providing a large number of pictures made either by the picture-a-second technique or continuous operation.

Motion pictures of a narcotic violation have an additional advantage in that they portray the complete sequence of action during a "pass" or "payoff."

In this type of operation, the ingenuity of the investigator is of utmost importance. In many instances, concealment for himself and his equipment will be required on short notice; however, on other occasions, the photographer can select his vantage point and plan his concealment well in advance.

In a protracted surveillance, a careful log should be included in the photographer's notes. The log should show the data concerning the photographic equipment, materials, and exposure, the identity of the person taking the photographs, the subjects in the picture, and the place and time of each film sequence. A simple way to record the time on the film itself is to photograph a clock and a calendar pad on a short length of film at the beginning or the end of each operating period. A shot of the day's newspaper headline (including the date) made at the beginning of the film will fix the earliest time of taking.

Conclusion

The officer should not be overawed by the seeming intricacy of modern photography. It is not necessary to be a "professional

Surveillance   241

photographer" to take a photograph that might send a criminal to the penitentiary.

As in any other technical field, the police photographer should endeavor to continue his education and further his technique. With the rapid advancements being made in the design of equipment and material, the police photographer should be alert for material both in photographic and police publications which might improve his efficiency.

As stated at the beginning of this section, the material presented here was not intended to be a treatise on photography, but it was intended to stimulate the imagination of the investigator to realize the important role that photogrophy can play in combatting crime.*

---

*Grateful acknowledgment is expressed to the Eastman Kodak Company for its permission to use material from the following publications: *Infrared and Ultraviolet Photography* and *Photography in Law Enforcement*.

9

THE COLLECTION AND PRESERVATION OF PHYSICAL EVIDENCE

THIS IS ONE OF the most important aspects of the criminal investigator's training and knowledge. It is important in all phases of crime inquiry; it is of paramount consideration in most narcotic cases. The nature of this crime, the law, and the court procedures usually make it necessary that narcotic drugs be introduced in evidence. While this is not invariably the case, it is almost the rule.

Perhaps more good narcotic cases have been lost in court through carelessness or ineptitude on the part of the officers and prosecutors in preserving and presenting narcotic evidence than for any other single reason.

Through the kindness of H. J. Anslinger, U. S. Commissioner of Narcotics, now retired, we reproduce here adaptations from an outline summary of instruction given at the U. S. Bureau of Narcotics Police Training School on the general subject of the collection and preservation of evidence. This outline is broad and general in scope. It goes to all types of physical evidence in all types of crime. This is a subject with which every police officer should be thoroughly acquainted. It is a body of knowledge which even the experienced investigator should constantly review until its application becomes an automatic, second-nature process. At the conclusion of this outline summary we will make comments on some of the special problems which confront the narcotic officer in collecting and preserving narcotic drugs for evidence.

THE COLLECTION AND PRESERVATION OF PHYSICAL EVIDENCE

I. **Procuring and Identifying Physical Evidence**

   A. *Definition*—Physical evidence is articles or material found in

The Collection and Preservation of Physical Evidence 243

an investigation which will assist in the solution of the crime and the prosecution of the criminal.
B. Every piece of physical evidence which could have any connection with the crime should be collected.
 1. Nothing should be rejected because it appears too big, too small, or too insignificant.
 2. Objects or material that seem insignificant at the time of discovery may later prove to be valuable evidence.
C. All physical evidence *must* be connected to the crime scene through photography, sketches, written descriptions and oral testimony.
D. The "chain of custody" must be maintained from the time physical evidence has been collected until it is presented in court.
 1. Physical evidence must be marked, labeled or physical characteristics recorded in such manner that it can later be positively identified.
  a. Identification marking must be permanent in nature.
  b. If the marks are placed in the evidence, care must be taken *not* to cover up or destroy items of evidential value.
  c. Identifying marks should include:
   (1) The officer's full name or initials (do not use an "X" or other common symbol that may be hard to identify).
   (2) The case number.
   (3) The date, time, and specific location where evidence was found.
   (4) Any additional information necessary to distinguish each item from all other evidence collected.
  d. Original notes should record markings used and any other appropriate identifying or descriptive information.
 2. Maintain a record of possession so that each item of evidence can be accounted for from the time of receipt until the time of trial.
  a. A system of receipts should be kept by the office to establish that each item of evidence was collected in connection with the crime scene and is in the same condition as found.

b. The description of receipts must be such as to distinguish each piece of evidence from all other similar evidence.
  3. Pack and store evidence carefully so that it will remain unchanged.
     a. Evidence may be excluded from exhibit in court if it has been improperly handled so that it is no longer in its original condition.
     b. Accurate laboratory conclusions may depend on receiving physical evidence in the same condition as when it was collected.
     c. Physical evidence should be stored in a secure place under the direct control of the person having custody.

II. Preservation of Evidence
  A. Packaging of evidence.
     1. Regardless of whether evidence is to be sent to a laboratory for analysis or storage pending presentation in court, it must be properly wrapped and packaged to insure its preservation.
     2. Certain types of evidence when submitted to a laboratory for analysis should be accompanied by a standard sample for comparison purposes, such as:
        a. Questioned documents.
        b. Mud.
        c. Dust.
        e. Abrasives.
     3. Wrapping evidence.
        a. Place a set of evidence receipts in duplicate with the evidence.
        b. Wrap evidence and receipts in paper, wood, or other type of covering material.
        c. Make wrapping tamper-proof by sealing with wax or Scotch tape.
        d. On the outside of this covering place the name and address of the person to receive the evidence and return address of the sender.
        e. Mark each side of the package with the words "Evidence

The Collection and Preservation of Physical Evidence 245

   —to be opened only by authorized laboratory personnel," or the equivalent.
   f. Affix to the wrapper a sealed envelope containing a letter of information.
   g. A final outside wrapping should be placed on the package.
      (1) Seal in a tamper-proof manner.
      (2) Plainly address to person or laboratory to whom evidence is to be sent.
      (3) Give return address of sender.
      (4) Give directions such as "Expedite," "Urgent," "Fragile," "Explosive," "Inflammable," "Perishable," or similar notation.
B. Letter of information.
   1. The letter should advise that the package contains evidence in a particular case (identifying case) and should only be opened by the intended laboratory or person.
   2. The request for laboratory services should consist of:
      a. A description of the package contents and anything special about them.
      b. The specific analysis desired.
      c. The conditions governing the laboratory analysis, such as:
         (1) Disposition of evidence after examination.
         (2) Whether or not evidence can be consumed in testing.
         (3) Whether or not evidence must be returned in the same condition as submitted.
         (4) Whether or not it is permissible for evidence to reveal signs that an analysis has been made.
   3. General information pertaining to the evidence, including collecting and handling, should be given.
   4. Give general history of case, which might aid the laboratory.
   5. Request the laboratory to acknowledge receipt of the evidence.
   6. Two copies of the letter should be mailed with the evidence, one copy should be mailed to the laboratory under

separate cover, and at least one copy retained by the investigator.

III. Processing Procedures for Specific Types of Evidence

A. Acids.
1. Ship in glass bottle, with glass stopper, sealed with wax.
2. Quantities up to one pint should be furnished laboratory.
3. For comparison a one pint standard sample should be furnished.
4. Bottles should be packed in glass wool, rock wool, or sawdust and shipped by railroad express.
5. Label "Glass," "Acid," "Corrosive," and "Fragile."

B. Alkalies, ammonia, caustic soda, carbonates, etc.
1. Pack, seal, and ship the same as for acid.
2. Label "Alkali," "Glass," "Corrosive," "Fragile."

C. Letters and documents.
1. Place identification markings on small blank space on each sheet.
2. Do not touch with bare hands.
3. Documents should be sealed in cellophane envelope, then sealed in manila envelope and mailed by registered mail.

D. Bullets and cartridge cases.
1. Place identification marks on base of bullets and on the inside of cartridge case.
2. All samples found should be furnished to laboratory for examination.
3. Shipment may be made by registered mail.

E. Casts.
1. Identification marks should be placed on plaster of paris casts before it hardens, and on moulage after hardening.
2. Wrap casts in soft paper and pack in wooden box with excelsior or sawdust.
3. Label "Fragile."
4. May be shipped by registered mail or railway express.

F. Clothing.
1. Identification marks may be placed directly on cloth or on tags that are securely attached.
2. If wet, dry before packing, but do not use excessive heat.

The Collection and Preservation of Physical Evidence

    3. Leave clothing whole—do not cut out stains.
    4. Wrap each article separately and identify on wrapper. Pack items securely in strong container for shipment.
    5. Ship by registered mail or express.
  G. Glass fragments.
    1. Identification marks may be placed on a piece of adhesive tape attached to each fragment of glass.
    2. Avoid chipping or further cracking.
    3. Keep questioned samples separate from known samples.
    4. Wrap each piece in cotton. Pack in strong container to prevent shifting and breakage.
    5. Label "Fragile."
    6. Ship by registered mail or express.
  H. Objects bearing latent fingerprints.
    1. Care should be taken not to add additional prints. Use gloves, forceps, or other similar aids in handling.
    2. If appropriate, include fingerprint cards of persons who might normally handle object, as well as prints of all suspects.
    3. Pack objects securely in a frame or other holder which will protect latent prints from damage.
    4. Label "Fragile."
    5. Ship by registered mail or express.
  I. Soil and mineral specimens.
    1. Pack in strong box and seal tightly. The use of envelopes or bags may result in crushing or disintegration.
    2. Ship by registered mail or express.

IV. General

  A. If valuable physical evidence is located at a crime scene, consideration should always be given to the practicability of having an expert remove and preserve it.
  B. Evidence that cannot be removed must be copied or verified by:
    1. Casts.
    2. Photographs.
    3. Drawing and sketches.
    4. Witnesses.

C. Photographs of evidence must be carefully documented by recording the following, if you expect to qualify as an expert photographer.
  1. Names of persons present when photograph was taken.
  2. Type of camera.
  3. Type of lens.
  4. The shutter speed.
  5. The diaphragm opening.
  6. Kind of film used.
  7. Time of day.
  8. Degree of light and whether natural or artificial.
  9. Details of processing.
  10. Chain of custody of negative and prints.

V. Crime Scene Searches—Introduction

A. Purpose of searches of crime scenes.
  1. To discover and seize contraband, means, and instruments used to commit the crime, and any other legally seizable articles.
  2. To discover information and clues relating to the crime.
B. Instances of how an officer may legally search a crime scene.
  1. By the authority of a legal search warrant.
  2. As incident to a legal arrest for a crime committed in the officer's presence.
  3. By a written or oral "waiver" of rights.
  4. Open fields.
  5. Probable cause as to automobiles.
  6. General right to search automobiles, vessels, trains, or aircraft entering the United States (Customs).

VI. Preparation for Search of Crime Scene

A. Organize officer group of proper number for each arrest.
B. Select equipment and material needed at each crime scene search.
  1. Evidence tags and labels, camera, compass, ax, pinch-bar.
  2. Assorted envelopes, paper cellophane containers, notebook.
  3. Watch, knife, file, string and cord, steel tape or ruler, flashlights.

The Collection and Preservation of Physical Evidence 249

    4. Latent fingerprint equipment, fingerprint kit.
    5. Evidence containers, specimen jars for liquids, sealing wax, paraffin.
    6. Shovel, probing rods, first aid kit and special equipment, such as metal detectors.
  C. Choose best time for search.
    1. As soon as possible after commission of crime; or,
    2. Time when evidence or contraband will most likely be present; or,
    3. When criminals will most likely be present.
    4. Dawn is usually a good time.
  D. Arrange for transportation to and from crime scene.
  E. Plan best approach to crime scene.
  F. The group leader should be an adept organizer.

VII. Procedure at Crime Scene

  A. Attitude of officer.
    1. He should be well poised.
    2. He should have ability to use right procedure.
    3. He should perform his duty in a professional manner.
  B. General procedure at crime scene.
    1. Make quick general survey.
    2. Segregate the scene, remove all unauthorized visitors.
      a. Defendants or known violators.
        (1) Secure names, addresses, and descriptions.
        (2) Put in custody of experienced officer.
      b. Suspects.
        (1) Secure names, addresses, and descriptions.
        (2) Arrange for interrogation.
      c. Witnesses.
        (1) Secure names and addresses.
        (2) Arrange for interview.
      d. Spectators.
        (1) Courteously ask them to leave.
        (2) If necessary, more forceful tactics may be used on the slow or stubborn ones.
      e. Newspaper reporters and photographers.
        (1) If any unusual problem, refer them to your public relations officer or your superior.

(2) Be courteous to them. Most newsmen are very cooperative. Courtesy begets courtesy.
(3) If newsmen happen to come by information which will injure the further development of your case if prematurely published, the reporters will usually go along in withholding for an appropriate time. Newsmen have high sense of public responsibility.
(4) Do not sacrifice any elements of investigation for the sake of a big story.
(5) Avoid photographing and giving names of officers who work undercover. Avoid exaggerated estimates of value of seized narcotics. Don't claim the narcotic traffic has been completely destroyed.
(6) Be sure to give cooperating police agencies due credit.
4. Have a definite plan of search, proceed in an orderly manner.
a. Begin at the point of entrance and search clockwise; or,
b. Start at a central point and proceed in ever-widening circles; or,
c. Use any plan which guarantees complete coverage.
d. The search must be thorough and complete.
5. Do not move any evidence or clues until viewed in original location by other officers and photographed.
6. Make drawings or sketches of the crime scene. (See outline on descriptions.)
7. Photograph the crime scene, generally and in detail.
8. Make accurate measurements of all distances to which later references may be made.
9. Keep proper notes or contemporaneous memoranda.
10. Search for latent fingerprints.
11. Determine the criminal's means of entrance and exit.
12. Observe the actions of the prisoner during the search.
13. Question neighbors as to location of missing objects.
14. Note missing objects and negative facts.
15. Look for tool marks caused by the criminal.
16. Examine objects moved in the commission of the crime.
17. Do not discuss the crime in the presence of violators, witnesses, spectators, etc.

18. Search for stains, such as ink, blood, mash, or any liquid having a bearing on the crime.
19. If automobile is used in crime, secure description of treads.
20. Make casts of footprints, tire tracks, etc.
21. Have an undercover officer mingle with spectators.
22. Look for special places of concealment.
23. Apply special search techniques.

VIII. Searching

  A. Common places of concealment in living quarters.
    1. Underside of tables.
    2. Behind mouldings.
    3. Behind and under drawers.
    4. In mattresses and bedding.
    5. Behind loose bricks and boards.
    6. Compartments and cabinets.
    7. Behind sections of mantles.
    8. Under sills.
    9. Around door and window casings.
    10. Under stairs.
    11. Stoves.
    12. Furnaces.
    13. Wastebaskets.
    14. Garbage pails.
    15. Flues.
    16. Behind plumbing fixtures.
    17. In clothing hung in closets.
    18. In and around iceboxes.
    19. In telephones.
    20. Behind pictures and mirrors.
    21. In boxes and cases in drawers.
    22. Underside of desks.
    23. Window shades and draperies.
    24. In trunks and boxes.
    25. Under lamp and light fixtures.
    26. In radios.
    27. Under floors.
    28. Folding pieces of furniture.

29. Under rugs.
30. Suspended down heating pipes, etc.

B. Common places of concealment in automobiles.
   1. In or behind cushions and upholstery.
   2. Under floor and mats.
   3. In radio sets, heaters, and heater ducts.
   4. Inside top lining.
   5. Behind rear vision mirrors.
   6. In and behind dash or glove compartments.
   7. Behind shells or reflectors of lights.
   8. In hub caps.
   9. Radio speaker.
   10. Behind door panels and fittings.
   11. Ash trays.
   12. Air cleaner and oil filter.
   13. In or around radiator.
   14. Recesses in and around engine.
   15. Bumper and underbody.
   16. Battery and battery box.
   17. Inside of tires.
   18. Fiberboard linings in truck.
   19. Trunk mats, floor, and tire walls.
   20. In or around gas tank.
   21. In or around muffler.
   22. In or behind sun visors.

C. Search techniques.
   1. Use flash or other lights to the maximum extent.
   2. Use metal detectors and other equipment where applicable.
   3. Bedding, cushions, upholstery, rugs, etc., can be checked to some extent by prodding deeply with fingertips or poking through the material with a needle-type probe.
   4. Look for areas that appear to have been recently disturbed, such as new nails or screws where you would expect to find

Figure 21. A large haul of Mexican marihuana seized in Illinois. This was concealed in the doors and framework of the automobile in which it was being transported. Photo courtesy Galloway News & Photo Service, Springfield, Ill.

The Collection and Preservation of Physical Evidence

them rusty, patches in plaster or cement, different colored paint in a small area and similar evidence of tampering.
5. Use mirrors to observe obscured areas.
6. Dismantle buildings or equipment to the extent necessary to assure location of all evidence.
7. Measure the inside and outside dimensions of buildings to locate hidden compartments.

Personal Search

There are few situations in police work where the search of the suspect's person is more important than in narcotic work. The immediate search must be rather thorough. Naturally, a first impulse of the suspect is to divest himself of any drugs which he may be carrying on his person. This is an impulse which often pays dividends to the investigator. On the approach of an officer the bad conscience of the trafficker or addict may cause him thus to bring drugs on his person to light, when otherwise there might not have been probable cause to arrest and search him. Under any circumstances the suspect should be closely and continuously observed and, when arrested, thoroughly searched as promptly as possible. When closing with the suspect the officer should be aware that there may be an attempt to throw away evidence, or to dispose of it by pushing it through a hole in the pocket or by swallowing it or in other ways.

Narcotic criminals develop an amazing ingenuity for concealing narcotics on the person. They may utilize the lining of coats, particularly the padding around the collar, sometimes that of the shoulder. The waistband of the trousers is a favorite place for concealment. Folds and seams of underwear may be utilized. Narcotics may be concealed in a packet attached to a cord fastened around

Figure 22. Photographs show a vest worn by hitch-hiker enroute from Mexico City to Chicago, Ill. The defendant, after being arrested in southern Illinois, stated that the bulge in the back of his jacket was "padding," but a search disclosed a large quantity of marihuana. He stated that he purchased the marihuana concealed in the vest in Mexico City and claimed the Mexican from whom he bought this marihuana sewed it in the lining of the vest. Courtesy Illinois Division of Narcotic Control.

the body next to the skin. A cache of drugs may be concealed in the knot of a necktie. A shoe heel may be hollowed out to provide a narcotic depository. Accessories like fountain pens, pencils, and knives may conceal hidden drugs. Under certain circumstances various of the body cavities may be employed for concealment. (See Fig. 4.)

Unless there is the sharpest vigilance there will continue to be repetitions of what happens too often in routine police operations. Narcotic drugs, presumably discarded by a prisoner, are found on the floor of the squad car, in an areaway in the police station or in the cell block, under circumstances where it is not possible to charge anyone with their possession.

The addict prisoner in jail requires special precaution. Confederates may attempt to smuggle narcotics to him in food, toiletries or other accessories or clothing, or they may be passed directly by visitors. His handkerchief, shirt, or pajamas might be saturated with heroin or morphine.

To the narcotic officer the collection and preservation of narcotic drugs as evidence present some special problems. He is handling potential "dynamite." If he is not scrupulously exact, meticulously careful and intelligent, he can be the victim of a serious explosion.

The first problem likely to perplex our officer is in the recognition of narcotics when he sees them. Is the powder, tablet, or solution a narcotic? Even with opiates and marihuana this is at times a difficult decision to make. If we are also enforcing the laws on other dangerous drugs, like the amphetamines and barbiturates, our problem is multiplied many fold. Some rules of thumb may be helpful here. The physical setting and circumstances may assist us in making the right decision. If a known narcotic addict has on his person or in his possession a folded paper containing a powdered chemical it is likely to be narcotics rather than something for his stomach ulcers. Admissions, explanations, or the lack of them, may assist in identifying or rejecting substances as narcotics. Special efforts to conceal or disguise drugs may indicate their contraband nature. As the narcotic officer gains experience he learns to observe the usual characteristics of narcotic drugs in the traffic. Some of these can be subjected to field tests for identification (page 92 et

The Collection and Preservation of Physical Evidence 257

seq.) Others he may be able to recognize as probably contraband because of the circumstances. If a drugstore is nearby and open he may be able to get an informed opinion from a pharmacist who has learned to recognize the gross appearance and special markings on tablets. One of the first statements made about the characteristics of an opium alkaloid is that it has a "bitter taste." Officers should not taste drugs! This accomplishes little. Many non-narcotic substances may be bitter. There is always the danger of tasting something that is highly caustic or corrosive or as lethal as potassium cyanide.

The investigator's recognition of a substance as narcotic is, of course, only on a tentative basis. Unless he has qualified as a chemist and as an expert in the field the officer should never be relied on or requested to testify to the fact that the substance is a narcotic. The chemical identification is a job of the laboratory technician. No matter how experienced, and how accurate his conclusions, attempts by a person not qualified in court as expert to identify substances as narcotics would lead only to confusion and embarrassment.

The officer's job then is a highly intricate and responsible one of connecting the presumed narcotics to a person or persons, preserving these drugs intact and safe, and establishing and maintaining a chain of custody which can be demonstrated when the drugs are offered as evidence in court.

When narcotic drugs are found on a search, the discovering officer will call this to the attention of the other officers present and will usually also confront the defendant or defendants with the fact. A field test will be made if necessary. The drug containers will be marked as indicated in the outline.

As soon as the narcotics can be taken to a headquarters office or other place where a scale is available they should be carefully weighed. No delay in this operation should be permitted. A seizure report must be promptly submitted. If it is necessary to hold the drugs seized at night until morning, their custody should be secure (not locked in an automobile, for example). At the first opportunity the suspected narcotics should be taken to a chemist.

Law enforcement agencies have varying procedures for the safekeeping of seized properties and other physical evidence. Narcotic drugs must be handled only under the most strict security routine. The small department, and even some larger ones, may find it most advantageous to promptly send all of a narcotic seizure to a chemist. If this is the procedure, let there be no delay. The chemist might hold the drugs in his custody until required to produce them in court to establish the chemical analysis. In case of a continuance it might be advisable that the drugs stay in the chemist's possession.

When narcotics go into the possession of the court as evidence there should be a follow-up procedure for the recovery and destruction of the drugs. Many prosecutors will ask that drugs be preserved after conviction until the appeal period is over. The object should be to dispose of the narcotics with the least delay. Any accumulation of these drugs should be regarded as a mounting danger. In most state jurisdictions narcotics are disposed of under court order with witnesses certifying to the fact. This should be a meticulously careful procedure. Knowledge by all concerned that there is a final audit will forestall abuses.

Should there be a retrial after appeal in a case in which drugs have been destroyed, it is a relatively simple matter to prove in court the fact of their existence and identity from official records.

We have found one of the most effective devices employed in the preservation of drug abuse evidence to be the "lock seal" envelope. This is simply a manila paper type envelope which can be ordered in varying sizes. In addition to the conventional adhesive, it has a metal interlocking fastener which, once closed, cannot be reopend without breaking. The "lock seal" envelope had been standard equipment in the old Federal Bureau of Narcotics for many years and we adopted this in the Division of Narcotic Control in Illinois. It is now used in the Federal Bureau of Narcotics and Dangerous Drugs. These envelopes may, of course, be overprinted to show pertinent information as to the case and defendant to which the narcotic evidence relates. At this writing one supplier may be Security Envelope Co., 406 Portland Ave., Minneapolis, Minnesota 55415.

Why do we emphasize this care in the handling of narcotic evidence? Simply because experience, sometimes bitter, has shown it to be one of narcotic law enforcement's "stickiest" problems. There are strains and situations in the handling of narcotics which require that we be more careful with their custody than in the handling of diamonds and rubies. Narcotic evidence is subject to all the dangers of loss or misplacing as is other physical evidence. In addition its care presents its own peculiar problems.

For example, the usual operations of a narcotic enforcement agency require that narcotic addicts, either as prisoners, witnesses, or informers, be about the premises. A narcotic addict will do, literally, almost anything to supply himself with narcotic drugs. Many of these addicts are master thieves, master pickpockets and quite a few are master con men. Any lapse in rigid custody procedures for the narcotic drugs is likely to produce losses. More dangerous and more insidious than the thief is the wheedling addict who wants "a shot to keep him on his feet." His request is not based on anything as simple as the merely humanitarian ground that without narcotics he is going to be a very sick man. In these days he might be told that when he gets to the jail doctor he will receive a dose of methadone to tide him over if his withdrawal symptoms are severe. Seldom would the request of the addict for narcotics be so crassly put as to be in the nature of a proffered bribe. But often the request for a "shot" does come. "If you will give me some stuff so that I can stay on my feet I will make you a case on Mr. Big."

Since "Mr. Big" is someone whom the boss would give his eyeteeth to put away, because the great desideratum of narcotic enforcement is to reach the higher-up, the inexperienced or wrongly informed officer might find himself intrigued with this sort of proposition. He looks only at the ultimate objective. He may not stop to consider that he has no right to administer, or to sanction the use of narcotics by anyone; that should he give an addict narcotics under any circumstances whatsoever, he, the officer of the law, is in the exact legal category of the foulest dope peddler. Because the ultimate end, he hopes, will be good he may consider the employment of the illegal means. He may not stop to consider other implications. Once he has furnished narcotics to an addict he has mortgaged his official future to that junkie. He has sold his birthright as an officer of integrity, often for a mess of pottage, since the addict's performance may not have measured up to his glib preliminary promises.

Fortunately we are discussing something of rather rare occurrence now. It was an aberration more common in the earlier days of narcotic law enforcement, knowledge which has caused some amateur pundits to write disparagingly of official practices of this sort as if they were common today. They are not. The experienced narcotic officer quickly comes to realize that if the addict really had a big "connection" he would not need to apply to the officer for drugs. However, there still may be seen the occasional lapse, usually by the inexperienced and unwary. But even experienced officers have been trapped by the juxtaposition of available drugs and the importunities and blandishments of the astute addict and have gone down to disgrace and imprisonment. To avoid accidents of human frailty in a profession where such accidents are infrequent in proportion to the great temptations involved, we must follow rigid procedures for safeguarding narcotics which come into our possession. This program should be as comprehensive as possible. For example, the possession of narcotic diluents like sugar of milk in the desk or lockers of narcotic officers should be completely proscribed.

Having set up our procedures for the safe custody of narcotics and having made them as foolproof as our ingenuity can devise, we are then foolhardy if we disregard the human factor and assume that the system is always working. The narcotic officer in charge is derelict in his duty if he does not make it his continuing business to check to see that his protective system is being followed in all respects.

Another facet of the collection and preservation of physical evidence, requiring meticulous attention, is seen in the occasional case where money and other valuables are encountered upon a search. Where jewelry, valuable watches, and other such property are found, the officers should be sure to see that they are put in the hands of the owner at once for his disposition (unless they are to be held as suspected stolen goods) lest a future claim be made that these articles are missing with the implication that the officers had something to do with the disappearance. Money found on a search presents some particular problems. If a defendant is present it should be counted before him and his agreement obtained to the amount, if possible. His signature or initials on a memorandum would be desirable. Much use is made in narcotic investigations of "marked" money, particularly currency identified and recorded by serial numbers. This requires that all funds on the search premises be carefully examined. This should be done in such a way as to minimize any contention that some money has been improperly retained by the officers. When a defendant thinks that some of his money may be identifiable currency, he sometimes will refuse to admit ownership of any currency found on the premises. Such monies should also be counted in the presence of the defendant and available confirmatory facilities used. Sometimes money found in substantial amounts may be the subject of proper levy by the Internal Revenue Service on jeopardy assessments because of failure of the owner to pay income taxes, or the like.

In any case where money or substantial valuables are taken for safekeeping it is the part of wisdom for the officer to immediately notify a superior by telephone or other communications of the amount and circumstances leading to the detention of these properties. Such precaution may forestall need for much explanation and possible trouble. Third parties left at a searched premises should be at the owner's approval and risk. These may make away with property. Of course the officer should give or leave receipts for any property taken from a premises not included in the return on a search warrant.

When defendants and defense attorneys observe that officers are following business-like routine in connection with the custody of money, few complaints will be heard. On the other hand, defendants are quick to sense careless or sloppy practice by police. Defense counsel often takes this opportunity to inject extraneous issues into a narcotic case. Careless practices may expose officers to undue temptations which occasionally have had disastrous results.

After seizure, either for evidence or for safekeeping, monies should be the subject of rigid custodial procedures looking toward their correct disposition at the earliest opportunity.

For some reason firearms, particularly pistols, found on a search often are handled carelessly. If seized, either as a precaution or for evidence, their custody should be a matter of careful routine.

10

SPECIALIZED ILLEGAL ACTIVITIES: CRIMINAL GROUPS IN NARCOTIC TRAFFIC

AMERICA IS THE GREAT melting pot. We are a synthesis of many peoples. We know that the foreigner, the immigrant, the "newcomer," the striving "greenhorn" of yesterday, is the solid, smug American of today. It is the American way—usually—to adapt the best from any old culture. Perhaps it is not always the best which is adapted but that is American too.

The American way is not to stigmatize people because of origin, nationality, race, religion, color, etc. If there are derelictions noted among special groups we are careful not to disparage whole segments of the population because of the illicit activity of a comparative and unrepresentative few. However, this wholesome conception of our society should not blind the professional law enforcement officer from observing that certain specific types of criminal operations may have a specialized race or nationality aspect. In making his personnel dispositions and planning his actions, it was important to the narcotic policeman in the 1920's to know narcotic addiction, rather widespread throughout the whole country, was confined primarily to Caucasians and Chinese. It was important to him to know that perhaps 50% of the whole Chinese population—mostly adult males—were addicted or were casual narcotic users, mostly opium smokers. It was of significance to the narcotic officer to know in the 1920's, again if for no reason than to intelligently plan his activities, that opiate addiction then was practically nonexistent among Negroes. Likewise, it was important for the narcotic investigator in 1960 to know that narcotic addiction, once so widely and more evenly spread throughout the country, was then, practically speaking, confined to a few of the larger cities, that even there the relative incidence among Caucasians was down, that the Chinese narcotic addiction had practically disappeared, and that the majority of our opiate addicts then were Negro. And of course it is vitally important to the enforcement officer of the early 1970's to know the picture now has changed to show the development of a polydrug abuse culture, to reflect a rising, more general country-wide distribution of drug abuse with a higher percentage of Caucasians and a younger group of addicts. The why and wherefore of these transitions, and speculations on changes in the future, are beyond the scope of this paper. Our point is that the enforcement officer, as a realist, notes these things and adjusts his programs and his personnel to suit. Some of our most interesting work has been in connection with two manifestations in this area. One of these has been the Chinese tong, the other is the so-called Mafia.

THE CHINESE TONG

As described herein, the tong is now primarily of historical interest. The Chinese tong is, of course, Chinese. It is also very American. We are not aware that its exact counterpart existed anywhere else than in America.* The Chinese "tong" or "hong," is a very definite entity. It should be by no means confused with the Chinese name societies, family associations, or the like. It owes its development to peculiar circumstances surrounding the Chinese which developed in this country. Chinese were first imported in substantial numbers at about the time of the California gold rush and, later, just after the Civil War when there was a great demand for their labor in the building of railroads and great construction projects in the West. The Chinese man, primarily a hewer of wood and drawer of water (with the exception of an elite merchant class) then was a welcome asset to our economy. But when he began to compete with "native Americans" for jobs, because he could exist more frugally and was generally more industrious, he was pretty tough competition. Also, he spoke a mysterious language. The literate among him wrote (or drew) a still more mysterious picture alphabet. For his own purposes, the Chinese generally assumed a great unfamiliarity with the offical language

---

*Although we have read of somewhat similar organizations in Hong Kong and Singapore.

of the country. By necessity and by choice he tended to segregate himself strictly from the other elements of the population. Even though he himself might be an ignorant, illiterate peasant, he was quite conscious of the fact that his people had behind them a long, highly developed civilization. Compared to that, the period of removal from barbarism of his northern European fellow American might be brief indeed. So the Chinese could accept the opinion of his white neighbor, the Westerner, who considered him as a "dumb heathen," with the tranquillity of "The Superior Man."

Because he was different, because he represented economic competition, and for many other reasons, including the fact that a goodly number indulged in the much feared habit of smoking opium, there was a keen community resentment against the Chinese. By the 1880's it had developed into state discriminatory laws in California and a Federal Exclusion Act which forbade the immigration of Chinese laborers. This bar continued until 1943. Maisel, in his article in *The Reader's Digest* (February 1959), estimates that up to the time of the Exclusion Act a quarter million Chinese had come to this country, mostly all men. Many went back. He says that by 1920 there were barely sixty thousand. If this latter figure is based on census counts, it probably should be greatly increased, even doubled, because one of the characteristics of Chinese communities after the Exclusion Act was the large proportion there of smuggled aliens who were in this country illegally. That, again, was a factor contributing to the voluntary segregation of the Chinese who wanted the possibility of inquiry by prying officialdom reduced to the minimum.

The genius of the Chinese is no better illustrated than in the manner in which the Chinese community divorced itself from American law enforcement. It was more or less a matter of mutual consent. The police authorities didn't take too seriously any goings on in "Chinatown." The Chinese were pretty law-abiding anyway. They had high standards of personal honesty. If a Chinese were found dead in an alley, he was "just another Chink," and nothing for great official concern. The Chinese had his own simple effective way of evading offical interrogation—"No spik English." His confidence in American courts and American justice was nil. The American community recognized that his suspicions of our justice were well founded. "Not a Chinaman's chance," as part of the slang, was well understood to mean that the cards were completely stacked against him. (Incidentally, a Chinese usually resents being called a Chinaman.)

Under these circumstances it was natural that the Chinese felt it necessary to call on his own resources when there were disagreements among Chinese. The very wholesome principle of arbitration was invoked. But the Chinese, because of his long sojourn under imperfect governments, had a pretty well ingrained tradition that payoffs, the squeeze, "payola," were a natural part of life. When there seemed to be too much "fixing" in these impromptu conciliation courts, some of the cruder elements among California Chinese sought to counter bribery with force, "muscle." This had some elements of the rebellion of working groups against the merchant classes. Since muscle is a game two can play, the merchants soon retaliated with muscle organizations of their own. This was the genesis of the tongs.

These rival organizations resulted in some killings. The episodes were referred to as tong wars. Some of the killings were done by so-called "hatchet men." The authors' experience does not extend back to that day, but we strongly suspect that the hatchet may have actually been a heavy cleaver, an instrument with which the Chinese restaurateur attained the greatest dexterity. In our time the Chinese was sufficiently Americanized to have adopted the pistol. We recall a series of raids in the 1920's on opium dens on Wentworth Avenue in Chicago. In the course of one night more than a bushel and a half of loaded pistols, mostly of a tinny, Spanish vintage, were seized.

Although the immediate necessity for the tong disappeared, it continued as a self-perpetuating muscle group which took over certain territories and rackets among the Chinese. As a muscle agency in the Chinese community, the tong endeavored to extort a membership fee from all of the Chinese population. In many towns a Chinese could not obtain employment from another Chinese until he had exhibited a receipt for what was called "oil money." For this the criminally inclined Chinese did receive some benefits. He had the counsel of the "English speaking secretary," who often was a fixer with the law. A police official occasionally visiting Chinatown might be overwhelmed at the generosity—free meals, etc.—showered on him by Chinese restaurateurs. He might innocently conclude that the Chinese at least apprecitaed the sterling worth of their blue-coated protectors. He would have been less flattered had he realized that a fat chit for his entertainment promptly showed up for adjustment in the office of the English speaking secretary. When the Chinese tong member got in trouble, he had quick access to a lawyer and to a bondsman provided by the tong. However, when he was not involved in tong business, he paid for these out of his own pocket.

The areas of greatest tong interest were gambling, narcotics, and prostitution, in that order. In what was then for the Chinese a relatively womanless world, a Chinese prostitute was a commodity of great value. A tong war was fought when one of these decided to leave her exploiters and to become the honest concubine of a wealthy merchant. Gambling was, and in some places still is, the great racket possibility among Chinese. Not only was the Chinese engrossed by skillful games of chance, but gambling was one of the few diversions available to him. Opium smoking was another.

The Chinese brought the knowledge of opium smoking and the habit with him, and a large portion of the Chinese community either became addicted or were casual opium smokers. This illicit business among the Chinese was generally in the hands of important tong members who used the tong structure for the distribution of narcotics. When former Narcotic District Supervisor George H. White joined the Hip Sing Tong in the 1930's as one of the few non-Chinese ever to be admitted to the councils of this organization, he found the tong to be a country-wide narcotic distributing mechanism. Opium and heroin, brought from Japan on fast Japanese liners by Japanese crew members, were delivered at ports of entry like San Francisco, Seattle, and Vancouver to Chinese tong members who took care of distribution up and down the Pacific coast, also inland and cross country to New York City. Since only a combination of the greatest good fortune and undercover work of the highest order ever permitted outside penetration of a tong, the police problem presented by this distribution of narcotics was an extremely difficult one. The tong held most of the cards. The business was conducted in a restricted area in which the interest of any outsider would be quickly noted. While internal difficulties among the Chinese sometimes produced information, their general solidarity minimized this. There were a few exceptions, but generally it was extremely hard for the American police, federal or local, to recruit Chinese as law enforcement officers because of strong family pressures against such employment. We have indicated the Chinese had the protection of the language, mastered by few Westerners, and an unreadable alphabet. Centuries of oppression by the law had made him extremely resourceful and adaptive. The American police contributed immeasurably by a pre-Korean-incident attitude that Chinese were generally ignorant, unintelligent, and relatively harmless. However, at other times, the same police organization would have the conception that these wily heathens were so infernally clever in their illegal machinations that there wasn't much purpose in trying to compile evidence against them!

Contributing to the confusion respecting Chinese, particularly in the days when fingerprinting was not comprehensive as it is now, there was great mystery about the Chinese name. Unless too badly badgered, the Chinese wrote his three-part name in a logical man's sequence, i.e. with the surname first, then a middle name, and a given name. But Americanization pressures may have forced him to reverse the order. This might be most confusing in an American alphabetical index. Still more confusing was the actual spelling of the name. Suppose we have the family name of Eng. If we don't find it under Eng, a resourceful file searcher might think of looking under Ing, but he would hardly look under "N" for Ng, which is as it is usually written and may most closely represent Cantonese pronunciation. Innumerable local dialectical variations among the Chinese added to the confusion. We would have no difficulty in finding Wong under the "W's," but if somebody with a better ear heard the name more exactly as Huang, or Hwang, our filing might be out of whack.

Gon Sam Mue was one of our celebrated Chinese narcotic agents. One of us then in the Bureau in Washington received a "poison pen" letter about Gon. (The Chinese were adept at writing these.) The allegation was that Gon was improperly employed as a federal narcotic agent, since he wasn't a citizen. "He claims to have been born in Seattle in 19... They kept birth records in those days. You can't find his name in the records." We sent for Gon's file. In it was a birth certificate for "baby Kan," well authenticated by collateral information as being that of Gon Sam Mue. But this aptly illustrates the vagaries of the Caucasian ear in hearing the same name as Kan or Gon. Naturally, the Chinese law violators didn't feel too bad if these little details seemed to confuse the American policeman.

One thing did cause the Chinese violator to sit up and take notice. When one of these was asked to write his name in Chinese, he quickly concluded that he wasn't dealing with an innocent. Regardless of phonetic inflection, the ideographs, of course, remain the same and are almost invariably written in the proper Chinese order. We found a request to write his name in this manner to be a most effective first step in establishing the respect of the older Chinese suspect.

There is another interesting variation to this Chinese name business. The middle name in a Chinese family or clan often is predetermined by the generation in which the person is born. At appropriate intervals the elders of the tribe determined these names. The words and their sequence were established by utilizing a poem or similar beautiful saying, from which five words were selected in the order in which they appeared. The first generation would have the first word, the second generation the next, until five generations had exhausted the possibility that returning to the first word would result in duplicating the name of any living person. The middle name might be conferred on the male infant. Females did not count! Sometimes, apparently, it was not bestowed or not used until the boy married. So American Chinese might have variations between the man's "baby name" and his "married name." Confusion is compounded by the fact that as Chinese became more Americanized they abandoned or modified some of these principles.

We have been discussing this subject with police for some decades. Consequently it was with a great deal of interest and pleasure that we came on an exposition of Chinese thinking and Chinese nomenclature in Michener's book, *Hawaii* (published by Random House). The America-wise Chun Fat, who had returned to China from California as a rich man after the gold rush, advises his sharp, young nephew Kee Mun Ki how a Chinese could easily get rich in the United States. In his Polonius-like instruction to the young man, he tells Kee to take advantage of certain very firm views which Americans hold about Chinese, i.e. (1) Chinese are very stupid, and (2) Chinese are very clever. When Kee pointed out that it might be very difficult to reconcile such inconsistent opinions, Chun Fat said, "Not at all. One simply must not rely on both of them with the same person at the same time." Chun Fat then illustrated that as a cook in a gold camp, he was allowed to roam the mining countryside looking for gold claims on the theory that he was just a dumb Chinaman who wouldn't know a gold prospect if he saw one. However, when full of gold location knowledge Chun Fat sought to sell claims in San Francisco, he had great luck. The Americans there recognized that someone as clever as the Chinese would be bound to have the inside track on desirable mining locations!

Then Michener described how a new Chinese immigrant to Hawaii went about to select a "family name" for the new generations to which he looked forward when his first baby was born. He consulted a wise scholar, who after suitably invoking all the signs and omens, prognosticated great things for the baby and his descendants. A poem was constructed containing in proper sequence significant words one each of which would be applied as the "family name" to each of five succeeding generations. Because of the great things which the scholar saw in prospect, the import of the name words was that the baby and his descendants would be rulers of continents!

Small wonder then that when in the Federal Bureau of Narcotics we attempted to come to effective grips with the dope dealing tongs we, for a time, followed the Giles system for indexing Chinese names. This was the procedure developed by the British Foreign Office which eliminates some of the difficulty arising from varied pronunciations and spellings. Under the Giles code each pictograph component of a name was given a numerical value. The Chinese name was then set up and filed in a sequence depending on numerals rather than on the alphabet.

We have set down the foregoing realizing that most of it is history. But we have always been intrigued with the fact that conventional American police practices were here disarmed and frustrated by differences in language and culture. For no good reason, the American who has no close acquaintance with the Chinese regards them as stoic and unemotional. George White, in his sojourn with the Hip Sing Tong, saw some refutations of this. When a tong establishment was raided by the police and its fortifications were strong enough to delay entrance so that evidence could be destroyed, the identities of the proprietors and operators of the joint were concealed; the officers endured the usual "dumb Chinaman" and "No spik English" routine, and after the chagrined officers had left, it was then a time for jollification. Selected members of the audience would assume various parts. Someone would simulate the forced entrance, the gruff and abrupt demands of the police, the obsequious rejoinders of the Chinese, the dissimulation respecting the understanding of the language, the hopeless puzzlement of the law, and its frustrated, empty-handed retreat. Sometimes members of the group would be so impressed with their own histrionic ability that they would literally roll on the floor with laughter. The American Chinese had a great sense of humor with a tremendous capacity for playing it straight. We have seen them deny completely an understanding of the English language, a position from which they quickly retreated when we began to ask intelligent questions about their identity and residence status. On the way to jail the defendant might be discussing baseball scores in the best American vernacular. However, we were not surprised to find that when, weeks or months later, the case came to trial, counsel for the defendant would solemnly ask an interpreter be sworn. The defendant sometimes, with what we thought was a discernible twinkle in his eye, would sit impassively and avail himself of the opportunity for a studied reply on cross-examination as the question went from counsel to interpreter to defendant and back.

As we said, we found it difficult because of Chinese family solidarity and prejudice to recruit Chinese narcotic agents. We thought that after World War II we would be in a much better situation. We realized that the old, single, male Chinese narcotic addict was disappearing. It was no longer possible to run opium-smoking joints without fear of prompt detection, so most of the Chinese addicts had gone to the heroin needle. They were coming to the end of a life shortened by this vicious dissipation. Few of the family man type of Chinese were addicted and practically none of the younger generation. But we knew that Chinese officers might be very effective in undercover work against narcotic violators in other segments of society. Hundreds of our younger Chinese in the armed services had been in one type of intelligence organization or another. We thought that some of these having a taste of investigative work could be easily recruited. In this we were completely mistaken, but not for the old reason. A couple of instances will illustrate what happened.

George White directed our attention to a young Chinese who had been a brilliant operator with him in the OSS. The young man was most polite and appreciative and honored by our notice, he said. However, within a few weeks he expected to go to the Orient as a representative of a large American corporation. His initial net earnings would be in the $10,000 per annum area (circa 1946). As much as he liked police work, he felt it impossible to make the financial sacrifice. . . . A variation on this theme was a bright young Chinese from Boston who had been in one of the Army intelligence organizations. He too was polite and apologetic. "You see, the family owns these three restaurants in Boston. Father thinks I am of an age when I should be taking some of the responsibility for the business off his shoulders. . . ." Since we had some conception of the gross which these establishments represented, we had to agree that perhaps father did need a little help. Eventually we managed to recruit a fine Chinese officer or two. But the net result of our experiences in this field was to give us a firm conviction that the future of the Chinese in the United States as a law-abiding pillar in his community is assured.

THE SICILIAN MAFIA

No story of the narcotic enforcement problem in the United States today would be complete without mention of the Mafia. Any full history of this phenomenon is beyond the purview of this paper. Books have been written on the Mafia. One of the best on the Mafia operation in America is *Brotherhood of Evil: Mafia*, by Frederic Sondern, Jr. (Farrar, Straus and Cudahy). This should be read by any serious student of criminology.* We can only briefly summarize.

The Mafia is usually represented as an organization of great mystery and secrecy. Of secrecy certainly there is much; of mystery very little. The Mafia had its origin in the Sicilian mountains. As was once more demonstrated in World War II, Sicily is a stepping stone for the invaders of Europe. Continually overrun through the centuries by foreigners, the Sicilian developed a constitutional antagonism toward foreign government and alien intrusion into his affairs. Some of the most stalwart, brave, and uncompromising sought to hold out in the highlands. Commendable patriotic impulses to resist outside law degenerated into contempt and resistance to all law in some areas. When the alien invader was not present the Sicilian resented government from the Italian mainland. He had many other things to resent, political and economic, including exploitation of a poverty-stricken countryside by absentee landlords. So we find clans of independent and self-reliant Sicilian mountaineers working together in outlaw bands. As reasons or excuses for criminal conduct we find overtones of patriotism, i.e. independence for Sicily—"Sicily for the Sicilians." There was a Robin Hood motif—steal from the rich landlord and distribute the wealth (just a little) to the poor. To their credit it must be said that the Mafiosi in Sicily have been consistently anti-Communist. This was probably for no other reason than that they correctly evaluated another muscle organization.

Naturally, rejection of constituted authority is a serious business. It is one in which the participants must play for keeps with their lives at stake. Since the Mafiosi were greatly in the minority, they would have to substitute efficient procedures, guile, stratagems, courage, and endurance for force of numbers. Under these conditions over the generations these clans developed some very effective modus operandi for the successful perpetration of crime. In Sicily these crimes were generally kidnapping for ransom, extortion under threat of kidnapping, killing, or maiming, or extortion under threat of burning or other destruction of property. (Ameri-

---

*See also *The Informer in Law Enforcement* by Harney and Cross, Chapter 6.

Specialized Illegal Activities: Groups in Narcotic Traffic 273

can police won't have to scratch too deeply here to see our own "protection" racket.)

The Mafia in Sicily relied heavily on the solidarity of its members to cover up crimes. When there are no witnesses there are no successful prosecutions. The penalty for informing, for failure to carry out orders, even for carelessness leading to unfortunate consequences, was death. Assassins were selected by lot or similar assignment, so the victim generally would be struck down by someone having no discernible motive and at a time when persons having a motive might be fortified with a perfect alibi. Here we have the precursor of the American professional killer, the "torpedo" or, in another variation, the one-way ride in which the victim is killed by his "friends."

So much in short summary on the rise of an organization in the Sicilian mountains, primarily of interrelated families; on organization of no written rules or bylaws, no rituals (except as they might appear as local idiosyncrasies). But the Mafia was a tightly knit, tremendously effective combination for criminal purposes, cemented by a history of generations of outlawry, further buttressed by ties of kinship, and kept in order by the iron discipline of bloodshed for any serious infraction of the code. Among the more significant aspects of that code was the precept that the Mafioso was completely above and independent of the law. In no instances should he have recourse to constituted authority. The Mafia would be the law. One subtle and valuable aspect of this code is the principle that the injured party not show resentment for injury (Why indicate to the prosecutor a motive?). Furthermore, the Mafiosi need not necessarily be in a hurry for vengeance. Certainty of retaliation, not speed, was the thing. Let the offender live for a while. Let him live in fear perhaps. But when the passage of time had lulled that fear and made him careless, that was time enough to strike him down, an easy victim, a warning to all those who would dare cross the Mafia. But this retribution in point of time would be far enough removed from the actual offense so that reasons and motives would be obscured.

The Mafia, under one guise or another, has long been known to the American police. Some Mafiosi came in the natural tide of immigration. Some came for a specific reason—one jump ahead of the police who may have wanted them for capital crimes. Looseness in our earlier immigration procedures made America a haven for these criminals. In the United States the Mafiosi usually concentrated in the larger cities and in communities where they felt at home among non-Mafiosi Sicilians or other Italians. In the earlier days their depredations were mostly against fellow countrymen, with kidnapping and extortion, "black hand," being the principal crime.

One of the earlier and most sensational manifestations of the Mafia was in the killing of Chief of Police Hennessey in New Orleans in 1890 because Hennessey had been too active in his collaboration with the police of the Kingdom of Italy in returning fugitive murderers to the justice of the Old Country. The Mafia threw its crudest muscle into the defense of the accused. It apparently was partially successful in intimidating a jury. Public outrage was great. A disgraceful lynching episode ensued. Later the Mafia was very much in the public eye when a New York police detective named Joseph Petrosino, who had been active in operations against the Mafia in this country and in collaborating with Italian police, was assassinated in Palermo, Sicily, in connection with a visit to that country in the course of this collaboration, in 1909. From time to time in the early 1900's the Mafia came to the attention of the Post Office Inspection Service when occasionally the mails were used in its extortion attempts. The advent of Prohibition was a great financial boon to the Mafia. The "businessmen" of the liquor underworld, the bootleg barons, in their struggle for territory had need for disciplined and effective "troops." The Mafosi represented a superlative group for the purpose.

The Mafia also became acquainted with the possibilities of the illicit narcotic traffic during the Prohibition regime and when Prohibition went out they stayed with narcotics in addition to their wider fields of gambling, extortion, and Shylocking. In the narcotic traffic the Mafioso proved to be a dedicated man. When certain names appeared with impressive regularity, Commissioner Anslinger directed the compilation of a file to ascertain what interlocking relationships might be found. One of us then in the FBN had a secretary, the late Edna P. Maxon, a dedicated woman to whom this work had a particular appeal. As much as that of any one person, the efforts of this little 95-pound woman with Emmett (Doc) Corrick (Mails, Files and Records, FBN) contributed to the discomfiture of the Mafia. These files were much of the basis on which the Kefauver Committee dragged the Mafia from obscure shadows and gave it some badly needed publicity.

Of somewhat more recent history, of course, was the so-called Mafia meeting at Apalachin, New York, in 1957 and the subsequent conviction (since reversed) in New York in January 1960, of twenty of those who had been in attendance at the Apalachin meeting. Incidentally, the record of the hearings before the McClellan Committee (Part 32) is, in our opinion, one of the finest pieces of unconscious humor in Congressional investigation literature. John C. Montana, once man of the year in Buffalo, gives a deadpan account of his adventures while seeking repairs for his automobile and while drinking tea at Barbara's Apalachin hideout. The poignant exchanges between hoodlum Montana and Committee Counsel Robert Kennedy as to the difficulties which these wealthy men were having with minor mechanical failures of their deluxe, new Cadillacs is another demonstration that even the rich have troubles! One of the objectives of the Apalachin meeting, it is believed, was to withdraw members of that organization from participation in the illicit narcotic traffic, presumably because of the continuing spotlight focused on it by the Treasury Department. Narcotic police need not be too optimistic about the complete withdrawal of Mafiosi from this field. If drug traffic is not to be recommended as an organization project, there will undoubtedly be some Mafiosi so dedicated to this way of life that they will carry on as individuals. We could hope that with the passage of time the Mafia might lose some of its deadly efficiency as a criminal device in this country. As the old men die off, we could hope to find a younger generation taking more chances and disregarding the fundamental precepts and discipline which made the Mafia the sinister force which it has been.

There has been a strangely emotional quality about the evaluation of the Mafia in some police circles. There has been some tendency to decry it as nonexistent, to doubt it as a ghost or a phantom. That doubt, it seems, is forever dispelled by the November 1957, Apalachin conference of the Mafia, where ghosts materialized as some threescore very live and agitated hoodlums, who, for all that came past the plea of "Fifth Amendment," were out in the country waiting for a streetcar.

Some people in the law enforcement field have questioned why the Mafia was not subject to penetration from the outside. These persons disregard the obvious, that to be a member of the group one had to be born into it, and that, in effect, the only way to leave it was to die. The Mafia was a recognized fact of life in its native Sicily. It has been minutely described in decisions of the Supreme Court of Italy and by many responsible writers. It is still recognized as a present fact of life there. Some time ago, some pro-Communist politicians in Sicily were caught "in flagrante" buying Assembly votes. These ascribed their discomfiture to a "Mafia plot" (*Time Magazine*, February 29, 1960). Despite such evidences, there still was a disposition in some quarters in this country to deny that the American resident Mafioso utilized the hard-learned lessons of his Sicilian Mafia tradition.

It has been interesting to note a rather clever scheme to dissipate suspicion by attempting extension of guilt.* Part of this is the assertion that reference to the Mafia implies anti-Sicilian or anti-Italian bias. This is like saying that because a few residents of the southern Appalachians have for generations been dedicated to moonshining then all Southerners are liquor excise tax evaders! Following the Apalachin arrests and preceding the trial, apparently there was a studied campaign on the motif that persons intent on prosecuting the Mafiosi were anti-Italian. In the saloon press there suddenly appeared a rash of comments on that general theme. Some stories and editorial comment appeared in more staid areas. One might be justified in concluding that this had long-range defense possibilities for the Apalachin mob. One might also surmise that behind it was the fine Sicilian hand of such a "publicist" as the man who came to dinner with Frank Costello just before the most recent attempt to assassinate that notorious gangster. If so, "operation spread-the-blame" was unsuccessful. Here again is a curious incident of how history may repeat itself. Few policemen of this generation will remember the "Molly McGuires." These were Irish miners in the

---

*This continues intermittently to this date.

Pennsylvania coal fields who, about the 1870's after enduring oppression and discrimination, took the law into their own hands with dynamitings and killings. While these terrorists represented just a small proportion of the Irish miners, some contemporary newspaper writers soon were attempting to include as Molly McGuires all of the Ancient Order of Hibernians. To read this in some old files was just a little disconcerting to one of the authors, scores of whose forebears were prominent in that respectable Irish nationalistic and anti-British association.

Citing only Robin Hood and Jean Lafitte there is romantic appeal in the notion of the bad man doing good for his people's sake or his country's weal, and this always makes a good story. And so it is respecting the Mafia, particularly in the tale of the sought for and realized desire of the Mafia leader Salvatore Lucania (Lucky Luciano) to attain deportation to Italy, thereby gaining release from a long term in a New York penitentiary. Allegedly this favor was in return for services by the noble outlaw in facilitating allied military landings in Sicily in World War II, by intelligence obtained secretly through the Mafia.

Recently this story has been retold by two very prominent writers in the crime field, Hank Messick in *Lansky* (G. P. Putnam's Sons, New York, 1971) and Gay Talese in *Honor Thy Father* (World Publisher, Times Mirror, New York, 1971) who seem to give it a limited credence. Granting that there are circumstances which could seem to support the story we do not think there is factual basis for it. We had a considerable part in the Kefauver hearing when the matter was looked into closely with all the power then wielded by a U. S. Senate investigating committee under Senator Estes Kefauver. Col. George Hunter White, then a District Supervisor in the Federal Bureau of Narcotics, with a long wartime experience in the OSS, concluded that this was an invention, contrived at low level and accepted by nonreluctant higher-ups when they were convinced that deportation was a good way to save New York taxpayers penitentiary room and board money and to rid the country of Lucania's presence. White was able to report with some assurance that there was no information in the intelligence community to support the yarn. Of course the Federal Bureau of Narcotics has the outstanding record for bringing about the deportation of

Mafiosi. But when possible we chose to deport them after they had completed a penitentiary sentence. We had reason to conclude that Lucania's presence in Italy contributed knowhow to the illicit "milking" of heroin from Italian pharmaceutical works after the end of World War II and its smuggling into this country.

The Mafia has been the most formidable obstacle to law enforcement ever to come to the attention of these writers. Concrete accomplishments against these people require a tremendous output of investigative time and energy. Too often the best-planned compaigns have been barren of results. Too often has the Mafia been able to retaliate in the successful killing of an informer. But the work has had its compensations. It is some satisfaction to know that we have had a small part in the campaigns of the Federal Bureau of Narcotics against the Mafia. This little (less than 300 men) agency had convicted and its evidence caused the deportation of more Mafiosi than all other law enforcement agencies combined.

One of the incidental but very real satisfactions has been the opportunity to work in the Federal Bureau of Narcotics with its agents of Sicilian extraction who are some of the finest law enforcement officers in the world.

Addendum

We think it a matter of grave current concern to general law enforcement in this country that we are now seeing dangerous offshoots from groups originally formed for highly idealistic purposes. A few of these seem to be resorting to crimes—murder, extortion, robbery, drug traffic, and the like—for their own special purposes.

11

THE FORTIFIED ROOM

As with gambling, the narcotic traffic is one of those crimes in which sometimes the violators may elect to use what may be termed a fortified room. This is simply a euphemistic designation for a premises used as a base for criminal operations in which the criminal seeks to obtain the protection of locks, bolts, bars, and similar obstructions to enable him to successfully carry out his illegal operations.

To the narcotic offender the fortification of a premises is intended primarily to give him these advantages: (1) the time to destroy evidence of the commission of the crime, i.e. narcotic drugs, also possibly cutting and mixing apparatus and other incidentals, together with any records, notes, or other writings on the premises which might be incriminating; (2) the time and opportunity to permit the escape of violators on the premises by the use of concealed escape routes, or to take steps to confuse the identification of culprits on the premises. Bearing this in mind, it will be apparent that the approach of the law enforcement officers to this suspected narcotic cache, or "pad," may be different in many respects from the procedure taken where the intention is only to arrest a fugitive or other felon when it is suspected that he is hiding out, or can be found in a certain location. In the latter case, the accent is on the safe and sure securing of a person. In the narcotic case, while there must be regard for this, there must be emphasis on the swift approach, the prompt entry before evidence can be disposed of. We want to catch the culprit "with the goods." Therefore, the narcotic officer may seem to assume a few more physical hazards and take less precautions for his own safety in making the approach. This is counterbalanced by the fact that, although there have been tragic exceptions, we will find that when we near his premises the narcotic dealer will be engrossed principally with the attempt to destroy or conceal physical evidence rather than with physical resistance to the officer.

TYPES OF FORTIFICATIONS

The type of fortification will range from the very simple to the very complex. Obviously, the simplest obstruction we might find is an ordinary door, locked against casual opening. We can go from there in stages to a very complicated type of protection. The ordinary door fastener may be further reinforced by bolts, or by special devices like chain locks. Much further protection against a speedy forced entrance is obtained by barring the door. This type of protection may range from a simple crossbar to several of these, which may be supplemented by vertical, or crisscross barring. The construction of the door itself will vary considerably. There is a simple panel type, which is pretty much on the flimsy order. For this there might be substituted heavy doors of solid construction or rather elaborately built special doors. These might be in the nature of sheet iron covered construction which we usually look for in a fire door. Effective and deceptive is an innocent-looking type of door in which a sheet of metal is sandwiched between wood.

A further elaboration of door construction may be found in the old-time icebox, or in the conventional safety vault type of door construction. This door, swinging outward and fitting snugly into its frame, gives great resistance to battering from the outside. Then, we may find a reliance on a series of doors, a system comparable to submarine air locks series; when the outer door is entered there is another one or two barring passage.

Naturally, a fortified room is as strong as its weakest point. Sometimes criminals may put considerable time and effort into strengthening doors, at the same time displaying an ostrich-like disregard as to weakness in wall construction. Particularly in modern building, wall paneling is likely to be frail. A strong door may be immediately adjacent to a plasterboard or similarly constructed wall, which can be quickly broken through. Even brick walls can sometimes be readily broken down by battering. However, we will find the careful schemer behind walls of some substance.

It is likely that he also will have taken due precautions respecting other openings. The windows may be barred or, if not, protected by heavy mesh or otherwise. For reasons of seclusion and privacy, racketeers sometimes prefer to locate fortified rooms on top floors and this sometimes permits of a rooftop exit. Unless it is adequately protected, we may turn this exit into a ready means of entrance. Sometimes violators will make simple mistakes in the setting up of a fortified room; sometimes a transom above a door can be readily forced; sometimes hinges which can be easily stripped or unbolted will be placed on the wrong side of the door.

PLANNING THE ENTRANCE

One of us (M.L.H.) can attribute his most acutely embarrassing episode in a long investigative career to a failure to anticipate the fortified room.

In the waning years of the Prohibition Era we were in the Twin Cities, working on a combination alcohol and income tax case in which members of the so-called "syndicate" were involved. We got some evidence on a man named Conrad Althen who, reports had it, was some kind of a business manager in the crime syndicate. Con Althen was a successful golf pro; however, he had acquired rich tastes including one for expensive women, which made his ordinary earnings inadequate. He had had a brush or two with the police. We had evidence through which we obtained a preliminary indictment on Althen. Armed with a bench warrant, we went out to make the arrest with, of course, some hope that this sort of a fellow might eventually open up on some of the higher-ups.

The actual serving of a bench warrant, as was the routine in those days, was the province of a deputy marshal. Investigator Jimmy Hitsman and one of us went along.

Con was living in a scattered suburban area of South Minneapolis. Lulled with the complacency of many a routine foray, we figured that at about daybreak, seven o'clock of an early winter morning, a late sleeper like Althen would be just another pushover. A quick look at the house disclosed poor prospects at the back door; there was a rather formidable storm shed indicating we would have to get through a couple of doors, at least. Jimmy was posted to watch the rear. We went up the innocent-looking front stoop, rang the bell, and then knocked and demanded entry in the name of the law.

The aging marshal's ears may not have been as sensitive as ours then were. On our first announcement, we heard sounds of ominous activity which convinced part of the team that we were not going to be let in. The marshal said, "Take it easy. After all, I'm responsible."

Finally, when the delay became intolerable, it was suggested to the marshal that he go to the back door and send Jimmy up front. That was a mistake.

While Jimmy was coming, we went to work barehanded on the rather innocent-appearing storm door, resilient boards nailed in a solid sheet, opening outward, fastened from the inside with a special hook, and with a hasp handle on the outside. When we attacked this with a strength latent from early cow milking days, the hasp came off, leaving an intact door. By the time Jimmy had run to the automobile, extracted a tire iron, and we had pried open the storm door, broken the glass in an inner door, and reached through and turned a lock, some time had elapsed. As we entered the front door there was a terrific crash of breaking glass at the rear. The athletic Althen had thrown a chair through the back window, followed it in person, had bounded past the astonished marshal and, when we saw him, had a good 50-yard lead, leaping over some adjacent fences. As we dashed through the house, there was an odor of burning paper and a few charred scraps on a gas burner.

Feeling that we were no match for Con's agility on foot, we decided to pursue in the automobile; in this scattered settlement Con could not get far, we thought. That was another mistake. Our man disappeared completely. (It was as if the earth had swallowed him up.) Later we learned that as he rounded the corner of a neighboring house, a milkman was driving by. Con dove into the milk wagon with a story—his wife had had an attack, he gasped, with a request that he be driven posthaste to a suburban drug store. Some way we completely overlooked that milk wagon with Con lying exhausted on the floor.

When we got back to Althen's house where we had left the marshal on watch, in addition to the useless char, we found some cryptic documents which were incomplete keys to fragments of books of account, which we later found in a downtown hotel room office. But altogether these records were too incomplete to be of much significance. We never saw Con Althen again—alive. A couple of days later, his body riddled with .45 slugs was found in a roadside ditch in nearby Dakota county.

It was that way, as we recall it, that we first became acquainted with a bright young lawyer just making his start in public life— Dakota County Attorney Harold Stassen, later to become Governor of Minnesota and a prominent figure in the national scene.

The Althen killing, a typical Prohibition Era gang ride, was never solved. The believable street gossip was that after Con escaped from us he went to his principals in the syndicate for "getaway money"; his ideas as to how substantial this payment should be apparently differed radically from theirs. After some acrimonious discussions, but apparently an acceptance of his terms on the mob's part, Con was directed to report someplace to be paid off— in copper-jacketed bullets.

Some members of the syndicate were successfully prosecuted on liquor charges, and later some income tax cases were developed. But, over the years, this has been a matter of acute professional chagrin. If only we had made a prompt entry and had grabbed Con before he got his trousers on he would, perhaps, today be a healthy ex-convict. Members of the syndicate would have received more of a comeuppance than they did. For want of a nail, the horse was lost, etc.

As in any military or law enforcement operation, a primary consideration is prior intelligence. Naturally, the first thing which would be valuable to know is that we are, in fact, to encounter locks and bars in the room which we expect to enter. We then can approach the job mentally conditioned and, to the degree that circumstances allow, properly equipped physically. We can testify from personal experience that there is no more futile feeling than that of standing in front of a seemingly impregnable fortress, surprised and barehanded. Sometimes such an unexpected denouement is unavoidable. Often it can be anticipated that fortifications might be expected. Often we will know that we have a hard nut to crack. If this is a situation where we can somewhat control a time schedule, as is often the case in narcotic investigations, there are certain obvious things which we will do.

By preliminary scouting and observations we will ascertain as much as we can of the construction and layout of the room, with particular attention to its weakness. We will try to locate lookouts, hidden exits, and the operation of warning devices, if any. This will include due regard for determining whether avenues of approach are secure. The approach should offer the greatest concealment and the least possibility of premature warning to the violator. The identification and connections of possible violators on the premises should be ascertained as definitely as possible. This will serve many purposes. It will aid us in properly apprehending the right people, if both customers and operators are on the premises. Attempts to confuse in this situation once was a primary tactic of some of the Chinese tongs operating opium-smoking rooms or heroin-shooting pads. The Chinese assumed, apparently with some justification, that all Chinese would look somewhat alike to Caucasian police. So while there was the usual delay in parley at the door and in bringing siege weapons into operation, the boss might quickly change coats and identity with the floor swabber or dishwasher. Eventually, we might arrive at the police station with a very inconsequential prisoner, the principals having been permitted to depart as "innocent bystanders" or just customers.

Prior intelligence will aid in future apprehension if a violator should escape. It may assist in obtaining entrance to the premises by ruse. As complete information as possible concerning the interior of the fortified room should be obtained with a particular object of knowing in advance what methods of destroying or concealing evidence are available.

We emphasize the importance of obtaining prior intelligence because this is a field which, in practice, is often very much neglected. The officers are preoccupied with the fact that there are narcotics on the premises, or that narcotics were purchased from the premises. They may have a witness—sometimes quite an unwilling one—who is vouching for the fact. The fact being the justification for a proposed search and seizure, the officers naturally concentrate on it and may neglect or overlook the corollaries which will make the raid a real success. Close attention to these details is necessary, even when the information is supplied by a police officer who may be working undercover. One of the prime objectives of the raid may be to secure competent evidence on a search, thereby making it unnecessary to expose the identity of the undercover man. In such cases, we are likely to have good information as to the identity and importance of suspects on the premises. Many officers, however, will fail to make acute observations as to the physical aspects of the fortified room, as they relate to a successful entrance and search. Particularly, it should be borne in mind that warning devices are not likely to be immediately obvious. Police may be too likely to think of the one-way mirror as a device for police operation, or something by which lady apartment dwellers, by peeping out, may frustrate the too persistent efforts of the Fuller Brush man. We first became acquainted with the fact that there was a mirror through which one could see from the reverse side when it was planted in a door of a fortified room as a lookout against us. Actually, lookout devices may be very simple, very unobtrusive, and yet very effective. They may be nothing more than practically unnoticeable gimlet holes in what looks like the solid wall at the top of a staircase. The modern operator will be likely to use simple electrical devices activated by the pressure of the feet of approaching visitors on floor or staircase. In some cases, he might be expected to use the principle of the electric eye.

The astute officer will always have in mind that any system of physical protection is usually no better than the efficiency of its human operators. Preliminary undercover operation, or other inside information, might tell us when watchmen and lookouts presumed to be alert are "out for coffee," on the telephone getting a bet down, or similarly distracted. Prior observation on such aspects is invaluable.

ENTRANCE BY RUSE

Our observations may convince us that we should make our penetration by ruse. Entrance by ruse is just as good a tactic as it was when Agamemnon's Greeks "abandoned" the Trojan Horse with its belly full of Greek soldiers on the plains of Troy, to be towed within their indestructible walls by the curious and unsuspecting Trojans. The ruse might be very simple. Someone may have supplied us with a password. The most formidable door may swing open for some simple abracadabra like John-sent-me; sometimes sentry personnel, simply are sufficiently careless so that an officer may ghost-in on the lee side of a substantially built accepted habitué. And, sometimes, our intelligence will have disclosed a series of physical manipulations of signalling devices which indicate that we are accepted customers.

Classic in operations of this sort is the entrance by the undercover man, knowingly or unwittingly, introduced and vouched for by one of the regular customers. If his incognito is expendable we can, of course, depend on him to open the door for us on the right split second when the raiders arrive. As often is the case, he may not be considered expendable and we will have to resort to other stratagems. Used so frequently that it may be overdone, but still apparently effective, are such ruses as claiming to be a telegraph or special delivery messenger; sometimes, a pose as a utility representative is effective. We know an incident in which some ingenious narcotic agents in New York attained unobstructed entrance into a premises by pretending that they had had a slight accident with the operator's parked car and were coming up to adjust any damage. The telephone sometimes may be employed effectively to notify the occupants that some legitimate business caller is to be ex-

Figure 23. Attack on "John Brown's Fort" at Harper's Ferry. The celebrated incident of the capture of John Brown at Harper's Ferry, Va., in 1859, illustrates many of the principles of a police action against persons holding out in a barricaded room. Brown, with several of his armed followers and with prisoner-hostages, had "holed up" in a brick and stone fire house equipped with stout doors. The defenders could subject attackers to gunfire over only a limited field. However, the attackers could not use gunfire without risk of wounding hostages. Here, after a parley at the door under a flag of truce, "Jeb" Stuart had signalled by hat on ground that Brown would not surrender. Marines had attacked the doors with sledges but found them unbreakable. Lt. Israel Green directed a squad of his marines to pick up a fire ladder lying near by and employ it as a battering ram. Shown is the squad withdrawing the ram from the aperture smashed in the door and Green leading the attackers through to capture Brown. From an original sketch by Dorothea Dorge Kreitner as suggested by contemporary accounts. (Marine Corps Historical Reference Series No. 10. U.S. Marine Corps, Washington, D.C.).

The Fortified Room

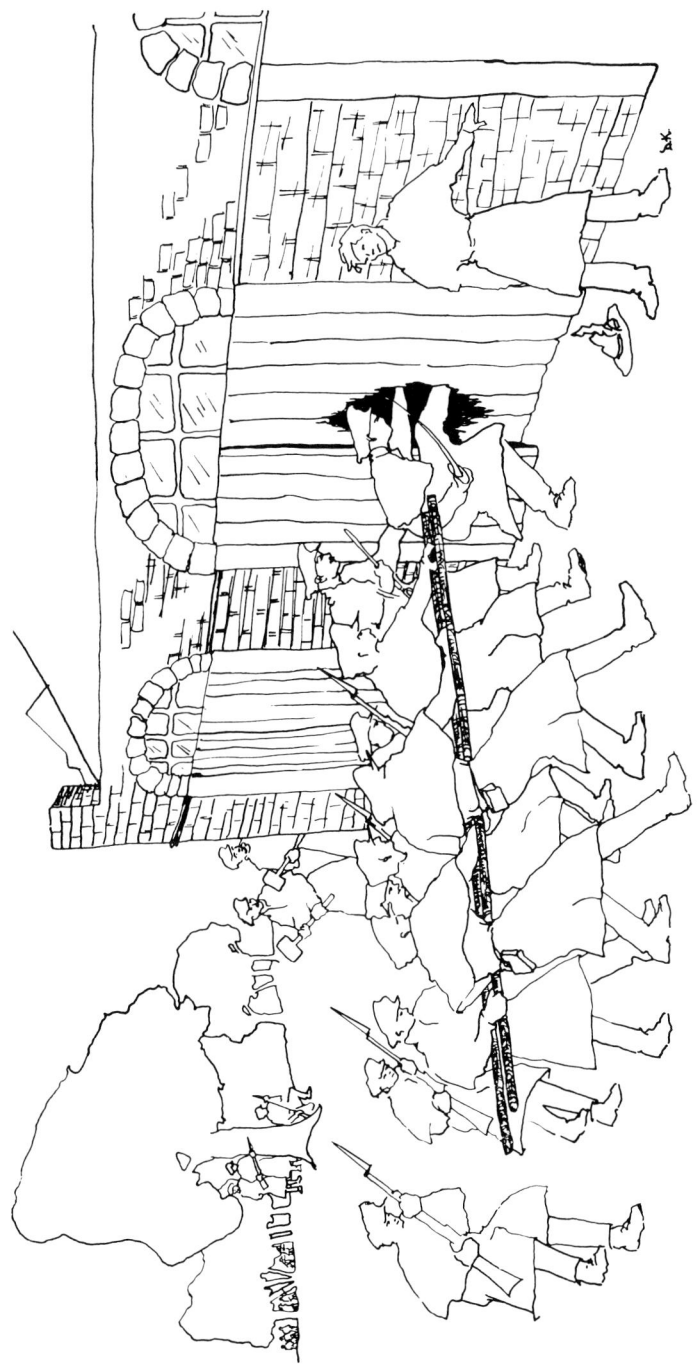

pected. A ring on the telephone on the split second when entrance is to be made is also good tactics, since it will tend to immobilize one occupant. We have known resourceful officers to bring about the quiet opening of a barred door simply by pouring a little water under the sill. When the curious occupant opened up to see where the small flood was coming from, he was a sitting duck.

ENTRANCE BY FORCE

If we decide that the fortified premises is not susceptible to entrance by ruse or that, for some other reason, it should be forced, we should make some careful plans. We should consider that we have the proper equipment. The ex-footballer can burst through most doors with a shoulder block. If he has been sitting in squad cars too long, he might resort to a tossed buttock. Since he may have great weight on this center of gravity, this is a fundamental approach. The foot is a splendid weapon for opening locked doors, although the slang phrase of "kicking in a door" is, of course, inaccurate. The leg is used in the same manner as a straight left (or right) is delivered with the arm, the door being hit with the flat of the foot with some emphasis toward the heel. There should be some care in aiming; if the foot encounters a knob, there may be some breakage. Naturally, younger members of the raiding squad should be given these honors. They are less likely to wake up the next day with strains and pains.

However, when the degree of fortification exceeds that which might successfully be met with nature's weapons, we should have the proper mechanism available. The first admonition here is a *Don't*. Do not, under any circumstances, attempt to shoot off locks. We have sometimes seen foolish young officers attempt this. Sometimes this might be successful; we know of several instances in which there was tragedy. An infant was killed in its mother's arms by an officer firing through a door under these circumstances. Spattering and ricocheting bullets have injured members of the raiding party. Here, his companions are likely to be in more danger than the trigger-happy pistol wielder. We know of one incident in the southern hills where an officer fired all his available ammunition unsuccessfully trying to break a lock on a root cellar door. Finally, he had to get a bar and pry the door open. When he did, his temperature dropped considerably to find that some of his ammunition had plowed harmlessly through a couple of cases of dynamite stored in the root cellar.

Sledges or hammers might be acceptable equipment for breaking into the fortified room. Generally, we prefer to shorten sledge handles somewhat—in the interest of easy portability. The handle however, should be long enough to permit of a vigorous swing. One of the oldest and most effective siege weapons is a battering ram, the capacity for destruction of which is all but forgotten in these modern days. At Harper's Ferry, Virginia, while an "army" of militia and Colonel Robert E. Lee stood by, with John Brown holding hostages under death threat in the Harper's Ferry fire house, a young lieutenant of the United States Marines found the key. First unsuccessful with sledges, his squad picked up a heavy fire ladder, drove this impromptu battering ram through the fire house door, rushed into the opening, and disarmed and captured Brown and his confederates with few casualties to the raiders and no harm to the hostages. Many ingenious battering rams have been devised. This weapon has some limitations. It should be long enough to accommodate adequate manpower, three or four or more men, but short enough to be reasonably portable and, of course, heavy enough to deliver a powerful blow. Another thing to be considered in the use of a battering ram is that one of any great length may be useless where it must be employed in narrow halls at an angle. We should always keep in mind the simple laws of physics. One of us recalls that we devised a very splendid weapon, short but of great weight, with adequate handholds, suitable for battering in a narrow hallway. The heavy scrap eye-bolt from which it was constructed was left in its natural state. The first thrust against the door produced a tremendous impact which drove the bolt through some inches of wood, where it stuck firmly in the still intact door until the proprietor of the joint, all evidence being disposed of, opened up and blandly inquired, "Why don't you ring the bell? You know you boys are always welcome." Thereafter some red-faced officers saw to it that a broad nose was welded to the battering ram, which then proved to be indeed a fearsome weapon.

The battering ram is, of course, primarily useful for breaking through a wall or breaking open a door which opens inward. To neutralize battering rams, sledges, or other blows from the outside, the criminal often will resort to the icebox door which swings out-

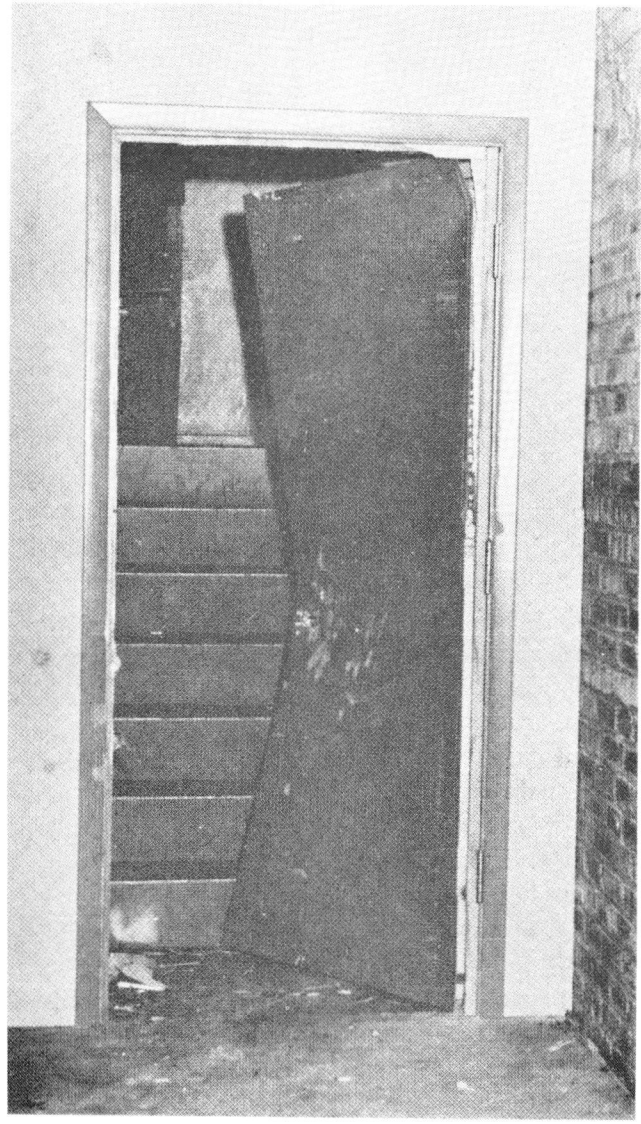

Figure 24. The effect of the hand battering ram. Metal sheath door broken and entrance gained. Photo courtesy State's Attorney of Cook County, Illinois.

The Fortified Room

ward, as we have mentioned. Battering from the outside only closes this door more firmly. Such a door is susceptible to quick opening by a sharp weapon which exerts a prying force. This might be a device similar to the usual wrecking bar. A most effective weapon is the pointed pick of the conventional fireman's ax, driven into the door crack at the vicinity of the lock. It is likely to spring it open quickly. An even better weapon, because of greater strength and leverage, is the conventional pick of the pick-and-shovel gang. With

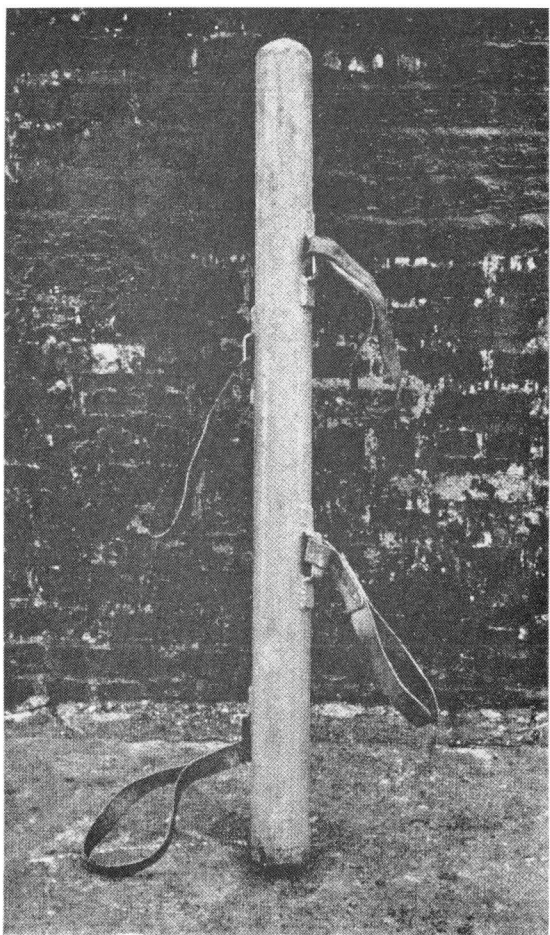

Figure 25. Hand battering ram. A powerful weapon against the fortified criminal. Weight 75 lbs., length 5 feet, it is 5 inches in diameter. The nose solid steel. Photo courtesy State's Attorney, Cook County, Illinois.

perhaps a handle shortened somewhat for convenience, this is a weapon which will pry most any door designed to open outward. Police supply houses sell special pry bars. When time is not critical, there are door frame spreaders, sometimes used by burglars, which, operating on the jack principle, can be used to force the door jambs apart until the locks disengage. An axe may be particularly useful where obstacles are constructed of wood. In emergencies, small tools like screwdrivers or automobile jack handles may be effective.

Figure 26. The battering ram, manned, being used to gain entrance into a building. Photo courtesy State's Attorney, Cook County, Illinois.

Where there is an opportunity for guile and stealth, locks might be picked or wax impressions made for the manufacture of keys.

Methods of forcibly entering into a premises, of course, can be as variable as the imagination and intelligence of the officers confronted with this problem. And the matter of using tear gas occasionally comes up for consideration. We have never thought of using it in a narcotic raid, unless the prime object is to secure the person of a dangerous felon. There are too many incidental disadvantages to the successful search to warrant the use of tear gas as a regular operating device.

The Fortified Room

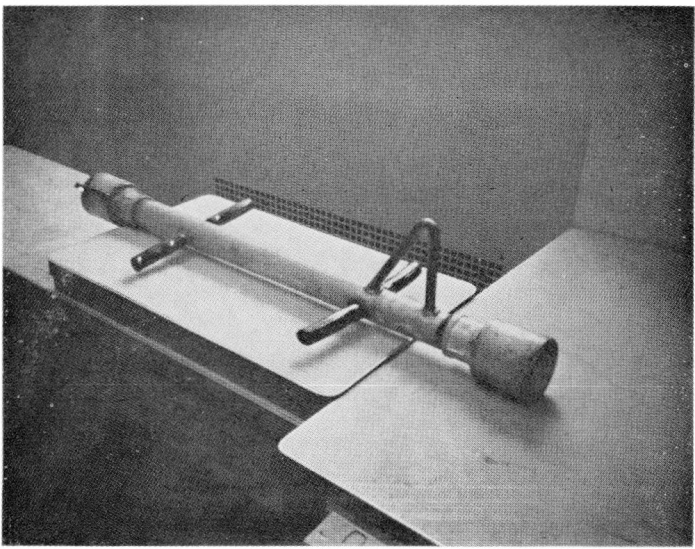

Figure 27. Battering ram of another type. This weighs about 55 lbs. and is about 4 feet long. In some cases it could be more maneuverable than ram pictured in Figure 25, more quickly directed and utilizing the "muscle" of the officers wielding it. Photo courtesy Metropolitan Police Department, Washington, D.C.

At one of the Bureau of Narcotics training schools at Washington, we heard Oklahoma police describe a quick entry into speakeasies there. It had become the practice for illicit liquor sellers to set up in a well-fortified house on the outskirts of town where the approach of raiders could readily be noted. With this warning, and the time necessary for breaking into a formidably buttressed house, any contraband on the premises could be disposed of. The officers evolved a technique whereby they approached the premises with a tow truck, with some length of a steel cable and hook unrolled. On being refused admission, they drove a vent into the door with an axe or pick, inserted a hook, and let the heavy tow truck take it away. Sometimes the door came off, sometimes the front of the building.

From Los Angeles police we heard an account of a wagering syndicate office set up in the center of a huge, strongly constructed warehouse building, where it was assumed the police would be delayed sufficiently for the disposal of evidence. Here, the police employed a heavy-duty truck with a protected front, and with this heavily loaded for proper inertia they drove it right through the doors of the warehouse.

We recall an unusual instance in Minneapolis. There was a fortified joint—a speakeasy—on the third floor of a building. Officers had obtained a search warrant for it, but were extremely anxious that their entrance could be made before evidence was destroyed. This presented a problem, since the only feasible approach was through a whole series of heavily barred doors with alert watchmen on guard.

On a hot August night, one of the officers went by the place and saw that in the interest of ventilation a couple of windows were wide open. In a short time, fire ladders were assembled and the law desended out of the blue on the startled operators. What makes this a case of keen recollection is that found on the premises were carpenter's bills for some $1400+ for work just completed in fortifying the speak's doors. And $1400 did a lot of fortifying in those days.

It might be well to mention some minor precautions: Criminals are not always sporting in their devices. We know of protective doors through which a whole series of nails had been driven from the inside, the sharp tips projecting through just a fraction of an inch, sufficient to tear a shoulder thrown against them. There is a precaution to be taken when a door containing glass is hit, either with the body or with a weapon. The glass may splinter and fall downward in a lethal shower.

ENTRANCE AFTER DELAY

Even if the entrance is delayed somewhat, and the occupant gives a self-satisfied indication of having disposed of evidence, the thoroughness of the search should not be minimized. Often the violators will destroy small, open "working plants" of contraband and will leave intact perhaps a much larger cache, depending on skill in concealment.

We recall a case in New York in which narcotic agents fruitlessly searched the premises, in which it appeared the violators had been successful in disposing of a quantity of heroin. As they were about to leave, they were stopped by another officer—a breathless

Paul Revere, whose underground source was so good that he was able to say the searchers should look more carefully and, specifically, under the kitchen linoleum, where they found a huge plant of drugs.

Even where the violator has been successful in dumping heroin, or other soluble narcotics, into a sink or bowl, it may sometimes be possible to salvage traces by shutting off the water and retrieving the solution in the trap.

Any open fires should be examined for evidence. All persons present should be searched for contraband. In addition to a minute inspection of the premises, the outside walls and the ground outside of windows and other openings should be checked for contraband that has been suspended by cord or thrown out.

INDIRECT METHODS

Sometimes when a crime fort seems impregnable there may be indirect ways of coping with it. These methods may be more applicable to gambling joints than narcotic establishments, but they are worth mentioning. One way, of course, to close up a joint is to station policemen at the doors. An effective way might be to identify visitors and customers by jotting down license numbers and by taking photographs. In this respect the motion picture camera is particularly valuable. It conveys the sense of furtiveness which is wonderful evidence when shown. In some cases witnesses have been subpoenaed before a Grand Jury on the basis of this type of evidence and successful prosecutions have resulted.

12

THE DOG AS A NARCOTIC DETECTOR

THE USE OF ARTIFICIAL AIDS in the locating of hidden treasure has long been a preoccupation of mankind. The gamut ranges from the dowser locating water with his divining rod to the geophysical scientific teams of today sounding out petroleum-bearing structures. Over the years the United States Treasury, of course, has long been concerned with concealed treasure, commodities hidden to escape customs duties or seizure as contraband. Many procedures and instruments have been suggested, some completely bizarre and unrealistic. Some highly successful devices have been developed to meet special situations. In the narcotic field some effective use has been made of the fluoroscope principle. This, as all such devices, has its limitations as to portability in that it does not easily indicate contraband except in metallic containers, and so on. The air transport industry is now confronted with a most serious detection problem arising from suspected intentional placing of lethal explosive devices on airplanes. Capitols and courthouses are being planted with bombs.

One of the extraneous instruments used by the Treasury with success in a limited area in the detection of concealed narcotics is the dog. Incidentally, the Treasury and dogs are not strangers. One of the original regulations of the Philadelphia mint provided that a watchman with a dog make regular nightly rounds of the mint and report it safe. There was a real "watchdog of the Treasury"!

As this was written in our first edition (1961) there was a considerable revival of interest in American police circles respecting the dog as a police auxiliary. Whether or not the considerable optimism respecting dogs was fully justified remains to be seen. However there is much more use of the dog in police work today. There are special conditions and special considerations where dogs

The Dog as a Narcotic Detector

have been found to be a great asset to police operations. It may be of interest and profit to narcotic investigators to have information respecting the rather limited experience of the then Federal Bureau of Narcotics in this field, and also to be cognizant of the later and much more extensive use of the dog as a narcotic detector by the U. S. Bureau of Customs.

Beginning about 1943, the Federal Bureau of Narcotics embarked on a substantial program for the use of the dog in developing narcotic evidence. Both of the authors were closely connected to this operation. We found there was considerable literature on the use of the dog to detect narcotic smuggling violations. Most of it was of the Sunday supplement type, but an occasional detailed foreign police report was also available, which convinced us we should proceed. The Royal Canadian Mounted Police had long experience with dogs and were of great assistance. After much trial and error, we determined that dogs could be expected to furnish certain specific performance in connection with two types of drugs, opium, as such, and cannabis (marihuana, hashish, etc.). Drugs of these types possess a certain volatility and have distinct and characteristic odors. In our project we experimented with many types of dogs: German shepherds, Doberman pinschers, fox terriers, the then newly stylish Weimaraner, and others. We concluded that the individual dog's intelligence, rather than breed, should be the strongest criterion for selection.

The best individuals developed were a German shepherd and a fox terrier. The eventual development and training of a dog which would perform suitably was a long and tedious process involving the rejection of dozens as lacking in stamina, lacking interest, too nervous, too susceptible to distraction (cat chasers), or for other reasons. The proper training of the animal and the dog master requires months. This must be done together. The best working relation is developed on long association between dog and dog master. The transfer of a dog from one person to another without loss of efficiency is difficult. It is well for persons contemplating the use of dogs in any type of police work to recognize the obstacles at the outset. Bringing dogs into a law enforcement organization is not just a case of "Let's get some dogs and some men."

We concentrated primarily on a training program which would

298 *The Narcotic Officer's Notebook*

let us utilize the dog in locating opium and marihuana. The dog first was trained on scent bags containing one of these drugs. Having very firmly learned to recognize and seek out this odor, he was taught to find concealed scent bags under increasingly difficult conditions. Since secrecy is generally an attribute in criminal investigations, the dogs were taught to refrain from their normal impulse to bark when they discovered the treasure trove. Put into actual service, some of them were noted for remarkable success, particularly a fox terrier, "Wolf," and a German shepherd, "Daro." For several years these animals worked all over the country, but particularly in New York City. Sometimes they were worked as a team. In this they developed a supporting camaraderie, but there

Figure 28. Detective dog (Wolf) with seizure of opium which he pointed out when concealed behind the bulkhead of a vessel. Photo courtesy U.S. Bureau of Narcotics.

was also an occasional professional jealousy, which has its human counterpart. In one instance, in searching a ship in the New York harbor, the big German shepherd, Daro, indicated a great interest in what might be down a long shaft-way. Fearing that the big dog would become wedged in the narrow space, he was held back and the little fox terrier allowed to proceed to discover a large opium cache behind a bulkhead. For hours thereafter the insulted big dog moped.

One of the most remarkable exploits of one of these dogs was in a large tenement house. The dog was called to search the premises of an arrested suspect for a concealed narcotic cache. He found nothing in the apartment, but continued to exhibit great interest. Taken out in the hall, he finally went to a floor below and strongly indicated at an apartment door. This proved to be an ostensibly unoccupied apartment. Part of the furniture was a large imitation marble pedestal supporting a fern pot. The dog strongly indicated at this, so much so that the officers, on meticulous examination, finally discovered that the cap of the pedestal could be unscrewed —something like a piano stool. Inside the hollowed-out column was a large metal receptacle filled with smoking opium.

During the period of the middle 1940's, a considerable amount of Mexican marihuana was being brought to New York in suitcases or similar receptacles, either shipped by express or transported as unaccompanied baggage. The narcotic dogs proved particularly adept in locating such shipments. It was a most rewarding experience to see these dogs taken into a baggage room where suitcases were piled as high as a man could reach, and to watch the dog finally determine an area of suspicion. There he would indicate at the bottom of a pile. But often when the bottom suitcase was separated, he would give it an indifferent sniff and immediately return to the baggage now at the bottom. There might be several repetitions of this process until, finally, a certain suitcase in that pile reached the bottom, whereupon the dog would indicate with unmistakable agitation and interest that that was the one. From this we concluded that the odor emanating from a suitcase high in a pile probably cascaded down to the floor.

As the opium traffic diminished in the later 1940's, and the racketeers concentrated on heroin, we began to find less use and value for the detective dogs. We had not been able to train a dog satisfactorily to recognize the odor of heroin or morphine. Heroin, in transport, was then usually in relatively small amounts which often were "bellied off" or otherwise carried concealed on the person.

Court decisions restricting the right of law enforcement officers promptly to follow their noses (and, inferentially, their dogs' noses) influenced the picture, and the Federal Bureau of Narcotics abandoned its dog program.

In our first edition we had speculated that the dogs might become valuable in marihuana intercept programs on the Mexican border. We also raised the point that the tracking-type dogs occasionally might be useful such as in back-tracking a suspect to his narcotic plant. The dogs we had been using apparently had not been interested in tracking and would not satisfactorily pursue that type of scent. We speculated that dogs bred for "nose" and trained only for tracking might have more potential in this field. And we recognized that a bloodhound on a track in Times Square, or in Harlem for that matter, might not escape unwanted attention.

The more recent experience of the U. S. Bureau of Customs in the detector dog field has developed many interesting answers. In response to the alarming increase of narcotic smuggling in the late 1960's the U. S. Bureau of Customs under Commissioner Myles Ambrose augmented or developed many countermeasure programs. These included authorization to Assistant Commissioner David C. Ellis to institute a comprehensive detector dog program. Messrs. Gene McEathron and James Cheatwood, dog-handling experts of long and extensive military experience, were chosen to design and implement the Customs Bureau detector dog program. It will be seen that the results have been most impressive. As in our earlier experience with dogs in the then Bureau of Narcotics, experts in Customs concluded that dogs could be trained to respond well to cannabis (marihuana, hashish, etc.) and to opium. However they do not rule that the dogs cannot also be trained to function well with some other smuggled commodities. As we had earlier concluded, Mr. McEathron reports "the individual dog's possession of specific traits, intelligence, 'self right,' natural inquisitiveness, restless nature, etc., rather than breed should be the strongest criterion for selection."

We note in passing that most of the Customs dogs now working are German shepherds. They are, however, experimenting with some Labradors. To illustrate the complexity and detail in selecting animals for a detector dog program, Mr. McEathron states

The Dog as a Narcotic Detector 301

that the acceptance ratio is about one dog out of every 125 evaluated.

The primary objective of the detector dog program was to train dog and handler as a team in locating marihuana and hashish. As stated earlier, this is an inseparable pair. If one of the partners must be removed it is necessary for a new team to be retrained to-

Figure 29. Albert, a German shepherd, on his first assignment in Laredo, Texas, detected marihuana concealed behind the door panel of a car, and has made other seizurers. Albert was trained at the Customs Detection Dog Training Center, San Antonio, Texas, by M/Sgt. Gene McEathron, on TDY from the U. S. Air Force. Photo courtesy U. S. Bureau of Customs, Aug. 1970.

gether. In our early experience with dogs we apparently overemphasized this togetherness in sometimes making the dog a household pet. Mr. McEathron reports that most professional dog trainers who deal with working dogs, field dogs, hunting hounds, civilian and military patrol dogs, and Customs narcotic detectors believe that the best performing animal is the one who is kenneled away from his handler when not in a working environment. The dog is not given a special reward for performance, like a tidbit; his reward is association with and the approbation of his handler. His appreciation is heightened when he rejoins the handler after being kenneled away from him.

Within the first nine months after the inception of the Customs detector dog program, 25 handlers and 39 dogs were employed in the New York, Miami, Chicago, Seattle, and San Francisco mail divisions and along the Mexican border.

As of March 12, 1971, U.S. Commissioner of Customs Myles Ambrose reported that the dogs and their handlers had made 255 drug seizures since August 1970. From August 1970 through February 1971, detector dogs and their handlers had discovered

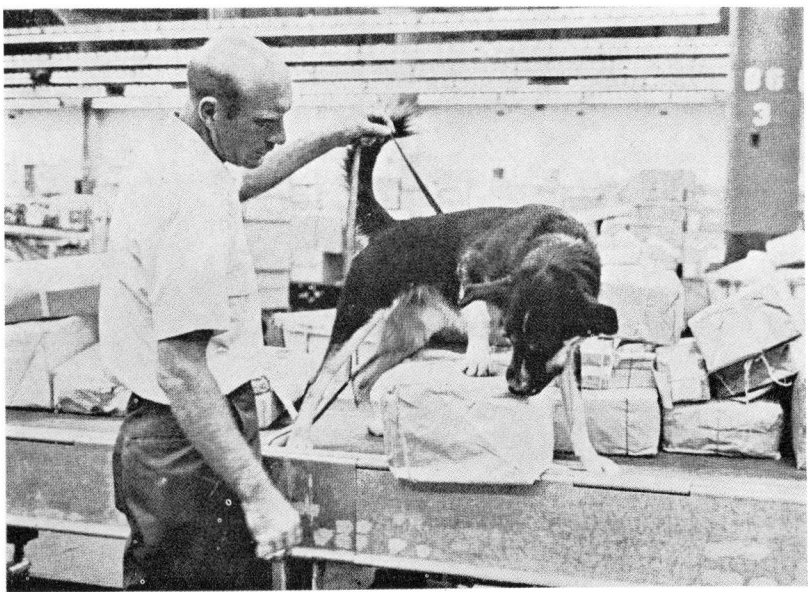

Figure 30. Kishi and Customs Dog Handler Witt detect a mail package containing marihuana. Photo courtesy U.S. Bureau of Customs, Aug. 1970.

approximately 1800 pounds of marihuana, 135 pounds of hashish, and 2600 marihuana cigarettes. During this period approximately 2,000,000 mail packages had been examined, 7000 vehicles screened, and 110,000 cargo units worked.

In Miami, Customs dog "Charo" alerted on a wooden table indicating the presence of hashish. The table was sent under surveillance to the addressee. The violator was arrested and 20 pounds of hashish were seized. On another occasion Charo, while searching a large freight warehouse, alerted on a large wooden crate which was found to contain 428 pounds of marihuana. In Laredo, Texas, detector dog "Scout" found 13.5 pounds of marihuana in a false compartment of a gasoline tank. In Nogales, Arizona, detector dog "Spunky" detected 306 pounds of marihuana that had been built into a compartment in a fiberglass boat. In San Francisco, during the months of November and December, Customs Dog Handler Harold Witt, with two dogs, detected 22 packages of marihuana weighing approximately 43 pounds, and three packages of hashish weighing about 17 pounds. Several of these finds were concealed in ceramic statues of Buddha. In El Paso, Texas, in December, Customs Dog Handler Joseph Hamilton and his dog found approximately 55 pounds of marihuana hidden under the floor-boards in the back of a truck. In Miami, during the first week of January, a detector dog found approximately 25 pounds of marihuana concealed in two stripped Cadillac automatic transmissions which were covered with Cosmoline and packed in heavy cardboard barrels. The transmissions were sent from Montego Bay, Jamaica, West Indies.

One of the detector dogs, "Kishi," showed his skill under highly publicized conditions. Because of some high-level interest in the anti-drug-abuse program, a demonstration of the detector dog was scheduled for the White House lawn. A parcel post package known to contain cannabis was "planted" among several other packages. Someone thought the dog's job should be made more intricate by augmenting the number of dummy packages and this was done from a ready source of miscellaneous, yet unscreened, packages in Customs process. In these prestigious surroundings Kishi commenced his examination of the mail. But before he came to the cannabis "plant" he indicated at one of the miscellaneous un-

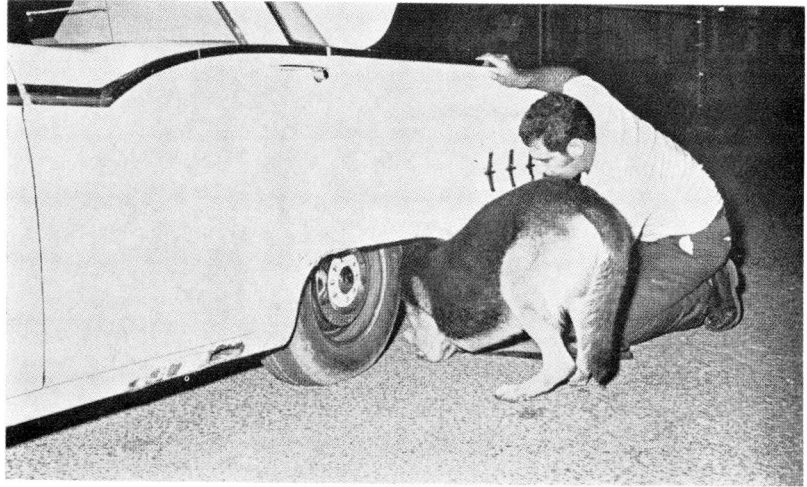

Figure 31. Jesse Sisnero, Customs Dog Handler, with Scout, conducting a search for concealed narcotics underneath a suspected vehicle at Laredo, Texas. Photo courtesy U.S. Bureau of Customs, Aug. 1970.

screened packages and it also proved to contain cannabis! After producing this unexpected dividend Kishi then proceeded to find the "planted" drug.

In October 1971 U. S. Commissioner of Customs Myles Ambrose reported that the detector dogs had been an outstanding success during their first year on the customs job. In that time their discoveries include 13,000 pounds of marihuana; 650 pounds of hashish; 4000 marihuana cigarettes; 35 pounds of opium and 300 grams of heroin. Currently there are 42 dogs and 28 handlers working at 22 ports of entry throughout the country.

At this writing the dogs are still hard at work. Our latest notice, from the San Francisco Chronicle, Nov. 19, 1971 is at that port German shepherd Pinkie sniffed out 80 pounds of hashish in a Volkswagen imported from Amsterdam the week before.

Apropos of our reference herein to the tracking dog, Mr. McEathron informs us "Since this book was published both civilian and military police train a multi-purpose dog that has a tracking capability. It is the general opinion of the instructors at the Customs Dog Training Center that the multi-purpose dog is a better detector, more highly motivated and his detection capability is easier to maintain."

No discussion of the detector dog program would be complete without mention of a hidden, unmeasurable, but logically a most substantial, dividend. That is the deterrent factor in the employment of dogs. It must deter many novice or would-be smugglers, and some professionals. The dedicated smuggler may be put to less simple, more difficult, more risky and expensive routes of entry.

Customs attributes much of its success in the establishment of its comprehensive detector dog program to assistance from the Department of Defense in acquiring and training dogs.* Through a cooperative arrangement the military provides dogs and training facilities. It also provides Customs with the names of veteran dog handlers discharged or about to be discharged from the armed services who might be interested in Customs law enforcement.

U. S. Customs has demonstrated that the detector dog is a potent weapon against the cannabis and opium smuggler, and it hopes to develop dog proficiency against other contraband such as heroin and cocaine.** It may well be, as goes the quip in its service quarterly, "Man's best friend becomes smuggler's worst enemy."

---

*Customs Today, Winter 1971.

**One pound of pure cocaine was discovered in a hollowed out book by a Customs drug-detecting dog and his Customs dog handler in Los Angeles on May 17, 1972 while checking a mail shipment. A suspected smuggler was later arrested. In making this announcement on May 26, 1972, U.S. Commissioner of Customs Vernon D. Acree stated that Customs dogs can positively identify cocaine and heroin regardless of purity or disguising odors. The special procedures used in training the dogs prevent them from becoming addicted to drugs they are seeking.

13

THE INFORMER IN NARCOTIC CASES

THE INFORMER HAS A valuable place in law enforcement, although generally unappreciated and usually much misunderstood. His contribution to the public good is seldom recognized.

A full discussion of informers is beyond the scope of this book. We long have considered this to be one of the most critical and essential fields of law enforcement operations and for law enforcement improvement. So convinced are we that we already have published a book, *The Informer in Law Enforcement* (see Bibliography) which we recommend to all law enforcement personnel, and particularly to all narcotic officers for whom it should be considered a companion work to this Notebook.

In this volume, then, we will make only brief reference to the informer. We must say at the outset that in obtaining evidence in narcotic cases the informer is perhaps more necessary than in the investigation of any other type of crime. The reasons will be fairly obvious. The narcotic traffic and narcotic addiction are particularly well hidden and relatively small social phenomena. Often it is necessary or most effective to use an addicted person to supply some of the evidence to establish a case, at least to furnish an opening wedge. The addict society and the narcotic drug peddling society are, in effect, secret societies into which one enters only if vouched for, and this often makes it necessary that we utilize an informer who already has an entree, a "membership." He can tell us who is dealing with drugs and how and where. He can introduce our undercover man to a peddler. He may perhaps be willing to purchase drugs for us to be used in evidence.

In general every peddler, every addict encountered by the narcotic officer, should be considered as a potential source of information, an informer. His information should be utilized in attempting to develop cases against others in the drug traffic, especially those in higher echelons. Obtaining and managing informers is a fine police art, a skill acquired with experience and understanding.

Many factors contribute to success in obtaining informers. Important in this area is the reputation of the law enforcement agency and the individual officer for integrity, fair dealing, and intelligent police operation. In many cases the informer takes a considerable personal risk. Like any of the rest of us, in danger he would want to put himself in the hands of competent people. The officer should be completely fair with the informer. He should not misrepresent nor hold out false promises to this person. He should not humiliate or degrade him. He should see that the full powers of all police agencies having jurisdiction are invoked if the informer is harmed or threatened.

The experienced officer knows that the first step to insure the safety of the informer from reprisal is intelligent handling which will conceal his identity and activities as an informer for as long as possible. Public policy requires that a citizen has a right and duty to inform his government of infractions of its laws, and that this be done in a confidential relationship. In recent years the federal courts and some others have weakened this rule somewhat in that they require the identification of an informer if it seems important in the establishing of a defense.

There was an old police maxim that a detective was as good as his informers. This was never wholly true, and is less so in these days of highly professionalized law enforcement officers. However, the saying always had some basis in fact and it still has weight. The ability to find, develop, and properly manage informers is one of the greatest assets a narcotic investigator can possess. We think that the full discussion in the book *The Informer in Law Enforcement* will prove of interest and some value to many law enforcement officers.

In several communities, including Fairfax Co. (Va.) a system has been devised whereby an informant can communicate information of suspected drug abuse offenses to the police by telephone without risk or necessity of having his identity disclosed. Rewards may be paid for information resulting in prosecution. This appears to be a device which, if handled carefully and intelligently, may be a considerable asset to drug abuse law enforcement.

14

OFFICIAL PRESCRIPTIONS FOR NARCOTIC DRUGS

IN OTHER CHAPTERS OF this book we have referred to the diversion to the illicit traffic of narcotic drugs from medical supplies. We have pointed out that in the early 1920's such diversion fed an addict population much greater in numbers than today's, and with a daily rate of consumption per addict several times as heavy as now seen. These diversions of medical drugs were brought under control by the setting up of administrative machinery which completely regulates the importing of opium and coca leaves into this country and assures their manufacture into finished drugs by only highly reputable firms operating under elaborate safeguards. Good control conditions prevail in the wholesaling and retailing of narcotic drugs. Physical safeguards are such that thefts of narcotics in substantial amounts rarely occur now. The forging of permits to divert narcotics in wholesale amounts, common in the early 1920's, now is practically impossible. We have pointed out that world agreements to limit the manufacture of finished narcotic drugs to medical and scientific needs have long ago dried up a source of diversion of narcotics from drug manufacturers abroad. (There was a disastrous exception to this in the late 1940's when, following World War II, a breakdown of controls in Italy allowed a flood of heroin to be released to the illicit market in this country. This source was finally detected and destroyed by cooperative efforts of Italian and American narcotic officers.)

We have mentioned doctors as a former substantial source of diversion of narcotics to addicts. A Report on Narcotic Addiction of the Council of Mental Health, American Medical Association (*Journal of the American Medical Association,* November-December 1957), quotes from a resolution of the American Medical

Official Prescriptions for Narcotic Drugs 309

Association House of Delegates in 1924, urging both federal and state governments to exert their full powers and authority to put an end to "all manner of so-called ambulatory methods of treatment of narcotic drug addiction whether performed by the private physician or by the so-called 'narcotic clinics' or dispensary."

Much of the supplying of narcotics to addicts by doctors was well intended, but there was enough carelessness or worse to bring about this most positive action by the medical profession. As a result of condemnation by the profession of the ambulatory treatment of an addict as improper medical practice and further definition as to when narcotics could be properly administered in ethical medicine, the narcotic prescription disappeared as a primary source of illicit narcotics. This process was also accelerated by the dying out or disappearance of older addicts in the late 1920's and in the 1930's. With them went a great fund of addict fraud and guile in "promoting" narcotic supplies from doctors and druggists for the satisfaction of addiction. Some of these addict operations we have referred to in Chapter 6.

The reader will remember that addiction here reached a rock-bottom low in World War II and for two or three years thereafter. But this was followed by a small explosion of addiction localized for the most part in a few of our larger cities. While much of the addiction, following the classic pattern, developed among criminal or delinquent persons, there were many young and relatively unsophisticated recruits. A large proportion were Negro. Up to this writing few Negro addicts have resorted to attempts to divert medical supplies for addiction. By necessity or choice they depend on the "street" market for drugs. However, with the acquisition of experience some of the newer addicts and, of course, a good representation of any old-timers seek to find drugs from medical stocks.

As we have pointed out, the federal narcotic control program, supplemented by state laws, requires careful channeling of legal narcotics. Pharmacists and physicians must purchase narcotics from manufacturers or wholesalers on official order forms, a copy of which is submitted to the Federal Bureau of Narcotics and Dangerous Drugs for a central audit. The more potent narcotic drugs may be prescribed by a physician only on a written prescription or administered in personal attendance and a record kept.

The professions of medicine and pharmacy naturally can be relied on to carry out their part of this program with meticulous care. Despite this there may be small leakages which can become appreciable. For that reason we include here a discussion of the official triplicate narcotic prescription as used in the states of California and Illinois. In essence, the narcotic laws of these states require that the more potent class of narcotic drug must be prescribed on a special form, fanfolded with the carbon paper to allow one writing to produce triplicate copies. One of these copies is kept by the physician as his official record. The two remaining copies go to the pharmacist who, after filling, files one for his records and sends the other on to the state authorities for an official audit.

California has had many years experience with this prescription. In Illinois it was provided for by a law which became effective in January 1958, and the authors had the responsibility for setting up the operating machinery. Our experience convinces us that this is a useful, valuable device where there is any appreciable amount of narcotic addiction. The program had been in effect only two days when an addict came into Illinois to lay a trail of forged narcotic prescriptions. His failure to have the proper official blank promptly disclosed a racket which hitherto he had been employing successfully for a long period. Later, teams of prescription forgers from Illinois were apprehended in adjacent Indiana. Frustrated in attempts to continue acquiring drugs by forgery in Illinois, because of the requirement for an official blank in that state, they had gone to the adjoining state. Here unfamiliarity with the territory brought prompt disclosure and arrest. One such team had employed several cripples to call on doctor after doctor to collect prescriptions for drugs. These were sold in several other states. Investigation by the Federal Bureau of Narcotics disclosed that one addict customer of this forgery team had mortgaged a valuable lumber yard and had dissipated most of the proceeds to buy drugs. In possession of one of the ringleaders at the time of his arrest was a letter from a confederate warning him not to resume his former narcotic forgery operations in Illinois since the official prescription blank would lead to immediate disclosure.

The official narcotic prescription blank then is a quick and convenient way of practically eliminating forgeries since the reproduction of the prescription booklet is beyond the technical resources of the addict. A little more slowly but almost as surely it eventually discloses the addict who goes from doctor to doctor with a fraudulent story and assumed symptoms to collect narcotic drugs. Rather quickly also it will disclose the person with a bona fide medical condition requiring narcotics who will not abide by his doctor's orders to limit his dosage, but who goes to one or several other doctors for his prescription without the knowledge of the other practitioners.

Audit of the official narcotic prescriptions and a companion audit of the federal narcotic order forms on which narcotics are purchased for office use and dispensing serve to quickly disclose any personal use of narcotics by physicians. These cases are very, very few. However they are very, very important from the standpoint of the doctor's patients, the medical profession, and the individual doctor concerned. There has been much discussion of addiction among physicians. The figures quoted (1% is a common guess) are, in our opinion, exaggerated. A generation ago, however, the number well exceeded 1%. In any event the offical narcotic prescription audit tends to disclose the addiction of a physician promptly before that addiction becomes massive and well settled as a way of life, and before the physician has seriously hurt himself and his patients. Prompt remedial measures can then be taken. In California the medical authorities claim that 92 percent of addicted doctors are rehabilitated, a splendid accomplishment considering the indispensable value of these individuals to the community. Our limited experience in Illinois indicates rehabilitation results there are just as successful.

As we have said, we think the official narcotic prescription program is valuable where appreciable addiction exists. We think it will become more and more valuable as the crop of addicts from the late 1940's and early 1950's become increasingly sophisticated and tend to turn to medical sources of supply.

We offer this suggestion for consideration in any area contemplating the adoption of this scheme. Medicine and pharmacy should be fully briefed on its value. Professional men are understandably impatient of anything which looks like more regulation or more government in medicine. However, convinced that a program offers something of value, they may be found quick to adopt it.

We made this suggestion in 1961. We think it has even more validity in 1972. Now we see what in the light of our experience in this field is an alarming tendency of a few physicians to "get on the bandwagon" to specialize rather promiscuously in writing prescriptions for methadone. This, we think, is bound to cause serious trouble (as it already has) in deaths of young people and the addiction of more. The existence of an auditing process would be of some protection to society and to the professions of medicine and pharmacy.

15
POLICE COOPERATION IN NARCOTIC INVESTIGATIONS

THE LARGEST PART of the American underworld opiate supplies come from abroad. This supply is diverted from the poppy fields of Turkey or some other Near East country where the plant is cultivated for the production of medical opium. Or the opium may originate behind the bamboo curtain of Red China or in contiguous countries in its orbit, with perhaps the official impetus of a regime capable of the foulest tactics to embarrass the West in every way. A relatively small stream of opiate drugs, a trickle, will come from adjacent Mexico. Some of this Mexican narcotic will be derived from opium poppies clandestinely grown in that country. More, perhaps, will be in the form of finished drugs in a traffic in which Mexico has been merely a way station for the transshipment of opiates from Europe or the Far East.

From the time the drug in the form of opium is scraped from the poppy heads in the fields, through its conversion into morphine base and then into heroin, and its smuggling out of and into various countries and to its final distribution, mainly in several large cities in this country to be shot into the veins of addicts, the flow of drugs follows a secret, devious, labyrinthian course compared to which the Cretan mazes were a child's puzzle. All of this, as we have emphasized, is a subsurface traffic carried on in a specialized underworld. It is an operation impervious to ordinary scrutiny. Usually its only surface manifestation is the discovery that some person has become addicted to narcotics and, when deprived of them through arrest or otherwise, begins to exhibit withdrawal symptoms at which time we find the other marks of his habit.

With this knowledge of the narcotic traffic it is obvious that, if they can be followed, there are threads of evidence leading from the street addict consumer back through various echelons of pushers, dealers, wholesalers, smugglers, clandestine heroin laboratory operators, the refiners of base morphine from opium, and the illegal diverters and exporters of opium from the poppy fields. The investigation of the narcotic case may in some respects be likened to a surgical procedure for removal of a cancer where there is only a small surface lesion but very extensive internal involvement. However, the indications often seen by the surgeon may not be available to the investigator. But the connected scheme of the traffic must be borne in mind always. It will be as involved and entwined as a pot of spaghetti. The investigator often will be puzzled as to where to start. Starting, he sometimes will be at a loss where and when to stop and may spend fruitless weeks and months on what

Figure 32. 1967 Citroen seized by U. S. Customs at San Juan, P. R., May 29, 1971. Factory-built panel between gas tank and rear seat and false rear floor compartment concealed over 248 pounds of pure heroin. Eighteen ½-kilo bags were found within the gas tank panel and fifty-six ½-kilo bags were found in the false rear floor compartment. U.S. Bureau of Customs photo.

will prove to be dead ends. But, inevitably, intelligent effort and some good luck will bring effective results.

A pill of opium found concealed in the crutch tip of a Seattle addict resulted in a wholesale roundup of dealers and the destruction of a country-wide narcotic distributing apparatus set up by a Chinese tong. The arrest of a small seaman peddler by a California sheriff's office eventually sent federal narcotic agents to Italy to unearth huge diversions of heroin there from a chemical factory. A story from the underworld resulted in the smashing of a "round the world" narcotic ring whose operation alone was bringing in enough drugs to supply a fifth of the addict population. Caught in this coup was Louis "Lepke" Buchalter, overlord of Murder, Inc., at the height of his vicious career. He was deposed as Emperor of Crime and sentenced to fourteen years in a federal penitentiary. From there he was soon taken to New York for trial by the state authorities for murder, and convicted and executed. Again in California, arrests by police of local peddlers set out a train of international investigation which in the following three years resulted in the arrest of an important dealer in Arizona and the arrest of wholesalers and smugglers in New York. Then, after a year-long pursuit of a fugitive, there was disclosed a Paris to Mexico City to New York heroin smuggling triangle, employing specially built baggage. The same inquiry resulted in the arrest of two Canadian fugitives considered to have been the most important traffickers in that country and the death of a third in an automobile pursuit in Mexico.

All this comes about after much trial and error, many blind alleys, many frustrating delays and legal obstacles, and sometimes just heartbreaking bad luck. But the only valid investigative concept is that each grain of heroin in the local traffic may be the key to the breaking of an interstate or international operation. Every case should be examined from that standpoint. In most instances it will quickly be apparent that the thread of continuity is broken. In some it can be pursued to a higher echelon or two and then must stop. But every once in a while will come the case that can be exploited to classic completion. This means, of course, that all narcotic officers, all enforcement officers for that matter, must work as a team against this traffic, something often hard to bring about in a profession which has its fair share of prima donnas. But the

American law enforcement officer generally knows that his best recourse in our decentralized law enforcement system is the highest degree of unselfishness in official cooperation. In this we are the source of wonder and amazement to foreign police accustomed to a monolithic law enforcement structure.

In the effective cooperation of local, state and federal agencies we should stress this point. Every addict, pusher, or peddler, great or small, should be considered a source of information and his possibilities in this direction exploited to the fullest. Every bit of documentary evidence, every scrap of paper containing writing, telephone numbers and the like, all evidence of communication may prove important. If not immediately pertinent to the present case this information should be placed in the file and catalogued as much as facilities permit. Background files are often the foundation of the most important narcotic investigation.

While there have been some lapses, it is our experience that some of the best history of international police cooperation has been in the narcotic drug field. Generally the police have been quick and eager, willing to perform, even when in some instances the statesmen's efforts seem to lag. We can take some personal pride in the fact that beginning in 1951 we had something to do with establishing good working procedures with the International Criminal Police Organization (INTERPOL), a French-based group which has proved of great value in the apprehension of international narcotic criminals.* The American-based International Association of Chiefs of Police (IACP) makes a potent contribution to the war against narcotics, particularly in the light of the great decentralization of the American police establishment. In a more highly specialized sense the International Narcotic Enforcement Officers Association (INEOA), membership in which is open to all active narcotic officers, performs some excellent services. For example, it distributes to members a roster of membership, facilitating prompt communication among personnel. It holds an annual conference at which the papers presented have, in our opinion, constituted one of the best seminars on current drug problems in this country and the world.

---

*The Hon. Eugene T. Rossides, Assistant Secretary of the Treasury for Law Enforcement, is U. S. representative and a vice-president of INTERPOL.

At this time there is an unprecedented drive to perfect the most formidable anti-drug-abuse law enforcement machine ever contemplated in this country, and with emphasis on a world-wide attack. The Department of Justice and the Treasury Department are greatly enlarging their forces and these will continue to build. Unfortunately, this takes time. The BNDD has greatly expanded its drug abuse training program for local and state officers. LEAA is supporting ambitious projects to enlarge the local efforts against narcotic drugs through such devices as the Metropolitan Enforcement Group (MEG). The primary mission of a MEG is to detect, investigate, and apprehend narcotic and dangerous drug traffickers within a metropolitan area.* States, cities, towns, and counties are increasing and training narcotic officers. If this effort can be paralleled by the establishment of prosecution and judicial efforts which will keep the courts functioning on a realistic basis there should be a crushing effect on the drug traffic. This accompanied by rehabilitative and public opinion efforts of demonstrated worth, vigorously and extensively pursued, should ease our situation.

The international program against narcotics and other dangerous drugs is being vigorously developed and pursued under the leadership of John E. Ingersoll, Director of the U. S. Bureau of Narcotics and Dangerous Drugs and U. S. Representative to the United Nations Commission on Narcotic Drugs. At the 1970 Atlantic City conference of the International Association of Chiefs of Police, Mr. Ingersoll said, "The [narcotic] problem will never be solved until the producing countries stop, once and for all, uncontrolled production and flow of illicit drugs. The time for just deploring the problem is at an end. The time for action is overdue" (*Police Year Book 1971,* IACP, p. 119).

As we indicated in Chapter 2 a new international convention to include the psychotropic drugs is being sought. Attempts are being made to expand the role and effectiveness of the United Nations in drug abuse control. Substantial financial support is being given toward this end. Direct working relationships with other nations

---

*In early 1972, the Hon. Myles Ambrose was reassigned from his post as U.S. Commissioner of Customs to that of Assistant Attorney General and Special Assistant to the President to head a country-wide special narcotic enforcement program. This contemplates the employment of selected teams of investigators, local, state and federal, and prosecutors in an intensified and concentrated attack on narcotic trafficking rings in our most sorely afflicted areas.

are being extended and intensified in an increasing degree. The effectiveness of continuing cooperation among countries is illustrated by such cases as the following:

French-American. George Roupinian. On July 26, 1969, Roupinian was arrested in New York City in possession of 2 kilograms of heroin. Roupinian consented to a search of his apartment in New Jersey where the agents seized an additional 8 kilograms of heroin. The heroin had been smuggled into the U. S. in 200 ski poles. The French police are attempting to develop a case against the source of supply in France through a Rogatory Commission.

French-American-Spanish-German-Swiss. Christian Hysohion *et al*. This was an extended investigation jointly conducted in several countries in 1969 as a result of leads obtained from other investigations. The traffickers in looking for new means to smuggle heroin into the U. S. devised a plan to pack the heroin in cans marked fish. The investigation led to a seizure of 30 kilograms of heroin and arrests in France, United States, Spain, and Switzerland.

French-Italian-American. Halit Elik *et al*. During June 1970, the Marseille District Office and Marseille police initiated an investigation of Halit Elik, Abdul Raghib-Ismael, and Franz Plezl. While under surveillance they were observed to meet with Turkish narcotic violators Ihsan Ferat and Halil Copuroglu. On June 24, 1970, Elik, Raghib, and Plezl were arrested in possession of 48 kilograms of morphine base which was hidden in traps in a Volkswagen. Later that day American agents met with Ferat and Copuroglu and negotiated for 100 kilograms of morphine base, which was in an automobile in Milan, Italy. U. S. agents coordinated the investigation with the French and Italian police and then travelled to Milan with the suspects. In Milan, Ferat, Copuroglu, and Omar Hussein were arrested in possession of 101 kilograms of morphine base, which was hidden in traps in a Goleath automobile.

German-American-French-Italian-Lebanese-Greek-English. John Moore *et al*. Information was received in 1970 that Moore and his associates were preparing to fly to Beirut to purchase a large amount of hashish. When the airplane left the U. S. the air control of all the countries was alerted to monitor the flight. When the plane landed in Lebanon the Lebanese police attempted to arrest the suspects. A gun battle ensued and the plane took off and headed toward Greece. Over Greece the plane was forced down and the Greek police arrested Moore and four associates and seized 670 kilograms of hashish and $50,000.

We have been told that Japan stopped its methamphetamine epidemic with intensive law enforcement combined with propaganda (Brill and Hirose). The problems are not identical but may suggest areas for the greatest corrective effort.

To us, one of the most pressing needs in the present worldwide narcotic drug abuse epidemics is herculean worldwide law enforcement effort against the drugs that threaten us. This is the essence of sound prevention. We have the ability to develop this effort. Let us hope that we continue to have the will to make the effort.

In the preface of this book we mentioned the recent and sudden change in the social climate in this country—and elsewhere—which makes tolerable and acceptable a drug culture which heretofore was unthinkable. Somehow, in some way, we must find means to correct this, to restore a balance of sanity.

Banker-Lawyer J. L. Robertson, vice-chairman of the Board of Governors, Federal Reserve System, is an articulate and penetrating commentator on the state of law enforcement in this country. At an observance of Law Day in Dallas, Texas, on April 29, 1971, Mr. Robertson made a speech, from which we extract a few sentences: "The notion that use of narcotics was not bad, but perhaps even good, began to appear in various media of communication: newspapers, magazines, books, motion pictures and popular songs. The advocates of drug use acquired sufficient respectability that they were able to spread their message with relative ease and in many cases to their own substantial pecuniary profit . . ." And Mr. Robertson cited Judge Learned Hand: "The hand that rules the press, the radio, the screen and the far-spread magazine rules the country. Whether we like it or not, we must learn to accept it".

In this area, certainly, the well-being, the future, and the very lives of so many never have been so dependent on so few.

Far off from these, a slow and silent stream,
Lethe, the River of Oblivion, rolls
Her wat'ry labyrinth, whereof who drinks
Forthwith his former state and being forgets.
                                   Milton, *Paradise Lost*

BIBLIOGRAPHY

American Journal of Orthopsychiatry, October 1958.

Anderson, William R., M.C.: *International Narcotic Enforcement Officers Association Annual Conference Report,* September 1971.

Anslinger, Harry J., and Tompkins, William H.: *Traffic in Narcotics.* New York, Funk & Wagnalls, 1953.

Ausubel, David P.: *Drug Addiction: Physiological, Psychological and Sociological Aspects.* New York, Random House, 1958.

Ball, John C., and Chambers, Carl D.: *The Epidemiology of Opiate Addiction in the United States.* Springfield, Thomas, 1970.

Barnes, Robert Earl: *Are You Safe From Burglars?* Garden City, N. Y., Doubleday, 1971.

Becker, H. K.: Carl Koller and cocaine. *Psychoanalytical Quarterly, 32:*July, December 1963.

Bejerot, Nils: *Addiction and Society.* Springfield, Thomas, 1970.

Bludworth, Edward: *300 Most Abused Drugs, A Pictorial Handbook.* Tampa, Fla.

Brill, Henry: Pro-drug dialectic communication on drug abuse and the marihuana red herring. In Wittenborn, J. R., Smith, J. P., and Wittenborn, Sarah A. (Eds.): *Communication and Drug Abuse: Proceedings of the Second Rutgers Symposium on Drug Abuse.* Springfield, Thomas, 1970, Chapter 3.

Brill, Henry, and Hirose, Tetsuya: The rise and fall of a methamphetamine epidemic, Japan, 1945-55. *Seminars in Psychiatory, 1(2):*179-194, 1969.

Caldwell, A. E.: *Origins of Psychopharmacology from Chlorpromazine to LSD.* Springfield, Thomas, 1970.

Connell, P. H.: Adolescent drug taking. *Proceedings of Royal Society of Medicine, 58:*409-412, 1965.

Connell, P. H.: Amphetamine dependence. *Proceedings of Royal Society of Medicine. 61(2):*178-181, February 1968. (Section of General Practice, pp. 4-7.)

Connell, P. H.: Amphetamine misuse. *British Journal of Addiction*, *60*:9-27, 1964.
Connell, P. H.: Clinical aspects of drug addiction. *Journal of the Royal College of Physicians, (London)*, *4*:254-263, 1970.
Connell, P. H.: Clinical manifestations and treatment of amphetamine type of dependence. *Journal of American Medical Association*, *196*:718-723, 1966.
Connell, P. H.: Drug addiction and its treatment; selected list of references on treatment. *Maudsley Bequest Lecture Course*, Maudsley Hospital, London, Feb. 3, 1969.
Connell, P. H.: The drug dependence clinical research and treatment unit. *Bethlem Maudsley Hospital Gazette*, *9(4)*:4-8, 1968.
Connell, P. H.: Drug dependence in Great Britain, a challenge to the practice of medicine. In Steinberg, Hannah (Ed.): *Scientific Basis of Drug Dependence*. London, 1969.
Connell, P. H.: Drug taking in Great Britain, a growing problem. *Royal Society of Health Journal*, *89(2)*:92-96, March-April 1969.
Connell, P. H.: The impact of the new approach to the problem of drug dependence in Great Britain. *Proceedings 29th International Congress on Alcoholism and Drug Dependence*, Melbourne, Australia, 1970, pp. 55-62.
Connell, P. H.: Some observations concerning amphetamine misuse: its diagnosis, management, and treatment with special reference to research needs. *Proceedings of Rutgers Symposium on Drug Abuse*, June 1968.
Connell, P. H.: Treatment of narcotic and non-narcotic drug dependence: The need for research. In Phillipson, Richard V. (Ed.): *Modern Trends in Drug Dependence and Alcoholism*. Butterworths, London, 1970.
Connell, P. H.: The use and abuse of amphetamines. *The Practitioner: Symposium on the Problem of Addiction*, *200*:234-243, February 1968.
Council on Mental Health: Report on narcotic addiction. Journal of American Medical Association, November-December 1957.
Ding, L. D., and Chan, L. Y.: A study of ex-prisoner female addicts in Hong Kong. *Bull Narcotics*, vol. XXII, No. 2, 1970.
Dobbs, W. H.: Methadone treatment of heroin addicts; early results

provide more questions than answers. *JAMA, 218*:1536-1541, (Dec. 6) 1971.

Eastman Kodak Company. *Basic Police Photography.* Rochester, N. Y. 1968.

Eastman Kodak Company. *Infrared and Ultraviolet Photography.* Rochester, N. Y.

Eastman Kodak Company. *Photography in Law Enforcement.* Rochester, N. Y.

Fleming, T. J.: *The Trial of John Brown.* American Heritage, August 1967.

Flynn, Errol: *My Wicked, Wicked Ways.* New York, G. P. Putnam, 1959.

Fraser, Havelock F., and Grider, James M.: *American Journal of Medicine,* May 1953.

Freud, Sigmund: *Uber Coca,* 1884-1885.

Friendly, Alfred: *Washington Post,* Dec. 12, 1971.

Fulton, Charles C.: *The Opium Poppy and Other Poppies.* Washington, D.C., U. S. Bureau of Narcotics, 1944.

Gardner, Ramon: Deaths in United Kingdom opioid users 1965-69. *The Lancet,* Sept. 26, 1970, pp. 650-653.

Gardner, Ramon, and Connell, P. H.: One year's experience in a drug-dependence clinic. *The Lancet,* Aug. 29, 1970, pp. 455-459.

Goodman, L. S., and Gilman, A.: *The Pharmacological Basis of Therapeutics.* New York, Macmillan, 1970.

Harney, Malachi L.: *Chicago Police Digest,* August 1959.

Harney, Malachi L.: Statement at Medicolegal Symposium of American Medical Association. Cleveland, Ohio, April 1959.

Harney, Malachi L.: *Wayne Law Review, 106*:278-279, 1971.

Harney, Malachi L., and Cross, John C.: *The Informer in Law Enforcement,* 2nd ed. Springfield, Thomas, 1968.

Horan, Robert F.: *Testimony before U. S. House of Representatives Select Committee on Crime.* Washington, D. C., April 28, 1971.

International Association of Chiefs of Police: *Police Year Book 1971.*

International Narcotic Enforcement Officers Association: *Annual Conference Report,* 10th, September 1969; 12th, September

1971.
International Narcotic Enforcement Officers Association: *International Narcotic Report,* October 1971.
Isbell, H., and Fraser, Havelock F.: Addiction to analgesics and barbiturates. *Journal of Pharmacology and Experimental Therapeutics, Part II, 28*:355, 1950.
Isbell, H., *et al.* Studies on tetrahydrocannabinol: I. Method of assay in human subjects and results with crude extracts, purified tetrahydrocannabinols and synthetic compounds. Committee on Problems of Drugs Dependence, National Academy of Sciences, National Research Council, 1967, p. 4844.
Isbell H., *et al.*: Tolerance of methadone. *JAMA,* December 6, 1947.
Jaffe, J. H.: Narcotic analgesics. In Goodman, L. S., and Gilman, A. (eds.): *The Pharmacological Basis of Therapeutics,* 4th ed. New York, Macmillan, 1970.
King, Alexander: *Mine Enemy Grows Older.* New York, Simon & Schuster, 1959.
Kolansky, H. and Moore, W. T.: Effects of marihuana on adolescents and young adults. *JAMA, 216*:486-492, (April 19) 1971.
Kurland, Albert A.: The deceptive communication and the narcotic abuser. In Wittenborn, C., Smith, J.P., and Wittenborn, S. A. (Eds.): *Communication and Drug Abuse: Proceedings of the Second Rutgers Symposium on Drug Abuse.* Springfield, Thomas, 1970, p. 265.
Levine, Samuel: *International Narcotic Enforcement Officers Association Annual Conference Report,* September 1969.
Lewin, Louis: *Phantastica, Narcotic and Stimulating Drugs, Their Use and Abuse.* London, Routledge & Kegan Paul, 1964.
Lieberman, Carl M., and Lieberman, Beth: Marihuana a medical review. *New England Journal of Medicine,* January 14, 1971.
Lynch, Vincent de Paul: *International Narcotic Enforcement Officers Association Annual Conference Report,* 1969, pp. 65-66.
Lynch, V. de P. Marihuana research. Twelfth Annual International Narcotic Enforcement Officers Association Conference Report, Albany, New York, September, 1971.
Maher, John T.: Resume on the Abolition of Opium. U. S. Bureau of Narcotics and Dangerous Drugs files.

Maisel, Albert: *Reader's Digest,* February 1959.
Maurer, David W., and Vogel, Victor H.: *Narcotics and Narcotic Addiction,* 2nd ed. Springfield, Thomas, 1967.
Messick, H.: *Lansky.* New York, G. P. Putnam's Sons, 1971.
Musto, David F.: The Marihuana Tax Act of 1937. *Archives of General Psychiatry,* 26, February 1972.
Nalty, B. C.: The Marines at Harpers Ferry. Marine Corps Historical Reference Series No. 10. Headquarters, U. S. Marine Corps, Washington, D.C., May 1959.
National Observer, May 19, 1972.
Nyswander, Marie: *American Journal of Orthopsychiatry,* October 1958.
Nyswander, Marie: Interview. *Modern Medicine,* October 1, 1957.
Nyswander, Marie: *The Drug Addict as a Patient.* New York, Grune & Stratton, 1956.
Pope Pius XII. Address Sept. 14, 1952 at First International Congress on the Histopathology of the Nervous System. Reprint of an article from *L'Osservatore Romano.*
Powelson, D. Harvey: *Clinical Notes on the Use of Marihuana.* University of California, 1970.
Schmidt, J. E.: *Narcotics: Lingo and Lore.* Springfield, Thomas, 1959.
Sondern, Frederic: *Brotherhood of Evil: The Mafia.* New York, Farrar, Straus & Cudahy, 1959.
Stephenson, Owen H.: *International Narcotic Enforcement Officers Association Annual Conference Report,* September 1971.
Talese, G.: *Honor Thy Father.* New York, World Publisher, Times-Mirror, 1971.
Terry, Charles E., and Pellens, Mildred: *The Opium Problem.* New York, Bureau of Social Hygiene, 1928.
Terry, James G.: Ten-year report on the Santa Rita Rehabilitation Center, Alameda, California, 1949-1959.
U. N. Commission on Narcotic Drugs: Report of 1958 session.
U. S. Bureau of Customs, *Customs Today,* Winter 1971, Washington, D. C.
U. S. Bureau of Narcotics Police Training School: *Outline Summary of Instruction.*

U. S. Bureau of Narcotics and Dangerous Drugs, Department of Justice: *Glossary of Terms in the Drug Culture.*
Vogel, Victor H., and Vogel, Virginia E.: *Facts About Narcotics.* Science Research Associates, Inc., 1951.
Wikler, Abraham: Clinical and social aspects of marihuana intoxication. *Archives of General Psychiatry, 23*:322, 1970.
Wikler, Abraham: A psychodynamic study of a patient during experimental self-regulated re-addiction to morphine. *Psychiatric Quarterly, 26*:270, 1952.
Wittenborn, J. R., Smith, J. P., and Wittenborn, S. A. (Eds.): *Communication and Drug Abuse: Proceedings of the Second Rutgers Symposium on Drug Abuse.* Springfield, Thomas, 1970.
Wolfe, P.: *Marihuana in Latin America, the Threat it Constitutes.* Washington, D.C., The Linacre Press, 1949.
Zelson, C., Rubio, E., and Wasserman, E.: Neonatal narcotic addiction: ten-year observation. *Pediatrics, 48*:178-189, (August) 1971.

Appendix

A FEDERAL SOURCE BOOK: ANSWERS TO THE MOST FREQUENTLY ASKED QUESTIONS ABOUT DRUG ABUSE

Note: Produced jointly by the Department of Defense, Department of Health, Education, and Welfare, Department of Justice, Department of Labor, and Office of Economic Opportunity. U. S. Government Printing Office, 1970.

THE WHITE HOUSE

March 11, 1970

Drug misuse is a growing national problem. Hundreds of thousands of Americans—young and old alike— endanger their health through the inappropriate use of drugs of all kinds. More than 100,000 of these Americans lead totally unproductive lives because of their addiction to narcotics.

The blight of illegal drug traffic—the lives it ruins and the lives it takes—is a serious concern for every American. It especially concerns American parents.

This publication presents the latest scientific answers to some of the questions most frequently asked about drug misuse. For the first time, all of the concerned Federal agencies and departments have pooled their knowledge to produce a single source book on the national drug problem. The answers are based upon the latest research findings of the National Institute of Mental Health and are presented in accord with the policies and programs of the Defense Department, the Department of Health, Education and Welfare, the Department of Justice, the Department of Labor and the Office of Economic Opportunity.

Unfortunately, this book does not provide all of the answers to all of the questions about drugs. The causes and consequences of drug abuse are not yet fully understood. But the concerted pursuit of knowledge by all concerned Federal agencies continues. As new facts—and new answers—are discovered, they will be incorporated into revised editions of this publication and, more importantly, into programs to curb the misuse of drugs. We will need more research, greater control of illegal drug traffic, and intensified information and education efforts.

This publication will reach several million readers throughout the country. Let it be a symbol of our determination to unify and help support the efforts of State, community and voluntary agencies in the control and prevention of drug misuse, and in the rehabilitation of the addict.

RICHARD NIXON

GENERAL QUESTIONS ABOUT DRUG ABUSE

What is a drug?

A drug is a substance that has an effect upon the body and mind. This publication deals only with those drugs that have a potential for abuse because of their mind-altering capability.

What is drug dependence?

Drug dependence is a state of psychological or physical dependence, or both, which results from chronic, periodic, or continuous use. Many kinds of drug dependence exist; they all have specific problems associated with them.

Not everyone who uses a mind-altering chemical becomes dependent upon it. Alcohol is one common example of this point. The majority of persons who drink do not harm themselves or those around them. However, more than five million Americans are dependent upon alcohol.

What is habituation?

Habituation is the *psychological* desire to repeat the use of a drug intermittently or continuously because of emotional reasons. Escape from tension, dulling of reality, euphoria (being "high") are some of the reasons why drugs come to be used habitually.

What is addiction?

Addiction is *physical* dependence upon a drug. Its scientific definition includes the development of tolerance and withdrawal. As a person develops tolerance he requires larger and larger amounts of the drug to produce the same effect. When use of the addicting drug is stopped abruptly, the period of withdrawal is characterized by such distressing symptoms as vomiting and convulsions. A compulsion to repeat the use of the addicting drug is understandable because the drug temporarily solves one's problems and keeps the withdrawal symptoms away.

Drugs other than narcotics can become addicting. Some people have acquired an addiction to sedatives and certain tranquilizers. Stimulants in very large doses are addictive.

Whether the person is physically addicted or abuses drugs for psychological reasons, he is dependent upon drugs. Drug dependence of any kind is a serious problem for the individual and society.

Are all drugs harmful?

Every drug is harmful when taken in excess. Some drugs can also be harmful if taken in dangerous combinations or by hypersensitive people in minute or ordinary amounts.

The fact that certain drugs can produce enormously beneficial results has produced the false notion that pills will solve all problems. Society must develop a new respect for all drugs. Drugs that affect the mind can have subtle or obvious side effects. These can be immediate or may become evident only after long, continuous use.

Why are drugs being abused these days?

Drug abuse is not a new phenomenon. Varying forms of drug abuse have been present for years in the United States and other countries. There are many reasons for the current epidemic of drug misuse. Very broadly, drug abuse can be described as an effort by individuals to feel different than they do. Many drugs temporarily allow their users to evade frustrations, to lessen depression and feelings of alienation, or to escape from themselves. Such misuse of drugs, of course, does not produce any improvement in the problems of the individual or society. Rather, it is a flight from problems.

Some of the factors in the great "turn on" of recent years are:
1) The widespread belief that "medicines" can magically solve problems.
2) The numbers of young people who are dissatisfied or disillusioned, or who have lost faith in the prevailing social system.
3) The tendency of persons with psychological problems to seek easy solutions with chemicals.
4) The easy access to drugs of various sorts.
5) The development of an affluent society that can afford drugs.
6) The statements of proselytizers who proclaim the "goodness' of drugs.

What is meant by a drug culture?

A drug culture or subculture is a group of people whose lives are committed to drugs. The members of any subculture may congregate in a particular geographic area, such as the Haight-Ashbury district in San Francisco.

Marihuana is almost invariably smoked in such communities, but hallucinogens, sedatives, stimulants and narcotics are also used. It has been demonstrated that these subcultures are transient in nature; only a minority of the members remain for more than a year.

Where are most drug users located?

The location of users varies with the drug in question. Until recently, almost all heroin use was confined to males in urban ghettos. Now this pattern is changing. A few young people in suburban areas use heroin. Marihuana formerly was seen primarily in disadvantaged areas, in certain Mexican-American communities, and in some groups of jazz musicians and similar persons. Today, marihuana smokers and users of hallucinogens are found among middle and upper class young people and other groups. Barbiturates and amphetamines were once abused primarily by middle and upper class adults. Now, many youngsters of all classes are misusing them. The important thing to keep in mind is that drug use patterns are changing rapidly in the United States.

Why do dependency producing drugs have such a wide range of effects upon different users?

The effects of mind-altering substances are related to the expectations of the user, the setting in which the use takes place, and the potency of the drug. Mind-altering substances can have vastly different effects upon different people because such drugs release individual underlying personality traits that are ordinarily covered up. Internal controls are diminished or eliminated; one person may become angry, another amorous, a third happy, others disoriented, confused, or depressed, and so on.

Even the same person taking the same dose of a drug on a subsequent occasion may have an entirely different response. As self-control is lost, the person reacts to suggestions from people around him and the setting in which the drug is taken. These factors can markedly alter the drug's effects.

Do drug abusers take more than one drug at a time?

People who abuse one drug tend to take all sorts of drugs. Some of them say they are looking for a new "high." Some will take any drug to get outside themselves. Some play chemical roulette by taking everything, including unidentified pills.

Why do some affluent people become involved in drug usage?

At one time we thought that if we could eliminate poverty, drug abuse would fade away. This notion was obviously erroneous. In a world where changes are rapid and yesterday's faiths and values may erode, affluence allows the time and finances to support drug excesses. Loss of goals and drive can be a by-product of affluence. When a person no longer needs to work in order to eat and clothe himself, he may develop problems of leisure. If he has no viable goals, no motivation or drive to create, to study or to help others, he may become bored or alienated, and vulnerable to the temptation of using chemical substitutes for productive living.

Can the effects of drug abuse be passed on to the unborn?

Some babies born to heroin-addicted mothers have shown withdrawal symptoms. Not enough is known about the genetic effects of other drugs. Taking drugs without careful medical supervision during pregnancy is extremely risky.

What is wrong with taking any drug I want as long as I do not hurt anyone else by doing so?

Society has duties to the individual, and the individual has certain responsibilities to the society in which he lives. A responsible social system provides its citizens with information about the dangers facing them, including the possible dangers of drugs. When a drug has both a harmful and a beneficial potential, regulations about the manner in which the drug is used should be formulated.

It is difficult for an individual to do something to himself that has consequences upon himself alone. Inevitably, the act will have an impact on those who are close to him and those who are dependent upon him. To "drop out" via drugs means that the person becomes dependent upon the social structure for a variety of services and supplies. Someone has to pay the bill.

Where does one go if he is becoming or is dependent upon drugs?

If the user wants help, one's family, a friend, physician, or minister could be asked to help find the best resource in the community. The family doctor, mental health professionals, or school counselors should be among the first to be contacted. Some community self-help groups are effective. Many community mental health centers have special drug abuse units; all centers should be able to provide services or referral to an appropriate resource.

What can a parent do to help a child who is abusing dangerous drugs or narcotics?

Talk about it and try to understand why this behavior is taking place. Ideally, a relevant alternative to drug misuse can be figured out. Increased family interest and involvement in the child's daily activities will help. Professional advice may be desirable. Some communities have programs run by ex-users.

When the youngster is intent upon continuing his drug taking, the problem is much more difficult. Solutions must be individualized. In some instances, it may be desirable to point out that the family cannot be expected to support the drug-taking activity. Psychotherapy may be necessary, but it usually is not successful if the patient is resistant to change. Arbitrary restriction of the youngster may or may not work. If he runs away or is apprehended in some illegal act, he should know that the family will support and help him as soon as he decides to alter his destructive pattern of drug taking and antisocial behavior.

What are the best counseling procedures to use for drug abusers?

In general, the counselor whose approach is punitive is unlikely to succeed. Channels of communication must be opened, and the patient must acquire some measure of trust in the counselor. By listening to the drug abuser's story, the counselor should not give the impression that he is condoning the behavior because he is listening without judging. He must try to understand what the drug means to the patient, and then determine what non-drug alternatives are available.

Group therapy is often successful. Many treatment programs are very effectively using ex-abusers as part of their counseling staffs. Naturally, the skill of the therapist is an important element in achieving success, but the most important factor is the desire of the user to stop using.

Is it possible to obtain medical help without incurring legal penalties?

A certified physician or psychologist can generally assure patients that discussion of drug abuse problems will be kept confidential. Practically all enforcement agencies cooperate with the person who wants help.

What more can be done to curb the misuse of legally obtained drugs?

The family medicine chest may be a source of initial drug trials by children. It should not be used as a stockpile of drugs that are no longer needed. Physicians and pharmacists must carefully watch the renewal of prescriptions of drugs that can cause dependence. The patient should be warned about using such drugs exactly as prescribed.

All manufacture, transportation and distribution of large quantities of drugs in legal commerce should be controlled by adequate safeguards. Large amounts of stimulants and sedatives are being diverted into illegal channels by theft and fraudulent orders.

What sort of program could make a real impact on our drug abuse problem?

1. Society should judge adults who misuse liquor or drugs by the same standards it judges young people. A double standard produces a credibility gap.

2. Children should not be continually exposed to the idea that the stresses of daily life require chemical relief.

3. Factual information about drugs should be stressed rather than attempts to frighten people.

4. Respect for all chemicals, especially mind-altering chemicals, should be instilled in people at an early age.

5. Efforts to detect all manufacturers and large scale traffickers of illicit drugs should increase.

6. Further research in prevention, education and treatment techniques should be carried out.

What can one do to help prevent the spread of drug misuse?

There are a number of things an individual can do:

1. He can set a good example by not abusing drugs himself. Since he can expect his children to model their drug-taking behavior after his, he can either refrain from drinking socially accepted alcoholic beverages, or drink in moderation.

2. He can learn as may facts as possible about drugs so that he will understand the problem and be equipped to discuss it in a reasonable manner.

3. If he learns that someone is peddling drugs, he should notify the authorities. It is the responsibility of both the individual and the community to keep the dealers out.

4. He should do what he can to assist anyone wanting help for a drug problem while awaiting additional aid from a trained person or a treatment facility.

5. Most important of all, he can strive to meet the ideals of parenthood, trying to rear his children so that they are neither deprived of affection nor spoiled. He should have a set of realistic expectations for them. He should give his children responsibilities according to their capabilities, and not overprotect them from the difficulties they will encounter. A parent should be able to talk frankly to his children, and they to him.

QUESTIONS ABOUT MARIHUANA

What is marihuana?

Marihuana is Indian hemp (*Cannabis sativa*). The parts with the highest tetrahydrocannabinol (THC) content are the flowering tops of the plant. The leaves have a smaller amount. The stalks and seeds have little or none. THC is believed to be the active ingredient in marihuana. Many other compounds are present in marihuana, but they do not produce the mental effects of the drug.

Does marihuana vary in strength?

Yes. Some marihuana may produce no effect whatsoever. A small amount of strong marihuana may produce marked effects. The THC content of the plant determines its mind-altering activity, and this varies from none to more than 2 percent THC. Because THC is somewhat unstable, its content in marihuana decreases as time passes.

The plant that grows wild in the United States is low in THC content compared to cultivated marihuana, or the Mexican, Lebanese, or Indian varieties. Climate, soil conditions, the time of harvesting and other factors determine the potency.

What is hashish?

Hashish (hash) is the dark brown resin that is collected from the tops of potent *Cannabis sativa*. It is at least five times stronger than marihuana. Since it is stronger, the effect on the user is naturally more intense, and the possibility of side effects is greater.

Answer to Questions About Drug Abuse 335

Is marihuana an addicting drug?

Marihuana does not lead to physical dependence. Therefore, it cannot be considered addicting. Chronic users become psychologically dependent upon the effects of marihuana. Thus, it is classified as habituating. The fact that a drug is not addicting has little relationship to its potential for harm, since dependence, whether psychological or physical, is a serious matter.

Is marihuana a stimulant or a depressant?

Because it affects the individual's self control, the effects of marihuana vary so widely that it can be either a stimulant or a depressant. THC is a strong hallucinogen with some sedative properties. Occasionally, a person intoxicated with marihuana will become stimulated and overactive.

How is marihuana used?

In this country, it is generally smoked in self-rolled cigarettes called "joints." It is also smoked in ordinary pipes or water pipes. Marihuana and hashish can also be added to foods or drinks.

What are the immediate physical effects of smoking a marihuana cigarette?

Reddening of the whites of the eyes, an increased heart rate, and a cough due to the irritating effect of the smoke on the lungs are the most frequent and consistent physical effects. Hunger or sleepiness are reported by some individuals.

How long do the effects of marihuana last?

This depends upon the dose and the person. A few inhalations of strong marihuana can intoxicate a person for several hours. Weak marihuana will produce minimal effects for a short time. When a large amount is swallowed, the effects start later but persist longer than when the same quantity is smoked.

How does marihuana work in the brain?

This is not known. Studies attempting to clarify the question are underway.

Does the individual's tolerance to marihuana vary with repeated use?

The development of tolerance to marihuana does not occur. Some people speak of "reverse tolerance." By that they mean that a person may require less marihuana in order to reach a specific "high." This is basically a matter of learning how to smoke the drug, and of learning what effects to look for.

Do heavy users suffer physical withdrawal symptoms like the narcotic addict?

No. Sudden withdrawal may provoke restlessness and anxiety in a few persons who daily smoke large amounts of hashish, but true withdrawal symptoms as seen in the heroin addict do not develop.

What are the long-term physical effects of extended marihuana use?

These are not precisely known. Extensive scientific research is underway to answer this most important question.

What are the psychological effects of marihuana?

The psychological effects of marihuana are variable. They include distortions of hearing, vision and sense of time. Thought becomes dream-like. The belief that one is thinking better is not unusual. Performance may be hampered or unchanged. Illusions (misinterpretation of sensations) are often reported, but hallucination (experiencing non-existent sensations) and delusions (false beliefs) are rare. Unfounded suspicion may occur, and this may be accompanied by anxiety. More often the feeling is one of a passive euphoria or "high." The individual tends to withdraw into himself. Occasionally, uncontrollable laughter or crying may occur.

What kinds of emotional problems can the marihuana user have?

Anxiety reactions and panic states have been noted. Accidents have occurred due to impaired judgment and time-space distortions. The user, especially if he is inexperienced, may become excessively suspicious of people and take action that leads to injury. A toxic psychosis consisting of mental confusion, loss of contact with reality, and memory disturbances has been recorded.

The effects of prolonged use are not scientifically known. In those countries where *cannabis* use has been traditional, excessive amounts are claimed to induce loss of motivation, apathy, memory difficulties and loss of mental acuity. Reports of psychotic breakdowns from the extended use of marihuana are frequently found in the medical literature of the Near and Middle East, but these require further scientific investigation.

Does the heavy use of marihuana affect the personality development of the young person?

It can. By making marihuana use a career, the young person avoids normal life stresses and the problems that are an intrinsic part of growing up. He therefore misses the opportunity to mature to his full physical and mental potential. In addition, the developing personality is known to be susceptible to the effects of all mind-altering substances.

Does marihuana lead to increased sexual activity?

Marihuana has no known aphrodisiac property. At various times in the past, both promiscuity and impotence have been attributed to the use of marihuana without scientific basis for either allegation.

Why do people continue to use marihuana?

The consistent user, the "pothead," is likely to be emotionally disturbed, according to many studies of this group. He is using the drug to treat his personality problems.

How much marihuana is being used in this country?

The use of marihuana is increasing. In a recent nationwide survey, 4 percent of those queried responded affirmatively to the question, "Have you ever used marihuana?" That would mean that more than 8 million people have tried the drug. Twelve percent of the young people indicated that they have tried it. Exact statistics are difficult to obtain because of the legal penalties.

In college surveys, two-thirds of those who said that they had tried the drug did so less than a dozen times. Another quarter are occasional users, and the rest—less than 10 percent—may be considered daily or heavy users.

Why are so many adolescents experimenting with marihuana now?

In part this is because marihuana is "in." Peer group pressures have led many to try "pot." Some use it as an act of defiance. Some are curious. While most adolescents do not continue using the drug, 5 to 10 percent become heavy, daily users.

How are teenagers introduced to marihuana?

In general, adolescents are introduced to marihuana by others in their group. There is little evidence to confirm the belief that "pushers" need to "turn on" a novice. His "friends" do it for him.

Heavy marihuana users may go on to more dangerous drugs as a result of group pressures or of their own volition. Occasionally, a "pusher" will persuade the buyer to try a more dangerous drug.

How does marihuana get onto the black market?

Although truckload lots are sometimes detected, most marihuana smuggling and sales are small-time operations of a few pounds or less. Organized criminal syndicates have not been involved to date.

About 80 percent of the marihuana comes in from Mexico. The rest is acquired locally. Hashish is made in the Near East and is smuggled into the U. S. Young people themselves account for most acquisition and sales, according to the Bureau of Narcotics and Dangerous Drugs.

What is the relationship between marihuana and criminal or violent behavior?

Any drug that loosens self-control may contribute to criminal behavior. Persons under the influence of marihuana tend to be passive, although some crimes have been committed by persons while they were "high." The personality of the user is as important as the type of drug in determining whether chemical substances lead to criminal or violent behavior.

Can one smoke a little marihuana, equivalent to a drink of alcohol, and not become intoxicated?

Some people familiar with the drug are able to control its effects to permit only a feeling of relaxation. However, the usual intent of the user is to become "stoned." As a rule, either no effect or an intoxicating effect is obtained from the use of marihuana.

Is marihuana less harmful than alcohol?

The results of intoxication by both drugs can be harmful.

We know that alcohol is a dangerous drug physically, psychologically or socially for millions of people. There is no firm evidence that marihuana would be less harmful if used consistently. In countries where alcohol is forbidden by religious taboo, skid rows based on marihuana exist. The "rumhead" and the "pothead" are both unenviable creatures.

If alcohol is legal, why not marihuana?

It would seem more logical to deal with our millions of alcoholics than to add another mind-altering chemical to our existing problem. Whether another intoxicant should be accepted into the culture is the question.

Only during the past 3 years has the sophisticated, scientific study of marihuana been underway. It would seem prudent to await the results of ongoing and planned studies before treating marihuana as we do alcohol.

Does marihuana have any medical uses?

Marihuana has no approved medical use in the U. S. Some re-

searchers are attempting to determine whether THC may have appetite-enhancing, anticonvulsant, or antidepressant capabilities.
What research is being done on marihuana?
A considerable amount of research with marihuana and THC is underway or planned. These investigations will help provide answers to many questions about the drug.

With the recent availability of synthetic THC and the ability to determine the amount of THC in marihuana, it is now feasible to know the exact quality of the substance being studied. This permits precise analysis that was not possible before in such ways as the following:

1. An examination of the changes that occur in the body when marihuana is smoked, as well as the observation of the metabolic changes that take place in THC.

2. The labelling of THC with radioactive material in order to learn the distribution and excretion of the drug.

3. The effect of marihuana on the chemical components of the brain and other tissues.

4. A testing of the acute and chronic toxicity of marihuana.

5. Research to discover the physiological and psychological changes in man caused by varying doses of marihuana. This ranges from studying brain-wave patterns to testing a subject's ability to perform complex tasks.

6. An examination of the effects of THC and other marihuana components upon chromosomes.

To determine the effects of the long-term use of marihuana more accurately, negotiations are now underway with qualified scientists in countries where the use of the drug has been customary for years. Groups of long-term, daily users will be compared with matched groups of non-users. The results of physical and psychological examinations will be studied for the two groups.

Is there anything in marihuana that leads to the use of other drugs?
There is nothing in marihuana itself that produces a need to use other drugs. Most marihuana smokers do not progress to stronger substances. Some do. Surveys supported by the National Institute of Mental Health show that the "pothead" does tend to experiment with other drugs. Hashish is frequently tried, and large numbers of "potheads" later use strong hallucinogens, amphetamines, and,

occasionally, barbiturates. Some try opium and heroin.

In one college survey, 1 percent of the "potheads" became addicted to opium or heroin. In surveys of heroin addicts, 85 percent had previously tried marihuana, but a still larger percentage had used alcohol before heroin.

It appears that the person who becomes seriously overinvolved with any drug is likely to have the emotional need to seek other kinds of drugs and to try them repetitively.

QUESTIONS ABOUT HALLUCINOGENS

What are hallucinogens?

Hallucinogens (also called psychedelics) are drugs capable of provoking changes of sensation, thinking, self-awareness and emotion. Alterations of time and space perception, illusions, hallucinations and delusions may be either minimal or overwhelming depending on the dose. The results are very variable; a "high" or a "bad trip" ("freakout" or "bummer") may occur in the same person on different occasions.

LSD is the most potent and best-studied hallucinogen. Besides LSD, a large number of synthetic and natural hallucinogens are known. Mescaline from the peyote cactus, psilocybin from the Mexican mushroom, morning glory seeds, DMT, STP, MDA and dozens of others are known and abused. Along with its active component THC, marihuana is medically classified as an hallucinogen.

Is it true that any drug will make you hallucinate if taken in sufficient amounts?

Many drugs will cause a delirium, accompanied by hallucinations and delusions, when taken by people who are hypersentitive to them. Extraordinarily large amounts of certain drugs may also produce hallucinations. However, the mind-altering drugs are much more likely to induce hallucinations because of their direct action on the brain cells.

What is LSD?

Lysergic acid comes from ergot, the fungus that spoils rye grain. It was first converted in 1938 to lysergic acid diethylamide (LSD) by the Swiss chemist, Albert Hoffman, who accidentally discovered its mind-altering properties in 1943.

What are the immediate physical effects of LSD?

A person who has consumed LSD will have dilated pupils, a flushed face, perhaps a rise in temperature and heartbeat, a slight increase in blood pressure, and a feeling of being chilly. A rare convulsion has been noted. These effects disappear as the action of the drug subsides.

What is the LSD state like?

The LSD state varies greatly according to the dosage, the personality of the user and the conditions under which the drug is taken. Basically, it causes changes in sensation. Vision is most markedly altered. Changes in depth perception and the meaning of the perceived object are most frequently described. Illusions and hallucinations can occur. Thinking may become pictorial and reverie states are common. Delusions are expressed. The sense of time and of self are strangely altered. Strong emotions may range from bliss to horror, sometimes within a single experience. Sensations may "crossover," that is, music may be seen or color heard. The individual is suggestible and, especially under high doses, loses his ability to discriminate and evaluate his experience.

What is a "Good Trip"? A "Bad Trip"?

In the parlance of the LSD user, the "good trip" consists of pleasant imagery and emotional feelings. The "bad trip" or "bummer" is the opposite. Perceived images are terrifying and the emotional state is one of dread and horror.

What are some of the more harmful effects of LSD?

During the LSD state, the loss of control can cause panic reactions or feelings of grandeur. Both have led to injury or death when the panic or the paranoia was acted upon.

The prolonged reactions consist of anxiety and depressive states, or psychotic breaks with reality which may last from a few days to years.

What is a "Flashback"?

A "flashback" is a recurrence of some of the features of the LSD state days or months after the last dose. It can be invoked by physical or psychological stress, or by medications such as antihistamines, or by marihuana.

Those individuals who have used LSD infrequently rarely report flashbacks; intensive use seems to produce them more frequently.

Often a flashback occurring without apparent cause can induce anxiety and concern that one is going mad. This can result in considerable fear and depression and has been known to culminate in suicide.

Can LSD damage chromosomes?

A number of reputable scientists have reported chromosomal fragmentation in connection with LSD exposure in the test tube, in animals, and in man. A similar number of equally capable scientists have been unable to confirm these findings. The question whether LSD itself can induce congenital abnormalities remains unresolved. Further work is continuing and will clarify this question.

Is there any evidence that heavy LSD use causes brain cell changes?

In experiments designed to answer this question, some changes in mental functions have been detected in heavy users, but they are not present in all cases.

Heavy users of LSD sometimes develop impaired memory and attention span, mental confusion, and difficulty with abstract thinking. These signs of organic brain changes may be subtle or pronounced. It is not known whether these alterations persist or whether they are reversible if the use of LSD is discontinued.

Are people more creative under or after LSD?

People who have taken LSD feel more creative. Whether they actually are or not is difficult to determine. In studies done to compare individuals' creative capabilities before and after LSD experiences, it was found that no significant changes had occurred. Creativity might conceivably be enhanced in a few instances, but it is diminished in others because LSD may reduce the motivation to work and execute creative ideas.

Is the LSD state like the mystical state?

The transcendental or mystical state includes feelings of wonder or ecstasy, a sense of perceiving beauty, the absence of rational thought, a sense of discovering great meaning. Many of these phenomena can be mimicked by the LSD state, which is why it has been called a "religious" drug. The LSD-induced mystical state differs as significantly from the natural one as an artificial pearl from the real thing.

Do you really get to know yourself after LSD?

The *illusion* that one obtains insights about one's personality and behavior while under LSD may occur. From an analysis of these "insights" and of subsequent behavior, it is doubtful that true insights happen with any regularity.

Why would anybody try a drug like LSD?

People give many reasons for trying LSD, ranging from curiosity to a desire to "know oneself." The overwhelming majority of people take the drug for the "high"—to feel better. This may be because they are unable to deal with life's frustrations, or feel alienated. If the LSD state were not accompanied by a "high," it would never have become popular.

What percentage of students have tried LSD?

Most surveys indicate that about 4 percent of college students have tried LSD at least once. This figure has remained relatively stable for the past three years. However, numbers of high school and junior high school students are known to have tried this drug recently.

Is the use of LSD increasing?

The use of LSD has levelled off and may be decreasing. Although some very young people are turning to LSD, a number of the older users are discontinuing its use. This shift is probably due to the growing knowledge of the side effects, the "flashbacks," the possibility of chromosomal changes, or simply because the users finally have come to recognize the illusory nature of the LSD experience.

What have we learned from LSD?

LSD is the most potent of all hallucinogenic substances used by man. A minute amount reaching the brain produces striking effects on mental functioning.

From research with LSD we have gained much basic information about the nature of brain cell transmission, and how distortion of the chemical mediators of transmission can result in disruptive mental functioning. Experiments that have sought to find a use for this unusual chemical have been inconclusive. It has been tried for the severe alcoholic, in certain character disorders, in childhood autism and as an aid to psychotherapy. At present no medical usefulness has been found.

Is much research going on using LSD?

More than 300 investigators have been given supplies of this drug through the National Institute of Mental Health to carry out research in the past three years. Considerable important work is continuing.

What is the source of illicit LSD?

Almost invariably, illicit LSD comes from clandestine laboratories or is smuggled in from abroad. The precursors, lysergic acid and lysergic acid amide, can be converted into lysergic acid diethylamide (LSD) by a proficient chemist who has a reasonably well-equipped laboratory.

When obtained from illicit sources, the quality of LSD varies. Some LSD is fairly pure; other samples contain impurities and adulterants. The amount contained in each capsule or tablet usually differs greatly from the amount claimed by the "pusher." The user has no way of knowing the quality or the quantity of his LSD.

QUESTIONS ABOUT STIMULANTS

What is a stimulant?

Stimulants are drugs, usually amphetamines, which increase alertness, reduce hunger and provide a feeling of well being. Their medical uses include the suppression of appetite and the reduction of fatigue or mild depression.

Many stimulants are known, including: cocaine, amphetamine (Benzedrine "bennies"), dextroamphetamine (Dexedrine "dexies") and methamphetamine. The latter drug is commonly called "speed" or "crystal." Stimulants are also known as "uppers" or "pep pills."

How do amphetamines work?

According to current research findings, amphetamines increase the availability of noradrenalin at the nerve cell connections. This is particularly true in areas of the brain associated with vigilance, heart action, and mood. Excessive stimulation of these brain cells is normal under emergency life conditions, but when it is prolonged by amphetamines, undesirable secondary changes develop.

How are stimulants taken?

Usually stimulants are taken by mouth in the form of capsules or tablets. Crystal methamphetamine and cocaine can be inhaled or "snorted" through the nose. They can also be injected into veins, in which case the effects are immediate and more intense.

How many people are abusing amphetamines?

The exact number of amphetamine abusers is unknown, but the abuse of very large quantities of amphetamines is increasing. The drug-using subcultures, such as Haight-Ashbury in San Francisco, are now essentially "speed" subcultures. The abuse of amphetamines in weight-reducing pills is also on the rise. Approximately 10 billion amphetamine pills are legitimately manufactured every year, and a large amount of these will be diverted into illegal channels. Many illicit laboratories that manufacture stimulants have been discovered and seized.

What are the various types of stimulant abuse?

There is the occasional user who takes the drug to exert himself beyond his physiological limits. He may want to stay awake to drive, excel in an athletic contest, or cram for an examination. This type of abuse rarely leads to difficulties, but it may. Instances of death during athletic contests have been traced to amphetamine use.

A second type of abuse is taking 75-100 mg. per day (the average dose is 15-30 mg.) for long periods of time. These individuals are drug-dependent.

A relatively new type of abuse involves the injection of massive doses intravenously once or a dozen times a day. This produces practically the same effects as cocaine. These users are referred to as "speed freaks."

What effects do amphetamines have?

In ordinary amounts the amphetamines provide a transient sense of alertness and well being. Hunger is diminished, and short-term performance may be enhanced in the fatigued person.

When amphetamines are taken intravenously in large amounts, an ecstatic "high" occurs which decreases over a few hours. Re-injection is then necessary to reproduce the stimulation. This cycle can go on for days until the person is physically exhausted. Shakiness, itching, muscle pains, and tension states are common. Collapse and death have occurred.

Upon withdrawal the "speed freak" feels terribly depressed and lethargic. Re-injection of amphetamines relieves these symptoms. Since tolerance to high doses develops and withdrawal symptoms occur, large amounts of amphetamines are considered physically addicting. Small amounts are psychologically habituating.

What are the physical complications of amphetamine abuse?

In addition to those diseases which accompany the unsterile injection of material into the body, the excessive amounts of amphetamines can cause certain medical problems. Liver damage may result from the enormous quantities being taken. Brain damage from such quantities has been demonstrated in animals. Abnormal rhythms of the heart have occurred, and a marked increase in blood pressure is well known.

Neglect of personal hygiene can lead to skin infections or dental decay. Drastic weight loss, and malnutrition and vitamin deficiencies are part of the list of adverse physical complications.

What are the psychiatric complications of amphetamine abuse?

While under the influence of large amounts of amphetamines, the individual may become overactive, irritable, talkative, suspicious and sometimes violent. He reacts impulsively. This combination can lead to belligerent or homicidal behavior.

There is a deterioration of all social, familial and moral values. Like the heroin addict, the "speed freak" will do anything to obtain his supplies.

The paranoid psychotic state can last long beyond the period of drug activity and resembles paranoid schizophrenia.

What can be done about the "speed" problem?

The elimination of the large-scale illicit supplies and better controls over legitimate production are part of the answer. In addition, the consequences and complications must be made known as widely as possible. The user needs skilled treatment. It is likely that only the very disturbed person will become involved in the "speed" scene if the known effects of taking the drug are properly disseminated.

Are there any special difficulties in the treatment of stimulant abusers?

The "speed freak" is a difficult patient to rehabilitate. Although he may want to stop using the drug, his "high" is so intense that he is attracted to the enormous euphoria that he obtains from the chemical. Persons who seem to have broken the speed habit often relapse.

Treatment may require the close support of the user's friends and family, plus medical and psychological help. In some cases, closed-ward hospitalization may be necessary. One of the more successful forms of treatment is group therapy in which ex-users interact with "speed freaks." Those who have come through the "speed" scene are trusted, and their counsel is likely to be accepted by the person who wants to stop his destructive use of the drug.

Why has Sweden virtually abolished the medical use of amphetamines?

Sweden has a major problem with the amphetamine-like substance, phenmetrazine (Preludin). It was introduced as a "safe" weight reducing pill, but for the past 10 years its illicit use has been increasing. It is estimated that about 10,000 people (Sweden has a population of 8 million) use large amounts of this drug, most of it by intravenous injection.

At present only those few cases which are approved by a special commission can be legally treated with amphetamines. Despite this cutoff of legitimate supplies, the problem continues. Illegal laboratories still provide the material, and much is brought in from other countries where it is readily available.

QUESTIONS ABOUT SEDATIVES

What are sedatives and tranquilizers?

Sedatives induce sleep. When taken in small doses they reduce daytime tension and anxiety. The barbiturates constitute the largest group of sedatives. When used without close supervision, the possibilities of taking increased amounts and becoming dependent are present. In street parlance, the sedatives are also called "goof balls," "sleepers," and "downers."

The tranquilizers are drugs that calm, relax and diminish anxiety. Like sedatives, they may cause drowsiness. Tranquilizers that are used to treat serious mental disorders are not dependency producing. It is tranquilizers like meprobamate (Miltown, Equanil) to which dependence can be developed.

Are sedatives physically addicting?

Yes. Tolerance to the effects of barbiturates develops and withdrawal effects occur when the drug is stopped. A strong desire to continue taking the drug is present after a few weeks on large amounts. Addiction to 50 or more sleeping pills a day has been reported.

Are barbiturates the only group of sedatives with danger of addiction?

No. Other addicting sedatives include glutethimide (Doriden), chloral hydrate and many others. Everything that is said about the barbiturates can be applied to the non-barbiturate sedatives.

Who are the abusers of barbiturates?

People who have difficulty dealing with anxiety, or who have troubles with insomnia may become overinvolved with sedatives or tranquilizers and come to depend on them.

Barbiturates are taken by some heroin users either to supplement the heroin or substitute for it.

People under excessive stress, or those who cannot tolerate ordinary stress, are vulnerable. A few years ago sedatives were drugs of abuse for adults. Now they are being consumed more and more frequently by teenagers and pre-teenagers.

Persons who take amphetamines and become jittery might also take barbiturates to ease their tension.

What are the medical uses for sedatives?

In addition to inducing sleep and relaxing tensions, barbiturates are used for psychosomatic conditions such as high blood pressure and peptic ulcers. One barbiturate, phenobarbital, is useful as an anti-convulsant.

What happens if a barbiturate abuser suddenly stops taking the drug?

If the barbiturate dependence is severe, sudden discontinuance of the drug can be dangerous. A severe withdrawal state resembles delirium tremens. The patient is sweaty, fearful, sleepless and tremulous. He is restless, agitated, and may suffer convulsions. In addition, he may see things that aren't there and have delusional, confused thoughts. The amount of barbiturate must be slowly decreased; the patient requires considerable medical and nursing support.

Sudden barbiturate withdrawal is an acute medical emergency requiring hospitalization and intensive care.

Are sedatives taken in large quantities dangerous?

Yes. The most common mode of suicide with drugs is with sleeping pills. Accidental deaths due to taking a larger number than intended are not uncommon. In the latter instance, the person takes one or two pills at bedtime, falls asleep and then awakens. Not remembering that he has taken his sleeping medicine, he takes some more. If this is repeated a few times during the night a poisonous overdose may be consumed.

Do people fall asleep when they take large amounts of sedatives continually?

Ordinarily they go into a coma. If they are tolerant to large amounts, they may remain awake and appear intoxicated. Speech and movements may be uncoordinated. Skilled tasks are performed sluggishly and without precision. Judgment and perception are impaired. Confusion, slurred speech, irritability, and an unsteady gait are often seen in chronic users.

How can one break a large sedative "Habit"?

This should be done with the help of a physician. Sometimes hospitalization is necessary. Gradual reduction is safer than abrupt discontinuance.

Is it true that some people abuse sedatives and stimulants simultaneously?

Yes. Although the two types of drugs have opposite actions, some individuals become dependent upon the combinations. It might be imagined that an "upper" would completely neutralize a "downer," but this is not so. A desirable feeling is obtained, and large numbers of such combinations may be swallowed habitually.

Is it true that the combination of sleeping pills and alcohol is dangerous?

Yes. Taken together, less than lethal doses of alcohol and sleeping pills may be fatal. The person who is drunk may take a few barbiturate capsules and not survive. Barbiturates when taken with narcotics, anesthetics, and tranquilizers may also be fatal.

QUESTIONS ABOUT NARCOTICS

What is a narcotic?

A narcotic is a drug that relieves pain and induces sleep. The narcotics, or opiates, include opium and its active components, such as morphine. They also include heroin, which is morphine chemically altered to make it about six times stronger. Narcotics also include a series of synthetic chemicals that have a morphine-like action.

Which narcotics are significantly abused?

Heroin accounts for 90 percent of the narcotic addiction problem. It is not used in medicine, and all heroin in the U.S. is smuggled into the country. Morphine, methadone, and meperidine are used medically and are infrequently seen on the black market. Paregoric and cough syrups containing codeine are also abused.

Is narcotic addiction increasing?

As of December 31, 1968, the Bureau of Narcotics and Dangerous Drugs reported 64,011 narcotic addicts in the United States. This is an increase of 2,000 (3 percent) over the previous year. These figures include only those addicts who have been reported to the Bureau. The reporting system is voluntary on the part of the reporting agency and, as such, is not all inclusive. The New York State Narcotic Control Commission reports about 60,000 narcotic addicts in New York alone. The heroin abuse problem has been increasing since World War II and it continues to increase. Perhaps the most realistic estimate of the number of opiate addicts in the country is between 100,000 and 200,000.

Why do people take opiates?

People in physical or psychological pain may turn to heroin for relief, especially if their ability to endure distress is low. Many are introduced to the drug by "friends." Some youngsters mimic the behavior of grownups who are addicted. Certain addicts derive gratification from turning others on.

Many believe, "It can't happen to me." They think they can use heroin occasionally and not get hooked. These are often weekend "joy poppers." A good number of these individuals end up addicted.

Young males from minority groups who live in central city areas are most likely to become addicts. There is evidence that some middleclass youngsters in the drug-using communities have begun to abuse heroin. A small number of doctors and nurses who have the drugs available have become addicted.

What does the heroin addict look like?

He may appear normal. Some of the acute symptoms associated with heroin are sniffling, flushing, drowsiness and constipation.

Very contracted pupils are typical of opiate use. Some addicts may have an unhealthy appearance because of poor food intake and personal neglect. Venereal disease among addicts is not uncommon.

Heroin addicts appear at hospitals with blood infections, hepatitis, symptoms of overdose and, more rarely, lockjaw.

Fresh needle marks and "tracks" (discolorations along the course of veins in the arms and legs) are detectable during an examination.

A sample of the addict's urine will reveal heroin or quinine. Barbiturate and amphetamine abuse can also be detected by urine testing.

Can a person function while on narcotics?

If the person is tolerant to an opiate he can usually function satisfactorily. This assumes that he is on a constant dosage level, and that his body's reaction to the drug is minimal. It merely keeps him comfortable.

This ability to perform, stay awake and alert after being kept on a maintenance level has been demonstrated with the methadone maintenance treatment. An occasional person will be drowsy.

What is it like to take a shot of heroin?

Generally, there is a feeling of relaxation and of being "high." This is accompanied by an "awayness" or pleasant, dreamlike state.

As tolerance develops, the "high" is generally lost. The addict then requires heroin to avoid the withdrawal sickness. In other words, at this point he is using heroin to feel normal.

What are the physical dangers of addiction?

The physical complications are many and some are life endangering. An overdose, resulting in death, occurs when someone has lost or never developed tolerance because he was using very diluted heroin. If, by chance, he obtains pure heroin, he may die moments after injection.

Infections from unsterile solutions, syringes, and needles cause many bacterial diseases. Viral hepatitis can be epidemic among addicts. Skin abscesses, inflammation of the veins and congestion of the lungs are further complications. Venereal diseases, tuberculosis and pneumonia are not uncommon.

The life expectancy of the addict is much lower than that of the non-addict. Addicts of both sexes are less fertile, and infants born of addict mothers may suffer withdrawal symptoms.

What are withdrawal symptoms like?

When addiction exists, stopping the drug provokes withdrawal sickness some 12 to 16 hours after the last injection. The addict yawns, shakes, sweats, his nose and eyes run, and he vomits. Muscle aches and jerks ("kicking the habit") occur along with abdominal pain and diarrhea. Chills and backache are frequent.

Hallucinations and delusions can develop, and these are usually terrifying. An injection of an opiate brings about immediate relief.

What are the psychiatric complications of narcotic addiction?

The life of the narcotic addict is deplorable. His waking existence is centered around obtaining money to buy heroin ("hustling"), making a connection with a pusher ("copping"), and trying to avoid withdrawal.

The activities that an addict will resort to in order to obtain heroin are harmful to himself and those around him. He may steal from his loved ones, double-cross his best friend, or pander his wife. It is obvious that a career of heroin addiction must lead to personality decay and seriously impair emotional maturation.

Is there an addictive personality?

It has been demonstrated that anyone can become addicted if he takes opiates regularly for a few weeks. Even animals can become addicted. However, certain kinds of people are more likely to become involved with heroin than others under similar life situations. These individuals have a low frustration tolerance and great dependency needs. Impulsive, immature, inadequate individuals are likely candidates. Many are "now" oriented, seeking the immediate "high" without regard to future consequences. Some have a character disorder that permits deviant behavior without guilt feelings.

Should a reasonably mature, stable person become addicted, the prospects of his rehabilitation are much better than those of the immature, unstable addict.

What treatment procedures are available to the heroin addict?

"Once an addict, always an addict" is simply untrue. Many treatment procedures are possible for the heroin user. Ex-addict self-help groups have been useful for some. Others have benefited from methadone maintenance. This consists of the substitution of methadone, a narcotic, under close supervision. If the patient on methadone takes heroin he will notice no effect from it because of cross tolerance. Another approach uses cyclazocine, a narcotic antagonist, not a narcotic. If heroin is taken after cyclazocine, no effect is noted.

Taking the addict off heroin is not too difficult, but keeping him off is. He usually needs counselling, job training and other rehabilitative efforts. The Federal Government and some States have civil commitment and voluntary rehabilitation programs. Many more narcotic addict rehabilitation centers are coming into existence at the community level. At these centers the addict seeking help can be given all the rehabilitation assistance he needs.

Is there a relationship between heroin and crime?

Many addicts had criminal records before they became addicted. Nevertheless, a direct relationship between the addicted person and criminal activity does exist because of the need for large sums of money in order to support his "habit." Shoplifting, pimping, prostitution, peddling heroin, and car theft are some of the crimes to which the addict resorts. When he is feeling symptoms of withdrawal, he may commit more violent crimes in order to obtain his drug.

Addicts who are sufficiently affluent to buy heroin will not commit criminal acts. The opiate state is one of passivity rather than aggression.

What are the organized crime elements that deal in narcotics and dangerous drugs?

Trafficking in heroin is usually undertaken by the organized criminal elements based in major metropolitan areas throughout the country. These organizations have the manpower, financial ability, and international connections with which to procure and successfully smuggle large quantities of heroin into the United States from France and other countries. To a lesser extent, numerous individuals and independent groups smuggle illicitly produced Mexican heroin in small quantities across the Mexican border.

What is the quality of heroin bought on the street?

Heroin is invariably diluted with milk sugar, quinine, or other materials. Capsules or cellophane "bags" which may vary from 0 to 10 percent heroin are sold to users for $2 to $10. The material is unsterile. Some of the heroin has been "cut" so much that the addict has a "needle habit," not a heroin "habit." A "needle habit" is one in which the user obtains gratification from hustling for narcotics and injecting himself with the material even though it contains little or no heroin.

What about the "British System" of dealing with heroin addiction?

Until recently, English heroin addicts were able to obtain heroin by prescription after registering with a physician. During the past decade, however, the number of known heroin addicts rose from a few hundred to several thousand. The number of known addicts under 20 years of age increased from one in 1960 to 1,016 in 1969. (These figures are regarded as underestimates, since many addicts do not come to official attention.)

As a result of this increase, the "system" was changed in 1968. British physicians can no longer prescribe heroin. Instead, rehabilitation centers have been established for the treatment of drug addicts. In cases where total abstinence is not possible for an addict, some heroin or methadone may be prescribed. The British system is considered a failure and has been modified to meet the increasing problem of addiction. However, it has largely prevented the involvement of organized criminal elements in heroin traffic. At present, the illicit traffic consists of addicts selling their supplies to others.

QUESTIONS ABOUT OTHER SUBSTANCES OF ABUSE

Model airplane glue, gasoline, paint thinner and other volatile solvents have been reported as abusable substances. What are their effects?

These substances, which were obviously never meant to be taken by man, contain a variety of chemicals, some quite dangerous. Others are toxic only when used over long periods. They provide a clouded mental state that can develop into a coma. Temporary blindness has been reported. Death is known to occur when the solvent is inhaled without sufficient oxygen as, for example, when the individual loses consciousness and his mouth and nose fall into the plastic bag containing the solvents. Damage to bone marrow, kidneys and lungs has been described in autopsy reports.

What about over-the-counter medicines?

Certain over-the-counter medicines have been taken in excess and have been used to "turn on." Certain cough syrups and the stay-awake and go-to-sleep preparations are sold without prescription and may cause dependence. Paregoric (camphorated tincture of opium), which is available in some States with a prescription, is also being abused.

Another way in which over-the-counter medicines and other advertised products might contribute to the drug abuse problem is the implication of their message. When children or adolescents repetitively hear that it is all right to take substances for minor emotional difficulties, they may become conditioned to believe the idea. It is not desirable to promote the notion that taking a chemical will solve the difficulties of everyday life.

Can nutmeg be abused?

If large amounts of nutmeg or mace are taken, they can induce a drunken, confused state. This requires a substantial quantity, which can irritate the kidneys. Abuse has been reported in immature adolescents, and in prisoners who have access to these spices while working in prison kitchens.

What is known about belladonna and jimson weed abuse?

A large number of wild plants can cause delirium or death, depending upon the amount ingested. They include belladonna and Jimson weed (stramonium) which grow in many parts of the country. They have long been used as intoxicants; they were the constituents of the witches' brews of earlier days. The notion that witches flew on broom-sticks was the result of the hallucinations of those under the influence of these powerful plants.

Dryness of the mouth and skin, a high fever and dilated pupils are characteristic effects caused by these weeds.

Asthmador is a drug that contains a combination of belladonna and stramonium and is prescribed as an asthma remedy. It, too, has been occasionally misused.

DRUG GLOSSARY

Acid: LSD, LSD-25 (lysergic acid diethylamide).
Acidhead: Frequent user of LSD.
Bag: Packet of drugs.
Ball: Absorption of stimulants and cocaine via genitalia.
Bang: Injection of drugs.
Barbs: Barbiturates.
Bennies: Benzedrine, an amphetamine.

Bindle: Packet of narcotics.
Blank: Extremely low-grade narcotics.
Blast: Strong effect from a drug.
Blue angels: Amytal, a barbiturate.
Blue velvet: Paregoric (camphorated tincture of opium) and Pyribenzamine (an antihistamine) mixed and injected.
Bombita: Amphetamine injection, sometimes taken with heroin.
Bread: Money.
Bum trip: Bad experience with psychedelics.
Bummer: Bad experience with psychedelics.
Busted: Arrested.
Buttons: The sections of the peyote cactus.
Cap: Capsule.
Chipping: Taking narcotics occasionally.
Coasting: Under the influence of drugs.
Cokie: Cocaine addict.
Cold turkey: Sudden withdrawal of narcotics (from the gooseflesh, which resembles the skin of a cold plucked turkey).
Coming down: Recovering from a trip.
Connection: Drug supplier.
Cop: To obtain heroin.
Cop out: Quit, take off, confess, defect, inform.
Crash: The effects of stopping the use of amphetamines.
Crash pad: Place where the user withdraws from amphetamines.
Cubehead: Frequent user of LSD.
Cut: Dilute drugs by adding milk sugar or another inert substance.
Dealer: Drug supplier.
Deck: Packet of narcotics.
Dexies: Dexedrine, an amphetamine.
Dime bag: $10 package of narcotics.
Dirty: Possessing drugs, liable to arrest if searched.
Dollies: Dolophine (also known as methadone), a synthetic narcotic.
Doper: Person who uses drugs regularly.
Downers: Sedatives, alcohol, tranquilizers, and narcotics.
Drop: Swallow a drug.
Dummy: Purchase which did not contain narcotics.
Dynamite: High-grade heroin.
Fix: Injection of narcotics.

Flash: The initial feeling after injection.
Flip: Become psychotic.
Floating: Under the influence of drugs.
Freakout: Bad experience with psychedelics; also a chemical high.
Fuzz: The police.
Gage: Marihuana.
Good trip: Happy experience with psychedelics.
Goofballs: Sleeping pills.
Grass: Marihuana.
H: Heroin.
Hard narcotics: Opiates, such as heroin and morphine.
Hard stuff: Heroin.
Hash: Hashish, the resin of Cannabis.
Hay: Marihuana.
Head: Person dependent on drugs.
Hearts: Dexedrine tablets (from the shape).
Heat: The police.
High: Under the influence of drugs.
Holding: Having drugs in one's possession.
Hooked: Addicted.
Hophead: Narcotic addict.
Horse: Heroin.
Hustle: Activities involved in obtaining money to buy heroin.
Hustler: Prostitute.
Hype: Narcotics addict.
Joint: Marihuana cigarette.
Jolly beans: Pep pills.
Joy-pop: Inject narcotics irregularly.
Junkie: Narcotics addict.
Kick the habit: Stop using narcotics (from the withdrawal leg muscle twitches).
Layout: Equipment for injecting drug.
Lemonade: Poor heroin.
M: Morphine.
Mainline: Inject drugs into a vein.
Maintaining: Keeping at a certain level of drug effect.
(The) Man: The police.
Manicure: Remove the dirt, seeds, and stems from marihuana.

Mesc: Mescaline, the alkaloid in peyote.
Meth: Methamphetamine.
Methhead: Habitual user of methamphetamine.
Mikes: Micrograms (millionths of a gram).
Narc: Narcotics detective.
Nickel bag: $5 packet of drugs.
O. D.: Overdose of narcotics.
On the nod: Sleepy from narcotics.
Panic: Shortage of narcotics on the market.
Pillhead: Heavy user of pills, barbiturates or amphetamines or both.
Pop: Inject drugs.
Pot: Marihuana.
Pothead: Heavy marihuana user.
Purple hearts: Dexamyl, a combination of Dexedrine and Amytal (from the shape and color).
Pusher: Drug peddler.
Quill: A matchbook cover for sniffing Methedrine, cocaine, or heroin.
Rainbows: Tuinal (Amytal and Seconal), a barbiturate combination in a blue and red capsule.
Red devils: Seconal, a barbiturate.
Reefer: Marihuana cigarette.
Reentry: Return from a trip.
Roach: Marihuana butt.
Roach holder: Device for holding the butt of a marihuana cigarette.
Run: An amphetamine binge.
Satch cotton: Cotton used to strain drugs before injection; may be used again if supplies are gone.
Scag: Heroin.
Score: Make a purchase of drugs.
Shooting gallery: Place where addicts inject.
Skin popping: Injecting drugs under the skin.
Smack: Heroin.
Smoke: Wood alcohol.
Snorting: Inhaling drugs.
Snow: Cocaine.
Speed: Methamphetamine.

Speedball: An injection of a stimulant and a depressant, originally heroin and cocaine.
Speedfreak: Habitual user of speed.
Stash: Supply of drugs in a secure place.
Stick: Marihuana cigarette.
Stoolie: Informer.
Strung out: Addicted.
Tracks: Scars along veins after many injections.
Tripping out: High on psychedelics.
Turned on: Under the influence of drugs.
Turps: Elixir of Terpin Hydrate with Codeine, a cough syrup.
25: LSD (from its original designation, LSD-25.
Uppers: Stimulants, cocaine, and psychedelics.
Weed: Marihuana.
Works: Equipment for injecting drugs.
Yellow jacket: Nembutal, a barbiturate.
Yen sleep: A drowsy, restless state during the withdrawal period.

INDEX

Acree, Vernon D., 305
Adamowski, Benjamin, xiv
Adams, John Bodkin, M.D., 29
Adanon. (*See also* Dolophine, Amidone, Methadone), 68
Addiction and Society (book), 7, 39, 47, 78, 83, 91, 135, 137, 141
Addiction Research Center, U.S. Public Health Service Hospital, Lexington, Kentucky, 77, 147
Addiction to Analgesics and Barbiturates (article), 113
Africa, cannabis abuse in, 79
Alameda County, California, Sheriff, 169
Althen, Conrad, 281
Ambrose, Myles, xvii, 300, 304, 317
American Journal of Medicine, article in, 189
American Journal of Orthopsychiatry, article in, 115
American Medical Association, 22, 24
Report on Narcotic Addiction, Council of Mental Health, 308
Resolution eliminating heroin from medical preparations, 62
Amidone (*See also* Adanon, Dolophine, methadone), 68, 94
Amobarbital sodium (*See also* Barbiturates, Amytal, sedatives), 90
Amphetamine (*See also* Dextroamphetamine sulphate, Dexadrine, Dexadrine Spansule, Timcaps, Methamphetamine, 39, 91, 93, 96, 344
abuse in Japan, 91, 319
abuse in Scandinavian countries, 347
Sweden, 347
addiction, 118
clandestine laboratories, 100
dependence, 47
identification, 92, 256
sulphate, 92
tests for, 93, 96
Amsterdam, Netherlands, hashish smuggled from, 304
Amytol (*See also* Barbiturates, Amo-

barbital sodium, Tuinal), 90
Anderson, William R., Rep., 136
Anslinger, H. J., vii, xiii, 6, 28, 36, 41, 44, 50, 51, 79-81, 150, 166, 174, 242
A.P.C., 93
Archives of General Psychiatry, article in, 77
Are You Safe From Burglars? (book), 130
Argot, 147, 150, 355
Asia, cannabis abuse in, 79
Asia Minor, cannabis abuse in, 79
Asseltine, J. L., M.D., 86
Asthmador, abuse of (*See also* Belladonna, Stramonium (Jimson weed), 355
Ausubel, D. P., 7

Ball, John C., 7, 9, 189
Barbiturates (*See also* Amobarbital sodium, Amytal, "Blue Heavens, "Goof balls," Nembutal, Phenobarbital sodium, "Red birds," Secobarbital sodium, Seconal, Tuinal, "Yellow jacks"), 47, 90, 347
abuse, 39, 47, 90, 131
addiction, 347
dependence, 47
identification, 256
tests for, 97
Barnes, Robert Earl, 130
Battard, Robert, xvii
Becker, H. K., 124
Behrman, (Doctor) case, 23
Bejerot, Nils, 7, 39, 47, 78, 79, 83, 91, 135, 137, 141
Belk, George M., xvii
Bell, Joseph, 203
Belladonna, abuse of, 355
Bence, Dorothy, xiv
"Bennies," (*See* Amphetamines)
Benzedrine "Bennies," (*See* Amphetamines)
Berger, Herbert, M.D., 85

361

Bhang (*See also* Marihuana, Cannabis), 71
Bibliography, 320
Bludworth, Edward, 99
"Blue heavens," (*See* Barbiturates)
Bouck, Robert L., xiii
Bransky, Joseph, xiv, 178
Breidenbach, Samuel H., xiii
Bridges, Florence B., xiv
Brill, Henry, M.D., 31, 38, 75, 319
British Dangerous Drug Act of 1967, 38
British Foreign Office, 269
British police, cooperation of, 318
"British System," xii, 21, 26, 29, 31, 36, 354
Brotherhood of Evil: The Mafia (book), 271
Brown, Charles, M.D., 86
Brown, John, 286, 289
Buchalter, Louis "Lepke", 315
Bundy, Dorothy, xiv
Burglary, 130, 179
Bussler, Louis F., xvii
Butler, William P., xvii
Butler, William R., xvii

Cairo Institution of Social Research, 74
Caldwell, Anne, M.D., 80
California, drug addiction prevention, 174
  narcotic laws, 108
  narcotic prescription blanks, triplicate, 187, 310
  opium smuggling into, 207
California Narcotic Addict Evaluation Authority, 122
Canada, addiction in, 35
  illicit heroin traffic, 100, 315
Canadian Senate Committee Hearings, 28, 29, 111
Cannabis (*See* also Marihuana), 47, 70-99, 95
Carlisle, James, M.D., 86
Chadwick, Phillip, 165
Chambers, Carl D., 7, 9
Chan, L. Y., 37
Chapman, Kenneth, M.D., 7, 166
Charas (*See also* Cannabis, Marihuana), 71
Cheatwood, James, xvii, 300
Chicago, Illinois, murder of P. O.
  Inspection Service investigators, 167
  Opium drug raids, 265
Chicago Police Digest, article in, 165

Chinese Tong, 263, 284
  opium smoking, 265
Chloral hydrate (*See also* Sedatives, 93
Chlorpromazine, 177
Clandestine drug manufacturing laboratories, 99
Clinical Notes on the Use of Marihuana (paper), 83
Coca leaves, imports, 40
  international control, 40
Cocaine (*See also* Stimulants), 47, 70, 93, 173, 344
  dependence, 47, 124, 149
  tests for, 93
Cocteau, Jean, 35, 105, 167
Codeine, 46, 65, 93, 129
  in narcotic withdrawal, 190
  tests for, 93
Colao, Charles F., M.D., 132
Coleridge, Samuel Taylor, 143
Communication and Drug Abuse (book), 7
Compulsory Education: A Cause of Drug Addiction (paper), 85
Confessions of an English Opium Eater (book), 102
Connell, P. H., M.D., xviii, 37, 135
Controlled Substances Act of 1970, 40, 44
Copuroglu, Halil, arrest of, 318
Corrick, Harry Emmett, xiii. 275
Costello, Frank, 276
Cozzi, Mario, xvii
Cowden, Capt. James R., xviii
Crime, 76
  and addiction, 82, 84, 165, 353
  and marihuana, 76, 84
  burglary, 130
  Chinese tongs, 263
  criminal groups, 262
  scene searches, 248
Crookshank, Herman, xiv
Cross, John C., vii, 10, 104, 195, 198, 200, 204, 209, 272
Crutchfield Edith A., xvii
"Crystal" (*See* Methamphetamine)
Customs Today (quarterly), 305
Cyclazocine, narcotic antagonist, 136, 353

Dagga (*See also* Marihuana, Cannabis), 71
Darvon, 93
  tests for, 93
DeBaggio, Carl J., xiii

Define, Joseph, 212
Delaney, Austin, M.D., 86
Demerol, 46, 47
  addiction, 102, 121, 124
Dengler, Harry M., xiii
DeQuincey, Thomas, 102
Dexedrine (See also Amphetamines), 92, 344
  Spansule, 92
Dextromphetamine sulphate (See also Barbiturates, Amphetamine sulphate, Dexedrine, Dexedrine Spansule, Timcaps), 92, 355
Diacetylmorphine (See Heroin)
Dictionary of the American Underworld Lingo (book), 150
Dilaudid, 19, 46, 65, 94, 121
  addiction, 102
  forged prescriptions, 107
  tests for, 94
Ding, L. D., 37
Direct Sales Company, Inc., case, 25
District of Columbia, heroin addict survey, 82
  marihuana smoking, 82
  narcotic clinic, 82
  Narcotics Treatment Administration, 140
Diversion of opium, 313
  China, Mainland, 313
  Far East, 313
  Near East, 313
  Turkey, 313
Djamba (See also Cannabis, Marihuana), 71
DMT (See Hallucinogens)
Dobbs, William H., M.D., 140
Dogs as narcotic detectors, 296
  Royal Canadian Mounted Police, 297
  U.S. Bureau of Customs, 297
  U.S. Bureau of Narcotics, 297
Dole, Vincent, M.D., 132
Dollard, Inspector Robert L., xviii
Dolophine (See also Adanon, Amidone, methadone), 68, 94, 139
Doriden (See also Glutethimide, Sedatives), 348
Drug abuse, 326
Drug Addict As a Patient (book), 109
Drug addiction, 3, 5, 10-39, 102, 326
  and crime, 165, 353
  British Columbia, 35
  Canada, 35, 38
  characteristics of, 102, 145, 350
  definition, 46, 47

Drug addiction (continued),
  dependence, 46, 102
  drugs of, 46
  Europe, 173
  France, 173
  habituation, 328
  heroin, 5, 11-13, 19, 30, 34-38, 121, 132, 141, 145-149, 331, 350
  Hong Kong, 36, 37
  incidence of (chart), 8
  infant, 137, 177, 331
  Low Countries, 173
  management and treatment, 102, 188, 352
  medical profession, 24, 120, 311
  methadone, 121, 131
  prevention, 174
  Scandinavian Countries, 174
  United Kingdom, 36-39, 173
  Vancouver, B. C., 35
  withdrawal, 188, 352
Drug Addiction: Physiological, Psychological and Sociological Aspects (book), 7
Drug culture, 329
Drug glossary, 355
Drugs, dangerous, identification, 98
Drugs of addiction, dependence, habituation, 46, 328
Duguay, M. R., M.D., 86
Dunsworth, F. A., M.D., 86
Duquenois-Levine Test, 96
Duquenois Reagent, 96

Eastman Kodak Company, 241
Eddy, Dr. Nathan B., 7, 60
Egypt, hashish effects, 74, 79
Elik, Halit, arrest of, 318
Ellis, David C., xvii, 300
Englander, David M., 9
Enright, John R., xvii
Entrance, after delay, 294
  by force, 288
  by ruse, 285
  indirect methods, 295
  planning, 281
Epidemiology of Opiate Addiction in the United States (book), 7
Equanil (See also Tranquilizers, meprobamate, Miltown), 347
Esrar (See also Cannabis, Marihuana), 71
Evidence, crime scene searches, 248
  "lock seal" envelopes, 258

physical, collection and preservation, 242
processing procedures for specific types, 246

Facts About Narcotic Addiction (pamphlet), 46
Fairfax County (Va.) Police, 130, 307
Federal Exclusion Act, 264
Federal Source Book: Answers to the Most Frequently Asked Questions About Drug Abuse (book), 326
Ferat, Ihsan, arrest of, 318
Ferric chloride test, 94
Finlator, John H., xvii
Fischer, Joseph, M.D., 112, 120
Flanders, Joseph C., xvii
Fleming, T. J., 322
Flynn, Errol, 168
Fortified room, 279
France, clandestine heroin laboratories, 99
  cocaine use, 173
Frankau. Lady Isabella, M.D., 38
Fraser, Havelock F., M.D., 113, 189
French police, cooperation of, 318
Freud, Sigmund, 124
Friendly, Alfred, article by, 86
Fulton, Charles C., xiv, 49, 51, 64

Gaffney, George H., xiv
Gardner, Ramon, 37, 135
Gasoline, abuse of, 354
Gentry, Ernest, 198
German police, cooperation of, 318
Ginsberg, Allen, xi
Giordano, Henry L., xiii
Glaser, Frederick B., 189
Glossary of Terms in the Drug Culture (booklet), 151
Glue, model airplane, abuse of, 354
Glutethimide (*See also* Sedatives), 348
Gon Sam Mue, 267
Goodman & Gilman, 122
"Goof balls" (*See* Sedatives, barbiturates)
Gothenberg, Sweden, death from methadone poisoning, 135
Greece, Ancient, psychopharmacology, 80
Greek police, cooperation of, 318
Greenfield, Irwin I., xiv, 205, 210, 219, 223
Grider, James M., Jr., M.D., 189
Gunn, John W., xvii

Haislip, Gene R., xvii
Hallucinogens, 39, 88, 100, 340
  clandestine laboratories, 100
  DMT, 340
  LSD, 340
  marihuana, 340
  MDA. 340
  mescaline, 340
  morning glory seeds, 340
  psilocybin, 340
  psychedelics, 340
  STP, 340
Hamilton, James A., M.D., 116
Hamilton, Joseph, 303
Hand, Judge Learned, 319
Harney, Gladys M., xiv
Harney, Malachi L., vii, 10, 29, 87, 117, 142, 165, 230, 251, 272
Harrison Narcotic Law, 9, 11, 23, 45
Hashish (*See also* Cannabis, Marihuana, 71, 74, 88, 303
  production ban in Morocco, 74
  seizures, Greece, 318
Hawaii (book), 268
Helen of Troy, 3, 80
Hennessey, Police Chief, murder of, 274
Herndon, Charlie, 199
Heroin, 46, 60
  addiction, 31, 82, 100, 116, 131, 168, 350, 352
  clandestine laboratories, 99, 314
  deaths from overdoses, 132
  detection by dogs, 299
  illicit prices, 10
  illicit traffic arrests, 315
  seizures:
    France, 318
    Hong Kong, 30
    Spain, 318
    Switzerland, 318
    United States, 318
  smuggling from Japan, 266
  tests for, 92
Higgins, Dr. Lois, 37
Hildebrandt, William (Big Bill), 177-178, 193, 201
Himmelsbach, Dr. Clifford K., 7, 67
Hip Sing Tong, 266, 270
Hirose, Tetsuya, 319
Hitsman, Jimmy, 281
Homer, 3, 80
Hong Kong, addiction, 36
  narcotic arrests, 30
  seizures, 30
  White Paper on narcotic drugs, 36

Honor Thy Father (book), 277
"Hopeine", 53
Horan, Robert F., xviii, 132
Hussein, Omar, arrest of, 318
Hysohion, Christian, arrest of, 318

IACP (*See* International Association of Chiefs of Police
Illinois, drug addiction, 174
   prevention, 174
   treatment, 171
   narcotic law, 108
   prescription blanks, triplicate, 187, 310
Illinois Division of Narcotic Control, 121, 258
Indian hemp, (*See also* Cannabis, Marihuana), 78
India, opium imported from, 129
INEOA (*See* International Narcotic Enforcement Officers Association)
Infant addiction, 137, 177, 331
Informer, in narcotic cases, 198, 306
Informer in Law Enforcement (book), ix, 306
Infrared and Ultraviolet Photography (pamphlet), 239
Ingersoll, John E., xvii, 317
International Association of Chiefs of Police (IACP), 316, 317
International Criminal Police Organization (INTERPOL), 316
International Narcotics Enforcement Officers Association (INEOA), 316
   Annual Conference Reports, 78, 84, 124, 137
   International Narcotic Report, 136, 138
INTERPOL (*See* International Criminal Police Organization)
Isbell, Harris, M.D., xiv, 7, 77, 113, 124, 147
Italian police, cooperation of, 318
   Supreme Court, 276
Italy, clandestine heroin laboratories, 99

Jaffe, Jerome H., M.D., 122
JAMA (*See* Journal of the American Medical Association)
Jamaica, marihuana use in, 84
   smuggling from, 303
Japan, heroin smuggling from, 266
   methamphetamine abuse, 91, 319
   opium smuggling from, 266
Jimson weed, abuse of (*See also* Stramonium), 355
Johnson, Donald W., xvii
Journal of Pharmacology and Experimental Therapeutics, article in, 115
Journal of the American Medical Association, articles in, 20, 22, 24, 140, 308

Kansas City Syndicate, 212
Kee Mun Ki, 269
Kefauver, Senator Estes, 277
   Committee on Crime, U.S. Senate, 277
Kennedy, Robert F., 275
Kif (*See also* Cannabis, Marihuana), 71
King, Alexander, 105, 175
Kolansky, H., 323
Kreiger, Sheriff Ralph E., 139
Kreitner, Dorothea Dorge, xiv
Kublai Khan, 35
Kurland, Albert A., M.D., 127

Lafitte, Jean, 277
Lagaipa, Charles (Big Nose Charlie), 207
Lansky (book), 277
Larimore, Granville, M.D., 31
Law Enforcement Assistance Administration (LEAA), 317
League of Nations, 60
Leary, Timothy, xi
Lebanese police, cooperation of, 318
Lee, Howard B., M.D., 139
Lee, Col. Robert E., 289
Lenck, William M., xvii
Leritine, 46, 69
Levine, Joseph, xvii
Levine, Samuel, 124
Levine test, 96
Levo-Dromoran, 46, 69
Lewin, Lewis, 78
Lewis, Edward, M.D., xvii
Librium, 93
Lieberman, Beth, 80
Lieberman, Carl M., 80
Lipsius, Morris, 150
Los Angeles police, cooperation of, 293
Lowry, Dr. James V., 7
LSD, 39, 88, 100, 118, 340
Lucania, Salvatore (Lucky Luciano), 277
Lundell, F. W., M.D., 86
Lynch, Vincent dePaul, M.D., 78, 84

Mace, abuse of, 355
McClellan Committee, U.S. Senate, 275
McEathron, Gene, xvii, 300, 304

Maconha, 71
Mafia meeting, Apalachin, N.Y., 275
Mafia, Sicilian, 195, 271
Maher, John T., Jr., xvii, 129
Maisel, Albert, 264
Malherek, Paul F., xvii
Mann, Jean, xiv
Manzoul (*See also* Cannabis, Marihuana), 71
Marihuana, (*See also* Cannabis, Halucinogens, 47, 71-88, 117-118, 334-340
   and addiction, 83 ,149, 335
   and crime, 76, 84, 338
   brain damage, 86
   detection by dogs, 299
   habituation to, 335
   identification, 95, 256
   in Jamaica, 84
   research, 339
   smuggled from Jamaica, 303
   tests for, 95
Marihuana Tax Act of 1937, 45, 81
Marquis Test, 93
Martin, Paul, M.D., 31
Maryland Psychiatric Research Center, 127
Maurer, David W., 7, 79, 82, 123, 145, 150
Maxon, Edna P., 274
MDA (*See* Halucinogens)
Medicolegal Symposium, American Medical Association, Cleveland, 10
Meprobamate (*See also* Tranquilizers), 93, 347
Meredith, George, 144
Mescaline (*See also* Halucinogens), 93, 340
   clandestine laboratories, 100
   tests for, 93
Messick, Hank, 277
Methadone, 46, 68, 92, 129
   addiction, 100, 128, 131
   clandestine laboratoreis, 44, 100
   deaths from overdoses, 132, 135
   infant addiction, 137, 177, 331
   maintenance on, 121-140, 352
   prescriptions, 312
   production, 140
   substitution in withdrawal, 189-190
   tests for, 92
   treatment, 121-140, 189-190
Methadone in the Capital: Does It Really Work? (WTOP-TV), 132
Methadone Treatment of Heroin Addicts, Early Results Provide More Questions Than Answers (article), 140
Methamphetamine (*See also* Amphetamines), 97, 142, 344
   control in Japan, 319
   tests for, 97
Metopon, 46, 66
Metropolitan Enforcement Group (MEG), 317
Mexico, illicit heroin traffic, 99, 206
   marihuana production in, 45
   heroin smuggling from, 206
Michener, James A., 268
Michigan, drug addiction prevention, 174
Miller, Donald E., xvii
Milton, John, 319
Miltown (*See also* Tranquilizers, Meprobamate), 93. 347
Mine Enemy Grows Older (book), 105
Minneapolis, police, cooperation of, 294
Modern Medicine. article in, 115
Molly McGuires, 276
Montana, John C., 275
Moore, Ben, 201
Moore, John, arrest of, 318
Morning glory seeds (See Halucinogens)
Morocco, hashish (kif) production ban, 74
Morphine, 19, 47, 49, 51, 59-60, 93, 168
   and crime, 166
   base in illicit traffic, 314, 318
   death from poisoning, 136
   dependence, 46, 102, 121-124, 166
   detected by dogs, 299
   illicit traffic, prices, 10
   seizures, Hong Kong, 30
      Milan, Italy, 318
      Marseille, France, 318
   tests for, 93
Motion pictures in narcotic enforcement, 240
Murder, 31, 166
Murder, Inc., 315
Musto, David F., M.D., 81, 323
My Wicked, Wicked Ways (book), 168
Myers, William B. (Barney), xiv

Nalline (*See also* Nalorphine, Naloxone), 145, 170
Nalorphine, 145, 170
Naloxone, narcotic antagonist, 136
Narcotic antagonists
   cyclazocine, 136
   nalline, 145, 170
   nalorphine, 145, 170
   naloxone, 136

Nalty, B. C., 323
Narcotic drugs, 46, 349
  abuse, 46, 350
  international controls, 41
  legal control, 40
  prescriptions, 308
  withdrawal, 69, 188
Narcotic Drugs Import and Export Act, 45
Narcotic investigations, police cooperation, 313
Narcotic prescription blanks, triplicate, 187
  California, 187
  Illinois, 187
Narcotic withdrawal, 69, 188-190
Narcotics and Narcotic Addiction (book), 7, 145, 150
Narcotics, Encyclopedia of Chemistry (book), 64
Narcotics, Lingo and Lore (book), 150
Narcotics Treatment Administration, District of Columbia, 140
National Observer, article in, 135
Nelson, Tommy, 202
Nembutal (See also Barbiturates, Phenobarbital sodium), 90
Neonatal Narcotic Addiction: Ten-Year Observation (article), 138, 177
New York, drug addiction prevention, 174
New York Times, articles in, 31, 74
Newey, Paul, xiv
Nitric acid test, 94
Nixon, President Richard, 327
Nomoff, Norman, M.D., 112, 120
North Carolina Prison Administration, 200
Nowlan, Elizabeth J., xvii
Numorphan, 46, 66
Nutmeg, abuse of, 355
Nyswander, Marie, M.D., 109, 115, 133

Oakland, California, Chief of Police, 169
O'Carroll, Patrick P., xiii, 196
Opiate Addiction (book), 102
Opiates, 48
  identification, 92, 256
  synthetic, 67
  withdrawal, 188, 189
Opium, 46-66, 93
  camphorated tincture (paregoric), 59, 129, 131, 177, 355
  crude, 54
  diversions of, 313
  imported, 40, 129
  international control, 41
  powdered, 58
  production, 53, 128
  raids, 265
  smoking, 10, 15, 55
  smuggling from Japan, 266
    Mexico, 206
  tests for, 92
  tincture of, 59
Opium Poppy and Other Poppies (pamphlet), 49, 51
Opium Poppy Control Act of 1942, 45, 51
Opium Problem (book), 7
Origins of Psychopharmacology from CPZ to LSD (book), 80
Ostroff, Anne, xiii

Paint thinner, abuse of, 354
Pantopon, 46, 66
  addiction, 102, 121
Paradise Lost (poem), 319
Paregoric (See also Opium, camphorated tincture of), 59, 177
  abuse of, 129, 131, 355
Patton, Neil, xvii
Pediatrics, article in, 138, 177
Pellens, Mildred, 7
Pennsylvania Division of Drug Control, 124
"Pep pills" (See Stimulants)
Percival, Walter L., 86
Perillo, Joseph A., xvii
Petrosino, Joseph, assassination of, 274
Phantastica (book), 78
Pharmacological Basis of Therapeutics (book), 122
Phenmetrazine (See also Amphetamines, Preludin. stimulants), 347
Phenobarbital sodium (See also Barbiturates, Nembutal), 90, 93
Photography, infrared, 239
  surveillance, 237
Photography in Law Enforcement (pamphlet), 241
Physician addiction, 24, 120, 311
Physicians' Desk Reference (book), 99
Picini, Michael G., xvii
Pinckney, Charles Cotesworth, 127
Plezl, Franz, arrest of, 318
Pocoroba, Benedict, 207
Police, cooperation in narcotic investigations, 313
  Arizona, 315
  Beirut, Lebanon, 318

California, 315
Europe, 315, 318
France, 318
Germany, 318
Greece, 319
Italy, 318
Lebanon, 318
Marseille, France, 318
Mexico City, Mexico, 315
Milan, Italy, 318
New Jersey, 318
New York City, 315, 318
Paris, France, 315
Seattle, Washington, 315
Spain, 318
Switzerland, 318
United Kingdom, 318
Police Yearbook, 1971, 317
Pope Pius XII, 172
Powelson, D. Harvey, M.D., 83
Preludin (*See also* Amphetamines, phenmetrazine, stimulants), 142, 347
Prentice, Dr., 20
Problems of Narcotic Drugs in Hong Kong (White Paper), 36
Psilocybin (*See* Halucinogens)
Psychedelics (*See* Halucinogens)
Psychopharmacology, 80
Psychotropic Convention, 41

Raghib-Ismael, Abdul, arrest of, 318
Rapid Duquenois-Levine Test, 96
Reader's Digest, article in, 264
"Red Birds" (*See* Barbiturates)
Report on Narcotic Addiction of Council of Mental Health, American Medical Association, 308
Resume on the Abolition of Opium (report), 129
Rhodes, Charles D., xiii
Richmond, R. G. E., M.D., 29, 111
Robbery, armed, 76
Robertson, Guy, 198
Robertson, J.L., 319
Robertson, Porter, 199
Rosenstein, Jack, xvii
Rossides, Hon. Eugene T., 316
Roth, Martin, 39, 83, 91
Roupinian, George, arrest of, 318
Royal Canadian Mounted Police, 297
Rubio, Estrellita, 138, 177

San Francisco, heroin smuggling into, 266
opium smuggling into, 266

San Francisco Chronicle, article in, 304
Santa Rita Rehabilitation Center, Alameda County, California, 116, 170
Scandinavia, amphetamine abuse, 39, 142, 347
Schmidt, J. E., 150
Schwarz, Conrad J., 85
Searches. crime scene, 248-254
personal, 254
techniques, 252
Seattle, Washington, heroin smuggling into, 266
opium smuggling into, 266
Secobarbital sodium (*See also* Barbituartes, Seconal), 90, 136
Seconal (*See also* Barbiturates, Secobarbital sodium), 90, 136
Sedatives (*See also* Barbiturates, Tranquilizers), 348
Settel, Arthur, xvii
Shahbaugh, Junia E., xiii
Shen Nung, Chinese Emperor, 80
Siragusa, Charles, xiii
Small, Dr. Lyndon F., 7
Smith, C. Conway, M.D., 86
Smith, J. P., 7, 75, 127
Sondern, Frederic, Jr., 271
Soudoun Shiekhouni, 78
Spanish police, cooperation of, 318
"Speed" (*See* Methamphetamine)
"Speedball" (*See* Cocaine, heroin, morphine)
Speer, Wayland L., xiii
Stassen, Harold, 283
Stephenson, Owen D., 84
Stern, Bill, 105
Stimulants (*See also* Amphetamines, dextroamphetamine, methamphetamine), 344
STP (*See* Halucinogens)
Stramonium, abuse of (*See also* Jimson weed), 355
Studies of Tetrahydrocannabinol (book), 78
Study of Ex-Prisoner Female Narcotic Addicts in Hong Kong (article), 37
Sullivan, Marvene R., xvii
Sullivan Acts, 197
Surveillance, 214
automobile, 228
fixed point, 234
methods, 221
motion pictures, 240
photography, 237
special foot surveillance problems. 223

Index

Sweden, amphetamine problem, 39, 142, 347
  death from methadone poisoning, 135
Swiss police, cooperation of, 318
Synthetic opiates, 67
Synthetic Substances With Morphine-Like Effect (article,, 60

Takouri (*See also* Cannabis, Marihuana), 71
Talese, Gay, 277
Tate, Dr., case, 26
Terry, Charles, 7
Terry, James G., M.D., 116, 148, 169
Tetrahydrocannabinol (*See also* Cannabis, Marihuana), 78, 334
THC (Tetrahydrocannabinol), 78, 334
Three Hundred Most Abused Drugs: A Pictorial Handbook (book), 99
Timcaps (*See also* Amphetamines, Dextroamphetamine sulphate), 92
Time Magazine, articles in, 30, 276
Tompkins, William H., 6, 150
Toxic Theory Linking Acute Cannabis Intoxication and Regular Use (paper), 85
Traffic in Narcotics (book), 6, 150
Tranquilizers, 93, 190, 347
  Librium, 93
  Miltown, 93
Treadway, Dr., 7
Trial of John Brown (book), 322
Tuinal (*See also* Barbiturates, Amobarbital, Secobarbital), 90, 93
Turkey, diversion of opium, 313
  fixed point surveillance, 235
  opium imported from, 129
  production, 128
Turkish police, cooperation of, 235

Undercover investigations, 191
Uniform Narcotic Drug Act, 13
United Nations Bulletin on Narcotics, articles in, 37, 62
United Nations Commission on Narcotic Drugs, 7, 28, 30, 317
United States Bureau of Customs, 44, 45, 88, 300
  dogs as narcotic detectors, 296
United States Bureau of Internal Revenue, 23, 45
United States Bureau of Narcotics, 7, 21, 44, 45, 67, 73, 76, 100, 107, 120, 121, 124, 174, 194, 195, 198, 258, 269, 275, 277, 300, 310
  dogs as narcotic detectors, 296
  Police Training School, 191, 242, 293
United States Bureau of Narcotics and Dangerous Drugs, 7, 9, 44, 45, 96, 129, 151, 172, 188, 258, 309, 317
United States Congress. House of Representatives. Select Committee on Crime, 131, 136
  Appropriations Committee Hearings, 41
United States Congress. Senate Investigating Committee under Senator Estes Kefauver, 275, 277
  Senator John McClellan, 275
United States Department of Defense, 327
United States Department of Health, Education and Welfare, 7, 45, 327
  Food and Drug Administration, 45
  Bureau of Drug Abuse Control, 45
United States Department of Justice, 21, 317, 327
  Bureau of Narcotics and Dangerous Drugs, 7, 9, 44, 45, 96, 129, 151, 172, 188, 258, 309, 317
United States Department of Labor, 327
United States Marines, 289
United States National Institute of Mental Health, 327
United States Office of Economic Opportunity, 327
United States Post Office Inspection Service, 167, 274
United States Public Health Service, 124
  Hospitals, 21, 62, 67, 77, 107, 109, 121, 148, 170, 186, 190
United States Supreme Court, decisions, 23, 26, 192
United States Tax Court, 182
United States Treasury Department, 22, 211, 316, 319
  Bureau of Customs, 44, 45, 88, 297, 300
  Bureau of Narcotics, 7, 21, 44, 45, 67, 73, 76, 100, 107, 120, 121, 124, 174, 194, 195, 198, 258, 269, 275, 277, 300, 310
  Law Enforcement Officer Training Schools, 191, 214, 242, 293
  Narcotic Section, Bureau of Internal Revenue, 45
  Narcotic Unit, Bureau of Prohibition, 45
  Secret Service, 4, 180

"Uppers" (*See* Stimulants)

Vancouver, B. C., addiction in, 35
   heroin smuggling into, 266
   opium smuggling into, 266
Vogel, Victor H., 7, 46, 79, 82, 122, 145, 150
Vogel, Virginia E., 46

Walker, John H., 28
Washington Post, articles in, 35, 82, 86, 101
Washington Star, articles in, 76, 132
Wasserman, Edward, 138, 177
Wayne Law Review, article in, 87
Webb, Jack, 234
White, George H., xiv, 194, 235, 266, 270, 277

Wikler, Abraham, M.D., 77, 102, 103
Williams, Garland, xiv
Williamson, Marjorie, xiii
Witt, Harold, 303
Wittenborn, J. R., 7, 75, 127
Wittenborn, S. A., 7, 75, 127
Wolff, Pablo, 78
World Health Organization, 47, 137
Wren, Walter, M.D., 86
Wright, C. R., 61

"Yellow jackets" (*See* Barbiturates)
Yen shee, 57, 58
Zack, Jane N., xvii
Zelaska, Lieutenant John W., xviii
Zelson, Carl, 138. 177
Zwikker Test, 97